Autonomy and Armed Separatism in South and Southeast Asia

The **Institute of Southeast Asian Studies (ISEAS)** was established as an autonomous organization in 1968. It is a regional centre dedicated to the study of socio-political, security and economic trends and developments in Southeast Asia and its wider geostrategic and economic environment. The Institute's research programmes are the Regional Economic Studies (RES, including ASEAN and APEC), Regional Strategic and Political Studies (RSPS), and Regional Social and Cultural Studies (RSCS).

ISEAS Publishing, an established academic press, has issued more than 2,000 books and journals. It is the largest scholarly publisher of research about Southeast Asia from within the region. ISEAS Publishing works with many other academic and trade publishers and distributors to disseminate important research and analyses from and about Southeast Asia to the rest of the world.

Autonomy and Armed Separatism in South and Southeast Asia

EDITED BY
MICHELLE ANN MILLER

INSTITUTE OF SOUTHEAST ASIAN STUDIES
Singapore

First published in Singapore in 2012 by
ISEAS Publishing
Institute of Southeast Asian Studies
30 Heng Mui Keng Terrace, Pasir Panjang
Singapore 119614

E-mail: publish@iseas.edu.sg • Website: bookshop.iseas.edu.sg

All rights reserved. No part of this publication may be reproduced, stored in a retrieval system, or transmitted in any form or by any means, electronic, mechanical, photocopying, recording or otherwise, without the prior permission of the Institute of Southeast Asian Studies.

© 2012 Institute of Southeast Asian Studies, Singapore

The responsibility for facts and opinions in this publication rests exclusively with the authors and their interpretations do not necessarily reflect the views or the policy of the publisher or its supporters.

ISEAS Library Cataloguing-in-Publication Data

Autonomy and armed separatism in South and Southeast Asia / edited by
  Michelle Ann Miller.
  1. Southeast Asia—History—Autonomy and independence movements.
  2. South Asia—History—Autonomy and independence movements.
  3. Insurgency—Southeast Asia.
  4. Insurgency—South Asia.
  5. Southeast Asia—Politics and government.
  6. South Asia—Politics and government.
  I. Miller, Michelle Ann, 1974-
DS526.7 A93   2012

ISBN   978-981-4379-97-7 (soft cover)
ISBN   978-981-4379-98-4 (E-book PDF)

Cover photo: Indonesian soldiers dismantling pro-Acehnese independence flags that had been erected by Free Aceh Movement rebels the previous night in commemoration of the formation of their armed separatist movement on 4 December 1976. Photo taken by Michelle Ann Miller in Lhokgna, Indonesia on 4 December 2000.

Typeset by International Typesetters Pte Ltd
Printed in Singapore by Mainland Press Pte Ltd

For my beautiful husband,
Tim Bunnell

CONTENTS

Acknowledgements ix

About the Contributors xiii

1. The Problem of Armed Separatism: Is Autonomy the Answer?   1
   Michelle Ann Miller

2. Mediated Constitutionality as a Solution to Separatism   16
   Damien Kingsbury

3. Self-Governance as a Framework for Conflict Resolution in Aceh   36
   Michelle Ann Miller

4. Autonomy and Armed Separatism in Papua: Why the Cendrawasih Continues to Fear the Garuda   59
   Bilveer Singh

5. The Parallels and the Paradox of Timor-Leste and Western Sahara   77
   Adérito de Jesus Soares

6. Between Violence and Negotiation: Rethinking the Indonesian Occupation and the East Timorese Resistance   93
   Douglas Kammen

7. Struggle over Space in Myanmar: Expanding State Territoriality after the Kachin Ceasefire   113
   Karin Dean

8. Sri Lanka's Ethnic Conflict: The Autonomy-Separation Dialectic 136
   Jayadeva Uyangoda

9. Unitarianism, Separatism and Federalism: Competing Goals and Problems of Compromise in Sri Lanka 162
   P. Sahadevan

10. Autonomy and Armed Separatism in Jammu and Kashmir 177
    Bibhu Prasad Routray

11. Armed Conflicts and Movements for Autonomy in India's Northeast 196
    Shanthie Mariet D'Souza

12. Southern Thailand: The Trouble with Autonomy 217
    Duncan McCargo

13. The Last Holdout of an Integrated State: A Century of Resistance to State Penetration in Southern Thailand 235
    Thomas Parks

14. Interlocking Autonomy: Manila and Muslim Mindanao 256
    Steven Rood

15. History, Demography and Factionalism: Obstacles to Conflict Resolution through Autonomy in the Southern Philippines 278
    Ronald J. May

16. Conclusion 296
    Michelle Ann Miller

Index 305

ACKNOWLEDGEMENTS

I am grateful to the Asia Research Institute, National University of Singapore, which made possible the "International Workshop on Autonomy and Armed Separatism in South and Southeast Asia" that led to the production of this book. The project also benefited from the financial and logistical support of the Asia Foundation and the Lee Kuan Yew School of Public Policy. For their constructive feedback on earlier draft chapters of this book, I thank Tim Bunnell, Boyd Fuller, Ian Macduff, Michael Montesano, Ora-Orn Poocharoen, Anthony Reid and Tin Maung Maung Than. Thank you also to the anonymous reviewers of the ISEAS Manuscript Review Committee who helped to improve the overall quality of this manuscript. For their outstanding administration of this project, I thank Alyson Rozells, Valerie Yeo, Henry Kwan, Karita Kan, Ada Wong, Mike Li, Peter Lee and Jim Wu. For his valuable support in the editorial process, I am indebted to Sovan Patra.

ABOUT THE CONTRIBUTORS

Karin Dean is a senior researcher at the Estonian Institute of Humanities, Tallinn University. She is interested in various spatial practices and the dynamics of state and nation building at the margins of mainland Southeast Asia. As a consultant on Myanmar for the Henry Dunant Center for Humanitarian Dialogue (2002–06), she worked with the ethnic ceasefire and non-ceasefire groups at the Thai-Myanmar border. Her Ph.D. research at the National University of Singapore (1999–2002) and later research explore the Kachin spatial and social issues mostly at the Sino-Myanmar border.

Douglas Kammen obtained his Ph.D. at Cornell University and has taught at the University of Canterbury (Christchurch), Universitas Hasanuddin (Makassar), the National University of East Timor (Dili). He currently teaches in the Southeast Asia Programme at the National University of Singapore. He is the author of numerous journal articles and book chapters on social movements, military politics, and political violence in Indonesia and Timor-Leste.

Damien Kingsbury is Professor at Deakin University, Melbourne, and author and editor of a number of books on regional politics and security issues. In 2005, Prof. Kingsbury was political advisor to the Free Aceh Movement in the Helsinki peace talks which ended three decades of separatist conflict, and has since advised on models of autonomy and negotiation procedures to the West Papua National Coalition for Liberation, the Liberation Tigers of Tamil Eelam and the Moro Islamic Liberation Front.

Ronald J. May is an emeritus fellow of the Australian National University, attached to the State, Society and Governance in Melanesia programme, and an adviser to the Papua New Guinea National Research Institute. He has been a frequent visitor to the Philippines since the 1970s and has written extensively on the Mindanao conflict. He is a former member of the Advisory Editorial Board of the *Journal of Muslim Minority Affairs*.

Duncan McCargo is Professor of Southeast Asian politics at the University of Leeds. His books on Thailand comprise: *Chamlong Srimuang and the New Thai Politics* (1997); *Politics and the Press in Thailand* (2000); *Reforming Thai Politics* (2002) (edited with U. Pathmanand) (2002); *The Thaksinization of Thailand* (2005); *Rethinking Thailand's Southern Violence*, ed. (2007); *Tearing Apart the Land: Islam and Legitimacy in Southern Thailand*; and *Mapping National Anxieties: Thailand's Southern Conflict* (2012).

Michelle Ann Miller is a Research Fellow at the Asia Research Institute, National University of Singapore. She previously taught at Deakin University and Charles Darwin University. Dr Miller is the author of *Rebellion and Reform in Indonesia: Jakarta's Security and Autonomy Policies in Aceh* (2009), as well as a number of refereed journal articles and book chapters on decentralization, minority rights, conflict resolution, the politics of Islamic law and governance issues, especially in Indonesia.

Thomas Parks is Regional Director for Conflict and Governance of the Asia Foundation and has been based in Bangkok since February 2008. Mr Parks has twelve years of experience in international development, primarily focused on South and Southeast Asia. He is the Asia Foundation's regional expert for programmes in conflict management, state fragility, and civil-military relations. His primary regional focus is Thailand and the rest of Southeast Asia, though he has worked in South Asia, East Asia, and Africa.

Steven Rood is the Asia Foundation's country representative for the Philippines and Pacific Island Nations. In his concurrent role as Regional Advisor for Local Governance, he helps to build local government, decentralization, and municipal government programmes throughout the region. Dr Rood, an expert on local government, decentralization, and public opinion polling, has been a consultant to both government and non-governmental organizations, including Associates in Rural Development Inc., The Social Weather Stations in Manila, and USAID. Dr Rood served as professor of Political Science at the University of the Philippines College Baguio from 1981 until joining the Foundation in 1999, and was the only foreign faculty member with tenure in the University of the Philippines system. Dr Rood is the author of a number of works on Filipino politics, with a special focus on democracy and decentralization.

Bibhu Prasad Routray, a Singapore-based independent analyst, is a Visiting Fellow at the Institute of Peace and Conflict Studies (IPCS), New Delhi, a Visiting Fellow at the Centre for Land Warfare Studies (CLAWS), New Delhi, and a Fellow at the Takshashila Institution. He previously served as Deputy Director at the National Security Council Secretariat, Government of India and Director at the Institute for Conflict Management's Database & Documentation Centre, Guwahati, Assam. He received his doctoral degree from the School of International Studies, Jawaharlal Nehru University, New Delhi in 2001. Bibhu has written extensively in various edited books, journals, print media and on the internet on terrorism and internal security. His current projects include best practices in counter-terrorism response in South and Southeast Asia.

P. Sahadevan is Professor of South Asian Studies and former Chairperson of the Center for South, Central and Southeast Asian Studies, School of International Studies, Jawaharlal Nehru University, New Delhi. He is Editor-in-Chief of *International Studies,* a quarterly journal published by SAGE Publications. He was Leverhulme Visiting Fellow at the Department of Politics and International Relations, University of Kent at Canterbury, U.K., and Ford Foundation Visiting Fellow at the Joan B. Kroc Institute for International Peace Studies, University of Notre Dame, USA. He has published about fifty research articles and book chapters; authored *Politics of Conflict and Peace in Sri Lanka* (2006); *Coping with Disorder: Strategies to End Internal Wars in South Asia* (2000); *India and Overseas Indians: The Case of Sri Lanka* (1995), and edited *Conflict and Peacemaking in South Asia* (2001) and *Perspectives on India-Sri Lanka Relations* (2011).

Bilveer Singh is Associate Professor at the Department of Political Science, National University of Singapore, and is concurrently serving as Acting Head of the Center of Excellence for National Security, S. Rajaratnam School of International Studies, Nanyang Technological University. He returned to NUS in January 2012. He specializes in regional security issues with a particular focus on Indonesia. His recent books include: *Post-Cold War Australian-Indonesian Defense Relations* (2002); *The Talibanization of Southeast Asia: Losing the War on Terror to Islamist Extremists* (2007); and *Papua: Geopolitics and Papua's Quest for Nationhood* (2008).

About the Contributors

Adérito de Jesus Soares has worked for various international, Indonesian and East Timorese NGOs, and was a law and political science lecturer in East Timor from 1999 to 2007. He was a member of East Timor's Constituent Assembly which drafted East Timor's constitution. Adérito is the author of a number of journal articles and reports, and is a regular contributor to regional newspapers such as the *Jakarta Post*, *International Herald Tribune*, *South China Morning Post* and *Christian Science Monitor*. In 2010 Adérito was elected by East Timor's National parliament as the first Commissioner of the country's newly established Anti-Corruption Commission, and is currently on leave from his Ph.D. programme at the Australian National University.

Shanthie Mariet D'Souza is a Visiting Research Fellow at the Institute of South Asian Studies (ISAS), National University of Singapore. She is also affiliated with the Institute for Defence Studies and Analyses (IDSA), New Delhi. Shanthie has been a Visiting Fulbright Scholar at South Asia Studies, The Paul H. Nitze School of Advanced International Studies (SAIS), Johns Hopkins University, Washington D.C.; Research Associate at the Institute for Conflict Management, Guwahati, Assam; and Editorial Assistant at the United Service Institution of India, New Delhi. She has conducted field studies in the United States, Pakistan, Afghanistan, Jammu and Kashmir and India's North East.

Jayadeva Uyangoda is Professor and former Head of the Department of Political Science and Public Policy, University of Colombo, Sri Lanka. His recent research and writings have been on Sri Lanka's ethnic conflict and peace initiatives. Among his publications are *Ethnic Conflict in Sri Lanka: Changing Dynamics*, Policy Studies No. 32 (2007); *Sri Lanka's Conflict: Context and Options* (2000); *The Question of Sri Lanka's Minority Rights* (2001); *Sri Lanka's Peace Process of 2002: Critical Perspectives* (co-edited with M. Perera) (2003).

1

THE PROBLEM OF ARMED SEPARATISM: IS AUTONOMY THE ANSWER?

Michelle Ann Miller

Over recent decades a number of states in South and Southeast Asia have been troubled by armed separatist movements that have sought to create their own independent polity via physical separation from the parent state. Various forms of autonomy have been promoted by policy-makers and donors as the most democratic way of accommodating separatist insurgents in ethnically, religiously, politically and socially divided states. Despite this, remarkably few states in Asia have succeeded in winning over their aggrieved separatist minorities to the dominant nationalist cause. This situation has created a real dilemma for many states of how much freedom to grant nationalist minority groups without ceding control over their sovereign territories to separatists.

This central dilemma of conferring democratic freedoms to sub-state nationalists without compromising state sovereignty has been reflected in the policy choices of governments in South and Southeast Asia. On the one hand, some governments in the region have sought to divert secessionist demands through offers of autonomy and other forms of self-rule. On the other hand, policies of forced assimilation have frequently been employed in a bid to crush armed separatist movements militarily as a precursor to peace. In South and Southeast Asia, many national governments have pursued a dual-track persuasive-repressive policy approach aimed at compelling armed separatists to comply with unilateral offers of autonomy through state coercion and military conquest.

Resolving this dilemma of reconciling minority independence demands with state claims to sovereignty is by no means a simple or straightforward process. Even when parent states respond to secessionist challenges by de-emphasizing a military approach and adopting ameliorative policies aimed at winning would-be separatists back into the broader national fold, separatist insurgents can, and sometimes do, attempt to garner political leverage for their nationalist cause through violent means. Autonomy can strengthen armed separatist movements if they use their increased access to state power and resources to mobilize in opposition to state authority (Cornell 2002, p. 252). For this reason, as John-Mary Kauzya points out, "the difference between decentralization and disintegration is very thin" (2005, p. 4). Striking the right balance between competing nationalistic agendas depends upon a basic level of consensus among the key political actors about the sort of autonomy formula to apply in the realignment of centre-periphery power relations (Horowitz 1981, pp. 166–67). Achieving such a delicate equilibrium between these oppositional interests is contingent upon the suitability of any autonomy design to the conditions and circumstances for which it was created. It also depends on the extent to which promises made by the key political players are kept. In armed separatist conflicts, which are always bloody, often protracted, and usually driven by forces with intransigent and irreconcilable claims to territorial sovereignty, promises about autonomy are frequently broken, perpetuating deep mutual mistrust. Under such circumstances, the capacity and willingness of parent states to negotiate shared rule outcomes with their aggrieved minorities is especially uncertain (Varennes 2007, p. 50; Weller 2009, p. 114).

The contributors to this volume came together at the "International Workshop on Autonomy and Armed Separatism in South and Southeast Asia", held in 2008 at the Asia Research Institute, National University of Singapore. They considered the core question of whether autonomy can offer a viable substitute for self-determination for armed separatist minorities in Asian national contexts. The authors explored the nexus between government offers of autonomy and the rise or fall of armed separatism in seven South and Southeast Asian countries: Indonesia, Sri Lanka, Burma/Myanmar, the Philippines, Thailand, India and Indonesia's former province of East Timor. In terms of political geography, the region is awash with states that inherited national borders from former colonial masters in the post-Second World War period of decolonization (or, in the case of East Timor, experienced secondary colonialism under Indonesian rule, 1976–99). Even in Thailand, where no formal colonization took place, the borders of Siam (as Thailand was called until 1939, and from 1945 to 1949) were to some extent determined by independence settlements between British and French colonial powers and the newly independent nation-states of neighbouring Malaysia, Burma/Myanmar, Laos, Vietnam and Cambodia. Into these reconfigured independent states the incorporation of dispersed ethnic, religious, cultural and linguistic minority groups was neither a process of comfortable assimilation nor a natural catalyst for the production of a common national identity. Partly in recognition of this, and partly out of fear of a return to colonial rule, nascent post-colonial governments in the region tended to impose a rigid, homogenizing sense of national identity in a bid to strengthen internal cohesion while confining alternative constructions of ethnic identity and belonging to the symbolic realm (Miller 2011*b*, p. 807). These were the same practices that had been used in the past by colonial rulers to manage opposition and contain assertions of difference (Santamaria 2004, pp. 7–8; Thio 2010, p. 100).

For the contributors to this volume, an intellectual inquiry into the nature of the relationship between autonomy and armed separatism is timely and relevant. The two major precedents to this book, *Armed Separatism in Southeast Asia* (edited by Lim Joo-Jock and Vani Shanmugaratnam, 1984) and *Ethnic Conflict and Secessionism in South and Southeast Asia* (edited by Rajat Ganguly and Ian Macduff, 2003) offer valuable background analysis on many (but not all) of the conflicts reviewed in this volume. Yet these two books are now outdated and the nature of scholarship about contemporary conflict is such that writings on this subject are constantly being overtaken by events, thereby necessitating regular empirical and analytical revision of historical as well as more recent developments. This volume alone required major rewriting when dramatic changes in the field (such as the Sri Lankan Government's military defeat of the armed separatist Liberation Tigers of Tamil Eelam [LTTE] in May 2009) forced assumptions about the dynamics of the conflict to be reconsidered and conclusions to be redrawn.

In addition to building upon previous edited collections on the specific phenomenon of "armed separatism", this volume contributes to scholarship dealing with the broader categories of religious and ethnic conflict in South and Southeast Asia (for example, Snitwongswe and Thompson 2005; Bertrand and Laliberté 2010; Cady and Simon 2007; Anwar et al. 2005; Trijono 2004). To some extent, it also speaks to the literature on terrorism in the region, which has proliferated since the September 2001 terror attacks on the United States (John and Parashar 2005; Vaughn et al. 2009; Tan 2007; Smith 2005). It should be noted, however, that since the initiation of the U.S.-led "war on terror", many national governments in South and Southeast Asia (as well as a number of authors) have portrayed separatist movements as terrorists in an effort to discredit their cause in the eyes of the international community and to attract United States funding and diplomatic support for more repressive policies against political opposition.

By focusing on the dynamics of the relationship between autonomy and armed separatism, this book also adds a new dimension to studies of decentralization, federalism, autonomy and other forms of self-rule for minority regions within existing nation-states. In Asian contexts, a small but valuable body of work on the devolution of central state powers and resources has partially addressed the question of different types of conflict resolution through autonomy (for example, He et al. 2007; Ichimura and Bahl 2009; Bhattacharyya 2010). Other writings have focused on the broader question of minority rights accommodation in Asia, including through various forms and degrees of autonomy (Miller 2011*a*; Castellino and Redondo 2006; Hofmann and Caruso 2011). To date, however, this is the only volume that explores the issue of autonomy as a means of managing the particular phenomenon of armed separatist conflict in South and Southeast Asian contexts.

The timeliness of this volume is also related to recent developments and events in the region. Since the late 1990s, there has been a forceful resurgence of armed separatist movements across South and Southeast Asia. Like many Latin American countries over recent decades, where escalating internal conflicts have corresponded with and been integral to national democratization processes, the growth of separatist sentiment and activity in South and Southeast Asia was brought about, in the first instance, by the fallout from the 1997 Asian financial crisis and the subsequent wave of democratization across parts of Asia. These events created multiple fissures and weak points in central governmental authority, which generated space for different viewpoints to be heard, including the voices of separatists (Acharya 2003; Miller 2009; Heiduk 2009).

Prior to this period of political flux and opportunity, the region had been dominated by authoritarian regimes and military dictatorships which had shown their intolerance of separatism by relying heavily on statist violence and coercion. Authoritarian regimes also tended to benefit from the perpetuation of armed separatist disputes by imposing a standardized sense of nationalism that legitimized their continued rule while denying legitimacy to institutions not sanctioned by the state (Robison 1993, p. 42; Santamaria 2004, p. 8). Indeed, authoritarian forms of government have generally proven far more capable of retaining control over their sovereign territories than democratizing regimes. Between 1974 and 1997, 57 per cent of new states recognized by the

United Nations were established immediately before or after their parent states embarked on transitions to democracy, usually within three years (He and Reid 2004, p. 296). This pattern can be explained by the inherent instability of transitions to democracy, when the opening of political space presents numerous challenges to state authority. Yet while authoritarian governments in Asia generally succeeded in keeping their independence movements under control up until the 1997 Asian financial crisis, their capacity and willingness to respond to the underlying causes of regional grievances remained weak or non-existent. In other words, though the coercive capabilities of states in the region were strong, their power and authority derived largely from their ability to govern *over* society rather than *with* societal consent (Fritz 2003, p. 5; Rudland and Pederson 2000, p. 7). As a result, with the exceptions of Indonesia's westernmost province of Aceh (where Acehnese separatists were only successfully democratically accommodated after numerous failed attempts), and the regions of Satun and Isaan in Thailand, which have been relatively successfully integrated into the Thai state, the factors that had originally given birth to separatist sentiment have been left largely or entirely unaddressed and have not disappeared over time.

The first flush of democratization in the late 1990s brought new systems and political leaders who began to look beyond a "military solution" to their internal conflicts and towards different forms of autonomy. National political elites who emerged from the ashes of old authoritarian regimes were vulnerable to mounting societal pressure for democratic change, which impacted upon how they saw themselves and the range of opportunities available to them. At the heart of this reduced emphasis on interventionist state policies was the belief that if sub-state nationalists were granted certain rights and freedoms then they could be persuaded to abandon their independence cause and constructively participate in national democratization processes. The view that autonomy regimes could provide a panacea for self-determination conflicts formed part of a growing global trend in the 1990s, triggered by the 1994 United Nations General Assembly launch of *The Liechtenstein Draft Convention on Self-determination through Self-administration* (Cárdenas and Cañás 2002, p. 115; Kymlicka 2007, p. 208). Initiated by the State of Liechtenstein, this Draft Convention helped to render mainstream among the international community the idea that separatist movements can be accommodated without compromising the territorial sovereignty and national cohesiveness of parent states.

In South and Southeast Asia, the growing acceptance that autonomy could help to reduce social fragmentation in deeply divided societies was not accompanied by consensus among the key political actors in any national context about what autonomy meant, how it should be applied, or to what extent. For governments in the region, autonomy was a deeply uncertain experiment in which "too much" autonomy tended to be equated with national fragmentation or disintegration. As such, autonomy was approached with extreme caution and usually as a last resort after state and separatist forces failed to militarily defeat one another (see, for example, Snitwongse and Thompson 2005; Miller 2009).

DEFINING AUTONOMY

The problem with defining autonomy is that it can mean whatever the key parties decide it means. There is no uniform model or definition of autonomy, which is designed for and adapted to specific situations according to the nature of the demands and expectations of the key parties. Nor do autonomy packages necessarily reflect the aspirations of all key parties to a conflict as autonomy may be unilaterally imposed by the stronger party (usually the central government) onto the weaker party (the minority population or minority region, in which the national minority forms a majority), and often in conjunction with other methods of conflict management (mostly physical force or state coercion).

Insofar as autonomy may be defined by a core set of characteristics, then, there are two features that all autonomy arrangements have in common. The first is that every autonomy model is framed within the boundaries of the parent state and does not attempt to redraw those territorial borders. In other words, autonomy "is just one construction for the division of jurisdiction within a state", with the nature of that jurisdiction being primarily institutional and not prejudicial to the subject-matter content of the jurisdictional division (Packer 2007, p. 71). Such jurisdictional divisions are designed to harmonize the organizational and institutional correspondence between rulers and the ruled. Second, autonomy is about the division of power within a state. Autonomy involves the transfer of state power and responsibility in one or more area of state authority (for example, legislative, political, administrative, economic, cultural and religious affairs) from the central government to the minority peoples or region that comprise the autonomous entity. Substantive autonomy arrangements (that is, arrangements which are not hollowed out by empty promises or overshadowed by repressive policies that strip autonomous entities of practical meaning) tend to combine a number of key areas of state authority for delegation and transfer to the autonomous entity. In this, autonomy can be understood as the means whereby minority peoples or minority regions are empowered to determine separately the specific functions to which they are entrusted for their own use and well-being (Potier 2001, p. 54; Suksi 1998, p. 359).

Beyond these basic elements of autonomy, the design and degree of autonomy arrangements vary considerably within and between countries. The case studies in this volume attest to the sheer diversity of autonomy regimes in their empirical form. Just as there is no clear consensus on which type of autonomy is most conducive to the management of armed separatist conflicts, different groups and individuals tend to place greater emphasis on specific forms of accommodation (Cunningham 2007, p. 3).

There is, however, broad agreement among the international community and donor and lending agencies (such as The World Bank, the United Nations Development Program [UNDP], the International Monetary Fund [IMF], and the Development Assistance Committee of the Organisation for Economic Co-operation and Development [OECD]) about the desirability of autonomy regimes modelled on liberal democratic principles. This is because assuming that the rights to freedom of expression and association (including the right to express dissenting views) are integral to any meaningful definition of democracy, then it follows that liberal democracies are, or should be, more capable of achieving peaceful outcomes to their national identity problems due to their tendency towards the political processes of negotiation and compromise. Yet among liberal democrats themselves, there are varying motivations for supporting autonomy agendas. For the liberal democratic left, autonomy is associated with a process of deepening critical aspects of democratic procedure and good governance, accompanied by the creation of new opportunities for separatist forces to engage constructively with nation-state building processes rather than in opposition to them. For the neo-liberal right, autonomy involves a rolling back of central state powers in order to reform failed or failing areas of centralized authority, often via structural adjustment programmes aimed at stemming the specter of separatism by improving economic efficiency in the provision of public services and facilities (Crawford and Hartmann 2008, p. 12). Such economic rationalism certainly fuelled the push to decentralize in many parts of Southeast Asia following the 1997 Asian financial crisis, especially in Indonesia and the Philippines, and, to a lesser extent, in Thailand. Yet many donors and lending agencies, along with reform-minded civil society actors, also saw the opportunity presented by weakened centralized authority to strengthen good governance at the local level by bringing government closer to the people. Such normative discourses about improving the responsiveness of local government tend to privilege autonomy as the preferred means by which to "empower" local communities and increase the "voice" and "participation" of the marginalized and the poor.

In many parts of South and Southeast Asia, however, like elsewhere in the world where similar experiments with decentralization have been undertaken (especially in African, Latin American and Eastern European countries), such discourses have often created the illusion of a shared language and common set of priorities when in practice there has been a mismatch between decentralization agendas and societal needs and expectations.

IS AUTONOMY THE ANSWER?

Arguments about the unambiguous desirability of autonomy as the most democratic means of accommodating armed separatist minorities are rarely reflected in reality. For practical purposes, decentralization reforms aimed at managing armed separatist disputes always encounter obstacles and sometimes result in the formation of new states born from countries completely dismembered by secessionist movements (such as the former Soviet Union, Czechoslovakia and Yugoslavia). In many cases, autonomy initiatives are couched in weak or shallow legal frameworks that generate confusion over the roles and responsibilities of key parties to an autonomy agreement, leaving the implementation of decentralization vulnerable to diminution. Frequently, separatist minorities are not granted a sense of ownership over the drafting or implementation of autonomy "agreements", thus heightening the risk of alienation from the decentralization process and a return to violence (Boltjes 2007, pp. 17–22). Often, too, weak states lack the capacity and material resources to honour the terms of autonomy arrangements. In other cases, national political elites either lack the political will and acumen necessary to search for a shared-rule solution, or they are prepared to put the problem of autonomy on the table for discussion but ultimately find it too hard to deal with (Miller 2009, p. 185). In such cases, where there is a deficit in democratic procedure in the institutionalization of autonomy, states tend to combine autonomy arrangements with more coercive or militaristic forms of conflict management (Wolff and Weller 2005, p. 20).

However, even when parent states seek to democratically accommodate their aggrieved separatist minorities through the conferral of broad and inclusive forms of autonomy, nationalist minorities can, and often do, use their increased collective capabilities to pursue their independence agenda. Many secessionists see autonomy and other central government concessions as too little too late, especially after protracted periods of state-sponsored repression under authoritarian rule. Viewing any attempts to renegotiate their governing status within the parent state as a futile exercise, they regard the creation of an independent polity as the only means available to (re)gain control over their own lives and livelihoods. Yet when armed separatists refuse to abandon their absolutist ideology the question arises as to whether decentralization adjustments can continue, or whether coercion and force are the only means available to maintain the parent state in its existing form.

ORGANIZATION OF THE BOOK

The sixteen chapters in this volume explore theoretical questions and empirical conditions under which different forms of autonomy have or have not helped to resolve armed separatist conflicts in seven South and Southeast Asian states. Because the localized and contextual conditions within and between states and armed separatist movements in South and Southeast Asia vary considerably, the contributors to this volume do not propose a "one size fits all" model for resolving armed separatist disputes. Rather, they explore the conditions under which autonomy has or has not worked according to such variables as the extent to which autonomy has actually been implemented, regime type, state strength and structure (federal or unitary system), economic disparities within and between states and favourable conditions for insurgency and counterinsurgency, such as access to funding and mountainous or jungle terrain. Moreover, the cases assembled in this volume illustrate the dangers of casting armed separatist movements as undifferentiated and homogenous entities that are set in simple opposition to the central government. Sometimes government offers of autonomy may only satisfy one faction within a separatist movement while further alienating another faction or multiple factions.

The studies in this book, then, identify the conditions under which autonomy has, or could potentially serve as an effective mechanism for conflict resolution. To this end, in Chapter Two Damien Kingsbury examines the question of whether autonomy, as it has been variously defined and implemented in South and Southeast Asian countries, can adequately address separatist claims by opening political space for the mediated processes of greater participation, representation, accountability and equity. Considering the separatist claims in Indonesia's Aceh and Papuan provinces, Sri Lanka's Eelam, the Philippines' Bangsamoro and the failure of the autonomy option in East Timor, Kingsbury argues that separatist conflicts may be resolved through mediated approaches designed to protect and uphold the rule of law in democratic and democratizing polities.

A case exemplar in the mediation of autonomy arrangements is Indonesia's westernmost province of Aceh. In Chapter Three, I describe how the protracted armed separatist conflict in Aceh (1976–2005) was eventually resolved via the transfer of self-government to the Acehnese people within Indonesia. My chapter considers why previous Indonesian government offers of "special autonomy" to Aceh failed, and how the conferral of broader powers of "self-government" provided the least conflictual method of protecting the individual and collective rights of the Acehnese people, while enabling former Free Aceh Movement rebels to engage constructively with Indonesia's national process of political development rather than opposing it.

Democratic accommodation of nationalist minorities as has occurred in Aceh is extremely rare. At the time of writing, such accommodation has not yet occurred in any of the other case studies in this volume. In Chapter Four, Bilveer Singh examines Jakarta's less successful attempts to resolve the conflict in Indonesia's easternmost province of Papua. The 2005 settlement of the Aceh conflict raised hopes in some quarters that Papuan separatism might be similarly abated via an Aceh-style self-government framework within Indonesia's democratizing national framework. Yet as Singh explains, while special autonomy (*otnonomi khusus*) has somewhat diluted Papuan independence demands, it has by no means provided redress for Papuan grievances against the Indonesian state or responded to the root causes of the Papuan conflict.

In Indonesia's dealings with Papuan insurgents, like the other case studies in this volume, autonomy arrangements have often been applied in conjunction with military force and state coercion. Such repressive policies have helped to maintain the state's monopoly over the physical means of violence but have done little to strengthen central government political legitimacy in separatist regions. In Indonesia, excessive state violence has historically contributed towards a loss of faith in Indonesia's right to rule in Aceh, Papua, and East Timor. As the failed autonomy option in East Timor demonstrated, the more depredations were committed against the civilian population by Indonesian security forces, the stronger the desire for freedom from state repression became, such that Jakarta's offer in 1998 of "special autonomy" was seen by the East Timorese people as too little too late and an unacceptable alternative to independence. In Chapter Five, Adérito de Jesus Soares compares the case of East Timor with that of Western Sahara to argue that the value of autonomy as a solution to armed separatism must be gauged only after first considering the particular historical and political backgrounds of each case. Douglas Kammen, in his chapter, agrees, emphasizing that East Timorese resistance to Indonesian oppression was never a matter of "separatism", but rather one of armed struggle against illegal occupation as Indonesian sovereignty was never officially recognized by the international community.

Questions about spatialized politics and differing dimensions of sovereignty in assigning a role and value to autonomy arrangements are elaborated by Karin Dean in her grim assessment of the state-imposed ceasefire imposed on Kachin separatists in Burma/Myanmar. She examines *de jure* and *de facto* issues of autonomy in the borderlands of Burma/Myanmar, analyzing the intransigent nature of the military junta and the international sovereignty that the country continues to enjoy despite internally malfunctioning as a highly fragmented political entity. The case of Burma/Myanmar also underpins the weaknesses inherent in autonomy arrangements that reinforce ethnic divisions between groups by excluding instruments for inter-ethnic cooperation at the territorial level.

Another case of exclusionary settlements that offer insufficient space to non-dominant groups is Sri Lanka in its dealings with Tamil separatist insurgents. The defeat in 2009 of the Liberation Tigers of Tamil Eelam (LTTE) by Sri Lankan government forces marked the failure of several attempts to search for an autonomy arrangement that could have potentially accommodated Tamil ethnic minorities within the Sri Lankan nation-state. Yet while the military defeat of the LTTE brought an end to major confrontation, it did not offer any meaningful solution to the conflict. In their chapters, Jayadeva Uyangoda and P. Sahadevan explore the complex dimensions of the Sri Lankan case and the difficulties presented by the ethnic character of autonomy claims in which ethnic politics reinforce social relations of inequality. Such inequalities fuel regional autonomy demands along ethnic lines on the one hand, while generating a body of resistance to ethnic-based autonomy on the other hand.

Other case studies in this volume deal with democratic polities that have experienced little success with democratic accommodation of nationalist minorities. The chapters on India's armed separatist conflicts by Bibhu Routray and Shanthie D'Souza show evidence of the world's largest democracy forcefully repressing the demands for accommodation by ethnic minorities in Jammu, Kashmir and in India's northeastern provinces. These cases also highlight the weak governing presence of New Delhi in its armed separatist regions, with the result that disaffected indigenous and non-indigenous ethnic minority groups have remobilized in violent opposition to Indian state authority and eroded autonomy arrangements even as some elements of autonomy have been implemented.

In Thailand, a dominant national identity embodied in the shibboleth "Nation, Religion, King" has created a powerful political culture of opposition to autonomy and democratic accommodation of Muslim Malay ethnic minorities in the southern provinces. In Chapters Twelve and Thirteen respectively, Duncan McCargo and Thomas Parks explore approaches to autonomy and degrees of state penetration in southern Thailand. These varying approaches have developed from divergent historical trajectories of centre-periphery relations and range from the relatively successful policies of non-interference and inclusive integration in Satun and Isaan to an ongoing low-intensity violent conflict over Thai state legitimacy in the southern border provinces of Pattani, Yala and Narathiwat.

The trajectory of autonomy in the southern Philippines has been such that efforts by Manila political elites to accommodate the demands of Moro separatists in Muslim Mindanao were strongest immediately after the start of the Philippines' transition to democracy and have subsequently been diluted by limited unilateral offers of autonomy. This follows a broader pattern in other democratizing regimes across Asia and in parts of Latin America and Eastern Europe whereby central government actors have tended to reduce the content of autonomy packages the more time that elapses after the initiation of transitions to democracy.[1] In the final two substantive chapters of this volume, Ronald May and Steve Rood consider the historical and contemporary reasons for the persistent failure of successive governments in the Philippines to provide redress for the grievances of Mindanao Muslims and examine the prospects for a future settlement that might satisfy both sides. Finally, the concluding chapter examines these case studies in comparative context and makes the case for a rights-based approach to autonomy as the most desirable and viable method of resolution of armed separatist disputes in South and Southeast Asia.

What all of the chapters share is: (1) a concern with the conditions under which different forms of autonomy exacerbate or alleviate the specific phenomenon of armed separatism, and (2) the circumstances that lead men and women to take up arms in order to remove themselves from existing state boundaries in order to create (or recreate) their own nation-state. These conditions and circumstances vary considerably within and between national contexts, as do the types of armed separatist movements and the motivations and agendas of their leaders. The diversity of armed separatist movements assembled in this volume is reflected, at least in part, in the differentiated government responses to their demands. The extent to which "autonomy" as it is understood and applied in South and Southeast Asia is capable of ameliorating the grievances of armed separatists by providing less extreme forms of engagement with, and accommodation within the existing parent state, is the core concern of this book.

Note

1. In cases where states are divided by separatist conflicts, there is a greater likelihood that the end of authoritarianism will lead to revolution, a "hybrid regime" that "seems to be neither democracy nor dictatorship" or a return to dictatorship (Bunce 2000, p. 723; Edvardsen 1997, p. 213).

References

Acharya, A. "Democratization and the Prospects for Participatory Regionalism in Southeast Asia". *Third World Quarterly*, 24, no. 2 (2003): 375–90.
Anwar, D.F., H. Bouvier, G. Smith, and R. Tol, eds. *Violent Internal Conflicts in Asia Pacific*. Jakarta: Yayasan Obor Indonesia, 2005.
Benedikter, T. *The World's Modern Autonomy Systems: Concepts and Experiences of Regional Territorial Autonomy*. New Delhi, London and New York: Anthem Press, 2009.
Bertrand, J. and A. Laliberté. *Multination States in Asia: Accommodation or Resistance*. Cambridge, New York: Cambridge University Press, 2010.
Bhattacharyya, H. *Federalism in Asia: India, Pakistan and Malaysia*. London and New York: Routledge, 2010.
Boltjes, Miek, ed. *Implementing Negotiated Agreements: The Real Challenge to Intrastate Peace*. The Hague, Netherlands: T.M.C Asser Press, 2007.
Bunce, V. "Comparative Democratization: Big and Bounded Generalizations". *Comparative Political Studies* 33, nos. 6–7 (2000): 703–34.
Cady, L.E. and S.W. Simon, eds. *Religion and Conflict in South and Southeast Asia: Disrupting Violence*. London and New York: Routledge, 2007.
Cárdenas, E.J. and M.F. Cañás. "The Limits of Self-Determination". In *The Self-Determination of Peoples: Community, Nation, and State in an Interdependent World*, edited by W. Boulder Danspeckilogramsruber. Colorado and London, U.K.: Lynn Reiner Publishers Inc., 2002.
Castellino, J. and E.D. Redondo. *Minority Rights in Asia: A Comparative Legal Analysis*. Oxford and New York: Oxford University Press, 2006.
Cornell, S. "Autonomy as a Source of Conflict: Caucasian Conflicts in Theoretical Perspective". *World Politics* 54, no. 2 (2002): 245–76.
Crawford, G. and C. Hartmann. "Introduction: Decentralization as a Pathway out of Poverty and Conflict?". In *Decentralization in Africa. A Pathway out of Poverty and Conflict?*, edited by Gordon Crawford and Christof Hartmann. Amsterdam: Amsterdam University Press, 2008.
Cunningham, K.G. "Divided and Conquered: Why States and Self-Determination Groups Fail in Bargaining Over Autonomy". Ph.D. Thesis. San Diego: University of California, 2007.
Edvardsen, U. "A Cultural Approach to Understanding Modes of Transition to Democracy". *Journal of Theoretical Politics* 9, no. 2 (1997): 211–34.

Fritz, V. "State Weakness in Post-Communist Countries: The Concept of State Capacity". *Romanian Journal of Political Science* 3, no. 2 (2003): 5–21.
Ganguly, R. and I. Macduff, eds. *Ethnic Conflict and Secessionism in South and Southeast Asia: Causes, Dynamics, Solutions*. New Delhi: Sage Publications, 2003.
He, B. and A. Reid. "Special Issue Editors' Introduction: Four Approaches to the Aceh Question". *Asian Ethnicity* 5, no. 3 (2004): 293–300.
He, B., B. Galligan, and T. Inoguchi, eds. *Federalism in Asia*. Cheltenham, U.K. and Northampton, USA: Edward Elgar Publishing Limited, 2007.
Heiduk, F. "Two sides of the Same Coin? Separatism and Democratization in Post-Suharto Indonesia". In *Democratization in Post-Suharto Indonesia*, edited by M. Bünte and A. Ufen. London and New York: Routledge, 2009.
Hofmann, R. and U. Caruso, eds. *Minority Rights in South Asia*. Leipzig, Germany: Deutschebibliothek, 2011.
Horowitz, D.L. "Patterns of Ethnic Separatism". *Comparative Studies in Society and History* 23, no. 2 (1981): 165–95.
Ichimura, S. and R. Bahl, eds. *Decentralization Policies in Asian Development*. London and Hackensack, N.J.: World Scientific Publishing Co. Pte. Ltd., 2009.
John, W. and S. Parashar, eds. *Terrorism in Southeast Asia: Implications for South Asia*. Delhi, India: Pearson Education, 2005.
Joo-Jock, L. and V. Shanmugaratnam, eds. *Armed Separatism in Southeast Asia*. Singapore: Institute of Southeast Asian Studies, 1984.
Kauzya, M.J. "Decentralization: Prospects for Peace, Democracy and Development". Division for Public Administration and Development Management, United Nations Department of Economic and Social Affairs, Discussion Paper, 2005.
Kymlicka, W. *Multicultural Odysseys: Navigating the New International Politics of Diversity*. Oxford and New York: Oxford University Press, 2007.
Miller, M.A. "The Nanggroe Aceh Darussalam Law: A Serious Response to Acehnese Separatism?". *Asian Ethnicity* 5, no. 3 (2004): 333–52.
———. *Rebellion and Reform in Indonesia: Jakarta's Security and Autonomy Policies in Aceh*. London and New York: Routledge, 2009; reprinted 2010.
———., guest ed. "Ethnic and Racial Minorities in Asia: Inclusion or Exclusion? [Special Issue]". *Ethnic and Racial Studies* 34, no. 5 (2011*a*).
———. "Why Scholars of Minority Rights in Asia Should Recognize the Limits of Western Models". *Ethnic and Racial Studies* 34, no. 5 (2011*b*): 799–813.
Packer, J. "Reflections on Implementation Mechanisms of Selected Autonomy, Self-Rule and Similar Arrangements". In *Implementing Negotiated Agreements: The Real Challenge to Intrastate Peace*, edited by M. Boltjes. The Hague: T.M.C Asser Press, 2007.
Potier, T. *Conflict in Nagorno-Karabaklh, Abkhazia and South Ossetia: A Legal Appraisal*. The Hague: Kluwer International Law, 2001.

Robison, R. "Indonesia: Tensions in State and Regime". In *Southeast Asia in the 1990s: Authoritarianism, Democracy and Capitalism*, edited by Kevin Hewison, R. Robison and G. Rodan. Sydney, NSW: Allen & Unwin, 1993.

Rudland, E. and M.B. Pedersen. "Introduction: Strong Regime, Weak State?" In *Burma Myanmar: Strong Regime, Weak State?*, edited by M.B. Pedersen, E. Rudland, and R.J. May. Adelaide: Crawford House, 2000.

Rustow, D.A. "Transitions to Democracy: Toward a Dynamic Model". *Comparative Politics* 2, no. 3 (1970): 337–63.

Santamaria, M.C.M. "Framing Ethnic Conflict and the State in Southeast Asia". *Kasarinlan: Philippine Journal of Third World Studies* 19, no. 1 (2004): 4–36.

Smith, P.J., ed. *Terrorism and Violence in Southeast Asia: Transnational Challenges to States and Regional Stability*. New York: M.E. Sharpe Inc., 2005.

Snitwongse, K. and W.S. Thompson, eds. *Ethnic Conflicts in Southeast Asia*. Singapore: Institute of Southeast Asian Studies, 2005.

Suksi, M. "Concluding Remarks". In *Autonomy: Applications and Implications*, edited by Markku Suksi. The Hague: Kluwer Law International, 1998.

Tan, A.T.H. *A Handbook of Terrorism and Insurgency in Southeast Asia*. Cheltenham UK and Northampton USA: Edward Elgar Publishing Limited, 2007.

Thio, L. "Constitutional Accommodation of the Rights of Ethnic and Religious Minorities in Plural Democracies: Lessons and Cautionary Tales from South-East Asia". *Pace International Law Review* 22, no. 1 (2010): 43–101.

Trijono, L. *The Making of Ethnic and Religious Conflicts in Southeast Asia*. Yogyakarta: CSPS Books, 2004.

Varennes, F. "Recurrent Challenges to the Implementation of Intrastate Peace Agreements: The Resistance of State Authorities". In *Implementing Negotiated Agreements: The Real Challenge to Intrastate Peace*, edited by M. Boltjes. The Hague: T.M.C Asser Press, 2007.

Vaughn, B., E. Chanlett-Avery, B. Dolven, M.E. Manyin, M.F. Martin and L.A. Niksch. *Terrorism in Southeast Asia*. Washington, USA: Congressional Research Service, 2009.

Weller, M. "Settling Self-determination Conflicts: Recent Developments". *The European Journal of International Law [EJIL]* 20, no. 1 (2009): 111–65.

Wolffe, S. and M. Weller. "Self-determination and Autonomy: A Conceptual Introduction". In *Autonomy, Self-governance and Conflict Resolution*, edited by M. Weller and S. Wolff. Abingdon and New York: Routledge, 2005.

2

MEDIATED CONSTITUTIONALITY AS A SOLUTION TO SEPARATISM

Damien Kingsbury

The idea of autonomy or other forms of sovereign devolution has been proposed as a viable compromise model in the resolution of claims to separatism. This chapter will consider the meaning and method of application of autonomy or other sub-state political models, and assess whether a semi-independent status can adequately address separatist claims. It will consider the formation of post-colonial states, the failure of many such states to adequately represent ethnic minorities, and the so-called third wave of nationalism in which national or proto-national groupings seek territorial sovereignty. The chapter draws on case studies from Indonesia's Aceh and Papua provinces, Sri Lanka's Eelam and the Philippines' Bangsamoro, and the failure of the autonomy option in East Timor.

The idea of autonomy has been available to sub-state entities since before the period of Westphalian states, and can be seen as having its origins in the allocation of devolved local rule in empires, or points of local political organization within a wider and overarching political constellation. In the post-Westphalian world of sovereign states, autonomy has generally been allowed to accommodate sub-national or ethnically distinct geopolitical entities that, for strategic reasons, have been obliged to accept incorporation into larger states. That is to say, the idea of autonomy is neither new nor novel, and has been accepted as a viable method of securing regional strategic interests while at the same time encouraging state loyalty via a degree of political "looseness" on one hand while confirming a rationale for state cohesion on the other.

Where a state has been established without due regard for internally differentiated constituent parts, as in the case of many unitary and centrally administered post-colonial states, a devolution of centralized state authority to a variety of sub-state models may be undertaken through a process of mediation. Such mediation applies to both the process by which such a devolved sub-state outcome is achieved, and to the outcome which locates the devolved sub-state entity between the polarities of absolute self-determination and absolute state sovereignty.

This mediated compromise, usually around autonomy or a similar form of local self-government, has been proposed as a viable model for the resolution of claims to separatism, sometimes in its own right and sometimes as a step along the path to full independence.[1] The terminology that has gained recent currency in such a process is "earned sovereignty". Earned sovereignty is an attempt to construct a standardized model for conflict resolution of separatist disputes, although implying a number of criteria that are not always necessary and which may not assist in achieving the desired outcome. Moreover, the meaning of the term is problematic. A more useful term, if one not yet current in the literature, is "mediated constitutionality".

This underlying proposal of mediated constitutionality is based on the assumption that actions in order to achieve or oppose separatism are either unresolvable and/or create more harm than they resolve. That is, while there might be strong grounds for separatist claims or for opposing separatist claims, the conflict that can arise in support of or opposition to such claims can outweigh the benefit any such claims or opposition to it might propose to bring. Hence, addressing the first principle causes of conflict might be possible other than through the creation of a separate state.

In particular, the idea of autonomy or related forms of sub-state devolution of authority are generally intended not just as a compromise between competing or mutually incompatible positions, but also as attempts to redress some of the fundamental failures of a pre-existing state in its role as the institutionalized representative of its citizens. The state has, or should have, a series of civic responsibilities towards its citizens which might be regarded as first principle reasons for its existence. Such responsibilities include, or should include, equal and consistent rule of law (*lex* as the origin of legitimacy) guaranteeing freedom with domination.[2]

Within the context of self-identifying groups, where legitimacy is not established in either normative or positive terms, or where legitimacy is held to have been lost or to not apply in relation to a specific people or a specific territory, such people will tend to seek remedial action. For a given people or territory, the mandate for such remedial action might become more compelling when an alternative source of legitimacy is identified and acknowledged. This is, often, the case with self-identifying groups within a reasonably geographically coherent area that do not acknowledge the legitimacy of a ruler from a separate location over the claimed area, or amongst whom that sense of legitimacy as legal inclusion has never been adequately established or has since been lost.

The people of post-colonial states usually have high expectations of independence prior to independence being granted. Yet most post-colonial states usually do not have the capacity to meet pre-independence expectations, and in many cases, capacity is actually lower than under the colonial regime, following the withdrawal of skilled administration and capital, and often (although not universally) due to the destruction resulting from attritional wars of liberation.[3] In the face of rising popular frustration and limited institutional capacity to respond to it, many post-colonial states begin to limit political space, resorting to authoritarian or dictatorial political practices.[4]

Where the limitation of political space takes the form of a patron-client relationship with ethnic majorities, ethnic minorities can feel alienated (victimized, even) and thus retreat to the ethnically and geographically specific. It is but a short step from geo-specific ethnic identification to claims to alternative nationhood and, from there on, to the claim for a state as its geo-institutional manifestation. Separation as a solution to this civic shortfall frequently becomes a goal in its own right, in which the end of the process justifies the means by which it gets there. This may mean that the separatist movement loses sight of the reasons that gave rise to it in the first place. Regarding the case studies, they each conform to a more broad or general type of failure of the post-colonial state to adequately, evenly and consistently address the concerns and interests of a specific minority of its citizens (Kingsbury 2008).

However, if it is the intention of such separatist or sub-state actors to redress what might be termed a civic shortfall of the state, then the focus may shift from separatism as a goal in its own right towards addressing the shortfall that has originally motivated the separatist claim. This might be termed a return to first principles of conflict resolution, a logic that was brought to bear in the resolution of the Aceh conflict in 2005 (see Kingsbury 2006, pp. 20, 121–22), and has since been viewed by some as constituting a basis for a model to be applied in other conflict contexts: "the tremendous achievement of the Helsinki process is plain to see. Aceh has become a possible model for resolving conflicts in other parts of the world" (Aspinall 2006, p. 4).

AUTONOMY AS A SUB-STATE MODEL

The idea of autonomy has an ambiguous or variable meaning. This was noted in the Aceh peace talks, when Finnish mediator Martti Ahtisaari inadvertently used the Finnish term that translated directly as "self-government" (*erityisitsehallinto*) when intending to mean "autonomy" (*erityisautonomia*). Even the term "self-government", which was subsequently adopted by the Free Aceh Movement during the talks as the basis for its negotiable claim, was vague enough for both Indonesian negotiators and Acehnese to ask what it meant, prompting the quip that the meaning of "self-government" would be defined by the outcome of those negotiations.

Etymologically, autonomy derives from the Ancient Greek for "self" (*auto*) and "law" (*nomos*), and implies not independence in a geo-strategic sense, or other forms of absolute separation from another political community, but the ability to make laws (in practice, self-rule) for one's own community. In a more practical sense, the meaning of autonomy is that which is given to it via any mediated process. The specific content of autonomy is thus not fixed (autonomy can come in degrees), and is usually derived as a consequence of negotiation which, other than in distinctly unequal contexts, implies compromise and the consequent loss of elements of the competing claims, e.g. independence on one hand and absolute sovereignty on the other.

In Indonesia, where the principle of granting autonomy (lit. *otonomi khussus*, or "special autonomy") was applied in the cases of Aceh and West Papua from 2001, the term implied a constrained form of local administration, primarily in relation to the allocation of a promised increase in revenues. Autonomy was likely granted to the Bangsamoro homeland region of the southern Philippines but, similarly to Indonesia, has little substantive content and was undermined in practice. In Sri Lanka, autonomy has been suggested as a model for resolving separatist conflict and was promised under the 1987 Indo-Lanka Accord. However, it was not implemented and more recent models now fall short of the claim of complete independence by the Liberation Tigers of Tamil Eelam (LTTE, or Tamil Tigers).[5]

Accepting in a practical sense that, as a mediated political arrangement, autonomy means whatever the content of any agreement as to its implementation states it to mean, the next question is whether autonomy can adequately address the types of political claims that inspire separatism. Very often in order to promote their claims, separatist movements adopt absolutist rhetoric, such as "separatism/victory/freedom or death" and an ideology around sacrifice (consider, for example, the LTTE Black Tiger suicide battalion and the institutionally endorsed cult within the LTTE of suicide upon capture). This is necessary in order to establish a position from which to prosecute initial political claims. Very often, a nationalist ideology is built up around such claims, or is concomitant with them.[6]

Given the commitment of separatist movements to independence, then, there remains the question as to whether a lesser status such as autonomy or self-government can provide an acceptable mediated outcome. Moreover, questions arise as to whether acceptance of such a mediated outcome can be understood by separatist movements as just a step on a longer journey towards full independence, as per Finland's conversion of autonomy to independence from imperial Russia in 1920, and whether or not autonomy can be a ploy by central governments to buy off separatist claims and pacify a restive population on one hand while undermining both the substance and the spirit of any mediated promises on the other. This can be seen to have been the case in Bangsamoro under the agreement between the Government of the Philippines and the Moro National Liberation Front in 1996, and by the government of Indonesia in Aceh and West Papua in 2001. Similarly, autonomy was understood to be code for "integration" in the case of East Timor in 1999[7] and was rejected in favour of the alternative position of full independence. Governments may also not accept settlements aimed at producing autonomy, particularly if they might lose direct and complete control over vital strategic or economic factors. Beyond the political commitment of movements towards particular goals, and the bad faith that can accompany and undermine mediated compromise agreements, there is also doubt as to whether compromise solutions can adequately address the claims which give rise to separatism in the first place.

The claim of a self-identifying bonded political group in turn raises the question of "nation", while geo-institutional claims of such a nation constitute claims to statehood. Within the context of an established state, the claim is thus to one of separation and reconstitution under a distinct and separate state identity. There are three broad views on claims to nationhood. The first is primordialist; that particular nations have always existed and that they constitute an essentially unchanging social bond. The second, "modernist", view is that nations are relatively recent constructions either of industrial necessity (Gelner 1983), explicit state programmes (Hobsbawam 1983, 2004), or technologically induced cultural unity (Anderson 1991). A third view is that nations are "ethno-symbolic" unities that cohere around symbolic representations of common identification, including civic values (Smith 1998, 2003).

Most states are internally defined by how their social groups are organized, if with varying degrees of dynamism, as constituent parts. Post-colonial states in particular tend to exhibit vertical or regionally based group tendencies, especially where they are constructed from multiple pre-existing ethnicities.[8] That is, ethnic groups that existed prior to the colonial experience and which may have not enjoyed close or comfortable relations with other groups often found themselves conjoined in colonial entities which transformed, in the post-colonial era, as multi-ethnic states.

Few such multi-ethnic colonies have made a fully successful transition to becoming voluntary states (states in which an overwhelming majority of its members freely choose to be citizens); in most cases there has been an element of compulsion in accordance with an overt "nation-building" project. Where this nation-building project has been predicated upon a higher degree of compulsion, and especially where there has been a dominant ethnic group among less dominant groups, this has tended to produce a reaction, often by way of assertion of a separate identity equally but differently conceived as "nation". This then raises two questions, the first being what it is that constitutes a nation, and, relatively, how claims to nationhood can be assessed. The second question concerns issues of legitimacy, voluntarism and compulsion.

National identity as the basis for the assertion of nationalist claims can be characterized in two broad streams. The most common quality of national identity is, as noted, based on ethnicity (Smith 1986*b*, pp. 22–46). A common language is the principal mediator through which individuals who may not know each other but actually or potentially communicate across distance and hence perceive themselves as having a common interest (Anderson 1991). However, basing the national project solely on culture, without extending that to include wider civic values, raises the prospect of reifying a mythical "glorious past" (Smith 1986*b*, pp. 174–208). In reifying itself, ethnicity becomes inwardly focused, exclusivist and reactionary.

Nations have traditionally tended to exist in relation to a specific and usually contiguous and relatively demarcated or delineated territory. The territorial reach of nations, or proto-nations, has historically shifted, especially prior to the advent of Westphalian sovereignty, and populations were often fluid. A key quality necessary for continuing success in sustaining national identity is based on concordance around normative shared values or the positive codification of plural civil values. This extended idea of nationalism comprises what has been termed "civic nationalism", or "civic nationality" (Smith 1998, pp. 210–13). This concept corresponds to a more voluntary, inclusive, participatory and open political society (for example, liberal democracy). In this, national identity and citizenship are ascribed on the basis of commitment to core civic values rather than ethnic origin, thus returning to the original meaning of the term "legitimacy" (see Seymour 2000; Habermas 2001*a*, 2001*b*). Such societies are the ones in which voluntarism and legitimacy are joined.

However, where ethnic bonds are historically weak in relation to the state and civic bonds are not evident, states tend to compel "national" membership, following, rather than preceding, the creation of the state. Such compulsion tends to preclude civic values. That is, not being able to allow the full expression of social plurality, the state rules *by* (often oppressive) law, thus denying justice.

The association of a people with a territory is most likely to be successful in being able to assert a claim to that territory if it is relatively compact and largely contiguous (Gellner 1983, p. 46). A dispersed territory is, relative to population, less easily able to be controlled and hence claimed. Territory is identified as a source of livelihood and a site of mutual defence, overlapping in the analysis of nationalism by Hobsbawm (Hobsbawm 2004, chap. 4; Gellner 1983, chap. 3; Smith 1998, pp. 79–82). The centralized and externally focused nature of industrial organization and the standardization of language it requires can thus be seen as contributing or strengthening both the development of a national identity and providing a basis for subsequent statehood (Hobsbawm 1983, 1990). That being said, there have been instances, however, where the formation of nations and national identities has occurred in numerous pre or non-industrial circumstances.[9]

If "nation" implies some formalization of group identity around a particular programme, then defence and security systems of the state can contribute significantly to this formalization. The group is starkly delineated, while membership is often explicitly reconfirmed, and the group goes through a relatively high degree of social organization under a coherent executive leadership. In this, grievance by members of a particularly identified group which elicits a violent state response may itself be the catalyst for nation formation where previously a less formal group identity existed. The importance of this feature cannot be overstated, as where outsiders may argue that a "nation" has not historically existed, in the face of threat or challenge it can come into being relatively quickly and with a high degree of both coherence and commitment in cases of mutual preservation. What is important, however, is if a sufficient majority of members of a group that reflects a number of key characteristics claim for themselves a national identity, and, in particular, if they are prepared to fight for it, then the claim is ultimately their own to make.

SELF-DETERMINATION

The claim of self-determination assumes that the bonded political community of a nation has no prior capacity to determine its own affairs, but should do so. This is, at one level, a normative claim arising, in the first instance, out of the Wilsonian-Leninist reorganization of Europe into nations that had previously been subsumed under greater empires at the end of the First World War. The logic of this process flowed into the post-World War II period, in which Europe's overseas colonies sought independence. However, as many post-colonial states were based on colonies that did not necessary reflect the unity or distinction of pre-existing ethnic identities, and that many such states at best had difficulty in establishing a non-ethnic (i.e. civic) form of national identity, there have continued to be numerous unresolved claims to separate national identity.

This, then, leads to a potential for competition between the nation as a bonded political group, and the state (Griffiths 2003). A "state" may be confluent with, but is analytically distinct from, "nation". The state, as it is generally understood in the contemporary sense, refers to a specific and delineated area (Smith 1986*b*, p. 235) in which a government embeds institutionalized political and judicial authority (Evans 1995) and claims a monopoly over the legitimate use of force within its sovereign territory (Krader 1976, p. 13). States regard themselves, *prima facie*, as legitimate. Hence, any claim against the state is in their view, *ipso facto*, illegitimate. Claims against the state from within deny the state's implicit claim to representation on the basis of legitimacy. As defining and protecting territorial sovereignty is integral to their being, states, therefore, logically reject separatist claims. Further, while assertions of national self-determination may be supported in principle in international law and appear to reflect the claims of civil and political rights (in relation to self-determination), they are not explicitly supported. There is no international legal mechanism for redress of separatist claims, and if there was it would probably have little binding capacity given the relative weakness of international political institutions (for example, the United Nations) when compared to the specifically located power of states (Packer 1998, 1999, 2000*a*, 2000*b*). That is, as a reflection of *real politik*, claims to separation from the state are only as strong as their capacity to be asserted.

MEDIATED SOLUTIONS

Mediated solutions are therefore intended to act as a "compromise between self-determination and the sanctity of borders" (Graham 2000). In that mediated solutions based on political compromise have been proposed as a method for resolving separatist conflicts, they have increasingly come to take shape around a core set of ideas, commonly referred to as "earned sovereignty". Key characteristics of such mediated outcomes generally include:

1. a multi-stage process of implementation
2. the sharing of sovereignty, or constitutional authority, where the state (or, an international organization) and the sub-state entity may, each, exercise some sovereign or constitutional authority and functions over the territory in question
    (a) the conditional devolution of sovereignty or constitutional authority in a given territory through the phasing out of preceding sovereign authority and the phasing in of a local authority. This is intended to allow the ceding state both the opportunity for adjustment and to help provide surety around the intentions and capacities of the aspiring state. The second type of limit or conditionality placed on any arrangement constitutes conditional sovereignty, where the aspiring state is required to meet certain benchmarks such as human rights enforcement, respect for minority rights and so on before it may acquire increased sovereignty.
    (b) conditionalities placed upon the sovereign reach of the central government, and the extent of local powers. This implies limitations on the extent of the autonomous authority and some of the functions of the autonomous region.
    (c) constrained or limited sovereignty which may manifest as autonomy, federalism or confederation

3. the necessity of building new institutions or adapting existing institutions prior to the determination of the final status of political devolution, often with the assistance of the international community, by which a state is able to manifest its organizational capacity
4. a mechanism for the determination of the final status of the territory in question, where the relationship between the existing state and the aspiring state is articulated, usually by a vote of the aspiring state's population and with the consent and under the supervision of the international community (Williams and Pecci 2004, p. 4; Hooper and Williams 2004; Scharf 2004).

At its most basic, the "earned sovereignty" model entails the conditional and progressive devolution of sovereign powers and authority from a "parent" state to a sub-state entity under international, preferably multinational, supervision. This is generally made available through a peace process as a multi-stage approach to address the issue of the final political status of the sub-state entity, or as a peaceful recognition of the legitimacy of a claim to test sub-state desire for separate status. The case of East Timor reflects a number of elements of such a process.

While mediated solutions such as "earned sovereignty" are legitimate attempts to work past some of the problems of the state-secessionist dichotomy, it also has a number of negative features. These include it being reliant on international goodwill (which may be undermined by disinterest or "realist" strategic self-interest) and being reliant on the agreement of the sovereign state to cede authority. Very often, such an agreement is also reliant upon the majority peoples of the state to accept such an outcome. A further difficulty is the common and usually unresolved issue of minorities within the proposed new state.[10] And, not least, there is the problem of a mediated outcome not being the preferred method of achieving a resolution to competing claims as opposed to a settlement by force of arms.

The role of the mediator in the establishment of autonomy is also critical. A mediator may also have a role in seeking the participation of agreement monitors or peacekeepers, without who, breaches of agreements are possible and, in most cases, probable. Organizations providing such monitors or peacekeepers must be willing to commit them for an extended period, commonly of not less than two years. Mediators or peacekeepers can derive from a unilateral source but, given the potential for a conflict of interest, generally derive from a wider range of sources. The Norwegian role in the Sri Lanka Monitoring Mission was buttressed by monitors from other E.U.

states, while the Aceh Monitoring mission was an E.U. initiative, comprising monitors from most E.U. states but also from other ASEAN states. Similarly, Interfet in East Timor was led by Australian forces, but comprised forces from twenty-three states.

The UN as a source of peacekeepers in particular has been regarded as ideal on one hand, representing the global community rather than potentially narrow state interest. However, it has also had three key drawbacks; willingness of specific states to provide resources for such a mission, the often constrained rules under which the UN operates, and a more or less universal UN tendency towards bureaucratic inefficiency and, very often, incapacity. Potential contributor states may be unwilling to participate in UN-led missions, or may be unwilling to sustain commitment to such missions for an extended period (Guehenno 2008).

With the possible exception of strategic interest, the claim of a dominant constituent group has no rational prior claim to the territory occupied by another group. Should it assert such a claim, it then undermines the basis of its own claim to territory, and manifestation as a state. That is, if the idea of sovereignty is to assert authority over a specific territory in pursuit of the commonly identified interests of a politically bonded group of people then, short of strategic interest, a state should have little concern over whether or not a geographically specific, differentiated politically bonded group within its claimed territory seeks its own territorially based self-determination. Where claims against this are made, they generally reflect the above noted strategic interest, often combined with economic interest and concerns about the protection of minorities within the claimed territory, as has occurred in Sri Lanka, Aceh, West Papua and Mindanao.

While the case study countries formally recognize ethnic minorities, each has dominant ethnic majorities: Javanese in Indonesia, Sinhalese in Sri Lanka and Christians in the Philippines.[11] Where that civic national identity building project fails (e.g. Indonesia prior to 2004), or fails to maintain its earlier promise (e.g. Sri Lanka, Philippines), in so far as a national identity is constructed, it can in a functional sense tend to be ethnically or normatively exclusivist, and hence alienate minority ethnic groups from the national project.

By way of illustration, as noted by Miller in this volume, expectations within Aceh upon Indonesia's independence were that the post-colonial independent state would attain a high level of autonomy within a loose federal framework, so as to functionally determine its own affairs. However, Aceh's loss of provincial status and Indonesia's reorganization as a unitary state was regarded as betrayal, leading to rebellion (Reid 2004; Kell 1995). The failure of the "special administrative" status of Aceh intended to resolve this conflict led to the Free Aceh Movement (1976–2005) (see Miller in this volume).

The situation was somewhat different in West Papua, as a later inclusion into the state (functionally 1963, formally 1969) (see Singh in this volume). In this case, initial aspirations were oriented towards complete independence, rather than being subsumed into Indonesia (GoN 1961, pp. 10–14). Thus, the aspirations of independence were replaced by what many in West Papua viewed as a further form of colonialism. Similar was the situation of East Timor, which proclaimed independence on 27 November 1975, in the hope of achieving international recognition to deter an imminent Indonesian invasion. On 7 December 1975, however, Indonesia formally invaded East Timor,[12] ushering in a new era of colonialism, until 20 September 1999 (after which there was an interim UN administration until 2002) (see Soares in this volume). In Sri Lanka, initial hopes for post-independence development were in significant part met by a democratic government presiding over relatively high levels of human development.[13] However, an assertion of Sinhalese majority rights at the expense of the Tamil minority quickly alienated much of the Tamil population, leading to communal discord and violence (see Uyangoda and Sahadevan in this volume).

In East Timor, the UN mediator monitored and, following a UN-supervised ballot (and brief forced withdrawal), oversaw peacemaking, peacekeeping and institution building. Alternatives to this general model generally focus on other than complete independence, including types of partial devolution, including localized decision-making (Sri Lanka under the 1987 Indo-Sri Lanka Accord), regional autonomy (Aceh, Hong Kong and Bangsamoro[14]), federation (proposed by both the Government of Sri Lanka and the LTTE in March 2003 (RNMFA 2003) and confederation (as mooted by the LTTE until November 2007). The main difficulties with these alternatives, in particular with localized decision making and regional autonomy is that the devolved powers may be easily subverted in practice, meaning that the form but not necessarily the substance of separatist claims is addressed. A further implication of this is that separatist claims may continue or resurface.

In Aceh, international pressure for a resolution to that conflict quickly developed following the 2004 tsunami that left around 200,000 people dead or missing and destroyed much of its infrastructure. The Indonesian government had been seeking a resolution to the Aceh conflict under the terms of its "special autonomy" package, and sought mediation by the Helsinki-based Crisis Management Initiative. On 22 December 2004, GAM agreed to CMI mediated talks. The tsunami struck two days later, and while it was not the reason for the talks, it did act as a catalyzer and compeller. GAM accepted a more genuine autonomy under the term "self-government", including greater local democratization, with the government agreeing to external monitoring of the eventual agreement by an E.U.-led Aceh Monitoring Mission (Ahtissari 2006).

In West Papua, the Indonesian government has said it would talk with separatist leaders, but only within Indonesia and without international mediation. These two criteria were rejected by West Papuan separatist leaders.[15] In principle, however, negotiations had been agreed to. In Sri Lanka, however, negotiations had at best achieved a ceasefire (2002–January 2008) but, unlike the 2005 Aceh resolution, without attempting to address, substantively, the underlying causes of the separatist conflict. As a consequence, this ceasefire only entrenched existing positions and, when circumstances changed around the agreement, the agreement itself began to unravel. In this respect, peace agreements, regardless of whether they contain measures to address substantive claims, only succeed in so far as the parties to the agreement honour both the letter and the spirit of the agreement. If the agreement does not address substantive issues and there is no clearly identified mechanism by which the aspect is envisioned to proceed, it is commonly only a matter of time before the ceasefire collapses.

Other factors that also play a critical role in separatist conflict resolution include the capacity of the mediation party, the extent of the "parent" state government to negotiate sovereignty, the extent to which causal issues underlining separatist claims are addressed, international guarantees and sanctions, agreement monitoring, the capacity for extended multilateral peacekeeping operations, and the extent of commitment to institution and capacity building measures. It is also imperative that representative parties to the talks have the capacity to legitimately represent their constituencies, and are able to compel compliance with their decisions among potential or actual dissenters.

In summary, autonomy or other mediated solutions to separatist conflict appear to take a number of increasingly conventional features of negotiation processes intended to assist resolving separatist conflict. This idea has problematic features, these include a *prima facie* assumption that the complete or partial sovereignty for the autonomous region is a legitimate condition. While many and perhaps most separatist movements have some legitimacy to their claims, based on ethnicity, territory and a sense of lack of belonging to the "parent" state, the assumption that the parent state will negotiate away elements of its sovereignty contradict the conventional sense of state sovereignty. Few states are willing to do this, and most that do only do so through a lack of options. That is, mediated outcomes that reduce state sovereignty are implicitly pro-separatist in its outlook, which may be a legitimate perspective but is unlikely to earn the trust of guardians of parent states. To this end, autonomy proposals must be neutrally balanced to allow parent states to engage in negotiation without understanding that, to paraphrase Oscar Wilde, the status of the claimant state has been established, and they are only haggling over the terms.

The mediated model also aspires to a universality of application, especially in its "earned sovereignty" guise, which demonstrates both the strength and the weakness of the legal academics who have tended to dominate discussion of the idea. Attempts to codify a conflict mediation model appear to be intended to serve as a kind of statute for the resolution of separatist conflicts. Yet, while many and perhaps most of the abstract underlying features of such conflicts are common enough, short of a lack of self-determination being given the status of a crime against humanity, there is no global legal mechanism which could impose such a statute. Nor, in a world that to a large degree remains based on both the legal and practical inviolability of sovereign states, are states likely to recognize such a statute. As a consequence, one of the realities of conflict negotiation that remains intact, is that the negotiating table is the place where the rules of the game are made as the game progresses and are, in large part, determined by the respective capacities of the bargaining parties. In reality, a state in a relatively weaker position will concede more, and a state in a relatively stronger position will concede less (Habeeb 1988).

Finally, given that sovereignty is the principal reason for the being of the state, placing it on the table as a *prima facie* point of negotiation is likely to lead to automatic state rejection. It may be in practice that any negotiation, which implies compromise, will lead to a practical reduction in the extent of state sovereignty. But this need not be posited as an implied outcome in order to achieve a successful resolution. What is more of concern, and relevance, is that any negotiated agreement be codified in ways that are consistent and mutually agreeable and, so far as is able, enshrined. The principal method of achieving this enshrinement is through constitutional amendment or rewriting. Employing "constitutionality" rather than "sovereignty" then sidesteps the issue of sovereignty while at the same time formalizing and, in legal terms, guaranteeing the negotiated agreement.

This then brings the process of negotiation back to first principle issues; what does each party claim, why do they claim it, and can the underlying concerns that inform their claim be met by an alternative arrangement. In most cases of separatism, the claim for a new state is based on the failure of the existing state to adequately address the legitimate concerns of a territorially specific ethnic group. This is usually as a consequence of the failure of the state to regard, both, its citizens as equal and their concerns as equally important. This then raises the question of the origins and nature of the state, and whether this can be changed to accommodate the legitimate grievances of separatist claimants, whether there is sufficient capacity to change or trust in such change, or whether the conflict has become so bitterly entrenched that the only option is for a degree of separation or divorce. Assuming no or little capacity for state change, or a lack of trust in state change, then partial sovereignty, autonomy, federation or confederation may be acceptable solutions. In each of these circumstances, a return to and reliance upon law as the basis for legitimacy appears as a necessary precondition. This implies a focus on constitutionality as the primary guarantor of political arrangements, rather than the more blunt claims of sovereignty or its diminution. The proposal put here, then, is that separatist conflict can be resolved through a mediated approach intended to institute or re-institute state or sub-state rule of law. The outcome of such a process will, therefore, be what could be referred to as "mediated constitutionality".

Notes

[1] See Kirschner (2007), Williams and Pecci (2004), Scharf (2004), Williams (2003), Hooper and Williams (2003), Heyman (2003), Bugajski, Hitchner and Williams (2002).

[2] Larmore, in Weinestock and Nadeau (2004), p. 106, also Ober (2000), Cicero (1998).

[3] See Chand and Coffman (2008) on reduced state economic capacity.

[4] Luis (2000), Englebert (2000), Cornwell (1999) and Hirschmann (1987) discuss this phenomenon in relation to sub-Saharan African states.

[5] The claims of the LTTE have shifted at different times according to changing circumstances, and have included federalism, confederation and absolute independence.

[6] See di Tiro (1984), Prabhkaran (2006), Ondowame (2007), Lingga (2002), Joliffe (2001) in relation to the nationalist ideologies of, respectively, Aceh, Tamil Eelam, West Papua, Bangsamoro and East Timor.

7   By way of illustration of the local meaning of autonomy, the local military organized "pro-autonomy" militias referred to themselves, overall, as the *Pasukan Perjuang Integrasi* (Integration Fighting Force).
8   A similar claim can also be made for multi-ethnic states that are compelled through a variety of circumstances to come together as political unities, Boznia-Herzegovina being a case in point.
9   Payne (1969), for example, refers extensively to the post-revolutionary but pre-industrial nation of France.
10 This refers to both further minorities as well as residual elements of the original majority, e.g. Sinhalese and Muslims in the claimed Tamil Eelam and Gayo, Alas and transmigrant (predominantly Javanese) minorities in Aceh and similar transmigrant and economic migrant minorities in West Papua.
11 Assuming religious difference as the basis for cultural difference in this instance.
12 Indonesian forces had engaged in cross-border incursion for the previous ten weeks.
13 As defined by the Human Development Index.
14 Bangsamoro in the southern Philippines was, at the time of writing, being negotiated between the Government of the Philippines and the Moro Islamic Liberation Front, with agreement on the concept of an autonomous administrative region, but talks stalling over technical details, including seabed boundaries and division of economic resources.
15 This position was confirmed a number of times but, most uniformly, at a meeting of leaders of separatist groups at a secret location in September 2007, at which the author was present.

References

Ahtisaari, M. *The Helsinki Accord and Its Implementation*. Helsinki: Crisis Management Initiative, 14 August 2006.

Alatas, A. *The Pebble in the Shoe: The Diplomatic Struggle for East Timor*. Jakarta: JP/R. Berto Wedhatama, 2006.

Alfian, I. "Aceh and the Holy War (Prang Sabil)". In *Verandah of Violence: Background to the Aceh Problem*, edited by A. Reid. Singapore: Singapore University Press, 2003.

Anderson, B. *Imagined Communities*. Verso, 1991.

Aspinall, E. "Aceh: Elections and the Possibility of Peace". *Australian Policy Forum*. Austral Policy Forum 06-37A, 18 December 2006.

Avebury, E. *Hansard*. United Kingdom: House of Lords, 8 January 2007.

Broadlef. "Movements for National, Ethnic Liberation or Regional Autonomy", 14 February 2005. <http://www.broadleft.org/natliber.htm> (accessed 4 March 2008).

Bugajski, J., B. Hitchner, and P. Williams. *Achieving a Final Status Settlement for Kosovo.* Washington, D.C.: Center for Strategic and International Studies, 2002.

Chand, S. and R. Coffman. "How Soon Can Donors Exit From Post-Colonial States?". Working Paper no. 141. Washington, D.C.: Center for Global Development, February 2008.

Cicero, M. *The Republic and The Laws,* edited by J. Powell and translated by N. Rudd. Oxford: Oxford University Press, 1998.

Connor, W. *Ethnonationalism: The Quest for Understanding.* Princeton, NJ: Princeton University Press, 1994.

Cornwell, R. "The End of the Post-Colonial State System in Africa?". *African Security Review,* vol. 8, no. 2 (1999).

Derrida, J. *Writing and Difference.* Chicago: University of Chicago Press, 1980.

Englebert, P. "Pre-Colonial Institutions, Post-Colonial States, and Economic Development in Topical Africa". *Political Research Quarterly,* vol. 53, no. 1 (March 2000): 7–36

Evans, P. *Embedded Autonomy.* Princeton, NJ: Princeton University Press, 1995.

Foucault, M. *The Archeology of Knowledge and The Discourse on Language,* translated by R. Swyer. New York: Pantheon Books, 1982.

Gellner, E. *Nations and Nationalism.* Ithaca, NY: Cornell University Press, 1983.

Gibbs, P. "Resistance and Hope in a Theology of Land for Papua New Guinea". *Australian E-Journal of Theology,* issue no. 5, August 2005.

GoN. *Report on Netherlands New Guinea for the Year 1961,* presented to the Secretary-General of the United Nations, pursuant of Article 73 (e) of the Charter, Government of the Netherlands, The Haguem, 1961.

Graham, L. "Self-Determination for the Indigenous Peoples After Kosovo: Translating Self-Determination 'Into Practice' and 'Into Peace'". *ILSA (International Law Students' Association) Journal of International and Comparative Law* (2000): 455–65.

Griffiths, M. "Self-determination, International Society and World Order". *Macquarie Law Journal,* vol. 3 (2003).

Guehenno, J-M. "Under-Secretary-General Cites Lack of Sustained International Interest as Critical to Difficulties of Maintaining Peacekeeping Gains Made in Key Conflict Areas". GA/PK/196, Department of Public Information, United Nations, New York, 10 March 2008.

Habeeb, W. *Power and Tactics in International Negotiations: How Weak Nations Bargain With Strong Nations.* Baltimore: Johns Hopkins University Press, 1988.

Habermas, J. "A Constitution for Europe?". *New Left Review,* no. 11 (2001*a*): 5–26.

———. *A Postnational Constellation.* Cambridge, Mass: MIT Press, 2001*b*.

Heymann, K. "Earned Sovereignty for Kashmir: The Legal Methodology to Avoiding a Nuclear Holocaust". *American University International Law Review,* vol. 19, no. 2 (2003).

Hirschmann, D. "Early Post-Colonial Bureaucracy as History: The Case of the Lesotho Central Planning and Development Office, 1965–1975". *The International Journal of African Historical Studies*, vol. 20, no. 3 (1987): 455–70.

Hobsbawm, E. *The Invention of Traditions*, edited by E. Hobsbawm and E. Ranger. Cambridge: Cambridge University Press, 1983.

———. *Nations and Nationalism since 1870: Programme, Myth, Reality*. First published in 1990. Cambridge: Cambridge University Press, 2004.

Hooper, J. and P. Williams. "Earned Sovereignty: The Political Dimension". *Denver Journal of International Law*, no. 31 (2004).

Huntington, S. *The Soldier and the State: The Theory and Politics of Civil-Military Relations*. Cambridge, Mass: Harvard University Press, 1957.

Joliffe, J. *East Timor: Nationalism and Colonialism*. Brisbane: University of Queensland Press, 2001.

Kell, T. *The Roots of Acehnese Rebellion*. Ithaca, N.Y.: Cornell Modern Indonesia Project, 1995.

Kingsbury, D. *Peace in Aceh: A Personal Account of the Aceh Peace Process*. Jakarta and Singapore: Equinox, 2006.

———. "Secessionist Legitimacy: A Comparative Analysis". In *On the Way to Statehood: Secession and Globalization*, edited by P. Radan and A. Pavkovic. London: Ashgate, 2008.

Kirschner, N. "Making Bread From Broken Eggs: A Basic Recipe For Conflict Resolution Using Earned Sovereignty". 28 *Whittier Law Review*, vol. 11, no. 31 (2007).

Krader, L. *Dialectic of Civil Society*. New York: Prometheus Books, 1976.

Lacina, B. "Understanding and Explaining the Severity of Civil Wars". Paper presented at the annual meeting of the International Studies Association, Honolulu, Hawaii, 2005.

Lingga, A. "Democratic Approach to Pursue the Bangsamoro People's Right to Self-Determination". Statement on behalf of Bangsamoro People's Consultative Assembly, Geneva, 17 July 2002.

Luis, J. "The Politics of State, Society and Economy". *International Journal of Social Economics*, vol. 27, no. 3 (2000): 277–343.

Lyotard, J-F. *The Post-Modern Condition: A Report on Knowledge*, translated by G. Bennington and B. Massumi. Minnesota: University of Minnesota Press, 1984.

"Mine Kills 25 in Sri Lanka; Autonomy Bill Passes". *New York Times*, 13 November 1987.

Nessen, W. "Sentiments Made Visible: The Rise and Reason of Aceh's National Liberation". In *Verandah of Violence: The Background to the Aceh Problem*, edited by A. Reid. Seattle: University of Washington Press, 2007.

Ober, J. "Quasi-rights: Political Boundaries and Social Diversity in Democratic Athens". *Social Philosophy and Policy* 17, no. 1 (2000): 27–61.

Ondowame, J. "West Papua National Coalition for Liberation call for peace talks". Media Release. West Papua Peoples' Representative Office, Port Vila, 2007.

Open Directory Project. <http://www.dmoz.org/Society/Issues/Territorial_Disputes/> (accessed 4 March 2008).
Packer, J. "Autonomy within the OSCE: The Case of Crimea". In *Autonomy: Applications and Implications*, edited by M. Suski. The Hague: Kluwer Law International, 1998.
―――. "The Implementation of the Right to Self-Determination as a Contribution to Conflict Prevention". In *Report of the International Conference of Experts*, edited by M. Praag and O. Seroo. Barcelona: UNESCO, 1999.
―――. "Self-determination and International Law", "West Papua and the Quest for Self-Determination". *Self-Determination and International Law* Utrecht, (2000*a*): 6–11.
―――. "The Origin and Nature of the Lund Recommendations on the Effective Participation of National Minorities in Public Life". *Helsinki Monitor* 11, no. 4 (2000*b*): 29–61.
Payne, T. *Rights of Man*. Harmondsworth: Penguin Books, 1969.
Prabhakaran, V. Tamil Eelam Heroes Day Address. Undisclosed location, 2006.
Reid, A. *The Contest for North Sumatra: Atjeh, the Netherlands and Britain, 1858–1898*. Kuala Lumpur: Oxford University Press, 1969.
―――. *The Blood of the People: Revolution and the End of Traditional Rule in Northern Sumatra*. Kuala Lumpur: Oxford University Press, 1979.
―――. "Indonesia, Aceh and the Modern Nation-state". Speech to National Integration and Regionalism in Indonesia and Malaysia conference, University of New South Wales at the Australian Defence Force Acadamey, Canberra, 26–28 November 2004.
RNMFA. "Consolidation of Ceasefire Top Priority, Sri Lanka Monitoring Mission to be Strengthened". Press Release, Sri Lanka Peace Talks — Agreed Statement on behalf of the Parties. Royal Norwegian Ministry of Foreign Affairs, Oslo. 21 March 2003.
Scharf, M. "Earned Sovereignty: Juridical Underpinnings". *Denver Journal of International Law and Policy* 31, no. 3 (2004).
Seymour, M. "On Redefining the Nation", in *Nationalism and Ethnic Conflict: Philosophical Perspectives*, edited by N. Miscevic. La Salle and Chicago: Open Court, 2000.
Sjamsuddin, N. *The Republican Revolt: A Study of the Acehnese Rebellion*. Singapore: Institute of Southeast Asian Studies, 1985.
Smith, A. "State-making and Nation-building". In *States in History*, edited by J. Hall. Oxford: Basil Blackwell, 1986*a*.
―――. *The Ethnic Origins of Nations*. Oxford: Blackwell Publishers, 1986*b*.
―――. *Nationalism and Modernism*. London: Routledge, 1998.
―――. *Chosen Peoples: Sacred Sources of National Identity*. Oxford: Oxford University Press, 2003.
Tiro, di. H. *The Price of Freedom: The Unfinished Diary of Hasan di Tiro*. Ontario: The Open Press, 1984.

United Nations. "Declaration on the Granting of Independence to Colonial Countries and Peoples". General Assembly resolution 1514 (XV), UN document A/4684 (1960).

Waltz, K. *Theory of International Politics*. Columbus: McGraw-Hill, 1979.

Weber, M. *Social and Economic Organization,* edited by T. Parsons. New York: Oxford University Press, 1946.

———. *The Protestant Ethic and the Spirit of Capitalism*. Oxon: Routledeg Classics, 2006.

Weinstock, D. and C. Nadeau. *Republicanism: History, Theory and Practice*. London and Portland: Frank Cass, 2004.

Williams, P. "Earned Sovereignty: The Road to Resolving the Conflict Over Kosovo's Final Status". *Denver Journal of International Law and Policy*, June 2003.

Williams, P. and F. Pecci. "Earned Sovereignty: Bridging the Gap between Sovereignty and Self-Determination". *Stanford Journal of International Law* 40, no. 10 (2004).

3

SELF-GOVERNANCE AS A FRAMEWORK FOR CONFLICT RESOLUTION IN ACEH

Michelle Ann Miller

The signing of an historic peace agreement on 15 August 2005 in Helsinki by the Indonesian government and the armed separatist Free Aceh Movement (*Gerakan Acheh*[1] *Merdeka*, GAM) brought an end to one of the most enduring armed separatist conflicts in Asia. This agreement was strengthened by the introduction in July 2006 of a Law on Governing Aceh (LoGA), which incorporated many of the core components of the Helsinki agreement and conferred quasi-federal powers of "self-government" to Aceh within the Indonesian unitary state. Though Jakarta had in the past offered different forms of "special autonomy" to Aceh in an effort to win its would-be nemesis back to the Indonesian nationalist cause, this was the first time GAM had been persuaded to transform their militant movement into a political organization that could constructively engage with Indonesia's process of political development.

This chapter will consider the nexus between Jakarta's different offers of autonomy to Aceh and the growth and reduction of Acehnese separatist activity. It will examine how and why Jakarta's decision to grant Aceh self-government buttressed the Helsinki peace process when previous special autonomy packages had failed to abate hostilities between the warring parties. Finally, the chapter will consider what makes Aceh's self-governing status unique and assess the province's prospects for sustainable peace under the new system.

The central conclusion of the analysis is that the most critical variable in the resolution of the almost three-decade-old Aceh conflict was political will, or agency. This political will was certainly reinforced, if not to a great extent, created by particular circumstances such as the December 2004 Indian Ocean tsunami and by the international pressure and assistance that followed the natural disaster. Yet natural disasters do not end human conflicts, and without political determination Jakarta and GAM would have been unable to broker a negotiated settlement and remain basically committed towards the long-term project of establishing the self-government of Aceh in Indonesia. Without political will, Jakarta would also have been unable to subordinate the Indonesian military (TNI)[2] to civilian control at a time when its informal influence over central government decision-making was considerable, and when an unprecedented number of security forces personnel were engaged in counterinsurgency operations in the province. Though GAM's military and political reach into Aceh's countryside had been seriously attenuated by the Indonesian military operations against them, past counterinsurgency campaigns had shown that the rebels could not be defeated by force alone; conversely, military operations had consistently been the primary cause of GAM's regeneration due to depredations committed by Indonesian security forces against the local population. If not for their own commitment towards a lasting settlement to the conflict, GAM could have also used the cessation of hostilities under the terms of the Helsinki agreement to recruit new members and fortify their shadow civil administration, which performed certain Indonesian government functions.[3] But because both sides have remained committed towards the Helsinki peace process, self-government has continued to gain ground as a viable framework for conflict resolution in Aceh, even though the challenges that lie ahead remain substantial and the future sustenance of the peace process is by no means assured.

BACKGROUND TO ACEHNESE AUTONOMY

The collapse of President Soeharto's New Order regime in May 1998, after more than three decades, was accompanied by some new initiatives to depart from the authoritarian regime's repressive and military approach in dealing with Indonesia's armed separatist conflicts in Aceh, East Timor and Irian Jaya (now partitioned into "Papua" and "West Papua") by promoting dialogue, decentralization and "special autonomy". Most political leaders in Jakarta saw decentralization as the most democratic way of accommodating the country's centrifugal forces and were prepared to recognize a "special" place for Indonesia's troubled separatist regions within the unitary state. However, the remarkable decision by Soeharto's self-appointed successor, President B.J. Habibie, to resolve the national identity dispute in East Timor by granting that province a referendum on national self-determination was widely seen as unacceptable in Indonesia and contributed towards his political defeat in the 1999 presidential election. For Indonesian nationalists, any debate about the national identity questions in Indonesia's separatist regions had to be constructed within, and had to seek to strengthen the territorial integrity and national cohesion of the unitary state, not to weaken or destroy it.

Jakarta's different offers of "special autonomy" and "self government" to Aceh in the post-Soeharto era were set against a backdrop of broken promises of autonomy and systematic repression by previous Indonesian governments. In the 1950s and early 1960s, Acehnese involvement in a broader Darul Islam (House of Islam) rebellion had largely stemmed from regionalist anger over Aceh's incorporation into the neighbouring province of North Sumatra.[4] This rebellion was eventually resolved in Aceh through a combination of Indonesian military operations and negotiations after Indonesia's first president, Sukarno, responded in May 1959 to Acehnese demands to manage their own affairs in accordance with Islam by conferring in principle *Daerah Istimewa* (Special Region) status to the re-established province of Aceh.

In many ways, Aceh's first separatist insurgency grew out of Jakarta's failure to honour the terms of the Darul Islam settlement. The Acheh-Sumatra National Liberation Front (ASNLF, also called GAM)[5] was launched in December 1976 by Tengku Hasan Muhammad di Tiro, a successful businessman and former self-appointed Darul Islam "ambassador" to the United Nations.[6] Like the Darul Islam insurgents, Hasan di Tiro, who in his earlier writings had promoted a broadly federal-style arrangement in Aceh's relations with Jakarta[7], was angered by the growing centralization of state power under Soeharto's New Order regime, which gradually rendered Aceh's *Daerah Istimewa* status meaningless. The New Order's assimilationist nation-building project emphasized a rigid interpretation of national unity in which regional assertions of diversity and difference were either confined to the symbolic realm or were forcefully repressed.[8] Economically, too, the New Order's national development project did not lead to substantive improvements in the local economy, even after the 1971 discovery of vast oil and gas reserves in North Aceh. Most of the profits were siphoned out of Aceh to political, military and business elites in Java, which later fuelled dreams amongst many Acehnese secessionists of turning their province into an independent Brunei. As the site of lucrative national oil and gas assets, Aceh's natural resource wealth also influenced Jakarta's decision to deploy large numbers of security forces to the province, whose aggressive response to perceived security threats has produced thousands of civilian casualties.

Jakarta's ability to convince the Acehnese that it was worth remaining part of Indonesia was further undermined, and also complicated by the New Order's intolerance of separatism, as shown in 1989 by the launch of a counterinsurgency campaign against GAM. The establishment of a Red Net Operation Implementation Command (*Komando Pelaksana Operasi Jaring Merah*) in Aceh effectively transformed the province into a Military Operations Area (*Daerah Operasi Militer*, DOM) for the next decade.[9] The human rights abuses that accompanied these operations further alienated Acehnese society from Indonesian authority and created conditions ripe for the regeneration of GAM in the post-Soeharto era. By mid-1998, when DOM ended and "non-organic"[10] battalions were withdrawn from the province, Acehnese anger towards Jakarta had become deeply embedded and manifested into widespread demands for retribution, compensation and social justice.

By mid-1998, Indonesian state power and authority had been severely compromised on multiple fronts across the archipelago. The initiation of the national democratization process following Soeharto's resignation produced a highly fractured national political landscape that created space for different viewpoints to be heard, including those of separatists. Indonesia's armed forces were institutionally weakened by internal factional divisions and were widely discredited as the primary instrument of authoritarian repression by the newly liberated national media. Indonesia was also the country hit hardest by the 1997 Asian financial crisis, where rising unemployment and poverty levels and soaring food prices translated into a sharp increase in crime and general lawlessness across the republic. The social impact of the economic meltdown in Aceh, along with the island of Java, East and West Kalimantan, and parts of Sumatra and eastern Indonesia, was especially profound.[11] In Aceh, some seized this opportunity to pressure Jakarta into providing redress for their long-standing grievances in the form of demands for greater regional autonomy, while others began to look towards the creation of an independent polity in which they would be free to govern themselves without fear of statist violence and with control over their own lives and livelihoods.

SEARCH FOR A NEGOTIATED SETTLEMENT

It was within this volatile national context that Indonesia's ruling establishment began to look towards decentralization as a means of restoring political and economic stability to stem the possibility of the "Balkanization" of Indonesia. Following the 1997 Asian financial crisis, the push to decentralize was also influenced by international donor and lending agencies such as the World Bank and the International Monetary Fund (IMF), which exchanged policy advice for financial disbursements to Indonesia, and which tended to promote decentralization as a way of strengthening local institutional capacity and democratic governance. The loudest calls, however, came from the regions, where local political and business elites applied growing pressure on the central government for political change and the realignment of centre-periphery relations.

While there was broad consensus amongst Indonesia's political leadership that some form of decentralization was necessary to re-establish law and order, there was considerable disagreement about how much central state power should be devolved to the regions, and within which constitutional framework. By late 1998 a national debate was starting to take shape about the competing merits of Indonesia's existing unitary system versus federal statehood. Most Indonesians negatively equated the concept of federalism with the former discredited Dutch colonial system and with efforts to weaken Indonesia's nation-building project. Though federations and unitary states take many different practical forms — some federations are far more centralized (such as Russia and the Czech Republic) than decentralized unitary states (for example, the United Kingdom and the Netherlands) — the two-tier federal system suggests a certain level of decentralization, whereas unitary statehood implies a greater degree of centralized control. In Indonesia, too, unitary state proponents tended to promote a more limited form of autonomy than advocates of federalism, at least during the early years of the decentralization debate. Conservative nationalists often argued that granting "too much" autonomy to Indonesia's conflict areas was tantamount to returning to the Dutch colonial federation and posed a threat to Indonesia's territorial sovereignty and national cohesion. By contrast, Indonesian federalists (who only ever comprised a small minority) maintained that the centripetal tendencies of the unitary state precluded the consolidation of inclusive democracy, and that subscribers to the "kindergarten theory" that federalism would lead to national disintegration were not seriously committed towards providing redress for the grievances of ethnic minority groups in Indonesia's conflict regions.[12]

Related to this federal-unitary statehood debate was a central dilemma that would plague the Indonesian government for much of the first decade of Indonesia's transition to democracy in its efforts to resolve the Aceh conflict. This dilemma principally revolved around the issue of how much freedom to grant the Acehnese people without releasing control over the territory of Aceh. Jakarta's dilemma was reflected in the high level of disconnect between Jakarta's security and autonomy policies about Aceh under the first three post-Soeharto administrations. Under the successive governments of B.J. Habibie, Abdurrahman Wahid and Megawati Sukarnoputri, some efforts were made to search for a negotiated settlement to the Aceh conflict through different offers of "special autonomy" and limited peace talks with GAM. For the most part, however, the Indonesian state relied more heavily on "security operations" in dealing with Aceh's separatist insurgency. One reason for this was that the Indonesian military was able to claw back some of its former political influence from the New Order regime under weak civilian post-Soeharto administrations and reassert itself as the primary defender of national unity. The increasingly intractable Aceh conflict created opportunities for the Indonesian military to become embedded in the state's nascent democratic institutions and prevent Indonesia's political leadership from internalizing crucial aspects of democratic procedure.

In addition to their ambitions for a greater role in national political life, sections of Indonesia's military establishment also had vested economic interests in perpetuating the Aceh conflict. With the Indonesian state only providing one-third of the national defense budget, the armed forces remained heavily reliant on alternative funding sources, which Aceh's war economy and rich natural resources provided in abundance. Soldiers and police officers were involved in every sector of the local economy, such as providing private security services to multinational companies, participating in Aceh's illegal logging and marijuana industries, extortion, commercial agriculture, exporting native fauna such as Sumatran tigers and exotic birds, and selling arms to GAM (including the direct sale of weapons from the Indonesian military's PT Pindad arms factory in Bandung).[13] That these business interests operated outside state control encouraged security forces personnel to subvert or ignore central government policy directives that endangered benefits derived from the pre-existing order. Resolution of the Aceh conflict thus threatened to bring an end to these opportunities for personal and institutional enrichment.

Beyond the Indonesian military's political and business interests in Aceh, the sharp reduction in Indonesian state authority that accompanied regime change and the national economic collapse seemed to produce a system and political leaders who functioned on the assumption of limited state capacity. That is, even though some troublesome political issues such as the national identity problem in Aceh could be put on the table for discussion, they were ultimately seen as too hard to deal with. While Indonesia's civilian leadership remained divided and indecisive about how to deal with GAM insurgents, however, the TNI continued to offer its traditional, if disingenuous "solution": that any *end* to the Aceh conflict had to *begin* with the annihilation of the rebels.

Jakarta's first two offers of "special autonomy" to Aceh in the post-Soeharto era failed to achieve their goal of reducing centre-periphery tensions because of their ineffectual response to the underlying causes of the conflict and also because they were not properly implemented. The first offer of limited special autonomy to Aceh in September 1999 via the promulgation of Law No. 44/1999 formally recognized the "Special Status of the Special Province of Aceh" in the fields of religion (Islamic law), education, and customary law (*adat*). This formula, which was based on the terms of the 1959 Darul Islam settlement, reflected the prevailing belief in Jakarta at the time that the Aceh conflict had stemmed from centralized authoritarian rule and could be redressed accordingly through decentralization and democratization. Related to this perception was the idea that Acehnese support for GAM would wane if local *ulama* (Islamic religious teachers/ leaders) were restored to the position of sociopolitical influence that they had enjoyed prior to the New Order. It was this rationale that informed the decision to allow the Acehnese to start implementing Islamic law (*Shari'a*) and to create an independent *ulama* council with the same status and decision-making powers as Aceh's provincial legislature.[14]

Law No. 44/1999, however, responded to none of the primary causes of the conflict. Even Aceh's then governor, Syamsuddin Mahmud, who maintained close ties to Jakarta, expressed his disappointment with the legislation, claiming that it represented "a kind of statement about Aceh's special status ... [but] not really special autonomy".[15] Amongst the civilian population, the new special autonomy law was widely unpopular, especially within the context of Aceh's deteriorating security environment and the intensifying counterinsurgency operations against GAM in the countryside, where 75 per cent of the local population lives and where the worst of the fighting took place during the conflict. For many Acehnese, whose daily experience of Indonesian authority was of violence, the invocation of *Shari'a* through Law No. 44/1999 was seen an "unwanted gift" from Jakarta that did not promise to provide any relief from the fighting or facilitate the dispensation of justice for human rights victims and their families. Though

Aceh's population is almost entirely Muslim,[16] the demands by GAM and their civilian supporters were explicitly nationalist in nature. GAM based their claims to territorial sovereignty on the construct of a distinctive Acehnese ethnic, linguistic, cultural, historical and geographic specific identity, and never sought to establish ties with Islamic movements in Indonesia or elsewhere. According to GAM, the *real* reason why Jakarta was imposing Islamic law in Aceh was to attract international support for its plans to launch a full-scale military offensive against the rebels and to portray Islam in Aceh as being of a "fundamentalist" or "fanatical" type. Aceh's independence movement was certainly far broader than GAM, encompassing civil society groups and organizations across the entire political spectrum. Yet public opinion was overwhelmingly in favour of GAM's nationalist imperative and there was a strong lack of grassroots support for what was generally seen as a "concocted" government version of *Shari'a* like that which had been imposed in Aceh during Dutch colonial times. Importantly, Law No. 44/1999 was also hurriedly passed three weeks after the East Timorese voted to separate from Indonesia in a United Nations-monitored referendum on self-determination when concerns that Indonesia was on the verge of national disintegration peaked. In Aceh, where the outcome of the East Timor ballot had been eagerly awaited, there was considerable optimism amongst the local population that it was only a matter of time before the Acehnese would similarly be granted an East Timor-style exit option from Indonesia. The precariousness of Indonesian state authority in Aceh was shown on 8–9 November 1999 at a "rally of millions" in the provincial capital of Banda Aceh, when some 500,000 of Aceh's 4.2 million people gathered at the Baiturrahman Mosque to demand an East Timor-style referendum on Aceh's political status.

Like Law No. 44/1999 before it, Jakarta's second more comprehensive offer of special autonomy to Aceh in July 2001 lacked grassroots support and was hardly implemented amidst the escalating violence on the ground. Law No. 18/2001, which officially changed Aceh's name to Nanggroe Aceh Darussalam (NAD, lit., State of Aceh, Abode of Peace) granted Aceh significant political, economic and legal concessions, including the return of most of its natural resource wealth, the right to hold direct democratic local elections, and the establishment of new institutions to further the expansion of Islamic law. Except for *Shari'a*, however, which Acehnese *ulama* actively promoted in order to increase their own access to institutionalized power, the other key components of the NAD law were either mismanaged or never enacted. Jakarta continued to withhold most of Aceh's resource revenue under the new system and direct democratic local elections were indefinitely "postponed" after GAM argued that local elections would decide Aceh's political status, whereas Jakarta maintained that Aceh would only be allowed to participate in Indonesia's 2004 general elections.

One important explanation for the lackluster implementation of the NAD law was that the legislation was formally introduced under the administration of President Megawati Sukarnoputri, who was basically opposed to decentralization and refused to tolerate any attempts to break up the country her father, Sukarno, had founded. Megawati saw the unitary state as inviolable and her personal reservations about granting "too much" autonomy to the regions had been widely reported in her former capacity as Abdurrahman Wahid's vice-president. As president, Megawati selected ministers who shared her view that excessive autonomy was a recipe for national disintegration. Little wonder, then, that the Megawati administration relied far more heavily on military force in dealing with the Aceh problem than on remedial policies. Though Megawati had no choice other than to ratify the NAD law, which was passed by the national parliament days before her presidential appointment, she warned the Acehnese that if they abused special autonomy then her government would "initiate stern law enforcement measures in the province".[17] This unhelpful attitude, combined with Jakarta's growing reliance on counterinsurgency operations and its reluctance to assume responsibility for managing the decentralization process, served to delegitimize the NAD law even as aspects of it were implemented.

There were also serious structural constraints towards implementing the NAD law. Within the context of the worsening conflict in Aceh, the state infrastructure was destroyed at a faster rate than it could be rebuilt. Local government officials reported in mid-2001 that 12,275 buildings had been destroyed since 1999.[18] After the NAD law was passed, GAM demonstrated its total rejection of autonomy by increasing its attacks on Indonesian state facilities.[19] Many government officials at the sub-district and village levels either abandoned their offices or reached agreements with GAM members in rebel-controlled areas, while similar arrangements were made in areas dominated by Indonesian security forces. In large parts of the province, where both GAM and Indonesian security forces operated, extortion was a particular problem. Local government officials and businesspeople were extorted (or charged "income tax")[20] by GAM and Indonesian security forces personnel at a standard rate of 8 to 10 per cent, or 30 per cent for government projects.[21] The conflict economy also reduced governmental accountability and transparency as local government officials blamed the fighting for the diversion of state resources and their failure to implement community development projects.

Finally, the NAD law itself was restrictive as a conflict management tool. Although the central government portrayed the NAD law as a "comprehensive" political solution to the conflict, the legislation did not comprehensively address the entire spectrum of Acehnese grievances. In particular, it failed to respond to Acehnese calls for justice for human rights violations and to end the systematic state violence. Nor did the special autonomy law include any legal provisions to encourage GAM to transform its militant movement into a political campaign through the formation of local political parties. Amidst the intensive counterinsurgency operations aimed at destroying them, the rebels had no incentives to lay down their arms. The ongoing military offensive on the ground in turn dramatically reduced the chances of special autonomy gaining popular acceptance and of restoring Acehnese confidence in Indonesian rule.

TOWARDS A NEGOTIATED SETTLEMENT

Jakarta's pledge to grant "self-government" to Aceh at the signing of the Helsinki peace agreement on 15 August 2005 was made after more than two years of emergency rule and after several heated rounds of internationally mediated negotiations between GAM and Indonesian government representatives. Aceh had been under a state of emergency since May 2003, when President Megawati Sukarnoputri had acquiesced to the military's calls to "crush" GAM by pronouncing martial law via Presidential Instruction No. 18/2003. Despite the downgrading of martial law to civil emergency rule in May 2004, however, little had changed in terms of the unabated fighting on the ground. Indonesian security forces had severely weakened GAM's military capabilities during the intensive counterinsurgency campaign and forced the rebels to scale back their activities to the sub-district level,[22] but the military operations had failed to achieve their goal of breaking the separatist movement. This was shown three days before the 26 December 2004 Indian Ocean tsunami when Aceh's then regional military commander, Major General Endang Suwarya, announced that 2,500 GAM combatants with 844 guns remained at large in Aceh, indicating that the military saw its mission there as being far from over.[23] That GAM retained an active fighting force was confirmed at the signing of the Helsinki agreement, when the rebels committed themselves towards demobilizing all of their 3,000 military troops and to surrendering 840 weapons.

What, then, finally convinced Jakarta and GAM to put aside their differences to work towards a negotiated settlement? Certainly no single factor can be attributed to the success of the Helsinki peace process, which paved the way for the self-government of Aceh in Indonesia and granted the Acehnese people meaningful autonomy within the Indonesian state. The 2004 Indian Ocean tsunami, which introduced most of the world to Aceh, placed strong international pressure on Jakarta to search for a peaceful end to the conflict. An offer made two days before the tsunami by the former Finnish president Martti Ahtisaari's Crisis Management Initiative (CMI) non-governmental organization to facilitate and mediate peace talks between GAM and Jakarta also convinced both sides to return to the negotiating table after the disaster. The involvement of an international mediating body in turn influenced GAM's decision to engage in dialogue as the rebels had never agreed to negotiate with Jakarta based solely on their military capabilities (or lack thereof), in part because of their basic distrust that the Indonesian government would honour any peace agreement, and in part because GAM sought international recognition and support for their cause.

Although each of these factors was critical, the case put here is that political will was the most important factor in the peaceful resolution of the Aceh conflict.[24] This is because in post-New Order Indonesia, the level of political will to search for a negotiated outcome to Indonesia's territorial disputes has often hinged on the ability and desire by political actors to take advantages of windows of opportunity presented by disadvantageous material preconditions. Since 1998, the opportunity to search for a negotiated settlement to Indonesia's internal conflicts has been greatest at the two points when the state has been structurally extremely weak. The first point was in 1998 when Indonesia was embroiled in the political turbulence of regime change and bankrupted by the 1997 Asian financial crisis. Yet it was during this period that President B.J. Habibie seized the window of opportunity presented by the Indonesian military's internal factionalism and discredited public image to withdraw thousands of non-organic troops from Aceh and to make the remarkable (and widely unpopular) decision to resolve the East Timor conflict by offering that province a UN-monitored referendum on independence. As time elapsed after the change of regime, however, Jakarta's willingness and capacity to develop ameliorative policies gradually weakened as political and military hawks in Jakarta regained political ground and forced a return to the policy of repression in Indonesia's conflict regions.

The second point when the level of political will to peacefully end the Aceh conflict peaked in Jakarta was after the December 2004 Indian Ocean tsunami. Once again, Indonesian state power and authority was severely structurally compromised in Aceh. Not only was this because of the physical devastation wrought by the waves along Aceh's battered coastline, but also because of structural weaknesses caused by the conflict, as well as by the unaddressed problems of systemic state corruption and by Indonesia's unreformed security sector which often acted in ways that ran counter to state goals and objectives. Despite these structural constraints, Indonesia's political leadership and GAM elected to use the window of opportunity created by the tsunami to reconsider their respective positions. One or both parties could have chosen to miss this opportunity or to unilaterally withdraw from the Helsinki peace process at any stage. Instead, both sides seized the chance to negotiate and to use the international community's assistance (and pressure) before the political moment was lost.

Such political moments, or windows of opportunity, tend to appear during times of national crisis, when key political actors recognize that some critical aspect of the existing system has failed and decide to work towards instituting positive change. National crises are also sites of tremendous political flux and instability, which tend to impact upon how political actors see themselves and the range of opportunities available to them. Before the 2004 tsunami, the government of Susilo Bambang Yudhoyono had not exhibited any strongly reformist credentials in its handling of the Aceh conflict. Unlike the past three Indonesian presidents, Yudhoyono did not apologize to the Acehnese during his first 100 days in power for past atrocities committed against them by Indonesian security forces. Instead, like Megawati before him, Yudhoyono authorized a continuation of Aceh's civil emergency status and refrained from withdrawing non-organic troops from the province and from ordering investigations into human rights violations in Aceh. From Jakarta's perspective, there was no reason to radically change a policy that had by all accounts dealt a severe blow to GAM's military capabilities and to the rebels' shadow civil administration. When the tsunami hit Aceh, however, it triggered an immediate change of approach by both parties. The day after the disaster GAM declared a unilateral ceasefire to facilitate the massive tasks of collecting corpses and helping the survivors. Two days later the Indonesian government lifted its ban on foreigners from entering the province to allow humanitarian assistance to reach tsunami victims. By late January 2005, both sides had accepted the CMI's offer to mediate peace talks in Helsinki and returned to the negotiating table. Though the tsunami created a circuit-breaker, it did not in itself end the deep mutual hostilities between the warring parties. What it did was present a new window of opportunity for both sides to reassess their own positions.

In stark contrast to the previous limited peace talks with GAM under the governments of Abdurrahman Wahid and Megawati Sukarnoputri, which had prioritized a ceasefire with a view to addressing more substantive issues later, the five rounds of negotiations that took place in Helsinki between January and July 2005 set far more ambitious goals. From the outset, former Finnish President Martti Ahtisaari, who was actively involved in managing all the CMI-monitored talks, adopted the operating rule that "Nothing is agreed until everything is agreed". This procedural principle of obliging neither party to adhere to any agreement that was not final had previously been used at the July 2000 Camp David Summit, which had unsuccessfully attempted to negotiate a final settlement to the Israeli-Palestinian conflict. Unlike the Camp David Summit, however, during the Helsinki talks the Indonesian government and GAM proved willing to make considerable compromises and to adopt new terminology to debate sensitive issues. In particular, the concession by Jakarta in the second round of talks on 21–23 February 2005 to replace the highly politicized term of "special autonomy" with "self-government" provided an important breakthrough that allowed both sides to start focusing on the substantive issue of what self-government would mean in an Acehnese context, and how it could be achieved without compromising Indonesia's territorial sovereignty. There were, of course, significant hurdles in this process, especially in relation to GAM's proposal to form Aceh-based political parties, which in the past had been flatly rejected by Jakarta on the grounds that it contravened Indonesia's Law No. 31/2002 on political parties that required parties to have a national presence. Yet in Helsinki, the Indonesian delegation eventually agreed to allow Aceh-based parties, a commitment, which, when honored through the introduction of supporting legislation in the form of a new Law on the Governing of Aceh (LoGA), would help to strengthen and sustain the peace process by making Aceh's political system the most inclusive and participatory anywhere in Indonesia.

SELF-GOVERNMENT

Law No. 11 of 2006 on the Governing of Aceh (LoGA) was ratified by Indonesia's national parliament on 11 July 2006 amidst intense controversy. Although the new self-governing law conferred unprecedented powers of self-governance to Aceh, it drew protests in the province's urban centres. On the day the LoGA was passed, GAM, Aceh's university student-led referendum movement (*Sentral Informasi Referendum Aceh*, SIRA), and dozens of local NGOs organized a one-day general strike in condemnation of the legislation, which excluded or diluted several core provisions in the Helsinki agreement. In Jakarta, although the central government and national parliament promoted the LoGA as the key to ensuring peace in Aceh, malcontents in Indonesia's political and military establishment also viewed the concept of self-government with suspicion and expressed concerns that the Acehnese had been awarded too many concessions.

Although the LoGA delivered less than had been agreed upon in the Helsinki agreement, it granted Aceh far more autonomy than Indonesia's other provinces and provided redress for some of the key weaknesses in the NAD law before it. In particular, the provision for direct democratic local elections in the LoGA enabled GAM to reap political benefits from the new system and to work within its legal parameters to constructively engage in Indonesia's democratization process rather than in opposition to it. The new self-governing law also incorporated key provisions from the Helsinki agreement that allowed the Acehnese to field independent candidates in local elections and to form Aceh-based political parties. These provisions were instrumental to GAM's capacity and willingness to continue its transformation from a militant organization into a political movement. Other concessions included the return of most of Aceh's natural resource revenue and the right to implement Islamic law, although these provisions were essentially a reconstituted version of the NAD law. Unlike the NAD law, the LoGA also emphasized the defense of human rights in Aceh and incorporated legal mechanisms to enforce such rights, albeit in a limited form that remained vulnerable to diminution. Chapter XXXIV of the LoGA envisaged the establishment of a human rights court in Aceh and a Truth and Reconciliation Commission with a mandate to decide on human rights violations cases, although by mid-2008 no progress had been made towards creating either of these institutions amidst a series of squabbles and standoffs between Aceh and Jakarta over the scope of their jurisdiction. For GAM, SIRA, and many Acehnese NGOs, a key source of contention was the lack of retroactivity of the human rights court under the LoGA, which only covered offenses after the promulgation of the law, not crimes committed during the conflict (Article 228). Nor did the LoGA specify whether Aceh's Truth and Reconciliation Commission would be authorized to handle past atrocities committed against the civilian population during security operations.

GAM, SIRA, and several Acehnese NGOs also expressed valid concerns about other key issues arising from the LoGA that undermined the Helsinki agreement. In one violation of the Helsinki agreement, which required the Indonesian military to revert to a strictly external defense role in Aceh, Article 202 of the LoGA holds the military responsible for state defence, thereby blurring the distinction between its internal and external functions.

Though Jakarta honored its commitment to withdraw all non-organic military and police troops from Aceh and to only retain 14,700 organic military troops and 9,100 organic police officers in the province, the LoGA included no formal constraints on the remaining organic troops. The LoGA also omitted a provision in the Helsinki agreement requiring Indonesian security forces who committed crimes against Acehnese civilians to be tried in civil courts.

On Aceh's self-governing authority, the LoGA delivered fewer political and administrative concessions than had been envisaged in the Helsinki agreement, changing the word "consent" in the Helsinki agreement to "consideration" in the LoGA in relation to Jakarta's acceptance of Aceh government policies (Helsinki MoU, Point 1.1.2; LoGA, Article 8). Another dispute arose over the administration of Aceh's revenue-sharing arrangements with Jakarta. GAM interpreted the conferral of "jurisdiction" to Aceh over its living natural sea resources and the right to "retain" 70 per cent of natural resources generated within its borders to mean that Aceh's provincial government would completely control those resources and the profits generated by them. Under the LoGA, however, Aceh's natural resources continued to be collected by the Finance Ministry in Jakarta and redistributed back to Aceh. This issue had previously strained centre-periphery relations between Aceh's provincial government and Jakarta during the limited efforts to implement the NAD law because neither the Finance Ministry nor the state-owned Pertamina oil company had disclosed their oil and gas profits, with the result that Aceh's political leadership did not know how much revenue they were entitled to receive.[25] When the LoGA was introduced, GAM and local NGOs argued that in perpetuating this flawed administrative system Jakarta had violated the terms of the Helsinki agreement. The architects of the LoGA attempted to provide some redress for past problems arising from the transfer of funds to Aceh by including an accountability clause requiring the central government to hire an independent auditor nominated by the State Auditing Agency [*Badan Pemeriksa Keuangan*, BPK]. However, the BPK, which reports directly to the national parliament, has a reputation for failing to practice investigative auditing in major graft cases.[26] As such, its capacity to recruit efficient independent auditors to monitor the disbursement of funds to Aceh remains questionable.

Although the LoGA failed to adhere to the letter and spirit of the Helsinki agreement, it did grant Aceh greater self-governing powers than the NAD law, especially in relation to political rights and representation. Aceh's first ever direct democratic local elections that were held on 11 December 2006 were largely a peaceful affair, being described by the European Union's

Election Observation Mission in Aceh (EUEOM) as "competitive, transparent and well administered" and compliant with international standards of democratic systems.[27] In an outcome that surprised most outside observers, as well as many Acehnese, GAM won the top gubernatorial position. Aceh's new governor, former GAM rebel Irwandi Yusuf, and his vice governor, SIRA leader Muhammad Nazar, won a landslide electoral victory with 38.2 per cent of the Acehnese vote, more than double their nearest rivals. GAM also performed well at the sub-provincial level, winning six districts in the first round of sub-provincial elections and another one in a run-off election on 4 March 2007.[28] Though few predicted their stunning success, the Irwandi-Nazar team was bolstered by their capacity to tap into their pre-existing grassroots support networks, as well as by GAM's eagerness to claim credit for the Helsinki peace process, by their appeals to Acehnese nationalist sentiment, and by their self-portrayal as a fresh alternative to the incumbent Jakarta-based party candidates. Under different conditions and circumstances, vote buying by powerful Jakarta-based parties may have been just as rampant in Aceh as it is elsewhere in Indonesia. But the collective memory of the recent conflict remained alive and well in the minds of the local population, and the national-based parties lacked GAM's structural and political reach into the countryside. There were, of course, negative reports that people only voted for GAM because they feared a return to violence and that GAM candidates had used their influence in villages to coerce or intimidate villagers into voting for them. According to the International Crisis Group, there was also a belief amongst sections of the local population that GAM would end their system of collecting "state taxes" (*pajak nanggroe*) if they were elected to official positions.[29] On the balance, however, the elections were open and transparent, as reflected in a post-poll survey by the non-governmental organization IFES (International Foundation for Election Systems), which found that 94 per cent of 1,203 Acehnese respondents were satisfied with the electoral process and felt that it had been conducted fairly.[30] This creation of a democratic framework to allow former separatist rebels to transform their militant struggle into a political campaign has so far been the crowning achievement of the LoGA. It has also led to the creation of an Acehnese society that is genuinely civil in the sense that for the first time since the start of the conflict, political actors have been able to debate difference in the public domain without recourse to, or, fear of violence. In this, Aceh's 2006 local elections have been one of the greatest, and least anticipated, success stories in Indonesia's transition to democracy.

CHALLENGES AHEAD

While the Helsinki peace process has continued to hold and gain strength since the 2006 direct local elections, the establishment of self governance in Aceh has by no means ended all of Aceh's political and structural problems, which remain substantial. Since his election, Aceh governor Irwandi Yusuf has retained a clean reputation untainted by allegations of corruption and continues to enjoy broad popular support. His government, however, has been accused of demonstrating preferential treatment towards former GAM rebels by awarding them official positions and government contracts over potentially more suitable candidates. Though providing business opportunities has helped to dissuade many ex-combatants from resorting to crime or returning to fighting, nepotism and patronage networks equally threaten to impede the development of good governance practices as Aceh struggles to continue rebuilding itself. There have also been occasional reports of violent attacks against more senior ex-combatants who have received land and financial compensation by disaffected foot soldiers who have not.

With the withdrawal in 2009 of foreign donors and Indonesian government agencies that were involved in Aceh's large scale post-tsunami, post-conflict effort, the management of fiscal decentralization continues to play an important role in the future security and stability of Aceh. If Jakarta continues to honor its commitment to the LoGA and return the increased revenues to which Aceh is entitled, then the provincial government could improve public service delivery and create better employment and business opportunities. Given the outcomes of the large-scale reconstruction effort, however, which have been mixed at best, Aceh's provincial government will inevitably encounter serious social and structural obstacles in this pursuit. Of the 30,000 Acehnese workers who were employed by foreign NGOs after the tsunami, 20,000 are expected to lose their jobs upon completion of the reconstruction effort.[31] Despite the massive injection of capital into Aceh since the tsunami, it remains the fourth poorest Indonesian province after Papua, Maluku and Gorontolo, and second only after Papua if the 13 per cent of Acehnese who became vulnerable to poverty after the tsunami are included.[32] If regulatory mechanisms are not introduced to minimize corruption and to hold local governments accountable for managing and spending their increased budgets, then Aceh's democratically elected leadership may lose legitimacy, as occurred under past Aceh administrations. The Aceh government's capacity to rebuild the local economy is especially important in a society with a recent history of social trauma, and where criminal activity is more likely to spread if state institutions fail to provide adequate public services and facilities and employment and business opportunities.

The other risk, of course, is that the outstanding points of contention between Aceh and Jakarta concerning discrepancies between the terms of the Helsinki agreement and the LoGA could fester and lead to new centre-periphery tensions if left unaddressed. Yet while the LoGA represents a watered-down version of the Helsinki agreement, it has also created a democratic framework within which to debate and work towards resolving problems arising from the implementation of self-government. The commitment towards creating this democratic framework was brought about, in the first instance, by the political commitment of the Indonesian government and GAM towards the Helsinki peace process. It was strengthened through the institutionalization of critical aspects of democratic procedure in the form of direct local elections and the introduction of Aceh-based political parties. Jakarta's acceptance of the election of former GAM rebels as the legitimate political representatives of the Acehnese people marked a leap forward in Indonesia's process of political development. The continued political will and commitment by both Jakarta and Aceh's directly elected government towards protecting the Helsinki peace agreement will have ongoing implications for Indonesia's transition to democracy, and more broadly, for the future direction of Indonesia's process of political development.

Notes

[1] The original British spelling of "Acheh" is generally preferred by GAM, reflecting the rebels' rejection of the Indonesian spelling. Despite his outspoken opposition to most other things Dutch, GAM's founding leader, Hasan di Tiro, also used the old Dutch spelling of "Atjeh" to establish the Atjeh Institute in America and GAM's Ministry of Information of the State of Atjeh Sumatra (*Kementerian Penerangan Negara Atjeh Sumatra*). See, for example, H.M. Tiro, *The Political Future of the Malay Archipelago* (New York: Atjeh Institute in America, 1965).

[2] TNI is an acronym for *Tentara Nasional Indonesia*, which literally translates as Indonesian National Army. Since 1999, when Indonesia's armed forces were officially separated, the Indonesian military's formal title has been TNI-AD (*Tentara Nasional Indonesia Angkatan Darat*, lit; Indonesian National Army-Land Force).

[3] For example, from late 2000, GAM administrative officials (called *ulee sagoe*) began registering the sale of land and issuing identity cards (called *tanda peuturi droe*) and marriage license certificates (*kaleuh meunikah*, lit., already married), which created a dilemma whereby many Acehnese civilians who held two sets of documentation risked being accused of being GAM members or their

supporters by Indonesian security forces. Arif Zulkifli et al., "One Province, Two Bureaucracies", *Tempo,* vol. I, no. 23, 13–19 February 2001.

4   The Darul Islam Rebellion began in West Java under the leadership of S.M. Kartosuwirjo, who pronounced an "Islamic State of Indonesia" (*Negara Islam Indonesia*, NII) in West Java on 7 August 1949. It later spread to Central Java, South Sulawesi, Kalimantan and Aceh with loosely integrated agendas for the formation of an Islamic state. A.R. Kahin, *Rebellion to Integration: West Sumatra and the Indonesian Polity, 1926–1998* (Amsterdam: Amsterdam University Press, 1999), p. 175.

5   On 21 July 2002, the ASNLF changed its name to GAM through the signing of the "Stavanger Declaration", which reflected GAM's changing vision from the re-establishment of an Aceh sultanate to an independent State of Acheh based on democracy. GAM's military wing, AGAM (*Angkatan Gerakan Acheh Merdeka*) was also changed to TNA (*Tentara Neugara Aceh*, Aceh National Army). *Stavanger Declaration*, Stavanger, Norway, 21 July 2002.

6   When the Darul Islam Rebellion erupted in Aceh in September 1953, Hasan di Tiro was working at the Indonesian Representative Office to the United Nations in New York. He resigned from that position to appoint himself the Darul Islam "ambassador" to the United Nations, a move that was supported by Acehnese Darul Islam leaders, and later those in South Sulawesi. Nazaruddin Sjamsuddin, "Issues and Politics of Regionalism in Indonesia: Evaluating the Acehnese Experience", in *Armed Separatism in Southeast Asia*, edited by Lim Joo-Jock and S. Vani (Singapore: Institute of Southeast Asian Studies, 1984), p. 115; Hiorth, F. June 1986. 'Free Aceh: An Impossible Dream?' in *Kabar Seberang: Sulating Maphilindo*, no. 17, p. 182.

7   See, for example, Hasan di Tiro, *Demokrasi Untuk Indonesia* (Banda Aceh: Penerbit Seulawah, 1958).

8   Despite this, the New Order's nation-building project was largely successful given Indonesia's dispersed geographical composition (with more than 17,000 islands) and ethnic, cultural, religious, and linguistic diversity (with 737 listed living languages). Aceh is not representative of Indonesia's national-building project and until 1998 was one of only three of Indonesia's then twenty-seven provinces with an independence movement.

9   Although the military operations in Aceh during this period became commonly known as "DOM", the "Red Net" operations and command structure formed their legal basis. For more detailed analyses of the DOM period, see for example, Al Chaidar, *Aceh Bersimbah Darah. Mengungkap Penerapan Status Daerah Operasi Militer (DOM) di Aceh 1989–1998* (Jakarta: Pustaka Al-Kautsar, 1998); F.W. Eda and S. Satya Dharma, eds., *Aceh Menggugat. Sepuluh Tahun Rakyat Aceh di Bawah Tekanan Militer* (Jakarta: Pustaka Sinar Harapan, 1999); L. Jones, *The Security Disturbances in Aceh During 1990*, Working Paper 104, Amnesty International (Clayton, Victoria: Center of Southeast Asian Studies, Monash Asia Institute, 1997); *Indonesia: "Shock Therapy" Restoring Order in Aceh, 1989–1993*

(London: Amnesty International, 1993); G. Robinson, "*Rawan* is as *Rawan* Does: The Origins of Disorder in New Order Aceh", *Indonesia*, vol. 66 (1998): 127–56.

10   "Non-organic" refers to troops deployed to a province on a short-term basis for specific combat exercises and counterinsurgency operations. "Organic" denotes troops recruited within their own province and permanently attached to the local territorial command structure. In practice, organic troops have been deployed to provinces outside their recruitment area. In Aceh, for instance, the deep mistrust between the civilian population and the Indonesian military and police made it difficult to recruit ethnic Acehnese into organic battalions. As a result, troops organic to other territorial commands were deployed to Aceh to reinforce counterinsurgency operations against GAM.

11   According to one nationwide survey, Aceh was the province with the fewest "coping strategies" (measured by sale of personal assets in exchange for food and reduced participation in community activities) to deal with the crisis. S. Sumarto, A. Wetterberg, and L. Pritchett, "The Social Impact of the Crisis in Indonesia: Results From a Nationwide *Kecamatan* Survey", Development Economics Working Paper No. 112, East Asian Bureau of Economic Research, 1998, pp. 7, 9, 10, 21, 26. See also M.I. Sulaiman, "From Autonomy to Periphery: A Critical Evaluation of the Acehnese Nationalist Movement", in *Verandah of Violence: The Historical Background of the Aceh Problem*, edited by A. Reid (Singapore/Seattle: Singapore University Press, in association with Washington Univesity Press, 2006), p. 126; M. Ross, *Resources and Rebellion in Aceh, Indonesia*, paper prepared for the Yale-World Bank Project on "The Economics of Political Violence", Department of Political Science, UCLA, 5 June 2003, p. 24.

12   Amien Rais (then leader of democratic opposition party, PAN), "Pemilu 2004, tak Ada Kursi Gratis bagi TNI", *Kompas*, 5 December 1999.

13   See, for example, "Disinyalir Barter dengan Ganja, Senjata Ilegal TNI Mengalir ke GAM", *Indomedia.com*, 4 March 2000; "Peluru M-16 dan Granat dari Depok untuk GAM", *Kompas*, 7 April 2001; "Aceh dalam Genggaman GAM dan TNI", *Pikiran Rakyat*, 16 December 2002; "Menghentikan GAM dengan Senjata", *Kompas*, 4 May 2003; Fahmi AP Pane, "Kesalahan Pencegahan Teror Bom", *Republika*, 11 August 2003.

14   *Undang-Undang Nomor: 44 Tahun 1999 tentang Penyelenggaraan Keistimewaan PropinsiDaerah Istimewa Aceh*, Chapter III, Article 3(d) and 5(1), (2).

15   Interview with Syamsuddin Mahmud, Jakarta, 20 November 2001.

16   Ninety-eight per cent of Acehnese are Muslims, compared with the Indonesian national average of 88 per cent Muslims.

17   "Mega tells Aceh to focus on autonomy", *Jakarta Post*, 29 August 2001.

18   "More than 55,000 homes destroyed in Indonesian unrest", *Jakarta Post*, 17 June 2001.

19   "A Rejection of NAD law", *Kompas*, 27 August 2001.

20 From GAM's perspective, what constituted extortion for Indonesian authorities was their legitimate collection of "state taxes" (*pajak nanggroe*) for the Acehnese war effort. Similarly, GAM saw their attacks on Indonesian security forces personnel and state facilities as part of their nationalist struggle to destroy what they saw as the illegitimate Javanese-Indonesian neocolonial system.
21 International Crisis Group, "Aceh: Can Autonomy Stem the Conflict?", ICG Asia Report no. 18 (Jakarta/Brussels: International Crisis Group, 27 June 2001), pp. 12–13; R. McGibbon, *Secessionist Challenges in Aceh and Papua: Is Special Autonomy the Solution?*, Policy Studies 10 (Washington, D.C.: East-West Center, 2004), p. 15.
22 International Crisis Group, "Aceh: A New Chance for Peace", Asia Briefing No. 40 (Jakarta/Brussels: International Crisis Group, 15 August 2005), p. 5.
23 "Pangdam: Kekuatan GAM Tersisa 2.500 Orang", <www.dephan.go.id>, (accessed 23 December 2004).
24 This argument is developed in M.A. Miller, *Rebellion and Reform in Indonesia: Jakarta's Security and Autonomy Policies in Aceh* (London and New York: Routledge, 2009).
25 "Dana Migas tak Jelas, Aceh Lapor ke MPR", *Serambi Indonesia*, 23 May 2002.
26 Richard Holloway, "Indonesia: Integrity Assessment", *Global Integrity Report*, 2004, <http://www.globalintegrity.org/reports/2004/2004/countryc6dc.html?cc=id&act=ia>.
27 European Union Election Observation Mission (EUEOM), *Statement of Preliminary Conclusions and Findings*, Banda Aceh, 12 December 2006.
28 International Crisis Group, "Indonesia: How GAM Won in Aceh", ICG Asia Briefing No. 61 (Jakarta/Brussels: International Crisis Group, 22 March 2007), p. 1.
29 Ibid., p. 6.
30 IFES, "Acehnese Satisfied with Election Process, Urge Government to Address Economy", *Press Release*, 23 February 2007.
31 *Jakarta Post*, 29 October 2007.
32 The World Bank, *Aceh Public Expenditure Analysis: Spending for Reconstruction and Poverty Reduction* (Washington, D.C./Jakarta: The World Bank, 2006), p. xiv.

References

Amnesty International. *Indonesia: "Shock Therapy" Restoring Order in Aceh, 1989–1993*. London: Amnesty International, 1993.
Chaidar, A. *Aceh Bersimbah Darah. Mengungkap Penerapan Status Daerah Operasi Militer (DOM) di Aceh 1989–1998*. Jakarta: Pustaka Al-Kautsar, 1998.
Eda, F.W. and S. Satya Dharma, eds. *Aceh Menggugat. Sepuluh Tahun Rakyat Aceh di Bawan Tekanan Militer*. Jakarta: Pustaka Sinar Harapan, 1999.

European Union Election Observation Mission (EUEOM). *Final Report, Governor and Regent/Mayor Elections*. Aceh: EUOM, 2007.
———. *Statement of Preliminary Conclusions and Findings*. Banda Aceh, 12 December 2006.
Government of the Republic of Indonesia. *Law on the Governing of Aceh* (LoGA), 2006.
———. *Republic of Indonesia Law No. 18 of 2001 about the Special Autonomy of Aceh Special Region as Nanggroe Aceh Darussalam*, 2001.
———. *Law No. 44 of 1999 about Implementation of the Special Status of the Special Region of Aceh*, 1999.
Hiorth, F. "Free Aceh: An Impossible Dream?". *Kabar Seberang: Sulating Maphilindo*, no. 17 (1986): 182–94.
Holloway, R. "Indonesia: Integrity Assessment". *Global Integrity Report*, 2004. <http://www.globalintegrity.org/reports/2004/2004/countryc6dc.html?cc=id&act=ia>.
IFES. "Acehnese Satisfied with Election Process, Urge Government to Address Economy". *Press Release*, 23 February 2007.
International Crisis Group. "Indonesia: How GAM Won in Aceh". ICG Asia Briefing No. 61. Jakarta/Brussels: International Crisis Group, 22 March 2007.
———. "Aceh: A New Chance for Peace". Asia Briefing No. 40. Jakarta/Brussels: International Crisis Group, 15 August 2005.
———. "Aceh: Can Autonomy Stem the Conflict?". ICG Asia Report No. 18. Jakarta/Brussels: International Crisis Group, 27 June 2001.
Interview with Syamsuddin Mahmud (former Governor of Aceh, 1993–98). Jakarta, 20 November 2001.
Jones, L. *The Security Disturbances in Aceh During 1990*. Working Paper No. 104, Victoria: Center of Southeast Asian Studies, Monash Asia Institute, 1997.
Kahin, A.R. *Rebellion to Integration: West Sumatra and the Indonesian Polity, 1926–1998*. Amsterdam: Amsterdam University Press, 1999.
McGibbon, R. *Secessionist Challenges in Aceh and Papua: Is Special Autonomy the Solution?* Policy Studies 10. Washington, D.C.: East-West Center, 2004.
Miller, M.A. *Rebellion and Reform in Indonesia: Jakarta's Security and Autonomy Policies in Aceh*. London and New York: Routledge, 2009; reprinted 2010.
———. "What's Special about Special Autonomy in Aceh?" In *Verandah of Violence: The Historical Background of the Aceh Problem*, edited by A. Reid. Singapore: Singapore University Press, 2006.
———. "The Nanggroe Aceh Darussalam Law: A Serious Response to Acehnese Separatism?". *Asian Ethnicity* 5, no. 3 (2004): 333–52.
Robinson, G. "*Rawan* is as *Rawan* Does: The Origins of Disorder in New Order Aceh". *Indonesia*, vol. 66 (1998): 127–56.
Ross, M. *Resources and Rebellion in Aceh, Indonesia*. Paper prepared for the Yale-World Bank Project on "The Economics of Political Violence". Department of Political Science, UCLA, 5 June 2003.

Sulaiman, M.I. "From Autonomy to Periphery: A Critical Evaluation of the Acehnese Nationalist Movement". In *Verandah of Violence: The Historical Background of the Aceh Problem*, edited by A. Reid. Singapore/Seattle: Singapore University Press, in association with Washington University Press, 2006.

Sjamsuddin, N. *The Republican Revolt: A Study of the Acehnese Rebellion*. Singapore: Institute of Southeast Asian Studies, 1985.

———. "Issues and Politics of Regionalism in Indonesia: Evaluating the Acehnese Experience". In *Armed Separatism in Southeast Asia*, edited by J.J. Lim and S. Vani. Singapore: Institute of Southeast Asian Studies, 1984.

Sumarto, S., A. Wetterberg and L. Pritchett. "The Social Impact of the Crisis in Indonesia: Results from a Nationwide Kecamatan Survey". Development Economics Working Paper No. 112. East Asian Bureau of Economic Research, 1998.

The World Bank. *Aceh Public Expenditure Analysis: Spending for Reconstruction and Poverty Reduction*. Washington, D.C./Jakarta: The World Bank, 2006.

Tiro, H.M. *The Political Future of the Malay Archipelago*. New York: Atjeh Institute in America, 1965.

———. *Demokrasi Untuk Indonesia*. Aceh: Penerbit Seulawah, 1958.

Print and Electronic Media Sources

Aceh-Eye.org
AcehKita
AcehNet
Aceh.Org
dephan.go.id
Detikworld.com
International Herald Tribune
Jakarta Post
Kompas
Kontras
Laksamana.net
Media Indonesia
Republika
Serambi Indonesia
Sinar Harapan
Suara Harian Merdeka
Suara Pembaruan
Tempo/ Tempo Interaktif

4

AUTONOMY AND ARMED SEPARATISM IN PAPUA: WHY THE CENDRAWASIH CONTINUES TO FEAR THE GARUDA

Bilveer Singh

Indonesian leaders are fond of referring to Papua's incorporation into their Republic as one of re-integration, colloquially known as *kembali ke Ibu Pertiwi*, or return to the Motherland. The term "reintegration" is designed to highlight that even though the territory was already "integrated" into Indonesia in the past, its hiving away by the Dutch colonialists from independent Indonesia from 1950 to 1962 qualifies the incorporation to be referred to as "reintegration". This is premised on the fact that Papua, referred by Indonesians as *Irian Barat* (West Irian) since 1950 or Dutch New Guinea throughout the colonial period, was supposed to be part of independent Republic of the United States of Indonesia (RUSI)/*Negara Kesatuan Republic Indonesia* (NKRI), the Unitary State of Indonesia, but due to Dutch manipulations and deceptions, supported by the West, this was denied. After continuing for another twelve years as a Dutch colony (January 1950 to August 1962), while the rest of Indonesia was independent, it was surrendered, by the Dutch, to the United Nations [United Nations Temporary Executive Authority, UNTEA], which in turn, transferred the territory to Indonesia in May 1963. Since then, Indonesia has ruled the territory with an iron fist, claiming many Papuan lives as well as causing damage to Indonesia's international reputation. The Papuan nationalists have been struggling for independent statehood since the early 1960s but despite the persistence of the aspiration, very little headway has been made. The various autonomy proposals made by Indonesia were partly aimed at defusing Papuan demands for independence as well as silencing the calls for separatism that have been ascendant since the fall of Soeharto in May 1998.

Papua was incorporated or reincorporated into Indonesia, first *de facto* and later *de jure*, largely due to the prominent role played by the Indonesian military. When Sukarno utilized *diplomasi* or diplomacy (as opposed to military combat) between 1950 and 1961, to regain the territory, he failed abysmally. However, where diplomacy failed, military brinkmanship has from the end of 1961, succeeded. Ever since, the Indonesian military has been a dominant player in Papua (as a symbol, consider that the *TRIKORA* Regional Command is located on a high ground overlooking the city of Jayapura, the provincial capital of Papua). Since May 1963, the Indonesian military's prominent role and the adoption of what has been described as the "security approach" have dominated Jakarta's policy towards the territory. Even though there have been fundamental changes since the collapse of the New Order regime in May 1998, and other approaches have supplemented, and, at times, even supplanted the military approach, the Indonesian military continues to have a major role in determining Jakarta's approach towards Papua.

PAPUAN GRIEVANCES

Since 1963, Papuan grievances have been adequately documented and expressed.[1] These, in one way or the other, stem from the territory's 2.5 million, largely Christian, population feeling politically, economically and socio-culturally threatened with the status of being minorities, of being "second-class" citizens of an internal colony of Indonesia. There is also a palpable fear of being oppressed, repressed and subjected to human rights abuses by the security apparatus.

The pro-autonomy and independence Papuan elites have identified a number of key issues.[2] These have been expressed differently on different occasions, depending on what is being emphasized. For instance, following the Second Papua Congress in 2000, Origenes Reagen Ijie identified the following as root causes of the Papuan conflict: Papua's historical past and the accompanying betrayals, the development of a Papuan national identity discordant with the Indonesian national identity, the wholesale injustices that Papuans have experienced at the hands of Indonesia, the violent exploitation of Papua's natural resources without any major benefits for the indigenous

Papuans, the increasing dominance of the transmigrants (referred locally as *pendatang*), the rising dominance of Indonesian culture that is undermining and threatening Papuan culture, the large-scale violation of human rights and repression by the security apparatus since 1963, and finally, the widening perception gaps between the Papuans and various key non-Papuan actors with a stake in the territory (be they Indonesians or foreign investors or other powers that have supported Indonesia's occupation of the territory).[3] A study by the Indonesian Institute of Social Sciences similarly concluded that the key sources of conflict in Papua relate to the illegal and unfair manner in which Papua was integrated into Indonesia without the involvement of the Papuans themselves, the fraudulent and unjust manner in which the Act of Free Choice was conducted to ascertain Papuans' willingness to be part of Indonesia, the manner in which Papua's wealth has been exploited with little or no benefits for the locals, the manner in which Papuan culture and traditions are viewed as backward and hence, threatened by Indonesian way of life, the violent manner in which the Indonesian military has treated Papuans, resulting in the death and suffering of thousands of Papuans for their alleged opposition to the Unitary State of Indonesia, and finally, the sense of betrayal by the international community, which to safeguard its own interests, has ignored the plight of the Papuans for more than four decades.[4]

Against this backdrop, identifying the main sources of conflict in Papuan is imperative as addressing the causes of the conflict is necessary for lasting peace to be achieved in the territory. First, there is, what is called, the need to "straighten history".[5] This refers to the lack of Papuans' participation in the independence struggle against the Dutch, the unwillingness of key Papuan leaders to join the Sukarno-Hatta proclamation of independence in August 1945, the belief that Papua already possessed the wherewithal of statehood in the early 1960s in line with the United Nations General Assembly's declaration on self-determination and most important of all, the non-participation of Papuan elites in the Bunker's negotiation that eventually resulted in the Dutch abandonment of the territory. The Papuans were never given the opportunity to determine their own future and this was instead done by those with vested interests in the territory; the latter ensured that Papua remained part of Indonesia. The pro-independent Papuan elites who refer to this as the "historical conspiracy to stab it in the back" by the West (especially by the Netherlands and the United States) want this to be reviewed and redressed. Even though the Dutch had promised Papuans their independence, the Papuans were marginalized from the consultations that led to the transfer of their territory from the Dutch to Indonesia under the Bunker Agreement (agreement brokered by American diplomat Ellsworth Bunker through the

United Nations between Indonesia and the Netherlands in August 1962). Another great sense of injustice concerned the manner in which the Act of Free Choice (the process by which Papuans' self-determination wishes were ascertained about whether they wanted to be part of Indonesia or exist separately) was implemented. Not only was the Indonesian security apparatus used to intimidate the Papuans to opt for remaining within Indonesia, more insulting was the process itself, whereby only 1,025 hand-picked Papuan leaders unanimously agreed to join Indonesia even though this was something, many would say, most Papuans disagreed with.[6] As a result, a low-intensity insurgency has been in progress ever since.

An additional source of unhappiness was due to Jakarta's (which Papuans have described as Javanese-led Muslim leadership) attempts to politically micro-manage the territory. Papuan traditional sources of authority and structures have been replaced by what are viewed as essentially Javanese-political structures from the village level to the provincial centre. As Papua is characterized by tribal diversity and the tribe occupies the centre stage of each Papuan community, what Indonesia has imposed on the territory is something that is alien and which Papuans view as an imposition and, more importantly, an insensitive one, at that. Papua's politics have mainly been determined by and from Jakarta, regardless of the wishes of the Papuans; any dissension that is expressed is usually dealt with brutally. Papuan challenges to Jakarta are simply described as expressions of separatism, threats to the Unitary State of Indonesia that deserve to be put down violently. The assassinations of Arnold Ap, Thomas Wanggai and Theys Eluay were examples of this policy.

The economic dimension of Papuan's discontent with the Indonesian state also deserves mention. Though richly endowed with various strategic resources, the Papuans are among the poorest people in Indonesia. More than forty years of integration into Indonesia has not brought any major material benefits to the indigenous people while the territory's natural wealth has been, largely, appropriated by either foreigners or non-Papuan Indonesians. It is due to this that Papuans view themselves as being colonized to satisfy the greed of Indonesians and their foreign backers, best symbolized by the economic activities of PT Freeport (the America-based company that is among the world's largest copper and gold producers as well as the largest tax payer in Indonesia). Massive ecological and environmental degradation has accompanied the economic activities of the major corporations, contributing to the Papuan's disillusionment; forests are important for Papuans spiritually and viewed as ancestral and communal lands.

At the same time, supplementing the political and economic threats, socio-culturally, the Papuans believe that what has transpired in their homeland is an invasion of an alien people, culture and religion. As the Papuans are essentially Melanesians, not of Malay stock, and mainly Christians, unlike the majority of Indonesia who are primarily Muslims, the territory has become a stage for a sort of a "clash of civilizations". Increasingly, the "island" of Melanesian Christians finds itself swarmed by the "sea" of Muslim Malays, and worse still, as these Muslim Malays also wield political, economic and military power, a siege mentality has emerged, with increasing fears of a "cultural genocide".[7] This is especially so in view of the various policies supporting transmigration that have fundamentally altered the ethnic-religious demography of the territory.

Finally, the pre-eminent role of the Indonesian military in the "re-integration" of Papua into Indonesia, mainly through the Soeharto-led *Mandala* Command, the host of military operations to exterminate the threat posed by the Papuan Independence Organisation (which, through military struggle, aims to win independence for the territory), the declaration of military emergency and primacy of the military in the politics of Papua under Soeharto, has led to large-scale violations of human rights, with allegedly more than 100,000 Papuans killed since May 1963.[8] While the scale of violence has decreased since the fall of the New Order, on a smaller scale, this has continued, with the *Cendrawasih* (the bird of paradise that is regarded as the national bird of Papua as well as of Papua New Guinea), continuing to fear the Indonesian *Garuda* (the mythical bird-like creature that is half-bird and half-human that is found in Indian and Buddhist mythology and that has been adopted as the national symbol of Indonesia). The metaphor is not an exaggeration; Papuans fear the Indonesian military, especially the Indonesian army and its special branch, KOPASSUS, because of its violent repression of separatist activity and targeting of Papuan civilians.

INDONESIA'S SPECIAL AUTONOMY PACKAGE

Papua's integration into Indonesia was undertaken by Sukarno. However, it was left to Soeharto, the main architect of Indonesia's Papua policy, to structure the main policies that eventually culminated in losing the battle of hearts and minds in the territory. Soeharto's successors, in turn, were compelled, in order to safeguard the integrity of the Unitary State of Indonesia to implement an array of measures, including, Special Autonomy in Papua. All being equal, the political entity under challenge, on its own or in consultation with the challenging party, often initiates various moves to achieve peace. This usually comes following the failure of the "military solution" to eradicate the threat and where, more often than not, there is increasing public support in the conflict territory for the opposition rather than the government. This can result in various arrangements ranging from a referendum to ascertain whether the territory wants to remain part of the state to various forms of local autonomy arrangements. Even though the New Order under Soeharto, through Law No. 5 of 1974[9] and the *Reformasi* (Reform Era) Order following it, committed themselves to some form of "Special Autonomy" for Papua, in reality, laws formalizing it were only passed by the Indonesian Parliament on 22 October 2001 and later, sanctioned by the President on 21 November 2001 under the Law No. 21 of 2001. Since then, technically, Papua has been under a special autonomy administration within the framework of the Unitary State of Indonesia. The process by which this came about, the concept of special autonomy, the dialogue process and the consensus that eventually emerged within Papua and how the Papuan leaders subsequently dialogued and reached a new *modus vivendi* have been aptly captured by one of the leading intellectuals in Papua, Agus Sumule, currently teaching at the University of Papua, Manokwari and who has adopted a neutral stance on the issue of independence.[10]

Viewed historically, Jakarta's promise of special autonomy to Papua was not new or unexpected. When the territory was incorporated into Indonesia the people of Papua were promised special autonomy by President Soeharto, who argued that the backward and underdeveloped economic situation as well as the wide socio-cultural differences between the Papuans and the rest of Indonesia demanded a special way of administering the territory.[11] However, it was only under President Habibie and his successor, Abdurrahman Wahid, that this was robustly pursued, culminating in the passing of a new law by the Indonesian parliament that transformed Papua into a province with special autonomy within Indonesia's unitary framework, along the lines of Jakarta, Yogyakarta and Aceh, the other provinces where some form of special autonomy has been operating.

More specifically, the special autonomy package that was eventually agreed upon was a function of developments in Indonesia, in general, and the increasing restive stance of the Papuans who wanted a separate and independent existence, especially following East Timor's secession from Indonesia in 1999. Following the collapse of the Soeharto regime in May 1998, Indonesia went through the *Reformasi* phase of political change, with authoritarian practices discarded and various aspects of democratization implemented. President Habibie's willingness to agree to a referendum for East Timor, conducted under the auspices of the United Nations, also provided an important catalyst, with Papuans believing that a similar opportunity would be made available to them.

The pro-independence Papuans, using the opportunity provided by the climate of political change and openness, expressed their desire for independence and total sovereignty through public demonstrations. For the first time, thousands of Papuans openly celebrated Independence Day on 1 December 1998 with the Morning Star flag being flown. In February 2000, the Papuan Peoples' Convention was held, followed by the convention of the Second Papuan Congress from end May to early June 2000. It was in view of this watershed development, where demands for independence were unanimously put forward, that special autonomy was viewed as "a win-win solution for Indonesia and Papua". For Indonesia, special autonomy was "viewed as a way out in holding on to or maintaining Papua as part of Indonesia". For Papua, special autonomy was "expected to provide answers to various problems faced by the Papuans".[12] At the same time, sensing that a clash was inevitable between Indonesia's need to have Papua as part of the Unitary State of Indonesia and the desire of many Papuans for independence, a group of Papuan intellectuals based at the University of Cendrawasih decided to come up with a compromised solution that would accommodate both sides. The then Governor of Papua, Jacob Solossa tasked Frans Wospakrik, as leader of a team, to draft a special autonomy proposal that would encompass the aspirations of all Papuans as the first step in Papua's transition to a province with special autonomy.

PAPUAN ATTITUDES TO SPECIAL AUTONOMY

The law drafted by the Papuans was titled "Special Autonomy for the Province of Papua in the Form of a Separate Government". According to Agus Sumule, the starting point was a simple one: what is special autonomy? For the Papuans, with their abundance of natural resources, autonomy "meant the freedom to organize and manage their own lives, including the right to their own internal government, to organize the society, its resources for the prosperity and well-being of the Papuans while not ignoring the interest of others within Indonesia".[13] On the other hand, there was national consensus that Papua's autonomy had to be "special". What this meant was that it would involve "a strategy to develop socially, culturally, economically and politically in a manner appropriate with the uniqueness and characteristics of the Papuan people, in view of the special conditions and environment found in Papua".[14]

With these parameters in mind, Frans Wospakrik's (then Rector of the University of Cendrawasih based in Abepura, near Jayapura, an intellectual respected for his neutrality) team developed a document that was later submitted to Jakarta for approval. It contained many revolutionary ideas, indicating that what the Papuans had in mind as far as special autonomy was concerned was very much different from what Jakarta leaders were prepared to concede. In some ways, the special autonomy package developed by the Papuans was more akin to the Bougainville and New Caledonia formula rather than say, what was then practiced in Jakarta, Aceh and Yogyakarta.[15]

Frans Wospakrik's special autonomy package included a number of important proposals. First, as far as *Powers of Papua as a Province* (Art. 6.1) were concerned, these included all aspects of governance excepting foreign policy, external defence, monetary matters and judiciary control by the highest national court. Second, under security (Art. 47: 1–4), the Police Chief was to operate under the authority and report directly to the Governor of the province. The three armed services, Army, Navy and Air Force, were not to have any domestic security duties in Papua and would only be responsible for external defence. The deployment of Army, Navy and Air Force personnel would also need approval from the Governor and the Government of Papua. Third, human rights (Art. 41) was to be the responsibility of the national and provincial government, especially in view of the widespread violations in the past. An independent Papua Commission of Human Rights was to be established to investigate the past abuses since 1963 and cases were to be lodged in the Papua Human Rights Court of Justice so that appropriate action and compensation could take place.

Fourth, for the protection of indigenous Papuans (with regard to their status as a minority in Indonesia and on account of their demographic position being threatened by voluntary and state-sponsored internal migration), special measures were proposed. Key political, economic and security positions were to be reserved for indigenous Papuans (*putra daerah*), including the positions of Governor, Deputy Governor, Chairman of provincial parliament, *Bupatis* and Chief of Police. In terms of political administration, a bicameral structure was proposed: constituted by the Provincial Parliament and the Papuan Peoples' Council. As far as *cultural identity* (Art. 2–4) was concerned, land rights were declared an important aspect of Papuan cultural identity, especially with regard to the ownership of forests. Also, cultural and regional symbols such as name of the territory (West Papua), its flag (Morning Star), coat of arms (the *Mambruk* bird), anthem (O My Land Papua) and other attributes would need to be promoted and safeguarded as they formed an integral part of Papuan cultural identity. Next, in the arena of economy, policies had to be implemented to ensure that Papuans benefit from the abundant wealth that was found in the territory. A policy of affirmative action was recommended. In terms of revenue sharing, 80 per cent was to be reserved for Papua with 20 per cent allotted to Jakarta. Finally, as far as *Papua's integration into Indonesia* (Art. 43) was concerned, the team declared the need to rectify history, especially the manner Papua was integrated into Indonesia, first in 1962 and later, in 1969. A Commission for the Rectification of the History of Integration of Papua into the Republic of Indonesia was to be established for this purpose.

DILUTED SPECIAL AUTONOMY

The then Governor, Jaap Solossa, was tasked with bringing the Papuans' special autonomy proposal to Jakarta to convince central political elites of the merit in Papuan aspirations. After much debate, however, the Papuan proposal was heavily watered down, creating much disenchantment and resentment in Papua and fuelling the perception that Jakarta was not serious and sincere about granting special autonomy to Papua. For many Papuans, the final document was merely a tactic by the central government to take the wind out of rising Papuan demands for independence. To start with, the heading of the document, "Special Autonomy for the Province of Papua in the Form of a Separate Government" was changed to "Special Autonomy of Papua Province". More fundamental and substantive were the changes made to various proposals put forward by the Frans Wospakrik team. First, as far as political affairs were concerned, the proposal for a bicameral political structure was rejected. While it was agreed that the provincial government, DPRD, instead of a Papuan People's Representative Council, would be established as a local government, the MRP would only function as a cultural representative. It would have no decision making capacity or political powers. The MRP, to be made up of religious, traditional and women representatives, would only advice the national and regional governments on cultural matters.

Second, in the economic arena the Indonesian Government agreed that Papuans should benefit from the wealth in their own territories and support the proposed policy of affirmative action. Third, on security matters, most of the suggestions were rejected in favour of the security apparatus, especially Army, Navy and Air Force, continuing as in the past. Jakarta also rejected the proposal for a Papuan Police Chief, agreeing, instead, to consult the Governor if necessary. With regard to cultural matters, the Papuans' demand for the ending of transmigration programmes was rejected with Jakarta stating that this would continue with the approval of the Governor and the local government. On the need for a Human Rights Commission in Papua, most of the proposals relating to it were rejected. Instead of allowing an Independent Papua Human Rights Commission, Jakarta agreed to the creation of a representative office of the National Human Rights Commission in the territory. The proposal for a formal Human Rights Courts of Justice was rejected by suggesting an assimilation of its functions under those of existing bodies. The proposal to examine past abuses since 1963 and compensating the victims was also rejected. Finally, on the need to rectify history, the recommendation for the establishment of a Commission of the Rectification of the History of Integration of Papua into the Republic of Indonesia was rejected. Instead, Jakarta recommended the establishment of a Commission of Truth and Reconciliation. The Commission was to clarify the history of Papua, its integration and oneness with Indonesia as a step towards national reconciliation between Papua and Indonesia.

IMPLEMENTATION ISSUES

Following the collapse of the New Order in May 1998, many Papuans felt and believed that a historical opportunity had arrived for them to review their political fortunes, and hopefully, achieve sovereign statehood, something that had been socialized and aspired to since May 1963. However, sharp faultlines between the Papuans and Indonesia, were cemented over somewhat when both sides agreed in 2001 to some form of a special autonomy. For many Papuans, this meant an opportunity to achieve, if not total sovereignty, at least, internal sovereignty, whereby they would be able to rule themselves with minimal interference from Jakarta. Special autonomy was seen as a win-win solution, a perception engendered by the belief that a new dawn had set in Jakarta and a more hands-off, tolerant and detached policy would result once the special autonomy arrangements were in place. This is because many Papuans believed that Jakarta feared losing Papua, as had happened in East Timor, and hence, the greater accommodation being demonstrated by the post-Soeharto leaders. Unlike the past, where expression of things indigenous was viewed as telltales of separatism, special autonomy was to sanction and legitimize the expression of Papuans' identity in the political, social, cultural and economic arenas. These were the lofty expectations Papuans had of special autonomy and unfortunately the reality was far removed from their aspirations.

Papua's special autonomy status was legalized under President Megawati Sukarnoputri via Law No. 21 of 2001. Special autonomy under Megawati, however, existed, for the Papuans in name only. A number of major failings under the Megawati administration were noteworthy. Even though special autonomy was expected to be in operation for at least three years before any major change could be implemented, through the issuance of

Presidential Instruction No. 1/2003, Megawati gravely undermined the letter and spirit of the special autonomy law. This involved the unilateral sub-division of Papua into three provinces without consultation with local Papuan leaders, who had rejected a similar proposal under the Habibie presidency. Presidential Instruction No. 1/2003 also contravened Article 76 of the special autonomy law which stated that "expansion of the Papua Province into provinces shall be carried out with the approval of the MRP and Provincial Parliament, giving close attention to the special cultural unity, readiness of the human resources and the economic ability and development in the future".[16] It was not that Papuan could not be sub-divided but rather that it had to follow due process, which Jakarta simply ignored. Later, when the Constitutional Court decreed that the splitting of the Papua into three provinces, especially the establishment of West Irian Jaya based on Law No. 45/1999 was illegal, this was disregarded by the Home Affairs Minister. Since then, there have been two provinces in Papua, with their respective administrations in place.

The delay in the establishment of the MRP was another sore point among the Papuans. It was not established under Megawati's presidency. Instead, it was President Bambang Yudhoyono who sanctioned this in December 2004 through Presidential Instruction 54/2004 and it only came into being much later in 2005. Next, the Papuans, in view of the litany of human rights violations in the past, were annoyed as the appointment of the Police Chief was undertaken without consultation with the local leaders, indicating that the security apparatus, the police and military, would be able to act with impunity as in the past. Consequently, the Papuans' fear of Indonesia and its intentions remained. Papuans felt that special autonomy on paper was in practice a farce, especially as far as transmigration was concerned. This has remained a major grievance, fearing that Jakarta was bent on creating horizontal conflict between the indigenous Papuans and the transmigrants, all the more, as the latter were dominating the political, economic and social-cultural spaces in the territory. In this regard, Jakarta's earmarking of land in the Mimika region (in the coastal regions of central Papua that is suitable for agriculture) for transmigration, despite vociferous protests from the locals, was interpreted as an act in bad faith and one that would greatly disadvantage the locals. At the same time, the continuing strengthening of the military capacity in Papua as well as operations against suspected OPM insurgents continued to be of concern, with the Indonesian military viewed as a major threat to Papuans and their interests. The failure to allocate Special Autonomy funds in time also stalled many public projects, leading many Papuans to view Special Autonomy as being counter-productive for their interests.

In addition, there were other criticisms against the manner in which Special Autonomy was being implemented in Papua. These were, perhaps, a consequence of the excessive expectations that were raised in Papua by the prospect of "special autonomy", combined with what Papuans viewed as minimal trickle-down benefits for them from the new arrangement. While a lot of Special Autonomy funds had been allocated, corruption among the Papuan elites ensured that those deserving assistance, especially the poor, continued to benefit very little from Special Autonomy. As one Indonesian political observer noted, "the people who benefit from the special autonomy are a group of Papuan elites who hold various positions in various regencies which are expanded without following any procedure as regulated in the special autonomy law through the involvement of the MRP".[17]

Additionally, Jakarta has been blamed for the lack of guidance and initiative in implementing the Special Autonomy Law for Papua. As was pointed out by an analyst, "the Special Autonomy is not just a matter of money but rather a political commitment to address problems such as reconciliation, human rights violations, natural resources management, health, poverty, defense and security".[18] Jakarta's lack of commitment was also evident from the fact that even though the special autonomy legislation mandated Jakarta passing seven government regulations to actualize the new system, by mid-2008, only one regulation had been passed, namely with regard to the establishment of the MRP. In addition to the MRP, the special autonomy law mandated the issuance of government regulations on the other six areas: reconciliation and justice, human resource management, natural resources exploration, population affairs, provincial symbols, flags and other attributes of identity, and the protection of local cultures. The fact that there are many problems with Special Autonomy in Papua was best expressed by the Governor of Papua, Barnabas Suebu. He argued that "despite huge Special Autonomy funds being allocated over the last seven years, most people are still living in poverty and are uneducated. A bigger part of the funds have been used to finance bureaucracy".[19]

While Papuans believe that special autonomy is not working for them and has yet to be fully implemented, the central government has indicated an interest in revising the existing special autonomy system on the grounds that "too much autonomy" has already been given to Papuans, thereby adding fuel to the Papuan separatist cause. It was mainly due to this that the Indonesian Government, without consulting the Papuan political leadership, especially the MRP, decreed a new law PP77/2007 that banned the public display of "separatist symbols", something which most Papuan regarded as insulting and an attempt to renege on the Special Autonomy Law, all the more, when

Aceh was allowed to do so. This led the key leaders of the MRP, Agus Alua, Franz Wospakrik and Hana Hikoyabi to argue that PP77/2007 "contradicts Indonesia's Special Autonomy Law No. 21/2001 and also contravenes the fundamental rights of all indigenous Melanesian Papuans".[20] At the same time, proposals to sub-divide Papua further were still afoot, with the possibility of the territory being divided into six provinces along the lines of the Dutch administration from 1950 to 1962. That there is a wide gulf between Jakarta and the Papuans on special autonomy was evident when the *Dewan Adat Papua* (Papuans' Traditional Council) on 15 August 2005 rejected the special autonomy law on grounds that Jakarta was being inconsistent and not serious in its implementation. Similarly, in 2007, the Association of College and University Students of the Papuan Central Highlands, with the support of Cendrawasih University and the MRP, concluded that special autonomy had failed in Papua and that it brought no discernable benefits to Papuans. Finally, John Djopari, Indonesia's former Ambassador to Papua New Guinea and Chairman of the Papua Special Autonomy Evaluation Team, concluded that Papuans' expectations of autonomy had not been met and that the package had failed. In large part, this was because most of the special autonomy funds had been utilized to expand new regencies and their administrations with the result that hardly any funds were allotted to address the needs of Papuans who were supposed to be the beneficiaries of special autonomy.[21]

CONCLUSION

From Jakarta's perspective, special autonomy (*Otonomi Khusus*) was granted to Papua as a political package and in recognition that the central government needed to demonstrate greater magnanimity in the post-Soeharto *Reformasi* era, especially when Indonesia itself was undergoing a phase of democratization. Special autonomy was also a compromise approach between the existing system of strong central control and Papuan independence. Moreover, the package resulted from Jakarta's efforts to undermine the emerging independence movement in the province, especially following Indonesia's loss of East Timor.[22] Jakarta thus viewed special autonomy as a political measure to retain Papua within Indonesia while attempting to douse separatist tendencies and at the same time appearing enlightened, liberal and democratic in the international arena.

For the Papuans, except for those in power who benefited from it personally, special autonomy was perceived as an Indonesian tactic to weaken Papuans' aspirations for independence. Jakarta's motives were allegedly evident from the drastic watering down of the original Papuan proposal on special autonomy, the delayed establishment of the MRP, the failure to implement six other regulations to implement special autonomy in Papua, the continued effort to sub-divide Papua to create horizontal conflicts among the Papuans, the continued efforts to "export" transmigrants, mainly Muslims, into Papua to dilute the Papuan Melanesian majority, the continued strong presence of the security apparatus and most recently of all, the issuance of PP77/2007, aimed at stifling Papuan nationalism, even though these were recognized as "cultural attributes" of the Papuans earlier.

Has special autonomy short-circuited the pressures for separatism in Papua? The answer is unequivocally no, despite the agreement by both sides to implement some form of special autonomy in Papua in 2001. In the end, however, what was implemented was not what the Papuans hoped, thereby fuelling further unhappiness in the territory. In the first instance, Papuan separatism emerged the moment the territory was integrated into Indonesia. There were fundamental grievances that needed to be addressed and that this has not happened is evident from the continuation of the low intensity warfare, waged by the OPM as well as the rise of political separatism, with an increasing number of Papuans, especially younger Papuans, demanding the right to self-determination and independence. What has been the saving grace for Indonesia has been the sheer political, economic and military asymmetry that has prevented Papuan from breaking away from Indonesia. The deep-seated mutual distrust amongst more than 265 Papuan tribes, their demographic weakness (consisting of only 2.5 million people in a Republic of more than 240 million), the sheer power and brutality of the security apparatus, the economic importance of the territory (which has coalesced internal and external stakeholders' opinion in favour of maintaining the status quo), as well as the international community's recognition of Papua as part of Indonesia since 1969, have militated against Papua's struggle for independence. At the same time, unlike East Timor, Jakarta is determined (for historical, political, economic, social-cultural and strategic reasons), to retain the territory at almost any cost. This is evident from the continuous violence that is perpetrated by the security forces deployed in the restive territory. For instance, on 19 October 2011, when the Papuan leaders organized the Third Papuan People's Congress in Jayapura, soldiers and police moved in to break it up, resulting in the death of six Papuans with many more arrested for treason.[23]

All this has meant that the micro-nationalism that has been solidified and cemented by Indonesia's political, economic, security and social-cultural mismanagement of the territory has not been able to make much headway in providing answers to genuine Papuan grievances. The offer of diluted special autonomy, its lackluster implementation, and the likelihood of further splitting of the territory into additional provinces will only weaken the Papuan struggle. What has emerged is that through the offer of special autonomy, regardless of how flawed it is, Indonesia has projected itself as a democratizing nation, willing to surrender political powers to the Papuans and if problems still remain despite devolution of political authority, blame should squarely rest on the Papuans rather than on the Indonesians. Finally, as Indonesia remains geopolitically and strategically far more important than Papua, the interests of the former will always override the latter, condemning Papuans and their interests to marginality, and its people be sacrificed on the altar of domestic and international politics.

Notes

[1] For detailed studies, see John Saltford, *The United Nations and the Indonesian Takeover of West Papua, 1962–1969: The Anatomy of Betrayal* (London and New York: RoutledgeCurzon, 2003); Peter King, *West Papua and Indonesia Since Suharto: Independence, Autonomy or Chaos?* (Sydney: University of New South Wales Press, 2004); C.L.M. Penders, *The West New Guinea Debacle: Dutch Decolonization and Indonesia, 1945–1962* (Adelaide: Crawford House Publishing, 2002); Jim Elmslie, *Irian Jaya Under the Gun: Indonesian Economic Development versus West Papuan Nationalism* (Honolulu: University of Hawaii Press, 2002); Yorrys T.H. Raweyai, *Mengapa Papua Ingin Merdeka?* (Jayapura, Papua: Presidium Dewan Papua, 2002); Tuhana Taufiq Andrianto, *Mengapa Papua Bergolak?* (Yogyakarta: Gama Global Media, 2001); Origenes Reaen Ijie, *Kongres Rakyat Papua II Merupakan Resolusi Dasar Menuju Papua Merdeka* (Jakarta: PT Bumi Intitama Sejahtera, 2003); and Adriana Elisabeth, Muridan S. Widjojo, Rusli Cahyadi, and Sinnal Belgur, *Pemetaan Peran & Kepintingan Para Aktor Dalam Konflik di Papua* (Jakarta: Lembaga Ilmu Pengetahuan Indonesia, 2004).

[2] For example, see Jacobus P. Solossa, *Otonomi Khusus Papua: Mengankat Mertabat Rakyat Papua Di Dalam NKRI* (Jakarta: Pustaka Sinar Harapan, 2006), pp. 9–10, 91–115.

[3] See Origenes Reagen Ijie, op. cit., pp. 3–22.

[4] See Adriana Elisabeth, Muridan S. Widjojo, Rusli Cahyadi, and Sinnal Belgur, op. cit., pp. 1–16.

[5] Prior to his death, a key player from the Indonesian side, Foreign Minister Subandrio wrote a rebuttal to the Papuans' claim for a need to "straighten history". See H. Dr. Subandrio, *Meluruskan Sejarah Perjuangan Irian Barat* (Jakarta: Yayasan Kepada Bangsaku, 2001).

[6] As was stated in a confidential memorandum by the United States Embassy in Jakarta in 1969 that was released by the National Security Archive in 9

July 2004, 'The Act of Free Choice (AFC) in West Irian is unfolding like a Greek tragedy, the conclusion preordained. The main protagonist, the GOI, cannot and will not permit any resolution other than the continued inclusion of West Irian in Indonesia. Dissident activity is likely to increase but the Indonesian armed forces will be able to contain and, if necessary, suppress it." See "Indonesia's 1969 Takeover of West Papua Not by 'Free Choice'", available at <http://www.gwu.edu/~nsarchiv/NSAEBB/NSAEBB128/index.htm>; also see "Irian Jaya: How Canberra helped crush freedom quest", *Sydney Morning Herald*, 26 August 1999.

7   See Syamsul Hadi, Andi Widjajanto, R.P. Utomo, N. Rochayati, Supriyato, S. Maria and W. Addinata, *Disintegrasi Pasca Orde Baru: Negara, Konflik Lokal dan Dinamika Internasional* (Jakarta: Center for International Relations Studies, 2007), p. 116.

8   Even though there have been many allegations, no definitive study exists on this controversial matter. For references, see Allard K. Lowenstein, "Indonesian Human Rights Abuses in West Papua: Application of the Law of Genocide to the History of Indonesian Control", International Human Rights Clinic Yale Law School, available at <http://www.freewestpapua.org/docs/genocide.pdf>; also see "Papua Project", <http://www.arts.usyd.edu.au/centers/cpacs/research/wpp.shtml> and Jim Elmslie, "West Papua: Genocide, Demographic Change, the Issue of 'Intent', and the Australia-Indonesia Security Treaty", available at <http://www.arts.usyd.edu.au/centers/cpacs/docs/Indo%20Solidarity%20paper.pdf>.

9   Even though Soeharto's New Order decreed various regional autonomy regulations, such as Law Number 5, 1975, in reality, centralization rather than decentralization was strongly practised in the belief that any weakening of central control would lead to the Balkanization of Indonesia, especially in territories such as Aceh and Papua where there were ongoing low-level insurgencies. See M. Ryaas Rasyid, "Regional Autonomy and Local Politics in Indonesia", in *Local Power and Politics in Indonesia: Decentralization and Democratization*, edited by Edward Aspinall and Greg Fealy (Singapore: Institute of Southeast Asian Studies, 2003), p. 64.

10 See Agus Sumule, ed., *Mencari Jalan Tengah: Otonomi Khusus Provinsi Papua* (Jakarta: PT Gramedia Pustaka Utama, 2003).

11 See G. Dwipayana and Ramadhan K.H., *Soeharto: My Thoughts, Words and Deeds* (Jakarta: PT Citra Lamtoro Gung Persada, 1991), pp. 85–92.

12 See Octavianus Mote, "Special Autonomy Issue", Genocide Studies Program, Yale University, available at <http://www.etan.org/issues/wpapua/1207spaut.htm>.

13 Agus Sumule, ed., op. cit., p. 49.

14 Ibid., pp. 49–50.

15 See Karl Claxton, *Bougainville 1988–98: Five Searches for Security in the North Solomons Province of Papua New Guinea* (Canberra: Strategic and Defence Studies Center, Australian National University, 1998), pp. 1–151.

16 See "House of People's Representatives of the Republic of Indonesia Bill of Law of the Republic of Indonesia No. 21 Year 2001 on Special Autonomy for the Papua Province", accessed at <http://www.papuaweb.org/goi/otsus/files/otsus-en.html>.
17 Octavianus Mote, op. cit.
18 Ridwan Max Sijabat, "Govt blamed for stagnant Special Autonomy in Papua", *Jakarta Post*, 29 March 2008.
19 "Indonesian govt blamed for stagnant special autonomy in Papua", Radio New Zealand International, 31 March 2008, available at <http://www.rnzi.com/pages/news.php?op=read&id=38882>.
20 *Cendrawasih Pos*, 17 March 2008.
21 Ibid.
22 As was analysed by a report in late 2001, Papua was granted "over and above the normal autonomy to undermine independence movements wanting complete separation from Indonesia by granting local population a greater measure of self-government". See "Special Autonomy for Aceh and West Papua", *Down to Earth*, no. 51, November 2001, available at <http://dte.gn.apc.org/51Aach.htm>.
23 See Hamish Fitzsimmons, "Video shows aftermath of Papua Crackdown", *ABC News*, 28 October 2011, available at <http://www.abc.net.au/news/2011-10-28/video-shows-aftermath-of-Pa>; also see "Ending Conflict in Papua", *Down to Earth*, DTE 89-90, November 2011, available at <http://www.downtoearth-indonesia.org/story/ending-conflict-west-pap>.

References

Adriana, Elisabeth, Muridan S. Widjojo, Rusli Cahyadi, and Sinnal Belgur. *Pemetaan Peran & Kepintingan Para Aktor Dalam Konflik di Papua*. Jakarta: Lembaga Ilmu Pengetahuan Indonesia, 2004.

Andrianto, T.T. *Mengapa Papua Bergolak?* Yogyakarta: Gama Global Media, 2001.

Claxton, K. *Bougainville 1988–98: Five Searches for Security in the North Solomons Province of Papua New Guinea*. Canberra: Strategic and Defence Studies Center, Australian National University, 1998.

Dwipayana, G. and Ramadhan K.H. *Soeharto: My Thoughts, Words and Deeds*. Jakarta: PT Citra Lamtoro Gung Persada, 1991.

Elmslie, J. *Irian Jaya Under the Gun: Indonesian Economic Development versus West Papuan Nationalism*. Honolulu: University of Hawaii Press, 2002.

Hadi, Syamsul, Andi Widjajanto, R.P. Utomo, N. Rochayati, Supriyato, S. Maria and W. Addinata. *Disintegrasi Pasca Orde Baru: Negara, Konflik Lokal dan Dinamika Internasional*. Jakarta: Center for International Relations Studies, 2007.

Ijie, O.R. *Kongres Rakyat Papua II Merupakan Resolusi Dasar Menuju Papua Merdeka*. Jakarta: PT Bumi Intitama Sejahtera, 2003.

King, P. *West Papua and Indonesia Since Suharto: Independence, Autonomy or Chaos?* Sydney: University of New South Wales Press, 2004.
Penders, C.L.M. *The West New Guinea Debacle: Dutch Decolonization and Indonesia, 1945–1962*. Adelaide: Crawford House Publishing, 2002.
Rasyid, M.R. "Regional Autonomy and Local Politics in Indonesia". In *Local Power and Politics in Indonesia: Decentralization and Democratization*, edited by Edward Aspinall and Greg Fealy. Singapore: Institute of Southeast Asian Studies, 2003.
Saltford, J. *The United Nations and the Indonesian Takeover of West Papua, 1962–1969: The Anatomy of Betrayal*. London and New York: RoutledgeCurzon, 2003.
Sijabat, R.M. "Govt blamed for stagnant Special Autonomy in Papua". *Jakarta Post*, 29 March 2008.
Solossa, J.P. *Otonomi Khusus Papua: Mengankat Mertabat Rakyat Papua Di Dalam NKRI*. Jakarta: Pustaka Sinar Harapan, 2006.
Subandrio, H. Dr. *Meluruskan Sejarah Perjuangan Irian Barat*. Jakarta: Yayasan Kepada Bangsaku, 2001.
Sumule, A., ed. *Mencari Jalan Tengah: Otonomi Khusus Provinsi Papua*. Jakarta: PT Gramedia Pustaka Utama, 2003.
Yorrys T.H. Raweyai. *Mengapa Papua Ingin Merdeka?* Jayapura, Papua: Presidium Dewan Papua, 2002.

5

THE PARALLELS AND THE PARADOX OF TIMOR-LESTE AND WESTERN SAHARA

Adérito de Jesus Soares

This chapter is, via a comparison of the problems of Timor-Leste and Western Sahara, aimed at revealing the relevant experiences of the two cases that can be contextualized into efforts to understand contemporary problems of armed separatist movements. Resorting to this comparison rather than depending on similar comparisons from the region is interesting from an international legal perspective. The chapter aims to explore what factors lay behind the rejection of autonomy by the Timorese people in the 1999 referendum. It also examines the argument of many observers who suggested that, one of the underlying factors in the opposition of the Timorese toward the offer of autonomy by the United Nations was the strength of Timor's case in international law. Western Sahara is, however, a counter example to the latter argument since, despite having a strong case in terms of international law, a just and acceptable solution has eluded it. The chapter concludes by arguing that autonomy is not always a magic bullet. International legal elements can be effective should there be a move towards more open and democratic occupying force, as was the case of Indonesia in relation to Timor-Leste case.

BACKGROUND: THE CASE OF TIMOR-LESTE

Timor-Leste was a Portuguese colony for almost 450 years. Sporadic revolts by the Timorese people, such as the Manufahi revolt of 1910–1912 under the leadership of the King of Manufahi, Dom Boa Ventura, were finally crushed by Portugal.[1] The struggle for independence took shape in the 1970s, after the flower revolution in Portugal in 1974 paved the way for the people of Timor-Leste to form political parties as the beginning of the decolonization process. However, Portugal failed to shepherd the process of decolonization. Following this, the Indonesian regime under Soeharto invaded Timor-Leste on 7 December 1975, a day before the visit by the United States' State Secretary Henry Kissinger and President Gerald Ford to Jakarta.[2] During the Indonesian occupation, massive human rights abuses were committed by the Indonesian military regime resulting in the death of more than two hundred thousand Timorese.[3] The Revolutionary Front for the Liberation of Timor-Leste (Frente Revolucionária do Timor-Leste Independente or Fretilin) — the de facto government- fought against the illegal occupation. With the crackdown on its military wing Falintil (Forças Armadas de Libertação Nacional de Timor-Leste-the Defence Force of National Liberation of Timor-Leste) in the early 1980s, Xanana Gusmão,[4] the new resistance leaders managed to inspire the fighting spirit of the Timorese, and, most importantly, expanded the resistance to the whole Timor-Leste through a massive clandestine network and support in the international arena. Ultimately, the resistance movement was successful in gaining support both internally within Timor-Leste, and externally from the international community. One of the strategies of the National Council of Maubere Resistance (Conselho Nacional da Resistencia Maubere- CNRM) before it became the National Council of Timorese Resistance (Concelho National da Resistencia Timorense- CNRT) in 1998[5] was to break the political impasse between the Indonesian government and the Portuguese government, with the launch of CNRM's Peace Plan in 1992.[6] It was launched before the Human Rights Sub Committee of the European Parliament by the CNRM spoke person, José Ramos Horta.[7] Subsequently, the Peace Plan was endorsed in various international forums by the resistance movement.

In relation to the theme of this volume, it is relevant to look briefly at the substance of the CNRM's 1992 Peace Plan. The Peace Plan consisted of three phases. The first phase (one to two years) emphasized dialogue between the Indonesian government and Portugal under the auspices of the UN Secretary General. This dialogue was to cover issues such as ending armed activities in Timor-Leste; immediate and unconditional release of political prisoners; reduction of Indonesian military presence including its forces and heavy weapons (tanks, helicopters, etc.); reducing the number of Indonesian public servants; expanding the activities of the International Red Cross; opening up Timor-Leste to UN agencies such UNICEF, UNDP, WHO, UNESCO and FAO; a comprehensive census; the establishment of a Human Rights Commission in Dili; lifting press censorship; freedom of political activities and assembly; removal of a restriction on teaching Portuguese; and the appointment of a resident representative of the UN Secretary General. Phase two covered issues such as normalization of relations between Portugal and Indonesia; legalization of political parties; representation of Portugal in Timor; establishment of a Portuguese Cultural Institute; election for a local assembly by Timorese only; election by the assembly of an East Timor Governor; withdrawal of remaining Indonesian troops; and significant governmental powers to be vested in Timor. The second phase was to be carried out over two to five years. The third phase stressed the issue of self-determination. It covered issues such as: preparation for a referendum on self-determination, followed by general election for Constituent Assembly; transfer of power to the elected government; Timor joining ASEAN and the South Pacific forum; and lastly Timor acceding to and ratifying all international human rights instruments.

Although this was a comprehensive proposal, the Indonesian government did not give it any consideration and rejected it outright. However, at the UN level it did lead to dialogue between the Indonesian government and the Portuguese government, and another separate forum to facilitate dialogue between the Timorese people — both those who were residing in Timor and Indonesia and in the diaspora — was conducted. This forum, the All Inclusive East Timorese Dialogue (AIETD), was held several times in the 1990s to discuss cultural issues, but not political issues. Sadly, no tangible result emanated from AIETD,[8] perhaps because as CNRT leader, Xanana Gusmão said, AIETD was totally manipulated by the Indonesian government.[9]

The geopolitical and financial crisis in Asia in 1998 had a huge impact on Indonesian politics and eventually led the newly elected President Habibie of Indonesia to announce a wide ranging autonomy package for Timor-Leste in January 1999 and promise to reduce the military presence in Timor-Leste. The original plan was to grant a special autonomy to Timor-Leste, as a final solution announced by Habibie on June 9, 1998 before the meeting with the IMF regarding the economic crisis facing Indonesia. Ali Alatas, the Foreign Minister then, communicated the plan to the UN Secretary General. Several senior official meetings were held between Portugal and Indonesia under the auspices of the UN Secretary General to discuss the draft of special autonomy for Timor-Leste. Apparently, there was a fundamental difference in the two countries' views of autonomy. For Indonesia, autonomy had to be the final solution to the Timor-Leste problem; while, for Portugal, autonomy was only be a transitional phase to prepare for a referendum- a position supported by CNRT as well. Facing this predicament and concomitantly dealing with the dire economic crisis and international pressure related to human rights, especially on the Timor problem, Habibie then announced that a referendum would be conducted in order to ask the Timorese whether they wanted to be integral part of Indonesia by accepting the special autonomy or wanted to be independent.[10] Later, Habibie acknowledged that his decision was based on the rationale that there was no benefit at all for Indonesia to keep Timor in a transition to independence should they reject autonomy after all. As he pointed out in his memoir, "the primary focus was to ensure that the problem [Timor-Leste] would be resolved once and for all".[11] Although there was reluctance among the military leaders who supported Habibie's policy, they seemed convinced that should the referendum take place, the Timorese people would vote in favour of autonomy. Most importantly, as General Wiranto, the chief commander of the Indonesian Military (TNI), said to Habibie, there should not be questions about the correctness of the 1975 integration of Timor-Leste into Indonesia, given so many sacrifices by the TNI, with thousands of them dying during the 24 years of occupation.[12]

Finally a referendum was organized under the auspices of the United Nations Mission on East Timor (UNAMET) on August 30, 1999. The referendum asked the Timorese whether they agreed with the Special Autonomous Region of East Timor (SARET)[13] within Indonesia, or opposed it, which would lead to a transition to independence. According to SARET, Jakarta as the central government would have powers over a range of important functions such as foreign affairs, defence, currency and finance. The autonomous region of East Timor would have powers in areas like police force and judiciary, under the jurisdiction of the supreme court of Indonesia. It would elect its own governor and manage natural resources, except those considered to be strategic or vital under Indonesian law. The August 30th referendum resulted in 78.5 per cent of the Timorese people voting to reject the autonomy proposal, resulting to the independence of Timor-Leste in May 2002, after two years of transition under the UN. The reaction of the Indonesian military and its militias to the vote was devastating, with hundreds of civilians killed and massive destruction across the whole country.

BACKGROUND: THE CASE OF WESTERN SAHARA

The case of Western Sahara is quite similar to Timor-Leste. Since the 1960s it has been recognized, as in the case of Timor, a non self-governing territory under the UN Decolonization Committee. Western Sahara was colonized by Spain for decades and resistance towards Spain was sporadic. It was in the 1970s that the Polisario Front (Frente Popular para la Liberación de Saguia el-Hamra y Río de Oro-Popular Front for the Liberation of Saguia el-Hamra and Río de Oro) took the lead in the struggle against Spanish occupation. As with Fretilin, the Polisario Front was born in May 1973 when a small group of Saharawi people — as the people of Western Sahara people are called-launched an attack on a small colonial fort in what was then called Spanish Sahara.[14] As in the case of Timor-Leste, where Portugal failed to effectively decolonize, Spain failed to hold a decolonization process on self-determination for Western Sahara. This decolonization process which was supposed to be held in 1975, was based on the UN Decolonization Committee's first resolution in 1964,[15] and reaffirmed by the General Assembly a year later.[16]

Instead of conducting the decolonization process, however, Spain ceded Western Sahara to Morocco and Mauritania on November 14 1975 (through the secretive Madrid Accord). The Western Saharan people were excluded from the Madrid Accord which resulted in the division of the territory, with the southern half of the territory given away to Mauritania and the northern half to Morocco. With this handover, Morocco made a historical claim to its illegal occupation of Western Sahara. The Polisario Front, as in the case of Fretilin, then proclaimed the independence of the Saharawi Arab Democratic Republic (SADR) on February 27, 1976. Morocco's and Mauritania's historical claim to the territory was rejected by the decision of the International Court of Justice (ICJ) in its advisory opinion[17] on October 1976. The ICJ, instead, endorsed the right to self-determination of Western Sahara through a referendum. The advisory opinion boosted Western Sahara's case, and it had a huge impact on other struggles for self-determination, as it became a precedent for struggling territories in pursuing their rights of self-determination internationally, including for Timor-Leste before the referendum.

In 1992, the UN established the United Nations Mission for the Referendum in Western Sahara (MINURSO), in order to carry out the process of self-determination through a referendum, as mandated in the UN's earliest resolutions regarding Western Sahara. MINURSO was set up following the Peace Plan proposed by the UN in 1991 which was agreed on by both Morocco and Polisario Front.[18] The five stages of the Peace Plan were aimed at starting a ceasefire; confining both armies; reducing Moroccan troops; repatriating refugees; releasing prisoners; identifying Sahrawis eligible to vote; and finally, holding a referendum, that would result either in independence or full legal integration into the Kingdom of Morocco.

Unlike in the case of UNAMET, MINURSO has been in Western Sahara more than fifteen years, but it has not managed to fulfil its mission yet. This is partly because of the opposition of the Kingdom of Morroco to the plan of the referendum, and at practical level, it is due the problem of identifying who is eligible to vote. The problem "who are the Saharawi people" became an obstacle to conducting the referendum as there was intimidation and manipulation by Moroccan authorities during the registration process. MINURSO, which has been criticized for failing to prepare the ground for referendum, handed over many of its tasks to the Moroccan authorities, which resulted in the manipulation by Morocco, for instance, in the case of which Saharawis should be eligible to vote. Frank Rudy, MINURSO's former deputy chairman affirmed that, "the U.N. Mission was a laughing stock at diplomatic parties in Rabat-the capital of the Kingdom of Morocco. The Mission's abandonment of a free and fair referendum was common knowledge."[19] He goes on to say that "the UN mission's impotence to stop the abuse was open and notorious".[20]

The failure to hold the referendum as mandated by the UN resolution, resulted in the UN Secretary General, Kofi Annan, in 1997, appointing James Baker III, former U.S. Secretary of State, as his personal Envoy for Western Sahara with the special task of facilitating dialogue between the Kingdom of Morocco and the Polisario. On 20 June 2001, the UN Secretary General proposed to the Security Council what was known as The Baker Peace Plan. The Baker Peace Plan proposed the integration of Western Sahara into the Moroccan Kingdom with a degree of autonomy. This proposal was accepted by the Kingdom of Morocco, but rejected by the Polisario Front.

Today, Morocco's proposal for an autonomy package to be voted on by the region's residents — both Sahrawis and Moroccan settlers — would provide limited power to the Sahrawis. It is clear that Morocco wants the adoption of the autonomy package — in other words, a vote for the acceptance of autonomy package — as expected by the Kingdom of Morocco, with the backing of its strong western allies such as France and the U.S.[21] However, the Moroccan autonomy proposal keeps being rejected by the Polisario.

Notwithstanding this failure, since 2007 there have been direct talks and confidence building measures between Morocco and Polisario under the UN auspices. As noted, however, in the UN Secretary General's report, the talks have not touched on substantive issues and the political impasse between Morocco and Polisario has not been broken. In Resolution 1813 (2008)[22] the Security Council calls upon the parties to continue to show political will and work in an atmosphere propitious for dialogue in order to enter into a more intensive and substantive phase of negotiations, to ensure implementation of resolutions 1754 and 1783; and affirms its strong support for the commitment of Secretary General and his Personal Envoy towards finding a solution in Western Sahara. As a routine gesture, the Security Council also called for the extension of MINURSO until 30 April 2009. What will be happen next to the Western Sahara remains a puzzle.

PARALLELS AND PARADOXES

It is interesting to draw out the parallels and paradoxes evident in these two cases. As identified by Rigaux in his brief account of Timor-Leste and Western Sahara, the two cases have similarities and differences.[23] Both Timor-Leste and Western Sahara were occupied by Iberian countries (Portugal and Spain). Both invading countries have strong alliances with western countries (such as U.S. and France, in the case of Western Sahara and England, Australia, U.S. and others in the case of Indonesia). Both Timor-Leste and Western Sahara were invaded by neighbours at almost the same time. Under the Command of Moroccan King Hassan II, Western Sahara was invaded by Moroccan Army on 6 November 1975, while Timor-Leste was invaded by Indonesia army under General Soeharto on 7 December 1975. In both cases, the colonial powers agreed to the process of decolonization, but they failed to comply with international legal obligations on the decolonization process. However, while the referendum in Timor Leste in 1999 led to independence, Western Sahara is still in a state of limbo. The United Nations has been in the Western Sahara for almost two decades; yet no referendum has been held.

We can add to Rigaux's list by fleshing out five main differences between the two cases — firstly, the direct involvement of the Polisario Front with Morocco in dialogues facilitated by the UN. This happened after the failure of the Baker Peace Plan as mentioned above. This was not the case with Timor. While there were tripartite meetings between the Indonesian government, the Portuguese government and the UN, the Timorese resistance leadership were marginalized from this process. The lack of involvement of Timorese in the process of negotiations was pointed out by Marker, the UN facilitator for the tripartite dialogue:

> Despite the creation of the AIETD, I felt that the existing process of trilateral consultations — U.N., Portugal, and Indonesia — had in many ways marginalized the East Timorese...[24]

This does not mean, however, that the participation of the Western Sahara in dialogue was without problems, as the Kingdom of Morocco always tried to marginalize the Saharawi within the process of dialogue through various ways.

The second difference between these two cases is in the transitional aspect of the autonomy packages proposed by the UN. In the case of Western Sahara, autonomy was proposed as a final solution according to the Baker Peace Plan, after the failure to implement the first Peace Plan. However, in the case of Timor-Leste, autonomy was proposed with another option — the transition to independence — should autonomy be rejected. And in fact, as mentioned earlier, the proposed autonomy was rejected overwhelmingly by the Timorese. Western Sahara, however, had no other option for independence, should they accept the Baker Peace Plan.

The third difference is the cooperation between the occupying powers and the UN Mission. In the case of UNAMET, in spite of the "soft resistance" by the Indonesian government in the beginning of the process, eventually Indonesia did collaborate with UNAMET in order to conduct the referendum. Notwithstanding the violence that occurred in Timor prior to referendum, UNTAET was determined to carry out the referendum (Although, it must be noted that UNTAET and the international community did not anticipate and were too slow and too soft to prevent the wave of violence before and after the referendum.) Unlike UNAMET, MINURSO has not had any real support from the Kingdom of Morocco which has undermine its integrity, as explained earlier.

The fourth difference lay in the scope of the democrative process in Indonesia and Morocco. While the dire economic and financial crisis in 1997/98 opened up the democratic sphere in Indonesia, resulting in the Soeharto regime being replaced by the slightly more democratic regime under Habibie, nothing comparable happened in the Kingdom of Morocco, where there continues to be less democratic space. And, lastly, during the struggle CNRT enjoyed the full support of the Portuguese government, while Western Sahara does not enjoy any real support from the Spanish government.

THE HOPE AND MYTH OF INTERNATIONAL LAW

As has been noted by many observers, Timor-Leste was a different case in the context of self-determination. Its status as a non-self governing territory under the UN Decolonization Committee was crucial. Following the invasion, both parties (Indonesia and Portugal) were trying to argue from an international legal perspective — as they believed in the "efficacy" of international law

— to justify their stance. For Indonesia, the integration through the 1976 Balibo Declaration was a genuine expression of the Timorese people; hence it was an act sanctioned by international law.[25] With this in mind, the Indonesian government used the Balibo Declaration, to try to convince the international community that the integration of Timor-Leste was a genuinely popular expression of the Timorese people; and that the integration met the criteria of self-determination under international law. On the other hand, Portugal's stance was that the integration was illegal as it did not fulfil the criteria for self-determination under international law.[26] The right to self-determination is an international legal concept that is subject to a never-ending debate. Some, argue that the right to self-determination is vague and lacking in any clear practical meaning. Others argue that the right to self-determination is an inalienable right for colonized people. Having said that, however, it is beyond the parameters of this chapter to explore this controversy in depth.

Looking at the record of voting on the Timor case in the UN since 1975, one might reasonably wonder what exactly was the role of international law. From the first UN Resolution condemning the Indonesian occupation and demanding that Indonesia leave Timor, to the last resolution, the language changed dramatically.[27] The language of the last resolution merely focused on the procedural aspect of the Timor case in the UN, such as endorsing the UN Secretary General to facilitate talks between Timor and Portugal, even though the status of Timor-Leste as non self-governing territory remained important in the UN Let's compare these two resolutions in more detail. Article 1 of the UN General Assembly Resolution 3485 (XXX), 12 December 1975 stated in its most unequivocal language that:

> The General Assembly ... Calls upon all States to respect the inalienable rights of Portuguese Timor to self-determination, freedom and independence and to determine their future political status in accordance with the principle of the Charter of the United Nations and the Declaration on the Granting of Independence to Colonial Countries and peoples.

The last UN resolution concerning Timor, Resolution 37/30, and 23 November 1982, further stated in very procedural language (Article 1):

> The General Assembly ... request the Secretary General to initiate consultations with all parties directly concerned, with a view to exploring avenues for achieving a comprehensive settlement of the problem and to report thereon to the General Assembly ...

Subsequently, there was dialogue between Portugal and Indonesia, under the auspices of the UN, as well as parallel meetings between Timorese leaders in East Timor and Indonesia and those from the diaspora. There were no tangible results from these various talks, except that more talks were conducted. Concomitantly, there was no significant progress in terms of human rights, with growing support for the independence among young people through a massive clandestine movement both inside Timor-Leste and in various cities in Indonesia where Timorese students were studying. But interestingly, as the UN's resolutions on the case seemed to grow weaker, the Timorese people and Portuguese government still had great hope in the power of international law.

There were similar experiences in the Western Sahara case. Despite the establishment of MINURSO in Western Sahara, with the main task being to conduct a referendum for the non-self governing territory, the UN Security Council altered the tone of its earliest resolution to a more procedural tone, as in the case of Timor-Leste. Interestingly, in the process of negotiations, Polisario is involved directly with Morocco, as explained earlier, but only to discuss the offer of autonomy as proposed in the Baker Peace Plan.

Reflecting upon the change of language in the UN resolutions concerning the two cases, one might wonder, what exactly is the power of international law in settling such a dispute? In spite of some degree of the indeterminacy of international law in both cases, I agree with the argument proposed by Professor Falk — that in the case of Timor, international law gave hope to those struggling for justice.[28] In Falk's words, "it would be misleading to adopt a legalistic view of the right of self-determination and assume that because the grounds for its invocation are present the means for its implementation can be found."[29] However, Falk also reiterated the importance of international law itself especially in relation to the struggle for self-determination. He put it succinctly: "it would be a tactical error to dismiss the relevance of international law as an aspect of a resistance struggle that builds and sustains effective support."[30] Another critical international law practitioner and scholar, Marti Koskeniemmi affirms that: "International law's energy and hope lies in its ability to articulate existing transformative commitment in the language of rights and duties and thereby to give voice to those who otherwise routinely excluded."[31]

CAMPAIGN AND VIOLENCE

In the preparation for the referendum on 30 August 1999, both the supporters of the autonomy proposal and its opponents (I am using the term referred to in the May 5 Agreement[32]) were guaranteed the right to conduct public campaigns. The campaign was supposed to be conducted in "a peaceful and democratic manner" by both sides.[33] Unfortunately, that was not the case in the lead up to the referendum in East Timor.

Amidst the violence created by militias with the backing up of the Indonesian military, the CNRT organized a three-day training for CNRT campaigners in the Cannosian Sisters' venue in Dili at the end of July 1999. It was attended by about 250 participants from all over Timor-Leste.[34] One of the sessions during the training was to explain the content of the special autonomy package (SARET) and its consequences should the Timorese vote for it. One of the main materials for the training was a booklet title: *Jebakan Integrasi* (The Integration Trap).[35] *Jebakan Integrasi*, which is mentioned briefly by Ian Martin, the former Head of UNAMET in his book *Self-Determination in East Timor*,[36] was a critique of SARET[37] proposed by the United Nations. *Jebakan Integrasi* argued that SARET was a trap since the power it allowed the central government would enable the latter to control any aspect of Timorese life. Thus the Timorese people should reject it.

Following the training, the participants went back to each district, as they had to organize public campaigns based on the rules of procedure adopted by the UN, Portugal and Indonesia. Later, CNRT sent its campaigners to visit districts in Timor-Leste. One team of campaigners was in charge of covering very tense places such as Oecussi, Maliana, Ermera and Liquica in the Western part of Timor-Leste. These districts were known for their notorious militia groups. The team, which consisted of about ten people, reached Oecussi safely and their public campaign went very well — of course under the surveillance of Oecussi militias and the Indonesian military. The team also managed to escape from the planned attack of militias on the way back from Oecussi to Maliana.[38]

On August 17 the campaign team reached Maliana from Oecussi and in the evening they had a planning meeting with CNRT in its compound, with local CNRT leader Manuel Magalhães.[39] As the campaign team was planning to conduct the campaign in Maliana's soccer field — in the middle of the town — on July 18, they were suddenly attacked by militia early in the morning. Hundreds of militia members came and attacked, throwing rocks at the CNRT compound. In a very short time, the CNRT boys in the compound defended themselves before escaping. As a consequence the campaign had to be cancelled and the CNRT campaign team escaped by climbing Mount Loelaco and walking for two days, before reaching Bobonaro sub-district, and renting another mini bus to take them to Ermera district. As the team arrived in Ermera, they decided not to carry out a public campaign.

Instead they distributed CNRT symbols such as flags and the symbol for the UN referendum and sent these to Liquica district, through another CNRT courier. The team then drove back to Dili and had a very close escape, as they passed the Railaco sub-district where the pro-autonomy groups were holding their campaign. But no one stopped the minibus as they thought the passengers were ordinary civilians.

Of course, there were other widespread human rights violations prior to the referendum. However, these two events and the ups and downs of Timor's resistance demonstrate how international law played a significant role in achieving their right to self-determination and how the Timorese people had trust in the ability of international law to address their problem. In spite of the violence, the Timorese still believed in the international agreement worked out by the UN, Indonesia and Portugal, on conducting the public campaign for the referendum. Perhaps, hope in the role of international law was as significant as other factors which contributed to the independence of Timor-Leste.[40]

CONCLUSION

This chapter explored the parallels and paradox of the Timor-Leste and Western Sahara case. It highlighted the important role of international law, combined with a robust network of resistance, in sustaining and facilitating a solution in the case of Timor-Leste. However, it also exposed the limits of international law in both cases, especially Western Sahara where the UN, from 1992 to the present has attempted without success to organize a referendum.

The 1997 economic crisis which led to the democratization process in Indonesia eventually opened the door to the use of international law most effectively in the case of Timor-Leste. In March 2011, another round of talks between Morocco and Western Sahara were facilitated by the UN in Malta. There was no concrete outcome, notwithstanding the fact that the parties agreed to continue with talks.

As indicated earlier, the difference between the two parties in Western Sahara lies in the options for autonomy proposed by each. Should the proposed autonomy be the final option for Western Sahara? Or should it be just a transition period, as decided by the Saharawis via a referendum, as was the case with Timor-Leste in 1999? As with Timor-Leste, it seems likely that without any significant change inside the Morrocan regime, Western Sahara will continue to be in limbo. The wave of protests and calls for democratic change in the Middle East and North Africa in early 2011 is expected to have an impact on the Morrocan regime and in turn change the regime's stance on Western Sahara.[41] Only when this occurs will the UN have the courage to endorse the proposal for the referendum which has been postponed since 1992.

An autonomy proposal is not always a magic bullet. Western Sahara demonstrates well how the imposition of autonomy, even by the United Nations, can create an unresolved situation. Cases discussed in this book which have international legal elements, including the case of West Papua for example, need special attention *vis-à-vis* autonomy proposals. It is this international aspect which can always be capitalized on by opposition forces confronting Indonesian rule there, to challenge an autonomy solution. As for the case of Western Sahara, the failure of MINURSO so far is unfortunate. However, one might hope that the combination of international legal elements, a robust network of resistance from POLISARIO and the prospect of change on the part of the Moroccan regime may bring a just solution that is based on the principles of the right to self-determination.

Notes

[1] John G. Taylor, *East Timor: The Price of Freedom* (New York: Zed Books, 1999), p. 11. Manufahi was the old name of the same district located in the southern part of Timor-Leste.

[2] Ibid., p 64.

[3] These atrocities have been documented in the report of Timor-Leste's Commission for Reception, Truth and Reconciliation in East Timor, available at <http://www.cavr-timorleste.org/en/chegaReport.htm>.

[4] Following the 1999 referendum, Xanana Gusmão was elected President in 2002, and was appointed Prime Minister in 2007.

[5] For the shift of strategy by the resistance movement, see Douglas Kammen, "Between Violence and Negotiations: Rethinking the Indonesian Occupation and East Timorese Resistance", in this volume.

[6] The Peace Plan was originally launched by Xanana Gusmão as the resistance leader in 1989, but did not gain much attention or support at the time.

[7] Horta took up the position as Minister for Foreign Affairs after the referendum and during the political turmoil of 2006 was appointed Prime Minister. He was elected President of Timor-Leste in 2007.

[8] Jamsheed Marker, *East Timor: A Memoir of the Negotiations for Independence* (Jefferson, N.C.: McFarland Inc. Publishers, 2003), pp. 16–17.

[9] Ibid.

[10] The shift in Habibie's policy happened a few days before receiving a letter from the Australian Prime Minister, John Howard which took the same position as

Portugal, i.e. favouring a referendum. However, it should be noted that the Howard's government's intention was to resolve the Timor problem once and for all with the expectation that Timorese people would vote for autonomy within Indonesia, which might in turn pave the way for a better relationship between Australia and Indonesia. See, Clinton Fernandes, "The Road to INTERFET: Bringing the Politics Back", *Security Challenges*, vol. 4, no. 3 (Spring 2008): 86–87.

11 See Bacharuddin Jusuf Habibie, *Decisive Moments: Indonesia's Long Road to Democracy* (Jakarta: Ilthabi Rekatama, 2006), p. 243.

12 See, Wiranto, *Selamat Jalan Timor-Timor: Pergulatan Menguak Kebenaran* [Goodbye Timor-Timor: Struggle to Tell the Truth] (Jakarta: IDe Indonesia, 2002), p. 89.

13 See Agreement Between the Republic of Indonesia and the Portuguese Republic on the Question of East Timor, 5 May 1999, Annex on The Constitutional Framework for A Special Autonomous Region for East Timor (SARET), available at <http://untreaty.un.org/unts/144078_158780/7/2/1414.pdf>.

14 For a more comprehensive account see, Tony Hodges, *Western Sahara: The Roots of a Desert War* (Westport, CT: Lawrence Hill and Co., 1983).

15 GAOR, 19th Session, Annex No. 8 (part I), UN Document A/5800/Rev. 1 (1964), pp. 290–91.

16 UNGA Resolution 2072, 16 December 1965, GAOR, 20th Session, Supplement 14, UN Document A/6014, pp. 59–60.

17 ICJ Reports, October 1975.

18 UN Resolution 690/1991, ratified on 17 May 1991.

19 Frank Ruddy, "Western Sahara: Africa's Last Colony", address at World Affairs Council, 2 November 2007.

20 Ibid.

21 For the U.S. involvement in Western Sahara case, see Jacob Mundy, "Neutrality or Complicity: The United States and the 1975 Moroccan Takeover of the Spanish Sahara", *The Journal of North African Studies* 11, no. 3 (September 2006).

22 S/RES/1813 (2008), 30 April 2008.

23 Francois Rigaux, "East Timor and Western Sahara: A Comparative View", in *International Law and the Questions of East Timor*, edited by Pedro Pinto Leite (CIIR/IPJET, 1995).

24 Marker, note 8, p. 17.

25 Balibo is the name of a small town in the Western part of Timor-Leste near the border with West Timor, Indonesia. The Indonesian Government claimed that in the Balibo Declaration, Timorese leaders who supported Indonesia, proclaimed the integration of Timor-Leste into the Indonesian republic. In fact, the Bali Declaration was drafted in Bali by Indonesian authorities and was later declared by Timorese pro-integration leaders.

26 The right to self-determination is guaranteed in the 1945 UN Charter as well as some other UN instruments such as the Declaration on the Granting

of Independence to Colonial Countries and People of 1960; International Covenant on Civil and Political Rights and the Covenant on Economic, Social and Cultural Rights both adopted in 1966 and entered into force in 1976.
27 See Paula Escarameia, "The Meaning of Self-Determination and the Case of East Timor", in Leite, above 23.
28 Richard Falk, "The East Timor Ordeal: International Law and Its Limits", *Bulletin of Concerned Asian Scholars* 32, nos. 1–2 (2004): 53.
29 Ibid.
30 Ibid.
31 Marti Koskenniemi, *The Gentle Civilizer of Nations: The Rise and Fall of International Law* (Cambridge: Cambridge University Press, 2002), pp. 516–17.
32 See Agreement Regarding The Modalities for the Popular Consultation of the East Timorese Through A Direct Ballot, signed between the Indonesian Government, the Portuguese Government and the UN on May 5th Agreement, available in <http://untreaty.un.org/unts/144078_158780/7/2/1414.pdf>.
33 Point C of the Agreement, ibid.
34 It was organized by CNRT in Dili and participants came from all over Timor-Leste. I was privileged to be one of the trainers who explained the concept of SARET to participants; and later joined the campaign in the Western part of Timor-Leste in the lead up to the referendum.
35 See, *Jebakan Integrasi* (Jakarta: Sahe Study Club, 1999). *Jebakan Integrasi* resulted from a series of discussions between Timor-Leste pro-independence activists and Indonesian pro-democracy activists in Jakarta, after the the agreement on the referendum was reached by the United Nations, the Government of Indonesia and the Portuguese Government.
36 Ian Martin, *Self-Determination in East Timor* (Colorado: Rienner, 2001), p. 27.
37 "Appendix: A Constitutional Framework for a Special Autonomy for East Timor", available in <http://www.un.org/peace/etimor99/agreement/agreeFrame_Eng02.html>.
38 We were informed later that the militias were waiting for us in Kefa, West Timor, Indonesia, so we took a different route out of Oecussi, to Maliana.
39 Magalhães was later killed with eight other CNRT leaders in Maliana's Police Station. See, *the Report of KPP-HAM Indonesia* (2000).
40 See Kammen, note 5.
41 See *Huffington Post*, 4 March 2011.

References

Escarameia, Paula. "The Meaning of Self-Determination and the Case of East Timor". In *International Law and the Questions of East Timor*, edited by Pedro Pinto Leite. London: CIIR/IPJET, 1995.

Falk, Richard. "The East Timor Ordeal: International Law and Its Limits". *Bulletin of Concerned Asian Scholars* 32, nos. 1–2 (2004).

Fernandes, Clinton. "The Road to INTERFET: Bringing the Politics Back". *Security Challenges*, vol. 4, no. 3 (Spring 2008).
Habibie, Bacharuddin Jusuf. *Decisive Moments: Indonesia's Long Road to Democracy.* Jakarta: Ilthabi Rekatama, 2006.
Hodges, Tony. *Western Sahara: The Roots of a Desert War.* Westport, CT: Lawrence Hill and Co., 1983.
Koskenniemi, Marti. *The Gentle Civilizer of Nations: The Rise and Fall of International Law.* Cambridge: Cambridge University Press, 2002.
Marker, Jamsheed. *East Timor: A Memoir of the Negotiations for Independence.* Jefferson, N.C.: McFarland Inc. Publishers, 2003.
Martin, Ian. *Self-determination in East Timor: The United Nations, the Ballot, and International Intervention.* Boulder, Colorado: Lynne Rienner Publisher, 2001.
Mundy, Jacob. "Neutrality or Complicity: The United States and the 1975 Moroccan Takeover of the Spanish Sahara". *The Journal of North African Studies* 11, no. 3 (September 2006).
Rigaux, Francois. "East Timor and Western Sahara: A Comparative View". In *International Law and the Questions of East Timor*, edited by Pedro Pinto Leite. CIIR/IPJET, 1995.
Ruddy, Frank. "Western Sahara: Africa's Last Colony". Address at World Affairs Council, 2 November 2007, available at <http://www.arso.org/RuddyAlaskaspeech2007.pdf> (accessed January 2010).
Sahe Study Club. *Jebakan Integrasi.* Jakarta: Sahe Study Club, 1999.
Special Autonomous Region for East Timor (SARET). "Agreement Between the Republic of Indonesia and the Portuguese Republic on the Question of East Timor", 5 May 1999, available at <http://untreaty.un.org/unts/144078_158780/7/2/1414.pdf>.
Taylor, John. G. *East Timor: The Price of Freedom.* New York: Zed Books Ltd./Annandale, N.S.W: Pluto Press, 1999.
Walt van Praag, Dr. Michael C. van with Onno Seroo, eds. *The Implementation of the Rights to Self-Determination as a Contribution to Conflict Prevention.* Center UNESCO de Catalunya, 1999.
Wiranto, General. *Selamat Jalan Timor-Timor: Pergulatan Menguak Kebenaran* [Goodbye Timor-Timor: Struggle to Tell the Truth]. Jakarta: IDe Indonesia, 2002.

6

BETWEEN VIOLENCE AND NEGOTIATION: RETHINKING THE INDONESIAN OCCUPATION AND THE EAST TIMORESE RESISTANCE

Douglas Kammen

At first glance East Timor appears to be an awkward fit in a volume on armed separatism and autonomy. The reasons for this are quite straightforward, one stemming from the definition of separatism, the other reflecting the ultimate outcome of the conflict. The Indonesian invasion of East Timor in 1975 was a violation of international law and Jakarta's act of "integration" in 1976 was never recognized by the United Nations or the vast majority of member states. The resistance explicitly justified its use of arms in terms of the right to self-determination and the illegality of the Indonesian occupation. Hence, the twenty-four year occupation was technically never a case of separatism. Second, while both sides periodically made proposals for peace (including calls for autonomy), these were readily dismissed by the other party to the conflict. Viewing "integration" as final and irrevocable, Jakarta rightly suspected that the resistance's proposals for autonomy were disingenuous ploys to open the door to eventual independence. The one exception to this arose in 1999 when President Soeharto's chosen successor, B.J. Habibie, agreed to a United Nations-sponsored referendum in which the people of East Timor were given the opportunity to support or oppose "special autonomy" within Indonesia. With the vote overwhelmingly opposed to Jakarta's offer, the referendum led to the opposite outcome — Indonesia relinquishing its claim over the territory and international recognition of East Timor's independence.[1]

Despite these objections, the theme of this volume provides a useful opportunity to rethink the dynamics of the twenty-four year conflict and the reasons for the success of the East Timorese resistance.[2] Most scholarship on the conflict in East Timor has focused on either the heroic resistance to the illegal occupation or the horrific human rights abuses committed by the Indonesian military/state. Curiously, far less attention has been paid to the long-term logic of the occupying power, including fluctuations in the use of violence and periodic efforts to employ negotiation. And yet, careful scrutiny reveals that the twenty-four year conflict in East Timor was punctuated like clock-work by something entirely exogenous to East Timor: the Indonesian electoral cycle. Corresponding to the national electoral cycle, at regular five-year intervals the regime of occupation withdrew troops from the territory, reduced or altogether ceased combat operations, and attempted in one way or another to "normalize" the status of the territory.[3] When these efforts failed — and they invariably did fail — the Indonesian military responded with massive new military offensives. Remarkably, this regular pattern in the regime of occupation is neatly mirrored by peace proposals, which over time came to include calls for an interim period of autonomy, presented by the resistance.

This chapter will use the theme of violence and negotiation to explore the long-term logic of the occupying regime and the development of resistance policy. Focusing on the regime of occupation, the first section of the chapter argues that Indonesian policy in East Timor was characterized by a cyclical oscillation between violence and negotiation that reflects the logic of the national electoral cycle. It illustrates that while Jakarta was prepared to offer minor concessions in order to eliminate the armed resistance, as long as Soeharto was in power there was no willingness to consider autonomy or a change in the status of the territory. Turning to the resistance, the second section highlights the uses of negotiation (and to a lesser extent violence) by the East Timorese pro-independence movement, and in particular the role of tactical proposals for autonomy as a means to eventual self-determination.

A CYCLICAL OCCUPATION

When Indonesia launched its full-scale invasion in late 1975 of what was then legally still Portuguese Timor, the generals in Jakarta assumed that the forces of the hastily declared Democratic Republic of Timor-Leste (RDTL) would be no match for Indonesia's vastly superior military (ABRI).[4] "The whole business", a senior advisor commented, "will be settled in three weeks."⁵ Months earlier the Portuguese governor and his staff had fled to the island of Atauro, 16 kilometers from the capital. The Revolutionary Front for the Liberation of East Timor (*Frente Revolucionária do Timor-Leste Independente*, Fretilin), which had become the de facto government, had few resources and, despite Jakarta's propaganda about the threat of involvement by communist Vietnam or China, no real prospect of receiving foreign assistance. Fretilin's military, called the Armed Forces for the National Liberation of East Timor (*Forças Armadas de Libertação Nacional de Timor-Leste*, Falintil), established in August 1975 from the old colonial military, inherited an impressive arsenal but had few trained officers and absolutely no combat experience. Furthermore, the generals in Jakarta were confident that neither regional neighbours nor major international powers would raise any serious objections to their plan to annex the territory. One day before the invasion was launched United States President Ford and Secretary of State Henry Kissinger, on a state visit to Jakarta, had given their blessing to the plan.

The invasion of Dili on 7 December was poorly planned and badly executed, but the loss of several hundred troops was not a serious set-back. The officers in charge of the operation were frustrated by the fact that Fretilin leaders had managed to retreat into the mountains and surprised by Falintil's ability to put up a fight, but there was still little reason to think that predictions of a quick conquest were misguided. Over the next several weeks, as more battalions arrived by sea, Indonesian troops were soon in control of most of the major road running along the north coast from the Indonesian border to the easternmost town of Lospalos, while additional troops had landed at strategic points on the south coast. All that remained was for ABRI troops to seize control of the north-south roads, thereby carving the territory into bite-sized parcels within which localized mopping-up operations could be carried out. Although military operations took longer than anticipated, failure was inconceivable. After receiving a petition from the Indonesian-appointed East Timorese Popular Representative Assembly requesting that the territory become part of Indonesia, on 17 July 1976 President Soeharto signed Law No. 7 of 1976 formally "integrating" East Timor into the Republic of Indonesia. But neither military operations nor an act of integration could complete Indonesia's plan to swallow the territory and armed conflict dragged on for another twenty-four years.

Throughout 1976 ABRI had an estimated thirty battalions in East Timor at any given time, more or less evenly distributed across the three combat sectors (west, central, and east).⁶ Despite the Indonesian military's vast numerical and technological advantages, Fretilin/Falintil forces put up stiff resistance. In late 1976 Fretilin radio broadcasts began to report more and more military successes, and in mid-1977 Fretilin even claimed that the Indonesian military had been forced to withdraw troops.[7] Dismissed by many observers as propaganda, such reports were in fact accurate, though not for the reasons given. ABRI withdrew large numbers of troops so that these units could return to their home areas to carry out civic works projects as part of the regime's developmentalist propaganda and "safeguard" the May 1977 general election. An official history of the Indonesian Marines explains: "In the context of holding the 1977 general election the number of TNI [sic, ABRI] forces in East Timor was reduced to one third [the previous level] so that units could provide security for the 1977 general election in other parts of Indonesia."[8] This reduction in troops and lull in combat activities provided an ideal opportunity for Indonesia to invite foreign dignitaries to visit the territory (or at least Dili and those towns under Indonesian control) and prove the success of "integration".[9]

The temporary halt to military operations during the first half of 1977 and the completion of the national electoral exercise set the stage for Indonesia's next initiative. In an August 17 independence-day speech Indonesian President Soeharto offered an amnesty to Fretilin/Falintil personnel who surrendered by 31 December.[10] This carrot (which, as discussed in the following section, was to have major repercussions within the resistance) was quickly followed by the stick: in September 1977 the Indonesian military launched a massive new offensive. This campaign culminated in the fall of the last Fretilin base areas in the east in late 1978 and in the west in early 1979. With the majority of the population now under Indonesian control and the armed resistance reduced to small bands, in 1981 the Indonesian military launched a massive operation in which at least 60,000 civilians were forced to march in a "fence of legs" across the territory to flush out the remaining guerrillas.

In early 1982, ABRI again withdrew large numbers of troops from East Timor.[11] As was the case in 1977, this had little to do with the resistance and everything to do with national elections: military units serving in East Timor were needed back in their home areas to carry out civic works programmes as part of the regime's campaign strategy and to provide security — and intimidation — during the general election. This was also the first time Indonesia held the election in East Timor. The official returns showed that the regime's electoral vehicle, Golkar, won an astounding 100.5 per cent of the vote in East Timor.[12] The final phase in the quinquennial electoral cycle came in March 1983 when the People's Consultative Assembly reelected Soeharto to a fourth term as president. Soeharto again installed a new cabinet and appointed bellicose General Murdani, one of the architects of the 1975 invasion, to replace General Yusuf as ABRI commander-in-chief.

As was the case five years earlier, the period between the 1982 national election and Soeharto's reselection provided another opportunity for Jakarta to "normalize" the status of its troublesome 27th province. Troop withdrawals meant a virtual cessation in combat operations; the cessation of combat allowed the regime to counter adverse international reporting by once again inviting foreign diplomats and journalists to visit the territory.[13] But the most significant development during this period was initiated by middle-ranking military officers in East Timor who opened contacts with Fretilin/Falintil figures, leading to a series of low-level meetings in the easternmost districts (Lautem, Baucau, and Viqueque). At the time, East Timor Sub-Regional Military Commander Colonel Purwanto commented to the press: "When I was younger I was renowned for being fierce. But when it comes to eliminating the remnants of the Fretilin band being fierce is not the way. This requires a persuasive approach."[14] One week after Soeharto's reselection, Colonel Purwanto was given permission to put this "persuasive approach" into action by meeting with Fretilin boss Xanana Gusmão and a verbal agreement was reached for a temporary ceasefire.[15] During the ceasefire ABRI is reported to have sent a team to East Timor to assess the prospects of holding a referendum, but the team reached the conclusion that Indonesia would lose a truly free popular vote.[16]

For Indonesia the importance of the ceasefire was primarily external, not internal. In response to international criticism of the invasion and human rights violations, Jakarta sought to lobby key states to recognize the integration of East Timor into Indonesia. In mid-1983 Indonesia finally agreed to commence talks with Portugal, which under the Presidency of General Eanes sought to take a more proactive stance on East Timor.[17] Jakarta also sought to reach out to Australia, where the Labour Party's 1982 electoral victory had stirred internal debate over the issue of East Timor, an opportunity Jakarta hoped to exploit by agreeing to allow a diplomatic visit to the territory.[18] On 28 July 1983, an Australian Parliamentary delegation arrived in East Timor to assess conditions.[19] With the Australian visit completed and General Murdani's patience with the ceasefire at breaking point, resistance leader Xanana Gusmão called on East Timorese in the Indonesian military to defect. The ensuing uprising in Viqueque was a major embarrassment and provided the cue for General Murdani to unleash a new offensive. As was the case in 1977, the renewed round of combat operations led to a dramatic increase in human rights violations throughout the territory.

The next electoral cycle had a less immediate impact on the ground, but perhaps a greater influence on the long term development of the resistance. In early 1987 Indonesian troop strength in East Timor was again reduced (the total number of battalions posted in East Timor dropped from an estimated 16 in 1986 to 12 in 1987). In the May national election Golkar won 73.1 per cent of the vote nationally and 93.6 per cent in East Timor.[20] And in March 1988 the Indonesian parliament dutifully elected Soeharto to a fifth term as president. Once again, the completion of the national electoral charade set the stage for a new attempt to "normalize" the situation in East Timor. With backing from Minister of Interior (Ret. Gen.) Rudini, Governor Mario Carrascalão recommended to the president that East Timor be "opened", a position supported by prominent economists who argued that greater openness would reduce both economic distortions and political abuses.[21] Soeharto eventually agreed to the governor's proposal, and in late 1988 he signed into law a Presidential Decree normalizing administrative responsibility in East Timor.[22] This administrative change ushered in a new policy of openness. Sweeping changes in military personnel were made, the use of torture during interrogations was discouraged, and a number of political prisoners were released. Furthermore, for the first time Indonesian nationals were allowed to freely enter the territory, as too were foreign tourists (although restrictions were placed on which districts they could visit). In a bid to counter international concern about the right to self-determination and human rights abuses, foreign dignitaries were also allowed tightly supervised visits to the territory to witness with their own eyes the "success" of integration.[23]

The new policy, however, produced its own contradictions. While softer policies and diplomatic visits were necessary to assuage international concern about the human rights situation, these diplomatic visits became an occasion for civilian protest against Indonesian rule. Such protest, in turn, led to an increase in covert operations and greater use of East Timorese informants and thugs. In contrast to the 1977 amnesty and the 1983 ceasefire, this opening lasted for several years. It was eventually shattered, however, in late 1991 by the massacre of civilians during a funeral procession at the Santa Cruz cemetery in Dili.[24] The Santa Cruz massacre and ensuring international condemnation prompted Jakarta to make immediate, and in some respects quite drastic, changes in East Timor. The two most senior military officers directly responsible for the province were sacked, middle-ranking officers were quickly replaced, a host of new external military units were rushed into the territory to restore security, and a dragnet was set around Dili to arrest pro-independence activists. These measures bore fruit in November

1992 when resistance leader Xanana Gusmão was captured at his hide-out in Dili. The timing of this crackdown — a mere six months before the next election — would seem to indicate a departure from the cyclical openings in 1977, 1982–83, and 1986–87. And yet in almost all respects the 1992–93 electoral period conformed to the previous pattern.

Despite the military crackdown, Indonesian troop strength in East Timor was again reduced in the lead-up to the 1992 election. ABRI documents show that between August 1991 and April 1992 non-organic troop strength dropped from 11,000 to 8,444, while the strength of territorial units (including the police) increased modestly from 4,792 to 5,169.[25] When the national legislative elections were held in June 1992, Golkar handily won 68 per cent of the national vote and 82 per cent of the vote in East Timor. In mid-March 1993, Soeharto was once again reselected to the presidency and promptly appointed a new cabinet and a new military commander-in-chief. With the completion of these democratic formalities, Indonesia once again sought to address the East Timor problem. In November 1992 Indonesia agreed to reopen diplomatic talks with Portugal. And in late March the Military Operations Command in East Timor (Kolakops) was liquidated, leaving the territorial military command (Korem) with sole responsibility for security in the province.[26] This was the military equivalent to the administrative normalization of 1988. While military officers stated that the abolition of the Kolakops was a sign of "greater stability and security",[27] the decision was clearly made in response to the ongoing international criticism of the Santa Cruz massacre. Finally, in July 1993 Jakarta gave approval for "talks" between pro-integration figures and the Fretilin external delegation. These measures were largely cosmetic and the conflict continued into its third decade.

In 1997, Indonesian troops were again withdrawn from East Timor and the electoral exercise was conducted with predictable results. Aside from higher than usual levels of campaign violence elsewhere in the country, there was nothing (aside from Soeharto's advanced age) to indicate that political change was on the cards. The onset of the Asian economic crisis, however, changed everything. By the end of the year the collapse of the Indonesian rupiah and resulting hyper-inflation led to regional price riots in Java. In March, Soeharto's election to a seventh term as president and the announcement of a new crony-infested cabinet triggered a rising tide of protest and demands for Soeharto's resignation. In May, major riots erupted in Medan, Jakarta, and Surakarta. Soon thereafter Soeharto resigned, passing the presidency to his protégé B.J. Habibie. The economic collapse and political implosion in 1997–98 were so extraordinary that one would not expect to find similarities between 1998 and the election-year cycles described above. And yet, the cycle of troop withdrawals, elections and political openings continued.

East Timorese seized on Soeharto's resignation and the political crisis in Jakarta to stage free speech fora and demonstrations. President Habibie first responded to pro-independence demands by suggesting that the province be granted "special status" and "wide-ranging autonomy", whereby East Timorese would have control over all areas except "foreign affairs, external defense, and some aspects of monetary and fiscal policy."[28] This suggestion was accompanied by promises to withdraw ABRI troops and an offer to release Xanana Gusmão from prison in Jakarta. In August the Indonesian and Portuguese foreign ministers agreed to discuss the offer, but they continued to hold diametrically opposed views on the meaning of autonomy: "While for Indonesia this autonomy would be the final dispensation, Portugal was willing to consider autonomy only as an interim or transitional arrangement pending the eventual exercise by the people of East Timor of their right to self-determination."[29] The Portuguese position closely followed the long-standing proposal made by the East Timorese resistance for a transitional period under Indonesia that would eventually lead to a full act of self-determination.[30]

Meanwhile, the outpouring of pro-independence activity made the province virtually ungovernable. Pro-integration figures and the Indonesian military responded by organizing paramilitary groups. The situation on the ground made it increasingly apparent to Jamsheed Marker, the Personal Representative of the UN Secretary General for East Timor, Australian Prime Minister John Howard and others in the international community that there was little support among the East Timorese for autonomy, a point they impressed on President Habibie and Indonesia's foreign ministry. In January 1999, President Habibie made a surprise announcement that he would make a final offer of "broad autonomy" for East Timor. By April 1999 Indonesia had worked out the framework for the proposed offer of the Special Autonomous Region of East Timor (SARET), which included the creation of an East Timorese Regional Council, police and judiciary, but with Indonesia maintaining responsibility for external defense, monetary and fiscal policy, and enjoying ultimate authority over immigration and courts of final appeal.[31] Negotiations in New York led to an agreement that the offer of SARET be made via a direct popular ballot. Though unique in many respects, the national elections in 1997–98 had again set the stage for the familiar pattern of demilitarization, elections, and a political opening. The logic outlined here can be extended to help explain why in 1999, when observers around the world knew that the Maubere people would chose independence, members of the Indonesian military elite could believe that their brutish terror tactics could secure the day: they were reading the results of the June 1999 election, in which the vote for Golkar in East Timor ranked fifth highest in the entire country.

These brief vignettes illustrate that Indonesia's use of "violence" and "negotiation" in East Timor was patterned in an astonishing way by the often dismissed quinquennial Indonesian festival of democracy. At neat five-year intervals Indonesian policy in East Timor was characterized by troop withdrawals, elections, and an "opening" intended to normalize Indonesian rule over the territory. To be sure, the content of the "openings" varied: in 1977 it was an offer of amnesty, in 1983 a ceasefire, in 1988 the normalization of governance, in 1992–93 diplomatic talks with Portugal and the abolition of the combat command, and finally in 1998 the ill-fated offer of "broad autonomy."

THE RESISTANCE

Having outlined the surprisingly cyclical character of the Indonesian occupation of East Timor, it is now possible to turn our attention to the East Timorese resistance and the origin of proposals for autonomy. There are at least three different issues that need to be addressed. First, was the resistance aware of the influence that the Indonesian general elections had on Jakarta's policy in East Timor and the possibilities that this presented? Second, what impact did the cyclical pattern of openings/normalization have on the resistance's own use of violence and negotiation during the course of the occupation? Third, and perhaps of greatest interest, what impact did this have on the internal structure and organization of the resistance?

The answer to the first of these questions is relatively straightforward. The available documentary evidence indicates that the resistance consistently viewed Indonesian elections as little more than a political charade. Xanana Gusmão's writings provide ample illustration. In a letter written in October 1982 to the United Nations General Assembly, Gusmão pokes fun at the Indonesian electoral exercise held several months earlier: "Suharto's party won the elections again. In East Timor under the threat of weapons, all the population voted in favor of Golkar. East Timor and Irian Jaya, by a curious paradox, were the 'most dear provinces' of Suharto and the best supporters of Golkar!"[32] Ten years later, in a letter written to UN Secretary-General Boutros-Ghali, Gusmão again mocks the upcoming June 1992 national election: "... it will not be surprising to hear about a massive participation of the people who [will have] voted for the all-mighty Golkar. As a matter of fact, instructions were already issued to the effect that everyone should vote for Mr. Golkar, in order to avert retaliation."[33] There are no indications in Gusmão's writings (or elsewhere) that the resistance was aware of the impact that Indonesian elections had on East Timor.[34] The one exception to this is an extraordinary statement by former Falintil commander Taur Matan Ruak to the Commission for Reception, Truth, and Reconciliation:

> We evaluated the situation daily ... on the international scene, we especially evaluated important events, [Indonesia's] parliamentary elections, the [Indonesian] presidential election, the 20th of May [anniversary of the founding of ASDT/Fretilin], troop withdrawals. On those occasions we undertook small actions which would have a large impact.[35]

But that does not mean that the Indonesian electoral cycle did have an impact on the resistance. Closer examination reveals that there was a strong correlation between the electoral cycles outlined above and peace proposals made by the resistance. Of equal importance, this cyclical pattern was to have a profound impact on the development of the pro-independence movement in general and the relationship between its military and civil wings in particular. The following brief accounts highlight these two points.

From the time of its formation in mid-1974, there had been serious ideological and strategic debates within Fretilin. The Indonesian invasion and first year of the war exacerbated these tensions. Three issues were of particular importance: (1) while most Fretilin Central Committee (FCC) members insisted on a policy of no compromise, a minority led by Fretilin President Francisco Xavier do Amaral favoured negotiation; (2) while Fretilin leaders insisted on a policy of civilian supremacy over the military, officers who had served in the Portuguese colonial military often disagreed with the FCC on ideological grounds and resisted taking orders from civilians; and (3) while FCC leaders stressed the importance of the party's social and political programmes, a minority argued that the human cost of maintaining civilian base areas was unacceptably high.[36] The large-scale withdrawal of ABRI troops prior to the 1977 Indonesian national election allowed Fretilin to claim success and provided much-needed breathing room for political consolidation. However, Soeharto's offer of an amnesty in August 1977 brought political differences to a boil: on 7 September the Fretilin

Central Committee arrested Fretilin President Francisco do Amaral, who had favoured negotiation and allowing civilians to surrender.[37] While the debate over policy was not new, it is clear that Indonesia's post-election "opening" — the offer of an amnesty — was the immediate trigger for the arrest and the subsequent purge of dissidents within Fretilin.

The Indonesian military onslaught launched in early September 1977 was to have a second important affect on the resistance: it exacerbated long-standing tensions between Fretilin politicos and military officers. Most accounts of the resistance have uncritically accepted Gusmão's claim that Fretilin officially adopted Marxism-Leninism at the party congress held in October 1977, when in fact party documents clearly show that the ideological turning point came at the 1981 national reorganization congress (at which Gusmão presided as conference president, head of the newly-established National Council of Revolutionary Resistance (CNRR), national political commissar, and commander of Falintil) that officially changed the party name from Fretilin to *Partido Marxista-Leninista Fretilin* (abbreviated MLF).[38] One can read the internal party politics from October 1977 until the establishment of MLF in 1981 as an ongoing attempt to assert civilian supremacy of a broadly conceived national liberation movement over a partially recalcitrant officer corps.[39] Taken together, the 1977 debates within the resistance over negotiation/compromise and civilian supremacy were crucial for the future development of the movement.

The 1982–83 Indonesian electoral cycle and "opening" had an even more apparent impact on the East Timorese resistance. Despite the continued insistence that compromise was out of the question, the resistance made novel new uses of negotiation. As the low-level contacts between ABRI and the resistance proceeded in early 1983, one of the sticking points was who would be recognized to negotiate. Indonesia wanted newly-appointed Governor Mario Carrascalão to represent Indonesia, believing that this would grant greater legitimacy to the provincial government. Fretilin rejected this, insisting that it would only negotiate with the occupying power, in this case represented by ABRI. When Fretilin/Falintil leader Xanana Gusmão met with Sub-Regional Military Commander Colonel Purwanto on 23 March 1983, Gusmão presented a four point "peace plan" that included (1) withdrawal of all Indonesian troops, (2) deployment of a UN peace-keeping force, (3) a free and fair referendum, and (4) continued presence of Falintil, the armed wing of the movement. In April, Gusmão wrote a letter informing the UN Secretary General of the peace plan and in May the Fretilin external delegation released a document outlining Fretilin's demands.[40]

Both sides viewed the ceasefire agreement as a useful tool in international lobbying. While Indonesia portrayed the ceasefire as a "conciliatory gesture" and invited the newly-elected Labour Government in Canberra to send a delegation to visit the territory, for Fretilin the negotiations and ceasefire demonstrated the continued strength of the movement. The party's external delegation issued a communiqué proudly titled "Fretilin Conquers the Right to Dialogue."[41] For the resistance the ceasefire was equally important internally, providing a much-needed opportunity to reorganize its forces, strengthen clandestine networks, and build bridges with East Timorese serving under the occupying military, some of whom eventually defected in August 1983. The military aspects of this are readily apparent (medical assistance for sick/wounded guerrillas, re-supply of food and munitions, new recruitment, etc.), but Fretilin strategy was neither purely nor primarily military. Instead, party leaders recognized that the armed resistance could never defeat the occupying forces and party policy continued to reflect an understanding of civilian supremacy over the military wing (Falintil). That meant, by extension, that the civilian component of the struggle was of equal importance, and hence great effort was placed on building clandestine networks and spreading pro-independence propaganda amongst the younger generation.

The next Indonesian electoral cycle (1987–88) was once again the occasion for an historic turning point in the resistance. In December 1987 resistance leader Gusmão announced his resignation from Fretilin and pulled Falintil out of the party structure. Henceforth it was to be a non-partisan army of national liberation.[42] This policy had been debated during the previous several years. Available sources do not make any connection between the Indonesian election and opening, on the one hand, and Gusmão's decision, on the other, but there can be little doubt that reduction in Indonesian military operations between the April 1987 national election and the March 1988 session of parliament that reelected Soeharto to the presidency provided breathing space for resistance commanders from different regions to meet and for Gusmão to consolidate the new policy. This new policy made it possible for individuals from non-Fretilin families to join Falintil, but the addition of a few new recruits was of little real importance. The real significance of the structural readjustment lay in the establishment of a broad national coalition, fully realized in December 1988 when CRRN was transformed into a more inclusive National Council of Maubere Resistance (CNRM). One week prior to Pope John Paul II's October 1989 visit to Dili, Gusmão announced a new peace plan. The contents of the proposal were little more than a restatement of Gusmão's

1983 peace plan, but the initiative was portrayed as proof that the resistance was united across party lines and was willing to use dialogue to seek a solution to the conflict.[43]

Taking advantage of the intense international outcry over the November 1991 Santa Cruz massacre, the resistance unveiled a new call for negotiation. In April 1992 National Council of Maubere Ressitance (CNRM) representative José Ramos-Horta presented a revised version of Gusmão's 1989 peace plan to the European parliament. This plan envisaged a three stage process: a first stage lasting up to two years during which Indonesia would withdraw military personnel, a second stage lasting from five to ten years during which East Timor would be given full autonomy, and a third stage in which an act of free choice would be held and the final status of the territory decided.[44] This is remarkable because for the first time the resistance called for a transitional period of autonomy under Indonesia. Jakarta's support for "talks" between pro-integration East Timorese and the Fretilin external delegation, prompted CNRM to release its peace plan once again. In the words of CAVR, "[t]he plan was intended to put the Suharto Government under pressure by offering an honourable way out and to present the resistance as the more constructive of the two protagonists."[45] This offer reflected the broader shift in resistance strategy, already apparent in the late 1980s, toward building a broad national front and emphasizing the civilian over the exclusively military wings of the movement.

The dramatic events in Indonesia in 1998 set the stage for the final milestone in the development of the East Timorese resistance. In March 1998 Soeharto was reselected to a seventh term in office. One month later, representatives from all the major East Timorese political parties, the Catholic Church, and civil society organizations met in Portugal and established the National Council of Timorese Resistance (CNRT).[46] In May Soeharto resigned and a month later his successor, President Habibie, made his first, vague offer of "broad autonomy" for East Timor. Here, once again, was a post-election "opening". Pro-independence East Timorese responded with public demands for a referendum, students held open public dialogues at the village level on the future, and in September CNRT opened an office in Dili.[47] Despite a sharp increase in violence by military-backed pro-integration paramilitaries, by year's end East Timor had become ungovernable. In January 1999 President Habibie made his surprise offer of a popular referendum. In doing so, he was accepting the third point of the 1993 CNRM peace plan. But while Jakarta strove to fashion an autonomy package that would maintain East Timor within the Republic of Indonesia while not going so far as to encourage separatist movements in Aceh or Papua, the East

Timorese had their eyes on a bigger prize. The final outcome, of course, was not autonomy but independence. These accounts suggest that the key developments in resistance policy correspond to Indonesia's own post-electoral attempts to "normalize" its rule over the territory.

CONCLUSION

Whereas the first section of this chapter demonstrated that the rhythm of the 24-year Indonesian occupation of East Timor was patterned to an extraordinary degree by the logic of the Indonesian national electoral cycle, the second section has shown that the quinquennial Indonesian "opening" in East Timor was accompanied by corresponding changes in the resistance. On the one hand, in each instance the Indonesian election prompted a policy response from the resistance. In 1977 Fretilin responded to the threat posed by Jakarta's offer of amnesty by purging those within its own ranks. Thereafter, however, the resistance responded to each of Indonesia's post-electoral "openings" by offering its own peace initiative. The core element that emerged from the original 1983 peace plan was a period of autonomy under Indonesia, but this was always understood to be a transitional period leading to a full act of self-determination. When that moment arrived, the resistance was confident that the people of East Timor would favour independence. On the other hand, these periods of "opening" and periodic efforts by the resistance to exploit peace plans had a major impact on the long-term evolution of the resistance, repeatedly pushing it away from a purely military entity and helping to highlight the need for a corresponding civilian component. The fusion of the armed and civilian wings is perhaps the most unique feature of the East Timorese experience, and this may set it apart from a number of other "armed separatist" movements in South and Southeast Asia.

Notes

[1] The date of East Timor's independence remains a point of controversy. While the United Nations, foreign governments and most observers thought that the transfer of sovereignty from the United Nations to the Democratic Republic of Timor-Leste on 20 May 2002 would mark the beginning of independence, segments of East Timorese society argued that this was the *restoration* of independence proclaimed on 28 November 1975. Under domestic pressure, the Fretilin dominated Constituent Assembly adopted this line in the constitution, which states that independence was proclaimed on 28 November 1975

but "recognized internationally on the 20th of May 2002". See "Constitution of the Democratic Republic of East Timor" (no publication information), pp. 10 and 12.
2   Recognizing the significant organizational developments and ideological shifts, the term "resistance" is employed here to cover the pro-independence movement in East Timor: Fretilin/Falintil from 1975 until 1981; CNRN/Fretilin-Falintil from 1981 until 1987; CNRM from 1987 until 1998; CNRT and its constituent organizations for the period 1998–99.
3   In a 1999 publication I argued that since 1982 the Indonesian military's use of paramilitary forces was a response to these regular post-election attempts to normalize Indonesian rule over East Timor. I now realize that this argument did not go far enough for at least two reasons. First, despite the fact that Indonesia did not allow East Timor to vote in the 1977 election, the pattern still holds, and hence the argument needs to be pushed back to cover the entire occupation. Second, it is now clear to me that the singular focus on paramilitaries in that article was too narrow. See Douglas Kammen, "The Trouble with Normal: The Indonesian Military, Paramilitaries, and the Final Solution in East Timor", in *Violence and the State in Suharto's Indonesia*, edited by Benedict Anderson (Ithaca, NY: Southeast Asia Program Publications, Cornell University, 2001). Hereafter cited as "Trouble".
4   In anticipation of an Indonesian invasion, on 28 November 1975 Fretilin President Francisco Xavier do Amaral read a brief proclamation of independence of the República Democrática de Timor-Leste.
5   Statement by Liem Bian-Kie, quoted in Benedict Anderson, "East Timor and Indonesia: Some Implications", in *East Timor at the Crossroads: The Forging of a Nation*, edited by Peter Carey and G. Carter Bentley (Honolulu: University of Hawai'i Press, 1995), p. 137.
6   This is my count. Most sources cite a figure of 40,000 ABRI troops in East Timor in 1976. See, for example, John Taylor, *Indonesia's Forgotten War: The Hidden History of East Timor* (London: Zed Books, 1991), pp. 23, 80. Hereafter abbreviated as *Forgotten War*.
7   See *East Timor News*, 2 June 1977 and 16 June 1977.
8   *Korps Marinir TNI AL 1970–2000* (Jakarta: Dinas Penerangan Korps Marinir, 2000), p. 233. The anachronistic use of the initials TNI in this passage reflects the fact that this volume was published after the name of the Indonesian military had been changed from ABRI back to TNI. Troop withdrawals, however, did not prevent ABRI from announcing combat operations. In late 1976 ABRI announced that operation Baratayudha would commence in early 1977. This name, derived from the final war between the Barata clan at the end of the Mahabarata epic, may have been selected in recognition that in lieu of its own troops ABRI would have to rely on East Timorese "partisans" and civil defense forces (*hansip*).

9   In March 1977 ambassadors from the United States, Australia, Nigeria, Tanzania, and Spain were allowed to visit East Timor; the following month two U.S. senators were also allowed to visit. See *Album Kenangan Perjuangan Siliwangi* (no bibliographical information available), p. 599, and John Taylor, *Forgotten War*, p. 83.

10 Carmel Budiardjo and Liem Soei Liong, *The War Against East Timor* (London: Zed Books, 1984), pp. x and 28. Hereafter abbreviated as *War Against ET*. No information is available about how the amnesty was communicated within East Timor. According to Taylor, in 1978 leaflets were dropped; the same method may have been used at the time of the August 1977 amnesty offer. Taylor, *Forgotten War*, p. 97.

11 Interviewed in June 1982, Colonel Kalangie told journalists that there were only 2,000 ABRI troops in the province. Barry Wain, "East Timor is being developed but local support eludes Jakarta", *Asian Wall Street Journal*, 14 June 1982. Assuming the partial withdrawal (i.e. one or more company) of non-organic battalions, this figure seems low but not implausible.

12 Barry Wain, "East Timor is being developed but local support eludes Jakarta", *Asian Wall Street Journal*, 14 June 1982, which reports that "even when absentee ballots were separated, Golkar was credited with an amazing 99.4 per cent in the adjusted result."

13 In late August 1982 Indonesia orchestrated a visit by diplomats from Australia, Venezuela, Switzerland and Sweden. In February and May 1983 foreign journalists were allowed to enter the territory. See Taylor, *Forgotten War*, p. 205.

14 Quoted in *Sinar Harapan*, 24 January 1983.

15 Unfortunately there is still no comprehensive account of this process. Although highly inadequate, see CAVR, *Chega! The Report of the Commission for Reception, Truth and Reconciliation in Timor-Leste* (Dili, East Timor: 2005), pp. 101–6.

16 See Arnold Kohen, *From the Place of the Dead: Bishop Belo and the Struggle for East Timor* (Oxford: Lion Publishing, 1999), p. 171.

17 See Ian Martin, *Self-Determination in East Timor: The United Nations, the Ballot, and International Intervention* (Boulder and London: Lynne Rienner Publishers, 2001), p. 18. Hereafter abbreviated as *Self-Determination*.

18 See Taylor, *Forgotten War*, pp. 134–35.

19 This visit paved the way for Indonesian-Australian talks, culminating in the 1985 Australian-Indonesian Timor Sea agreement and the Labour government's *de jure* recognition of Indonesian sovereignty in East Timor. Taylor, *Forgotten War*, p. 170.

20 Ian Martin notes that "[i]n 1986, Portugal, encouraged by the UN and pressured by its European partners, came close to agreeing that East Timorese participation, with UN observation, in the Indonesian elections scheduled for 1987 would be treated as an expression of the wishes of the population of the territory. However,

21 after internal debate, the Portuguese government reasserted an insistence on a proper act of self-determination." *Self-Determination*, p. 18.
21 See "Interview with Mário Carrascalão", *Indonesia* 76 (October 2003), p. 11. On the economists, see Herbert Feith, "East Timor: The Opening Up, the Crackdown and the Possibility of a Durable Settlement", in *Indonesia Assessment, 1992: Political Perspectives on the 1990s*, edited by Harold A. Crouch and Hal Hill (Canberra: Research School of Pacific Studies, Australian National University 1992), p. 63.
22 "Keputusan Presiden Republik Indonesia, Nomor 62 Tahun 1988 Tentang Peylenggaran Pemerintahan dan Pembangunan di Propinsi Tingkat I Timor Timur", published in *Himpunan Peraturan Negara* (Jakarta: 1988), pp. 1103–5.
23 The most important visits were by Pope John Paul II on 12 October 1989 and U.S. Ambassador to Indonesia John Monjo on 17 January 1990.
24 This is discussed in detail in Kammen, "Trouble", pp. 160–65.
25 See data in Samuel Moore, "The Indonesian Military's Last Years in East Timor: An Analysis of Its Secret Documents", *Indonesia* 72 (October 2001): 25.
26 For a full discussion of these moves, see Kammen, "Trouble", pp. 165–69.
27 Quotation is from Brigadier-General Theo Syafei, cited in Kammen, "Trouble", p. 166.
28 Martin, *Self-Determination*, p. 19.
29 Ibid., 19.
30 See discussion in the next section of the 1989 and 1993 peace proposals.
31 Ibid., pp. 27–29.
32 "Message to the 37th United Nations General Assembly", dated 14 October 1982, in *To Resist is to Win! The Autobiography of Xanana Gusmão with selected letters and speeches*, edited by Sarah Niner (Richmond, Victoria: Aurora Books, 2000), p. 82. (Hereafter cited as *To Resist is to Win!*) Unfortunately the editor omitted the first part of the paragraph in which this sentence appears.
33 "Letter to Boutros Boutros Ghali [sic]", dated 31 January 1992, in *To Resist is to Win!*, p. 160.
34 Similarly, scholarship on the occupation has highlighted electoral irregularities and the statements by Indonesian officials about the importance of elections in East Timor, but does not suggest any connection between the elections and either Indonesian policy or the resistance. See Budiardjo and Liem, *War Against ET*, pp. 113–14, and Taylor, *Forgotten War*, pp. 132–33. Note, however, that the back cover of the volume of Gusmão's writings edited by Sarah Niner states that the book is "organized chronologically, in sections that represent distinct periods of Gusmão's leadership" — periods that correspond precisely to Indonesian elections!
35 Quoted in CAVR, *Chega!*, chapter 5, p. 41. 20 May is the anniversary of the founding of the *Associação Social Democrata Timorense* (Social-Democratic Association of Timor), renamed Fretilin on 12 September 1974. Although

36 Budiardjo and Liem, *War Against ET*, pp. 60–65.
37 It is curious that none of the major studies of the occupation make the connection between Soeharto's offer of an amnesty and Amaral's arrest. Budiardjo and Liem argue that Amaral "attempted with force to take over the Fretilin leadership" (p. 61). Taylor states that at the time Amaral had already entered into local ceasefires with ABRI (p. 96). CAVR does not discuss the amnesty offer in its account of events in 1977, but then mentions in passing that in 1978 the offer had "been extended". *Chega!*, chapter 3, pp. 77–78.

not stated explicitly, it appears that he is referring to the 1990s, not earlier periods.

38 For Gusmão's version, see *To Resist is to Win*, p. 47; Dennis Shoesmith, "Timor-Leste: Divided Leadership in a Semi-Presidential System", *Asian Survey* 43, no. 2 (2003): 231–52; CAVR, *Chega!*, chapter 3, p. 78. On the establishment of MLF, see República Democrática de Timor Leste/Frente Revolucionária de Timor Leste Independente, "Acta da 1a. Conferência Nacional", 1981, photocopy, in the author's possession. MLF was abolished in April 1984 and the party was once again simply called Fretilin.
39 Party-military tensions continued, however, until the 1984 showdown between Gusmão, on the one hand, and Mauk Moruk, Kilik Wae Gae, and Ologari, on the other.
40 Accounts of the talks and ceasefire vary slightly. See, for example, Budiardjo and Liem, *War Against ET*, pp. 72–73, 150–51; Taylor, *Forgotten War*, pp. 136–37; and CAVR, *Chega!*, chapter 3, p. 102.
41 Fretilin External Delegation, "Fretilin Conquers the Right to Dialogue", Lisbon, 1983, cited in Taylor, *Forgotten War*, p. 218; Douglas Kammen, introduction to "A Tape Recorder and a Wink? Transcript of the 29 May 1983, Meeting Between Governor Carrascalão and Xanana Gusmão", *Indonesia*, no. 87 (April 2009): 73–80.
42 See Edward Rees, "Under Pressure: Falintil — Forças de Defesa de Timor Leste: Three Decades of Defence Force Development in Timor Leste, 1975–2004", Geneva Center for the Democratic Control of Armed Forces, Working Paper no. 139 (2004).
43 An abridged version of the document in which Gusmão lays out the peace plan is in *To Resist is to Win!*, pp. 139–41. The peace plan is discussed in CAVR, *Chega!*, chapter 5, pp. 39–40, and Chapter 7.1, p. 88.
44 See CAVR, *Chega!*, chapter 3, p. 120, chapter 7.1, pp. 88–89. The CNRM proposal for a period of autonomy is remarkable given the vehement stand Gusmão had taken during the 1980s against any such proposal. See Xanana Gusmão, "A History that Beats in the Maubere Soul", in *To Resist is to Win!*, pp. 87–88, 104–6.
45 CAVR, *Chega!*, chapter 7.1, p. 88.
46 CAVR, *Chega!*, p. 126.
47 Kammen, "Trouble", pp. 170–79.

References

Album Kenangan Perjuangan Siliwangi. Jakarta: Badan Pembina Corps Siliwangi, 1991.

Anderson, Benedict. "East Timor and Indonesia: Some Implications". In *East Timor at the Crossroads: The Forging of a Nation*, edited by Peter Carey and G. Carter Bentley. Honolulu: University of Hawai'i Press, 1995.

Asian Wall Street Journal (Hong Kong).

Budiardjo, Carmel, and Liem Soei Liong. *The War Against East Timor*. London: Zed Books, 1984.

CAVR. *Chega! The Report of the Commission for Reception, Truth and Reconciliation in Timor-Leste*. Dili, East Timor: 2005.

East Timor News (Australia).

Feith, Herbert. "East Timor: The Opening Up, the Crackdown and the Possibility of a Durable Settlement". In *Indonesia Assessment, 1992: Political Perspectives on the 1990s*. Canberra: Research School of Pacific Studies, 1992.

Gusmão, Xanana. *To Resist is to Win! The Autobiography of Xanana Gusmão with selected letters and speeches*, edited by Sarah Niner. Richmond, Victoria: Aurora Books, 2000.

"Interview with Mário Carrascalão". *Indonesia* 76 (October 2003).

Kammen, Douglas. "The Trouble with Normal: The Indonesian Military, Paramilitaries, and the Final Solution in East Timor". In *Violence and the State in Suharto's Indonesia*, edited by Benedict Anderson. Ithaca, NY: Southeast Asia Program Publications, Cornell University, 2001.

———. Introduction to "A Tape Recorder and a Wink? Transcript of the 29 May 1983, Meeting Between Governor Carrascalão and Xanana Gusmão". *Indonesia*, no. 87 (April 2009): 73–80.

Kohen, Arnold. *From the Place of the Dead: Bishop Belo and the Struggle for East Timor*. Oxford: Lion Publishing, 1999.

Korps Marinir TNI AL 1970–2000. Jakarta: Dinas Penerangan Korps Marinir, 2000.

Martin, Ian. *Self-Determination in East Timor: The United Nations, the Ballot, and International Intervention*. Boulder and London: Lynne Rienner Publishers, 2001.

Moore, Samuel. "The Indonesian Military's Last Years in East Timor: An Analysis of Its Secret Documents". *Indonesia* 72 (October 2001).

Rees, Edward. "Under Pressure: Falintil — Forças de Defesa de Timor Leste: Three Decades of Defence Force Development in Timor Leste, 1975–2004". Geneva Center for the Democratic Control of Armed Forces, Working Paper no. 139 (2004).

República Democrática de Timor Leste/Frente Revolucionária de Timor Leste Independente. "Acta da 1a. Conferência Nacional", 1981. Photocopy, in the author's possession.

Republik Indonesia. "Keputusan Presiden Republik Indonesia, Nomor 62 Tahun 1988 Tentang Peylenggaran Pemerintahan dan Pembangunan di Propinsi Tingkat I Timor Timur". Published in *Himpunan Peraturan Negara*. Jakarta: 1988.

Shoesmith, Dennis. "Timor-Leste: Divided Leadership in a Semi-Presidential System". *Asian Survey* 43, no. 2 (2003): 231–52.

Sinar Harapan (Jakarta).

Taylor, John. *Indonesia's Forgotten War: The Hidden History of East Timor*. London: Zed Books, 1991.

7

STRUGGLE OVER SPACE IN MYANMAR: EXPANDING STATE TERRITORIALITY AFTER THE KACHIN CEASEFIRE[1]

Karin Dean

In the context of the Union of Myanmar/Burma, the application of several concepts that are suggestive of autonomy for ethnic minority regions can be misleading for the wider international community. In Myanmar, "union" reads as "unitary", illegitimate can be treated as "legal", and "legal" may actually mean "illegitimate".[2] In a similar vein, the term "ceasefire" as a stage in ethnic minority conflict resolution — as read by the international community — may have very different implications when it involves unilateral offers made by Myanmar's ruling military authorities to armed ethnic groups. For practical purposes, such "ceasefires" are simply aimed at enforcing authoritarian order while indefinitely staving off ethnic minority demands for greater political autonomy within their historic homelands.

The central argument in this chapter is that the establishment of ceasefires has made the task of achieving territorial control largely easier for the Tatmadaw.[3] It has also helped to bolster the military's ambitions of legitimizing its state-building efforts while depriving minority groups of any meaningful autonomy. To this end, the chapter will discuss the military's version of state-building in relation to the autonomy expectations of the Kachin ethnic minority. After a brief overview of the evolvement of the

Kachin armed resistance (1961–94), it will then focus on the trends and developments during the 1994–2011 ceasefire in Kachin State.

BACKGROUND

Myanmar is variously viewed as an authoritarian "ethnocratic" state (Brown 1994) or an "illiberal" and uncertain "unitary state" (Tin 2004). The malfunctioning of many of the institutions expected from a state (in the Westphalian sense) such as law enforcement agencies, ministries and executive branches, has prompted designations of "weak" or "failed" for Myanmar as a state, although never "un-sovereign". "… Myanmar is a juridical state rather than an empirical one. Or … it is a "weak" state because 'the institutions of the state are contested to the point of violence'" (Rajah 2001, p. 14 quoting Buzan). Or is it a weak state but a strong regime because its military regime has managed to hold on to power for almost fifty years? "Internal colonialism" has been used by some authors (Sidaway 2000, pp. 598–600; Brown 1994, pp. 158–205) to describe the situation where the exploitation/management of abundant natural resources is the driving force for the (central) state (government) to acquire and control territory, and for establishing communications and infrastructure to facilitate access, while economy and politics are utilized as measures of control over space. Regardless the designation, directly relevant to the ways how the armed conflicts and their resolutions are managed, have been the military's wants and its versions of analyses of the political situation.

The military seized power in Myanmar initially as a caretaker government in 1958. Between 1961 and 1988, General Ne Win ruled with force and thoroughly institutionalized the military until he was forced out of power, at great human cost, by popular street demonstrations. In 1990 the military allowed elections for constituent assembly for drafting a new constitution, where the opposition National League for Democracy (NLD) won in a landslide. The NLD victory was a miscalculation by the military authorities that had tried to prop up its own political party — and the then de facto government, State Law and Order Restoration Council (SLORC), maintained power. The constitution drafting process was started in 1993 under stringent military control and supervision, prompting the NLD to walk out in protest in 1996.

From 1988 until the elections of 2010 there have been no clear distinctions between the state, the government and the armed forces, all of which have been conflated (Selth 2002). The contested territorialities at Myanmar's ethnic borderlands and the low-intensity guerilla warfare continue to signify the lack of internal sovereignty within the internationally recognized boundaries.[4] Regardless that Myanmar today is more unified than it has ever been, its territories have never functioned as one, internally sovereign, political unit. Historically, there have been centuries of rivalry and expansion of various kingdoms (Mon, Shan, Bamar, Arakan), loosely connected tribal territories and zones of Chinese influence at the present borderlands. British colonialism created the boundaries for a future Burma, followed by the Second World War and turbulent years of independence premised upon a pact between the Burmese independence architect Aung San and some ethnic representatives to form a federal Union. While some of the largest ethnic groups (e.g. the Karen) did not agree to join the Union, others (e.g. the Shan, the Kachin, the Chin) who signed the pact were disappointed in what they viewed as increasing Bamarization and centralization during the first Burmese government. Protracted warfare has lasted for sixty years and is still persisting, although in greatly reduced capacity.

The consolidation of Myanmar is not a result of the kind of rigorous and premeditated State- and nation-building process encompassing language, education, rewriting of histories, ethnic/linguistic categorization and promotion of State nationalism — that has been pursued by the new governments in the neighbouring post-colonial States of Southeast Asia and in China. The State consolidation in Myanmar has largely been achieved through coercive methods by the military power elites since 1962, including the forceful appropriation of urban spaces and landscapes, and of various "symbolic, social, legal and even intimate corporeal spaces" (Hudson-Rodd and Hunt 2005). Through what Myanmar's ethnic opposition calls "divide-and-rule", but also rewards for compliance and direct occupation of territory, the ruling elites continue their quest for the strategically important resource-rich ethnic territories at the borderlands.

Between 1989 and 1995, a total of fifteen insurgent organizations agreed to brokered ceasefire arrangements with the then "Prime Minister" General Khin Nyunt (Smith 1999; South 2008). With different groups, the ceasefire terms have varied. Zaw Oo and Win Min (2007) argue that the ceasefires were negotiated in three waves, with the first wave (starting in 1989) garnering more rewards and fewer restrictions in hope of encouraging more ethnic groups to negotiate. This wave included mostly the groups formed by the ex-members of the Communist Party of Burma located in Shan State, plus the New Democratic Army-Kachin (NDA-K) in Kachin State. The second (1991–92) and third (1994–95) waves of ceasefire agreements were less accommodating (Ibid.), although the restrictions also depended on the size and type of the group. The largest and most significant of the later agreements were the ceasefires with the Kachin Independence Organization and Army (KIO/KIA) and New Mon State Party (NMSP) because of these groups' staunch political agendas and history of well organized armed resistance. However, the ceasefire deals were not made with the intention of proceeding to political solution acceptable to both sides, but rather to control the remaining territories and natural resources. During the KIO/KIA ceasefire, the number of the Tatmadaw battalions in Kachin State increased from 26 in 1994 to 41 in 2006 (KDNG 2007a), while the intensive resource extraction (teak and other old-growth forest, gold and jade) has lead to great damage to one of the last remaining natural eco-systems in Southeast Asian mainland. The military government's pressure since April 2009 to disarm and transform ceasefire groups, including the KIO/KIA, into Border Guard Forces (BGF) under its command, demonstrates the military's determination to opt for the solution suitable to its version of State building. Collapse of some of the ceasefires after 15–20 years of precarious persistence has been a real prospect since the start of the pressure for BGF and continues after the first sitting of the new parliament in 2011.

MILITARY STATE BUILDING

In 1990 it was suggested that by abandoning the military regime's policy of crushing the ethnic insurgencies, the then 200,000-strong army could be reduced to a border protection force as small as 20,000–30,000 (Selth 2001, p. 12). Instead, the number has doubled, and increasing amounts of troops are deployed in territories where the ruling government has gained control either by force or through ceasefire negotiations. Without an external enemy or security threats, the Tatmadaw has doubled in size since 1988 to active forces of about 428,250, ranking it twelfth in the world.[5] While the army has expanded, almost every other public institution has degenerated, maintaining only a name, with the situation being particularly grave in health and education.[6] The mishandling of economy by the military regimes is explicit in every economic indicator.

Myanmar's military power elites have been quite open about the kind of state that they want to have, a strictly centralized unitary state. Its three main "national causes" — non-disintegration of the union, non-disintegration of national solidarity and perpetuation of national solidarity — have been inscribed on many walls, posters and all printed media throughout the country. Since the 1990s the military, under international pressure, has launched a chain of legality related procedures from its "roadmap to democracy" to "constitution" and "elections" aimed at legitimizing its grip on power, which Smith (2003) has poignantly described as a transition from "warriors" to "state-builders." The 14-year long constitution-drafting process (1993–2007) produced a constitution draft in 2008 guaranteeing 25 per cent of the 440-seat new assembly for the military and giving wide powers to the head of the armed forces to declare a state of emergency, dismiss the government and dissolve the parliament — powers that can be evoked against any attempts to amend a law against the military's interests. Several ceasefire group representatives tried to "make" the constitution drafting National Convention "work" by submitting proposals with demands for ethnic states' autonomy with effective legislative powers — but to no avail. In the climate of fear, pressure and counterfeit that has been widely documented to mark the constitutional referendum in May 2008, the constitution was "overwhelmingly approved" and elections set for 2010. The referendum and constitution have been spurned as "sham" by most in the (Western) international community — a remark that has run through most international media in reference to the 2010 elections. Engaging the process of "militarization" in the name of "democratization" is how Sakhong (2011) describes the post-election switch of the military elites into civilian outfits.

Administratively, Myanmar has seven (ethnic) states and seven (Bamar) divisions, while the denoting of state to the existing administrative units has always been highly misleading in terms of actual autonomy. The SPDC administrative subdivisions have presided over the States and divisions, named after the corresponding ethnic state (e.g. Kachin State Peace and Development Council, Arakan State Peace and Development Council), or division (e.g. Irrawaddy Division Peace and Development Council, etc.). The head of any State/Division Peace and Development Council has generally hold two posts — that of the council chairman and that of the regional commander of the respective military command. Thus the chairman of Kachin SPDC has also been the Commander of Northern Command, the chairman of Arakan SPDC the Commander of Western Command, the chairman of Irrawaddy Division PDC the Commander of Southwest Command and so on. These commanders, mostly graduates of either Defence Services Academy or the Officers Training School, all have ranks of brigadier-general or major-general and have been appointed by the Senior-General Than Shwe, the paramount of the then ruling regime, in close consultation (and with occasional compromises) with his close aides and the army commander in order to keep them content. The military has shown zero tolerance for any constitutional element of political autonomy in ethnic States, presenting any such attempts as leading to disunity and disintegration. It has neither political will nor (what international community might think is rational) foresight to consider any of the "proposals concerning the distribution of legislative powers between the centre and the regions" (Bowman 2007) that the ethnic representatives, spearheaded by the two largest ceasefire groups, the KIO and the NMSP, proposed under the strict conditions of the national convention in 2004. In 2007, the KIO submitted a proposal based on the federal principles once again (known as the nineteen-point proposal) — that not only faced the refusal by the regime but a threat to break the ceasefire agreement with the KIO, declaring that "… they [the KIO/KIA — K.D.] can be pushed back to the mountain" (Sakhong 2011; EBO 2010). In parallel, the ethnic political organizations and Bamar opposition working out of Thailand have composed their own versions of state constitutions for the ethnic states for a truly federal and democratic union based on contributions from the populace within the respective states. The following response by a high ranking Myanmar government official to the ethnic ceasefire group representatives participating in the National Convention in 2004 clearly illustrates military notions of state-building that are set in opposition to ethnic minority autonomy expectations:

> Why do you want to build separate houses while we are building one house where everybody will have his room or his floor?
> (personal communication, Yangon, September 2005)

However, regardless the highly controversial administration of the elections and the intentions of the military elites, the 2010 election opened up a new political landscape in Myanmar. In addition to the (new) Government of the Republic of the Union of Myanmar, seven ethnic state assemblies and governments plus another seven regional assemblies and governments have been established, leading to a refurbished political scene and assumedly to some new political actors.

THE MOSAIC OF SPACES

The ceasefires with various armed ethnic groups have created a complex mosaic of continuously changing "autonomous" spaces in Myanmar's ethnic states, each with different types of authority and dynamics contingent upon the particular sets of actors and the political geography of the moment. Again, the conventional notions of autonomy or ceasefire do not apply, as these spaces may have multiple or overlapping authorities. First, several areas near the Thai- and Sino-Myanmar border are in fact out of the direct reach of the Myanmar government — these are the revolutionary spaces that the political opposition refers to as liberated areas. These areas with low-intensity warfare are controlled by the armed political opposition groups who see themselves as defending their land and civilians from the incursions of the Tatmadaw. Such liberated zones were much larger before the waves of ceasefires — in Kachin State swelling at times to include half of the State under the KIO administration and another 25 per cent as no man's land (Smith 1999, p. 401). Today the remaining zones of armed resistance are located mostly near the Thai-Myanmar border. There the Tatmadaw continues its tactics of designating "free-fire zones", where its soldiers are warranted to shoot on sight (Grundy-Warr and Wong 2002). This has lead to forced mass relocations of civilians and flows of refugees to Thailand. The largest ethnic armies still fighting the Tatmadaw are the armed wings of the Karen National Union (KNU), the Karenni National Progressive Party (KNPP) and the Shan State Army-South (SSA-South) in Karen, Karenni and Shan States respectively.

Aside from the war zones, the second type of spaces constitute ceasefire areas where the armed ethnic groups retain and administer the agreed "autonomous" territories through a system of state-replicating institutions overseeing education, health, communications, public and external relations, and so on. Their territories are explicitly manifested by army checkpoints and hoisted flags and an "official" channel of communication is open with the Myanmar government via the group's representative offices at the state controlled territories. The two largest and strongest ethnic ceasefire groups with a longish history of adherence to firm political agendas and determination to achieve "real" autonomy, are the KIO/KIA and the NMSP in Kachin and Mon States, respectively.[7]

The third type of spaces is the so-called semi-autonomous areas created for splinter groups of the ethnic political organizations/armies. Under the labels of "peace and development" several such ceasefire/peace groups and some local smaller militias engage in various "economic", "trade" and "business" activities that may include cross-border "trade" of timber, used motor vehicles, and, in certain documented cases, also narcotics (personal communication, Thai-Myanmar border, May and December 2003, June 2004, March and June 2005). The territories of these groups are smaller and less clearly demarcated, with the zones of influence overlapping with that of the regime authorities with who they closely collaborate in exchange for certain privileges. The military set these groups on high pedestal in the country, and engaged them as the main body of the ethnic representatives at the National Convention — an example of what the ethnic political opposition view as the junta's divide-and-rule policy. Groups such as the

Karenni National People Liberation Front, the Democratic Karen Buddhist Army, the Mon Peace Armed Group, the Kayinni National Progressive Party,[8] Kayinni National Solidarity Organization, belong to this type. Most of the smaller armed entities have accepted to become a BGF or are transforming themselves into the militia under the command of the regime's armed forces. A unique entity due to its history of formation, past and present geopolitical ties with China, and sheer size and wealth from widely documented opium production and the indictment of a number of its leaders by U.S. law enforcement authorities for alleged drug-trafficking, is the United Wa State Army (UWSA).[9] There are other groups gaining influence and enforcing good relations with the military junta in return for various privileges (for example, the Pa-O National Organization).

THE KACHIN AND KACHIN STATE: STRUGGLE OVER SPACE

Throughout the tumultuous years of British colonial rule and the Second World War, the Kachin nationalist movement was consolidated by the efforts of the Christian elites from the largest Jinghpaw tribe. Today the Kachin people tend to view themselves as a nation comprising six tribes: the Atsi, the Maru, the Lashi, the Jinghpaw, the Rawang and the Lisu – or the *Jinghpaw Wungpawng* in Jinghpaw, which is the modern lingua franca. The Jinghpaw elites have been at the centre of the nationalist movement until today, and also hold central leadership positions in what later became the Kachin Independence Organization.[10] During the formative years of the State-building era in colonial Burma, the Kachin representatives together with the Shan and the Chin representatives, and the Burman independence initiator Aung San, signed the historic Panglong Agreement on 12 February 1947 to form the Union of Burma, although the possibility of amalgamating with China had also been previously raised by some Kachin representatives (Smith 1999, p. 73).

Two inflammatory developments initiated by the democratic Burmese government in late 1950s lead to the Kachin armed struggle against the State, marked by the establishment of the KIO/KIA in 1961. One was the ceding to China of 153 square kilometers of Kachin State territory as a part of the settlement between Beijing and Rangoon of the Sino-Burmese border — a colonial heritage imposed by the British on China from its then power position. The second development that served as the last straw for the predominantly Christian Kachin community was the insensitive attempt by Rangoon to establish Buddhism as the State religion.[11] The embrace of armed struggle for a sovereign territory was a new and strongly unifying turning point in the Kachin nationalist movement. In their fight against the State of Burma, the KIO replicated typical State practices and manifestations, complete with regalia and symbols such as flags, logos, army/uniform, border-crossing checkpoints and gates, and other institutions of authority. The KIO was also characterized by an opaque style of leadership engendering corruption, which, post-ceasefire has eroded some of its popular support.

Against the backdrop of the many resistance movements and insurgencies in Burma, the KIO/KIA guerilla resistance was among the most successful. During its peak, the Burmese military government only ventured up to a quarter of the 89,000 square kilometer Kachin State (mainly towns and areas along the railway) and controlled only sixty kilometers of the 2,200 kilometer Sino-Burmese border (Smith 1999, p. 360). The area under the KIO's influence encompassed nearly 40,000 square kilometers and by the 1980s, over 30,000 people. The KIO ran five high schools, ten middle schools, 119 primary schools, and two hospitals complete with X-ray facilities and operation theatres (Lintner 1997). The KIA fielded more than 8,000 regular troops who were organized into four brigades, according to Jane's Intelligence.[12] The wide Kachin support, the effective organization and leadership of the army, and the rich revenues from jade (the largest jade resources in the world are found in Hpakant, Kachin State) contributed to its military success. In 1980–81, the KIO chairman Brang Seng negotiated autonomy in Rangoon with General Ne Win himself, with Beijing as the guarantor of the talks that scored the KIA a solid political victory. However, the KIO/KIA returned to the jungle as the ruling military junta offered no more than "rehabilitation" for the rebels (Lintner 1997). In a major offensive by the superior Tatmadaw forces, the then KIA's general headquarters at Na Hpaw and the KIO's political headquarters at Pa Jau, both near the Chinese border, surrendered in 1987. This weakened the KIO/KIA, and after being further undermined by the breakaway of its Fourth Brigade in Shan State in 1991 [that became the Kachin Democratic Army (KDA)], and under the Chinese pressure, it entered into a ceasefire agreement in 1994 with the State Law and Order Restoration Council or SLORC, the then government of Burma.

KACHIN GEOGRAPHIES OF MILITARIZATION[13]

The territories retained by the three KIA brigades under the ceasefire are some of the wildest, most remote and sparsely inhabited areas in Southeast

Asia. While the KIA Second Brigade in Western Kachin State (the Hukawng Valley and surrounding hills around Danai) is totally surrounded by the newly gained territories of the Tatmadaw, those belonging to the KIA First and Third Brigades, in Northern Kachin State and at the Sino-Myanmar border, respectively, provide an anomaly in the international system of sovereign states with an ethnic armed group controlling and administering sections of an international boundary. This dictates a rather curious dynamic on the Sino-Myanmar border, 900 kilometers from China's provincial capital Kunming and 900 kilometers from another sizeable urban centre, Mandalay. The Kachin State capital city of Myitkyina (with a population of about 140,000 people) has always been under the Tatmadaw's control and is within eighty kilometers of the largest KIO controlled town of Laiza on the Sino-Myanmar border.

The KIO headquarters, its sizeable town of Laiza and the KIA army camps are strategically located very close to the Chinese border, thus establishing enclaves between China and the SPDC-controlled territory in Myanmar. Typically, the border cuts through some uninhabited wilderness and mountainous terrain, thus the Chinese border checkpoints tend to be in administrative centres that are the closest to the border — not *on* the border — thus leaving portions of territory out of the sight of any State. The KIO/KIA has checkpoints, "gates" and border guards near its army headquarters and towns. The exact location of the border is not marked and smaller village roads between China and the KIO territories do not have checkpoints, although the Chinese authorities are increasingly patrolling these. On the contrary, the border between the KIO/KIA territory and the SPDC-controlled areas is more explicitly manifested, by both ceasefire parties, the Tatmadaw and the KIO/KIA. For example, gates with guards and hoisted flags confront each other within 100 m distance on the road from Myitkyina to Laiza near the junction where the KIO territory begins. The 188-kilometer-long Myitkyina-Bhamo road passes very close to the gate and used to be closely monitored by the government, involving different institutions (such as the police, army, security and investigation bureaus, intelligence and immigration), both for security and for generating revenues from various taxes.[14] Such checkpoints are the obvious markers of the Myanmarese State territoriality that the Kachin refer to as "Myanmar gates" in English. The most genuine *Myanmar gates* — in the literal meaning of the witty, although unintentional, allusion — are the Tatmadaw checkpoints between the government controlled areas and the KIO/KIA administered territories where identification is required and/or a fee extracted. For a traveling Kachin this means entering/exiting the military government controlled area and correspondingly, approaching/

leaving the KIO-controlled territory, which remains the only Kachin territorial place (Dean 2005). These checkpoints and the many army camps were not there before the 1994 ceasefire agreement. "No rural uprising would be successful under these circumstances of occupation by so many light infantry battalions. The countryside is literally one vast, strung out garrison.... One of the former most powerful ethnic armies is precipitously surrounded by dozens of Tatmadaw units, units which would have had no chance at all of establishing their presence here prior to the cease-fire agreement" (Matthews 2001, p. 11).

In what is unique political geography, the KIO/KIA high-ranking officials use the roads on the China side to travel between their territorial enclaves. The character and large share of the KIO/KIA spatial practices are defined by the presence of its headquarters in Lai Sin Bum near Laiza, and the location of the 3rd Brigade administration and some army camps along the Sino-Myanmar boundary. Communication and commuting often on daily basis take place between these locations — by crossing into China and re-entering into the KIO territory — due to the absence of proper car roads, particularly from the KIO/KIA headquarters to Laiza, or to other places inside Kachin State. Many ordinary Kachin also travel via China because of the better roads and public transportation, non-existent in Burma. In the KIO territory, Chinese currency, *yuan*, is widely used, while internet and phone lines and electricity are wired in. The phone numbers, including those of the mobile phones, have Chinese country codes — thus a Myanmar government officer who wants to contact the KIO from Kachin State capital Myitkyina, must make an *international* call.

Similarly as in trade, the Chinese officials up at to least the prefecture- and provincial level have not distinguished politically between the internationally recognized sovereignty granted to the State, and the self-government of the KIO/KIA, an ethnic armed organization that runs its border. The Chinese officials pay visits to the KIA army camps or brigade headquarters and are officially invited to formal social occasions such as festivals, various openings, VIP weddings and anniversaries, including the celebrations of the Revolution Day (the founding date of the KIO).

MILITARY'S POLITICAL ECONOMY

The ceasefire has changed drastically the political economy of the resource-rich Kachin State, to the advantage of the military regime. The ruling junta has been able to reinforce its forces in the absence of the KIA armed resistance resulting from the ceasefire agreement, and appropriate more space for control and extraction of resources. The most straightforward method for appropriating extra space is through coercive land confiscation from local populace "for the army".[15]

Along the territorial access to almost the entire State, the Myanmar's military government can command its rich natural resources such as jade, gold, forests and hydro-energy.[16] Among the various forms of resource exploitation, logging has been particularly pervasive, fuelled by the Chinese ban on logging in the adjacent Yunnan province in 1996, followed by a nationwide ban two years later. Extensive deforestation in Kachin State has gradually increased regardless its adverse impact on the livelihood of the farmers of the area, in addition to its negative environmental implications. In 2002, the military regime offered up to 18 per cent of the entire Kachin State for mining concessions that has transformed gold-mining from independent Kachin entrepreneurship providing livelihoods into a large-scale industry controlled by non-Kachin concession holders (KDNG 2007*a*). Mining concessions have been granted mostly to Chinese companies and military-allied groups from outside Kachin State, while state-sponsored infrastructure improvements such as the new roads that have been built in Kachin State and the upgrading of the World War Two Ledo Road, are intended to facilitate logging and resource extraction. In 2007, a project-launching ceremony was held for a 152-meter-tall hydropower dam at the Irrawaddy confluence, 40 kilometers from Myitkyina, intended to transmit electricity back to China (KDNG 2007*b*). While the local populace is being displaced from what the Kachin view as the heartland of their culture, in addition to the loss of livelihood, the dam would sit 100 kilometers from a major faultline in an earthquake prone area. The dam is the first in a series of seven large dams planned to be built by Chinese companies along the Irrawaddy.

Human rights advocates argue that large-scale conservation projects do not, primarily, aim to conserve nature but facilitate state-building and militarization by the "government" (Noam 2007). Without consulting or even informing the KIO, the military junta in collaboration with the World Conservation Society (WCS), established 3,800 square kilometer Hkakabo Razi National Park in 1998 in the northern tip of Kachin State. The establishment of this "protected area" has caused an increase in the number of Burmese military battalions stationed in the surrounding area to over ten (Ibid.).[17]

Largely untouched by Myanmar's military until mid-1990s was Hukawng Valley, recognized as one of the world's hotspots of biodiversity and the site for the world's largest tiger reserve established jointly by the junta and the U.S.-based WCS. During the establishment of the 22,000 square kilometers Hukawng Valley Tiger Reserve in 2004, the KIO was contacted. Alan Rabinowitz of WCS has confirmed that one of the reasons the military government was so enthusiastic about the Hukawng Valley Tiger Reserve was the opportunity to engage the KIO, who controls around 80 per cent of the valley, in negotiations (Noam 2007) — but from a position of power. The number of gold mining sites in Hukawng valley alone increased from 14 (in 1994) to 31 (in 2006) and migrants have been sweeping into the valley in search of quick profits from gold mining (KDNG 2007). Danai serves as the junta's centre for administrative and military activities in Hukawng Valley. Public and private buildings have been seized and one third of the surrounding farmland confiscated without any compensation since the ceasefire (KDNG 2007). Authorities also forcibly seized properties from local residents without compensation and then resold those properties for profit to non-local business (Ibid.). Causing disruption in rice economy and threatening the farmers' livelihoods was the order by the military authorities to grow 500,000 acres of physic nut trees (Jatropha Curcas) for bio diesel as a part of the nation-wide campaign where each State and division had to do the same. Since the launch of the campaign, farmers have been called by the local authorities to plant the trees without wages on days fixed by the administrators, at a time when they should be growing paddy.[18]

The politico-economic situation in Kachin State cannot be fully analyzed without considering opium poppy farming. Poppy cultivation that was banned by the KIO has been gradually increasing since the ceasefire. Under the military's political economy, many common people have lost their livelihoods, while the demand for drugs is high with gold and jade mine employers encouraging its consumption to ensure the workers' loyalty.[19] United Nations Office on Drugs and Crime (UNODC) reported in December 2009 that opium cultivation in Myanmar increased in the third straight year, especially in Kachin State and Shan State. Opium poppy is grown near the areas controlled by the Myanmar military army battalions, which commanders demand between US$4,167–15,625 as one-time tax from all poppy field owners around the base. Chinese businessmen in Kachin State and from neighbouring China's Yunnan province are attracted by the terms of the Myanmar Army. All poppy field owners and workers have to cross the Burmese Army base to go to their poppy fields, thus the workers are hired since the Myanmar military does not want the ethnic people to cross the army base territory.[20]

SECURITY THREATS

Although overt acts of war have been stopped by the ceasefire, the militarization of the entire Kachin State by the Tatmadaw and the proximity of the different armies have created new security threats while maintaining earlier tensions. While raiding and burning of villages have ceased to be sources of insecurity, the feelings of insecurity continue to persist in a state where arms have been exchanged for peace. The Tatmadaw presence has given rise to confiscations of property, extra-judicial arrests, forced labour, extraction of fees (or rice), and the potential for (and cases of) rape.[21] Forcible sales of rice to the Tatmadaw up to four times below the market price are commonplace at every harvest, while the villagers who cannot meet the army's quota of rice due to drought or other natural reasons, must buy rice at black market prices and provide it to the Tatmadaw in order to meet the quota (personal communication, Kachin State, 29 November 2000). Each year, farmers are ordered to sell paddy to the Myanmar military at prices lower than market rate. For example, after the latest harvest in December 2009 in Bhamo district, every farmer was ordered to sell 10.5 kilograms of paddy per acre to the local army base at a price of US$3.1 per 10.5 kilograms. The farmers are also required to transport the rice to the military base. The Kachin News Group, based at the border, quoted a farmer as saying "The fact is I don't want to sell paddy to the military because of the low price. But, it is an order and therefore compulsory".[22] In some reported instances, the farmers prefer to give the military the equivalent amount of cash and keep the rice. For a populace already living at subsistence level this contributes to food insecurity. In towns, although the uniformed army is usually present and visible, there is not a lot of social interaction between the soldiers and local residents other than in various services and daily interactions at marketplace. Many Kachin have never talked to a uniformed Tatmadaw soldier. Around the state capital Myitkyina, the numerous Tatmadaw soldiers have slightly withdrawn since the ceasefire. "They used to be more aggressive … but it is still better to keep away from them", an ethnic Burmese Indian pastor from Rangoon who regularly visits and services Kachin Catholic churches, noted (Kachin State, 17 December 2000).

The Tatmadaw has not tried to improve or rebuild its image during the time of peace. The villagers from the villages near the newly opened or existing army bases are called upon to work for the army in the construction of roads and new buildings, in clearing forests for new outposts and cultivating paddy during the hot season although the last is not a feasible practice. "It is ceasefire period now. The Army has no fighting to do and the soldiers are free but even petty work and odd jobs in the army area have to be carried out by the villagers ... At a time like this when the army should try and help the villagers and boost their morale, it is doing the very opposite by exploiting them", states an anonymous report from Kachin State.

CONTINUING POLITICAL STRUGGLE

The political struggle has expanded into many spheres and groups of society and the stakes are high. For the common populace and mushrooming civil society groups working half underground, the struggle over space has transformed into that for social and, even, long-term physical survival. Hazards from gold-mining where mercury is widely used and dispersed into the Irrawaddy river, the side effects of mining towns that spawn prostitution, drugs and an aggravating HIV/AIDS epidemic have become the main target of these groups that provide awareness-building, support and counseling for the people who have spiraled down the path of poverty, with no prospect for proper education and improvement of living standards in sight. Common people do not express political demands but lament about the total negligence by the regime. The cumulative fallout of the deteriorating political and economic situation in Myanmar has lead to large numbers of Kachin women being lured into China as workforce or brides where they end up as victims of human trafficking groups (KWAT 2008). The socio-economic situation in Kachin State has gravely worsened due to the large influx of migrants, the Chinese labour and investments, and increased opium production tacitly maintained by the Tatmadaw, as reported by the Kachin underground reporters. Kachin State capital Myitkyina is one of the hotspots in Southeast Asia for HIV/AIDS infection caused by the use of shared needles. Amongst the educated Kachin elites, the concerns are diverse — from the issues of culture, religion, environmental problems and conservation to problems of urbanization, brain-drain, education (personal communication, Kachin State 2004 and 2010). Although such concerns and feelings are essentially non-political, the ruling regime in Myanmar transforms these into politicized issues with references to the government (or rather, to its negligence). The need for a federal system under which the Kachin should have executive, legislative and judiciary power to address the concerns, emerges as a topic in discussions on the above listed issues very often (personal communication, Kachin State, January 2004 and 2010).

Similarly, the Kachin political struggle for autonomy after the ceasefire has greatly diversified and become sophisticated with vibrant political (re)mobilization taking place. In early 2000s, when the KIO/KIA popularity had declined amongst the general Kachin populace as a result of several factors, related to the establishment of the ceasefire, the Kachin National Consultative Assembly (KNCA) was established to bring together civilians represented by community leaders, the different religious denominations and the Kachin ceasefire groups. The KIO leadership has been involved in improving its public relations and publicly explaining the rather unpopular decision to participate in the National Convention, and in preparations leading to the formation of a Kachin political party to contest the military organized elections in 2010. The military authorities have exploited any crack and internal divide within the Kachin. For example, the Commander of Northern Command and Kachin State Peace and Development Council Maj-Gen Ohn Myint played a key role in 2005 in instigating an unsuccessful coup in the NDA-K to replace its leader by his rival and a Kachin businessman, and in 2006, he helped to set up a tiny militia group consisting of the members of one Kachin tribe, Rawang, with historic grievances against the KIO, called the Rebellion Resistance Force.[23] The most important political developments have been the continuous rejection by the KIA to transforming itself into a BGF and the formation of the Kachin State Progressive Party (KSPP) with a former KIO vice chairman as the leader to contest the 2010 elections. However, although the KIO has firmly gone along with the military government organized constitution drafting process, trying to make it into a chance to politically negotiate some degree of autonomy, the regime rejected the registration of the KSPP for the 2010 election and the situation remains extremely tense over the BGF issue.

CONCLUSION: CEASEFIRE AND CONFLICT RESOLUTION IN MYANMAR

In Myanmar the embodiment of the state has been its army, the Tatmadaw, enshrined in Myanmarese politics and the policies of the government, demanding regional and local compliance. The Tatmadaw's actions, practices and initiatives have exacerbated the ethnic nationalities' perceptions of the Union and helped to create an image of the Bamar as the enemy. It has been proved that many regional, local and/or lower-rank Tatmadaw personnel abuse their power. Atrocities and extra-judicial killings have been and continue to be recorded by ethnic governments and Amnesty International, which reveal, at most, the tip of the iceberg. Yawnghwe (1989, p. 92) regards the Tatmadaw, and not the centre-periphery disputes or imposition of Buddhism and Bamarization as a "major and very serious issue which threatened to, and did, in the final analysis, upset the intricately structured superordinate-subordinate relationship between the center and the states." Smith (1995, p. 223) also suggests that it is not the abuse of political rights but the Tatmadaw atrocities that have left a bitter legacy of resentment in many communities.

The Tatmadaw's efforts to achieve ceasefires with separatist groups in the troubled borderlands of Myanmar is a part of the military authorities' state-building process which is intended neither as a step towards conflict resolution nor as a strategy of addressing the concerns of the ethnic minorities. The regime has engraved its ambition — non-disintegration of the union and national solidarity — on the many walls and posters throughout the territory it controls. Its de facto practice of appropriating territorial, rural, urban, even symbolic and intimate spaces, as documented in various research, only reflects the singularity of its purpose.

As the ceasefire stops fighting, it is a step closer to permanent peace and appears to be a desirable development from a humanistic perspective and in the logic of conflict resolution. In Myanmar, the context of local political considerations and the nature of military regime — the embodiment of which is the Tatmadaw — in interaction with a multitude of local, state-level and geopolitical variables have produced a very different outcome. Unlike other post-colonial states such as India or Malaysia, the state in Myanmar has never pursued accommodationist policies towards opposition groups as a means of ending confrontation and certainly not by bringing them into representational government (Smith 2003; Callahan 2003). Of modern-day resonance is also the military's continuance of the same coercion tactics that the colonial state employed in counterinsurgency campaigns against communists (Ibid.). Smith (2003) points out that within the five decades of the KNU/KNLA armed resistance there have only been four initiatives at peace talks in the intervening years, while Callahan (2003) in her thorough study of the Tatmadaw has raised the possibility of the political inevitability of coercive solutions to internal crises. Certainly the military regime benefited from the KIO/KIA ceasefire (as did some KIO/KIA leaders) in the form of concessions and opportunities to do business.

Following the ceasefire agreement, hopes were initially high amongst common people in Kachin State that peace, improved living conditions and economic development would follow. But that, however, "turned out to be a curse" (KDNG 2007*a*) since the Tatmadaw has been expanding and acquiring territory through direct land confiscations and through control of territory in several other ways. In addition to establishing territorial military presence, the army pursues various other territorial practices that serve to denote control over territory. The control and exploitation of natural resources is the most politicized and contentious issue that has been linked to "internal colonization" (Sidaway 2000) in the context of the (post)modern era of sovereign state system where no "official" colonies exist. Communications and infrastructure, economy and politics can be utilized powerfully as devices of control over space by the state. Negligence, economic disparities and marginalization have resulted from the military political economy in Kachin State — and the money has flown into the coffers of the regional army commanders and the State, that has been the military. The spatial outcomes effected by the 2010 elections and the continuing pressure for the establishment of BGF at the Sino-Myanmar border are yet to unfold.

The ceasefire of 1994 greatly changed the structure of security/insecurity. The military government has succeeded in generating the feelings of insecurity amongst many Kachin who live in towns and villages in the Tatmadaw controlled areas. The physical presence of uniformed soldiers and the army camps in Kachin State serves as a constant reminder of direct Myanmarese State domination. Feelings of insecurity predominate as villagers remain vulnerable to the army's "legal" yet illegitimate practices.

Any "autonomy settlements" between the current military government and the armed groups benefit a selected small group of elites at power and their associates involved in the settlement. An autonomy settlement under the "arms for peace" ceasefire agreements has only resulted in the tightening of the military's grip on political and economic power. The ceasefires enable the military to achieve greater control over more territory and, importantly, its resources, as the situation in Kachin State demonstrates. Ceasefires also enable the leading generals to put more pressure on weaker parties to the ceasefire. The ultimate aim of the ceasefires has been to gradually disarm and weaken the ethnic political resistance groups.

Notes

[1] The Chapter was last updated in March 2011, and it thus analyses the Kachin armed resistance of 1961–94 and the following ceasefire of 1994–2011. The Kachin ceasefire discussed in the Chapter collapsed in June 2011, and the ensuing fighting has sent unprecedented numbers of refugees to the Sino-Myanmar border areas. The zones of armed resistance at the Thai-Myanmar border were turned into ceasefire areas in January 2012.

[2] For elaborations on the idea "illegal but licit" in Southeast Asia, see *IIAS Newsletter* 42 (2006) focusing on underworlds and borderlands, particularly discussions by van Schendel, Abraham, Walker and Smith.

3   Tatmadaw, meaning "armed forces", is the Burmese language reference for the Myanmar army, and will be used in the paper as such.
4   A political geographer Peter Taylor (1995, p. 6) has called upon to distinguish between the internal and external sovereignties of a State, using the term "internal sovereignty" to mean "effective [State] control of a territory" and noting that "external sovereignty" — recognition by international community — is the basis on which a State is considered sovereign.
5   <http://english.dvb.no/textonly/news.php?id=979>.
6   Estimations of expenditures spent on armed forces, health and education vary. According to a report by DLA Piper Rudnick Gray Cary (2005), an international law firm, 30–50 per cent of the government's budget is spent on the armed forces, while health receives 3 per cent and education 8 per cent of its budget. The IMF (1999/2000) estimate is 0.3 per cent of GDP on education, quoted in the same report. Another source quoted in the report is Social Watch that also shows how public health and education expenditures as percentage of GDP have decreased over the years: health from 1.1 per cent of GDP (1990) to 0.4 per cent (2001); and education respectively from 2.4 to 1.3 per cent of GDP.
7   The KIO and the NMSP are not representatives of the entire Kachin/Mon peoples or the respective States.
8   This should not be mixed up with its "mother" organization, the Karenni National Progressive Party, a politically and militarily staunch guerilla organization, whose ceasefire with the military government has broken down.
9   The United Wa State Army (UWSA) banned opium in 2005 in the pattern of earlier bans by other large opium-growing groups — National Democratic Alliance Army, ban in 1997; the Myanmar National Democratic Alliance Army, ban in 2003. These bans are attempts to gain international political recognition and support for the development of their impoverished regions after decades of war and isolation (Jelsma and Kramer 2008).
10 The Kachin "nationalist project" is successful in that it has managed to unite the people from a sundry of loosely affiliated tribes sharing many similarities in traditions and social order, under the single label Kachin. It has also suffered from internal divides along tribal affiliations and to a lesser extent, religious denominations. There are grievances amongst some "Kachin" individuals and tribal groups, particularly within the Lisu and the Rawang, towards the Jinghpaw.
11 See Tegenfeldt (1974), Smith (1999) and Lintner (1997) for wider discussions of the role of those events on the Kachin rebellion.
12 <http://www.janes.com/extracts/extract/jwit/jwita037.html>.
13 This section is based on fieldwork observations, communication and interviews conducted at the Sino-Myanmar border in January–February 2000, November–December 2000, March 2001 and August 2004; and in Kachin State in January 2001, January–February 2002 and January 2004. References to fieldwork are omitted to avoid repetition, except for quotes.

14 In 2000, there were about thirty checkpoints along the road "for the purpose of extracting money" as stated by a Kachin (personal communication, Kachin State, 2000). In January 2002, there were seventeen checkpoints and in 2010 this had been reduced to a few — which indicates a greatly improved security situation from the state perspective.

15 This happens on ad hoc basis and has been reported by the grassroots community and news groups. See KDNG (2007a) for land confiscations in Hukawng Valley, or "Burmese Army confiscates land and popular 'Stone Dragon'", Kachin News Group, 12 July 2008 <http://www.kachinnews.com/News/Burmese-Army-confiscates-land-and-popular-Stone-Dragon.html accessed 08.02.10> on land confiscations in Putao. Both areas have largely been opened up to the Myanmar military after the 1994 ceasefire.

16 An in-depth analysis of the adverse effects on the environment and local populace, caused by the various natural resource exploitations, is beyond the scope of this paper but is thoroughly reported by some environmental organizations and local community groups. The Global Witness, an international NGO, reports on logging (2003), based on its researchers' field interviews and observations. The eighty-one-page report by the Kachin Development Networking Group (KDNG 2007a) examines the impacts of gold mining in Hukawng Valley, and its sixty-four-page report (KDNG 2007b) considers the prospects of the planned dams on the Irrawaddy. The Kachin News Group (KNG) <www.kachinnews.com> reports regularly on new mining/logging concessions given out by the military authorities to the Chinese and other businesses, and has posted some videos on logging, mining and deforestation at the world's largest tiger reserve at Hukawng Valley, on its channel at Youtube <http://www.youtube.com/user/KachinNewsGroup>.

17 The Wildlife Conservation Society (WCS) based in New York City led the way into Myanmar in 1993, becoming the first INGO of any kind to initiate a programme inside Myanmar. WCS's primary aims are to work closely with the military regime (specifically the Ministry of Forestry), to increase the area covered under Myanmar's protected area system and engage in wildlife protection.

18 This is out of the eight million acres of physic nut trees the military plans to grow in the entire country, as reported by the Kachin News Group, 14 May 2009 in "Junta orders planting Physic Nut in northern Burma" <http://www.kachinnews.com/News/Junta-orders-planting-Physic-Nut-in-northern-Burma.html> (accessed 8 February 2010). About the local opposition to this project, read Nawdin Lahpai, "Students paste anti-Castor-oil-trees posters in Myitkyina (Special)", 3 July 2008 <http://www.kachinnews.com/Feature/Students-paste-anti-Castor-oil-trees-posters-in-Myitkyina-Special.html> (accessed 8 February 2010).

19 Reportedly some employers give money to miners to buy drugs <http://www.kachinnews.com/index.php?option=com_content&task=view&id=280&Itemid=149>.

[20] Kachin News Group, "Army allows only Chinese to grow poppy in Northern Burma", 25 January 2010 <http://www.kachinnews.com/News/Army-allows-only-Chinese-to-grow-poppy-in-Northern-Burma.html> (accessed 30 January 2010); see also Shyamal Sarkar, "Alarming rise in poppy cultivation and opium use in Kachin State", 30 June 2008 <http://www.kachinnews.com/Commentary/Alarming-rise-in-poppy-cultivation-and-opium-use-in-Kachin-State.html> (accessed 8 February 2010).

[21] An incident such as the gang rape and murder of a Kachin schoolgirl (27 July 2008) by Tatmadaw soldiers from Light Infantry Battalion (LIB) No. 437 in the territory jointly controlled by the Tatmadaw and the KIO, causing widespread condemnation by the Kachin from Tokyo to New Delhi, has been much politicized. The Tatmadaw arrested a soldier, apologized and provided some compensation. See Nawdin Lahpai, "Kachins protest schoolgirl gang rape and murder", 27 August 2008 <http://www.kachinnews.com/Feature/Kachins-protest-schoolgirl-gang-rape-and-murder.html> (accessed 8 February 2010).

[22] Kachin News Group, "Farmers ordered to sell paddy to army in Northern Burma", 20 January 2010 <http://www.kachinnews.com/News/Farmers-ordered-to-sell-paddy-to-army-in-northern-Burma.html> (accessed 30 January 2010).

[23] "Rebellion Resistance Force troops airlifted to Burma's new capital", Kachin News Group, 25 September 2007 <http://www.kachinnews.com/News/Rebellion-Resistance-Force-troops-airlifted-to-Burma-s-new-capital.html> (accessed 8 February 2010).

References

Bowman, Vicky. "The Political Situation in Myanmar". In *Myanmar: The State, Community and the Environment*, edited by Skidmore Monique and Trevor Wilson. Canberra: Australian National University E. Press and Asia Pacific Press, 2007. <http://epress.anu.edu.au/myanmar/pdf_instructions.html>.

Brown, David. *The State and Ethnic Politics in Southeast Asia*. London and New York: Routledge, 1994.

Callahan, Mary. *Making Enemies: War and State Building in Burma*. Ithaca and London: Cornell University Press, 2003.

Dean, Karin. "Spaces and territorialities on the Sino-Burmese boundary: China, Myanmarand the Kachin". *Political Geography* 24 (2005): 808–30.

DLA Piper Rudnick Gray Cary. *Threat to Peace: A Call for the UN Security Council to Act in Burma*. Washington, 2005.

Euro-Burma Office (EBO). "The Kachin Dilemma: Contest the Election or Return to Guerrilla Warfare". EBO Analysis Paper, no. 5 (2010), available at <http://euro-burma.eu/doc/EBO_Analysis_Paper_No_2_2010_-_The_Kachin%27s_Dilemma.pdf> (accessed 15 March 2011).

Global Witness. *A Conflict of Interests: The Uncertain Future of Burma's Forests*. A Briefing Document. London: Global Witness Ltd., 2003.

Grundy-Warr, Carl and Wong Siew Yin Elaine. "Geographies of Displacement: The Karenni and the Shan Across the Myanmar-Thailand Border". In *Singapore Journal of Tropical Geography* 23, no. 1 (2002).

Hudson-Rodd, Nancy and Myo Hunt. "The military occupation of Burma". *Geopolitics* 10 (2005): 500–21.

International Institute for Asian Studies (IIAS). "Underworlds and Borderlands". Newsletter 42, October 2006, available at <http://www.iias.nl/index.php?q=newsletter-42> (accessed 15 March 2011).

Jelsma, Martin and Tom Kramer. *Withdrawal Symptoms: Changes in the Southeast Asian Drugs Market*. Transnational Institute. TNI Debate Papers no. 16 (August 2008).

Kachin Development Networking Group (KDNG). *Valley of Darkness: Gold Mining and Militarization in Burma's Hugawng Valley*. KDNG Publications, 2007a.

———. *Damming the Irrawaddy*. KDNG Publications, 2007b.

Kachin Women Association Thailand (KWAT). *Eastward Bound*. Chiang Mai, 2008.

Lintner, Bertil. *The Kachin: Lords of Burma's Northern Frontier*. Asia Film House Pty. Ltd. under licence from Sollo Development Limited in conjunction with Robroy Management Pty. Ltd. and the Lua Publishing Services Partnership. A Teak House Publication, 1997.

Matthews, Bruce. "Ethnic and Religious Diversity: Myanmar's Unfolding Nemesis". *Visiting Researchers Series* 3. Singapore: Institute of Southeast Asian Studies, 2001.

Noam, Zao. "Eco-authoritarian conservation and ethnic conflict in Burma". *Policy Matters: Conservation and Human Rights* 15 (2007).

Rajah, Ananda. "Burma: Protracted Conflict, Governance and Non-Traditional Security Issues". Working Paper no. 14, Institute of Defence and Strategic Studies, Nanyang Technological University, Singapore, May 2001.

Sakhong, Lian H. "Burma At Crossroads". A presentation at the Forum for Asian Studies, Stockholm University, The Seminar Series, 1 March 2011, available at <http://euro-burma.eu/doc/Lina_Burma_at_Crossroads__110301_.pdf> (accessed 15 March 2011).

Selth, Andrew. "Burma's Armed Forces Under Civilian Rule: A Return to the Past?" Working Papers, The MyanmarFund, Technical Advisory Network of Burma, Washington, D.C., 2001.

———. *Burma's Armed Forces: Power without Glory*. Norwalk, Connecticut: EastBridge, 2002.

Sidaway, James D. "Postcolonial Geographies: An Exploratory Essay". *Progress in Human Geography* 24, no. 4 (2000).

Smith, Martin. "A State of Strife: The Indigenous Peoples of Burma". In *Indigenous Peoples of Asia*, edited by R.H. Barnes, Gray A. and Kingsbury B. Association for Asian Studies, Inc., Monograph and Occasional Paper Series No. 48 (1995).

———. *Burma: Insurgency and the Politics of Ethnicity*. Dhaka: The University Press; Bangkok: White Lotus; London, New York: Zed Books Ltd., 1999.

———. "The Enigma of Burma's Tatmadaw: A 'State' within a 'State'". Book Review. *Critical Asian Studies* 35, no. 4 (2003).

South, Ashley. *Ethnic Politics in Burma: States of Conflict*. Abington: Routledge, 2008.

Taylor, Peter. "Beyond Containers: Internationality, Interstatedness, Interterritoriality". *Progress in Human Geography* 19, no. 1 (1995): 1–15.

Tegenfeldt, Herman G. *A Century of Growth: The Kachin Baptist Church of Burma*. South Pasadena, 1974.

Tin, Maung Maung Than. "The Essential Tension: Democratization and the Unitary State in Myanmar (Burma)". *South East Asia Research* 12, no. 2 (2004).

Yawnghwe, Chao Tzang. "The Burman Military: Holding The Country Together?". In *Independent Burma At Forty Years: Six Assessments*, edited by Josef Silverstein. New York: Cornell University Southeast Asia Program, 1989.

Zaw Oo and Win Min. *Assessing Burma's Ceasefire Accords*. Policy Studies 39. Washington, D.C.: East-West Center, 2007.

8

SRI LANKA'S ETHNIC CONFLICT: THE AUTONOMY-SEPARATION DIALECTIC

Jayadeva Uyangoda

Do government offers for autonomy reduce the momentum for secession in a context of protracted civil war? Or, do incomplete autonomy measures provide new encouragement to secessionist projects? How can an autonomy solution be realistically feasible when the state emerges victorious in a protracted internal war against an armed insurgency launched on behalf of an ethnic minority? I explore these three questions in relation to the experience of Sri Lanka which has had an ethnic minority armed insurgency for secession spread over two and a half decades, from the early 1980s to 2009. The civil war came to an end in May 2009 when the armed forces of the Sri Lankan state militarily defeated the Liberation Tigers of Tamil Eelam (LTTE), which spearheaded the insurgency. Two factors concerning regional autonomy make the Sri Lankan case study interesting. The first is about the capacity/incapacity of the autonomy option to bring the conflict to an end when the civil war was raging. The second is the extent to which the government is willing to pursue the autonomy option after defeating the ethnic minority rebellion. This chapter explores the trajectories of the autonomy debate in Sri Lanka during and after the civil war.

Is regional autonomy a viable alternative to secession? The answer to this question emerged during the civil war has been a complex one. It had often been shaped by the ways in which the politics of the conflict was played out at the national, regional and global levels. Similarly, the secessionist project of the Tamil rebels and the limited autonomy offers made by governments have been two constitutive components of the protracted civil war. To elaborate on the point, the spread of the armed rebellion for secession in the Northern and Eastern provinces of the country compelled the governments of Sri Lanka to explore regional autonomy options. At the same time, half-hearted and minimalist autonomy offers by the government repeatedly reinforced the argument for secession. Thus, resistance to regional autonomy, offers of limited autonomy, and the escalation of the separatist rebellion have been two sides of the same process of civil war protraction. Sri Lanka's ethnic conflict has been replete with stories of autonomy denial in the early phases of conflict formation (from the 1950s to the 1970s), an intermediate phase of minimalist power-sharing (early 1980s), a moderate degree of power-sharing in response to armed separatism (the late 1980s), pressure for greater regional autonomy in the phase of protracted civil war (1990s) and, in more recent years, the resurgence of the argument for minimalist regional autonomy in the post-9/11 global context of the war against terror.

One way to understand this uneasy relationship between autonomy offers and secessionist agendas existed throughout the civil war in Sri Lanka is to re-frame the question of autonomy in terms of the larger question of state power. Thus, the autonomy debate in Sri Lanka was not only about refining a constitutional doctrine or designing a new institutional arrangement. Rather, it was essentially about the presence or absence of the will to share state power, share sovereignty, and re-define both the nationhood and statehood. Autonomy in that sense entailed re-arranging the politics of ethnic relations, re-structuring majority-minority relations, and re-working the ethnic foundations of the state on the basis of inter-group equality. It requires a strong commitment to pluralize the state. Thus, being more than an exercise in political engineering, the idea of autonomy has had a normative dimension too. It concerned itself with re-organizing the terms and conditions of political association among a plurality of ethnic communities in the transition from ethnic civil war to post-civil war peace. Against this backdrop, in exploring the autonomy-separation dialectic, we need to reflect on questions such as the following: What type of autonomy offers by governments can divert the trajectory of conflict away from war? What depth and thickness of regional autonomy could have been adequate to provide incentives to secessionist insurgents to give up the insurgency?

This chapter is an attempt to explore such a retrospective reflection. It is organized in the following manner. The central thesis of the chapter is built around the argument that the issue of regional autonomy in Sri Lanka is deeply embedded in the question of the limits of sharing state power and that ethnicity-based autonomy requires a programme of substantial state reform. The chapter begins with a discussion of this proposition. Then it provides an account of how the question of regional autonomy as demanded by the Tamil minority began to be entangled in a difficult process of state reform. This discussion also presents an account of the existing provincial councils system in Sri Lanka which was established in 1987 through Indian initiative. Then the chapter maps out different phases of Sri Lanka's state reform trajectory, highlighting some key contradictions developed between the limited autonomy politics of Sri Lankan governments and the separatist politics of Tamil nationalists. These developments are helpful to understand the mutually exclusive as well as mutually dependent processes of limited and incomplete autonomy on one hand and the quest for minority separation on the other. The sub-themes in this section are the limits of unilateral state reform initiatives, reform-weariness and its consequences, and Tamil perspectives on regional autonomy. This discussion emphasizes the point that any serious shift towards peace through a negotiated political settlement in Sri Lanka required the abandoning of autonomy-separation binary logic. The chapter concludes by suggesting that, for a political solution based on regional autonomy to emerge as a real alternative to the war, both the Sinhalese political establishment and the LTTE needed to radically re-frame and re-define their unilateral approaches to the outcome of the conflict.

AUTONOMY AS STATE POWER: THE "AUTONOMY TRAP"

Regional autonomy is essentially about the sharing of state power. In an ethnic conflict, it entails the sharing of state power on the basis of both ethnicity and territoriality. The embeddedness of both territoriality and ethnicity in the question of state power, as frequently demonstrated in Sri Lanka, has made ethnic conflict management through power-sharing doubly difficult. Thus, autonomy offers, although necessary, were not sufficient to transform the conflict from a civil war into a political settlement. In the context of a separatist armed insurgency against the state, an autonomy project capable of transforming the conflict should have presupposed a credible and substantial alternative to secession. It should have been strong enough to alter the trajectory of the conflict towards, both, ending the war and settling the conflict.

Two preliminary points stemmed from Sri Lanka's experience during the civil war in this regard are in order. First, although autonomy offers are necessary to mitigate ethno-political civil war, under certain circumstances, inadequate as well as extensive autonomy offers can even lead to conflict escalation and re-legitimation of secessionist goals of the aggrieved ethnic minorities. This points to a specific kind of "autonomy trap" emerged in Sri Lanka during the civil war. Inadequate autonomy offers made by the government frustrated minoritarian nationalists and reinforced their argument for secession. Substantial autonomy demands by minority nationalists angered the nationalist forces within the majority ethnic community, limiting the regime capacity even to pursue limited autonomy options. This is the essential dilemma of autonomy and power-sharing arrangements in majority-minority conflicts. As Bachler (2004) points out, state reform and conflict are closely related in a double sense. While state reform can be seen as a prerequisite for conflict transformation and sustainable peace, it can also easily become a new source of conflict (Bachler 2004, p. 274). Bachler warns that state reform must be seen as a "tightrope walk" always "seeking a fine line between conflict mitigation and crisis escalation." I take Bachler's insight to make the point that an incomplete and inconclusive state reform agenda made Sri Lanka's reform process doubly difficult to sustain. As I show in the following discussion on Sri Lanka's case, attempts at state reform in an ethno-political conflict, whether they are radical or moderate, can revitalize ethnic passions while making political trades off difficult, even impossible. If abandoned halfway through, inconclusive reform attempts may run the risk of transforming the state reform project itself into a new source of conflict intractability. I call this the dialectic of ethnic conflict and state reform.

The second point is that the capacity of any autonomy offer to alter the trajectory of the conflict in the direction of settlement depends largely on the extent to which the contestation for state power is embedded in the conflict process. Secessionist civil war provides the context for the highest form in which the state power is contested. This poses some more challenges. One is about the adequacy of any proposed autonomy package to reduce the commitment of the parties to the civil war, particularly the rebels, to seek unilateral outcomes to the intensely contested claims to state power. Another is about the regime's political will and capacity to implement autonomy arrangements. Some governments might formulate autonomy offers due to specific political circumstances, like compulsions of pre-election alliances and public clamour for peace under conditions of war weariness. But in deeply divided societies, autonomy packages are easier formulated than implemented. Thus, not all regimes can really implement and constitutionalize their reform wishes. The regime capacity for autonomy reform is often contingent on the unpredictable ways in which the politics of the conflict and war is played out.

Sri Lanka's conflict has been one in which three ethnically conceived state-formation projects were in contestation. One of them was majoritarian and the other two minirotarian. The majoritarian state-formation project was spearheaded by the Sinhalese nationalist forces and it was officially implemented by the regimes in power and state institutions, the bureaucracy, the state-controlled media, and the armed forces. For a large part of the post-colonial period, the majoritarian state formation project sought the consolidation of the unitary state. During the secessionist challenge by the Tamil state-formationists, it sought to re-establish the unitary state by military means. The Tamil state-formation project sought to carve out a territorial state in the Island's Northern and Eastern provinces. The Muslim minoritarian state-formation project did not seek secession. Its focus was on regional autonomy in the Eastern province. These three have had the following salient characteristics. The Sinhalese state formation project was about restoring the unitary state in a multi-ethnic social formation; the Tamil project was a state-seeking minority enterprise centred on a combination of nationhood and territorial statehood; and the Muslim project was about regional autonomy for a regional minority.

AUTONOMY AS STATE REFORM: THE DIFFICULT PATH

During the 1990s and after, Sri Lanka has had two levels of regional autonomy existing in a relationship of tension and conflict. The first was the official and constitutionally sanctioned system of Provincial Councils that have existed in seven provinces of the country since 1988. The other was the unrecognized regional autonomy which the LTTE had been maintaining for several years in the Northern and Eastern Provinces under the conditions of civil war.

Sri Lanka's official autonomy arrangement was established in 1987 through the 13th Amendment to the Constitution. The 13th Amendment introduced "devolution" by setting up a system of Provincial Councils. Each Council covered an administrative province. Altogether eight provincial councils were created. With regard to the two provinces of the North and East, a single council was set up in 1987 through the merger of the two provinces. The merger of the two units with a demographic majority of the Tamil-speaking people, including both Tamil and Muslim communities, was a demand made by the Tamil nationalist groups. In the ideology of Tamil nationalism, these two provinces were considered the "traditional homeland" of Sri Lanka's Tamil-speaking people.

In terms of its nature and powers, Sri Lanka's system of provincial councils was modeled according to the Indian system of federalism, with centralizing features dominating the power-sharing arrangement. The councils are elected every four years and each council is headed by a Chief Minister. The 13th Amendment to the 1978 Constitution defined the powers of the centre and the provincial councils through three lists — the central list, provincial list and the concurrent list. The provincial list includes police and public order, provincial education, planning, local government, housing, agriculture, and health. The concurrent powers are to be exercised jointly by the centre and the provinces, but in its actual operation, and in the context of asymmetrical power relations between the centre and the periphery, the scheme of concurrent powers favour the central government. The extent of regional autonomy offered in the provincial council system is not very wide, because of the "lack of clarity on the powers which are devolved" (Peiris 1996, p. 6). Because of this lack of clarity, the constitutional provisions themselves have permitted the central government "both to retain so much power" and at the same time "undermine devolved powers" so easily that there is no "substantial devolution" (Edrisinha 1998, p. 24).

The setting up of the provincial councils in 1987 was largely in response to the pressure exercised by the Indian government headed by Prime Minister Rajiv Gandhi on the Sri Lankan government. Gandhi became the Indian Prime Minister in 1984 after the death of his mother, Prime Minister Indira Gandhi who followed an approach sympathetic to the Tamil quest for autonomy in Sri Lanka. For political and strategic reasons, the Indian government had maintained a direct and indirect influence over the Sri Lankan conflict, initially even supporting the Tamil nationalists. However, when the war began escalating beyond any control in the mid-1980s, the Rajiv Gandhi government of India altered its policy towards Sri Lanka. A key feature of that policy shift was the decision made in mid-1987 to make a decisive intervention to stop the war and impose a political settlement to the ethnic conflict. The Indo-Lanka Accord signed by Prime Minister Rajiv Gandhi and Sri Lanka's President Junius Jayewardene in July 1987 was the outcome of India's direct entry to Sri Lanka's conflict.[1] The setting up of the Provincial Council system through the 13th Amendment to the Constitution was carried out by the Jayewardene regime in accordance with a key commitment made in the Indo-Lanka Accord. Thus, the impetus for regional autonomy came from outside, not from within. This has a continuing relevance to assessing the capacity of Sri Lanka's political class to constructively handle a secessionist threat through devolution of state power.

The impact of the setting up of Provincial Councils through Indian initiative in 1987 is quite significant. All the Tamil nationalist groups initially appeared to have accepted the political solution envisaged in the Accord and implemented through the new system of devolution. But in the ethnically-majority Sinhalese society, the reception it received was quite mixed. Only a section of the ruling United National Party (UNP) and a few Left-wing political parties welcomed it. The UNP government was initially divided on both the Accord and the Provincial councils. Among those who initially opposed it were the Prime Minister and the National Security Minister. The Sri Lanka Freedom Party (SLFP), which was the main opposition party at that time, also vehemently opposed the Accord, the Indian role in the conflict and the political solution through devolution.[2] The Sinhalese nationalist opposition was actually led by the *Janatha Vimukthi Peramuna* (JVP–People's Liberation Front), which had till then been proscribed by the government.[3] The nationalist resistance soon developed into a major anti-state armed insurgency, lasting for two years. Despite this opposition, the UNP government passed the 13th Amendment to the Constitution to establish Provincial Councils, held elections for the councils amidst massive anti-state as well as counter-insurgency violence and instituted the Councils.

The consequences of the Provincial Council system of 1987 for the trajectory of Tamil ethnic politics have been equally complex. The Tamil United Liberation Front, the mainstream, non-militant Tamil party in exile in India, and all the Tamil guerilla groups initially pledged to accept the Indo-Lanka Accord and the political solution offered by it. The armed groups generally agreed to surrender their weapons and join the "mainstream" of politics. But the LTTE, the dominant Tamil guerilla group at the time, soon began to show signs of dissent and within a few weeks of the Accord indicated their unwillingness to go along with the Indo-Lanka Accord. The LTTE also staged a fake surrender of weapons. The refusal by the LTTE to surrender weapons and disband its guerilla units created conditions for the Indian government to send its military forces to enforce peace in Sri Lanka. The Indian peace enforcement soon developed into a major war between the Indian troops and the LTTE in Sri Lanka's North and East. The LTTE's rejection of the Indo-Lanka Accord was partly due to the fact that the LTTE was not a direct party to negotiations. The parties that directly negotiated the peace deal of 1987 were the Sri Lankan and Indian governments. Meanwhile, the LTTE rejected the Provincial Councils, describing them as an inadequate model of regional autonomy. The LTTE's notion of an acceptable political solution was based on the concept of "self-determination" which, by that time, did not mean anything less than secession.

Despite opposition and rejection by important political constituencies in the Sinhalese and Tamil societies, the Provincial Council system began to work slowly. The initial difficulties it faced were two fold. The first was the opposition by Sinhalese as well as Tamil nationalists. The Sinhalese nationalists viewed "devolution" as a federal arrangement that would undermine Sri Lanka's unitary state and eventually pave the way for a separate Tamil ethnic state. The opposition by Tamil nationalists, as spearheaded by the LTTE, saw this particular model of regional autonomy as an inadequate political solution, arbitrarily imposed on the Tamil people by the Indian and Sri Lankan states. The second set of difficulties emanated from the reluctance of politicians and the bureaucracy to devolve to the periphery the powers they were constitutionally obliged to through the 13th Amendment. Reforming the state in the direction of regional autonomy against a culture of unitarism and centralization has been a difficult process in Sri Lanka. Even after two decades of their existence, the Provincial Councils have not yet been given powers relating to the police, the law-and-order and land.

Meanwhile, the Provincial Council of the Northern and Eastern province suffered a huge setback in 1990, within two years of its establishment, from which it has not yet recovered. The Council was dissolved by the central government in 1990 in the context of "peace talks" between the then President R. Premadasa and the LTTE. The coalition that had come into power in the North-East Provincial Council consisted of an alliance of several anti-LTTE ex-militant groups, the Eelam People's Revolutionary Front (EPRLF) being its main partner. When President Premadasa's regime began "peace talks" with the LTTE in 1989 the LTTE made use of that opportunity to target the EPRLF administration in the Province. Amidst the government's hostility, the EPRLF Chief Minister made the mistake of declaring unilateral independence soon after the government dissolved the Provincial Council. While the Chief Minister and his colleagues fled to India seeking political asylum, the Provincial Council was brought under the central government. Till May 2008, it was administered by a Governor appointed by the President, with no elected council. The elected provincial councils continued to function in other seven provinces where there was actually no popular demand for devolution.

The discussion above about the Provincial Council system, which was introduced in 1987 as the first measure of regional autonomy to provide an alternative to secession, encapsulates some major aspects of the politics of

Sri Lanka's ethnic conflict management through autonomy. A few of these aspects may be formulated as follows. Even when the ethnic conflict became a civil war, Sri Lanka's political establishment was not yet ready to accept regional autonomy as necessary to address Tamil minority grievances. In the absence of a domestic impulse for a political solution to the ethnic conflict through state reform, it was external intervention, by India in this particular instance that coerced the Sri Lankan government to institute regional autonomy. Similarly, regional autonomy even in a limited framework as embodied in the Provincial Council system was seen by influential segments of the Sinhalese polity, particularly the nationalist sections, as a threat to Sri Lanka's national sovereignty, territorial integrity and unity. It is also seen by them as a totally unnecessary concession to an ethnic minority whose representatives had resorted to war, violence and "terrorism" against the state. In Tamil society too, the reaction to the Provincial Council system was mixed. Some saw it as constituting an acceptable framework for a political settlement while others, the LTTE, rejected it as inadequate as a measure of self-determination. In the subsequent years, both the war and the Provincial Council system began a process of uneasy co-existence, with the Northern and Eastern provinces continuing to be the main theater of Sri Lanka's internal war. As a result, benefits of even the limited regional autonomy of the Provincial Council system did not reach the two provinces which, in fact, most needed devolution.

PATHS OF STATE REFORM

In order to place both the difficulties and the potential for regional autonomy to constitute the basis of a political solution to Sri Lanka's ethnic conflict, as demonstrated in the context of the Provincial Council system, it is useful to identify some dynamics of state reform politics in post-colonial Sri Lanka. Three distinct phases can be identified in the development of the government's official positions in relation to the ethnic conflict. During the first phase, which was the period up to the early 1980s, the idea of regional autonomy was given a narrow and restricted interpretation to mean administrative decentralization under strict political control exercised by the central government. The District Development Councils, introduced in 1980 in response to the early Tamil nationalist agitation for self-determination and separation, exemplified this perspective of autonomy as administrative decentralization. In the second phase encompassing the mid-1980s, the concept of "devolution" entered the autonomy debate and eventually led to its expansion to include semi-federalism in the mid-1990s. This semi-federalist orientation of the autonomy debate continued till 2003. The third phase began in 2005 during which the government's stand on regional autonomy has slipped back to limited autonomy with central control. The key phrase that captures the spirit of this third phase is "maximum devolution within the unitary state".

The Tamil minority project of autonomy and separation too has a history of altered trajectories. In the 1950s, within just a few years after political independence, a case was made for territorially-based federalist autonomy for the Northern and Eastern provinces. In the late 1970s, the project of independence replaced the federalist claim and in the early 1980s, it took the form of an armed insurgency for secession. After the mid-1980s, particularly after the introduction of devolution consequent to the Indo-Lanka Accord of July 1987, the Tamil nationalist project entered into two parallel and competing paths — secession by means of war and federalist regional autonomy through compromise. While the LTTE continued to pursue the goal of secession through armed struggle, a number of Tamil nationalist insurgent groups opted for regional autonomy in place of separation. The LTTE had claimed a number of times its willingness to explore options for compromise and a political settlement short of separation. However, its commitment to such a goal remained vague and suspicious throughout the civil war.

A question that arises against this backdrop is: what had the civil war done to the quest for a political solution to the ethnic conflict through regional autonomy? A brief account of the main developments that occurred during the post-1987 period of the ethnic conflict is useful to find an answer to this question.

One key development occurred in the period after the setting up of provincial councils in 1987 was the re-opening of the debate on autonomy. It developed around the efforts made by the Mangala Moonesinghe Parliamentary Select Committee which was established in 1991.[4] The mandate of this Select Committee was to "recommend ways and means of achieving peace and political stability in the country" (Loganathan 1996, p. 167). What this sanitized formulation actually meant was for the Select Committee to propose a political solution to the ethnic conflict through the consultation of all stakeholders, except the LTTE, to the conflict. The Select Committee also came into existence in the aftermath of the collapse in 1990 of the government-LTTE peace talks and the resumption of the war between the two parties. The strategy of the government, as it appeared, had a dual track. It sought to promote a consensus among Sinhalese, Tamil and Muslim political parties other than the LTTE on a possible political solution while engaging the LTTE militarily. The outcome the government wanted, perhaps, was to create a situation in which either the LTTE would be compelled by circumstances to accept the new political solution which the Moonesinghe Committee would propose, or be isolated when that solution was being implemented with the participation of other Tamil parties and the Muslim parties. The LTTE's strategy, on the other hand, was to continue the war and violence to make the point that no political solution was possible or viable without its participation in it as a key party to the conflict. As subsequent events indicated, the LTTE's strategy worked in this particular instance.

During the consultations of the Moonesinghe Committee in 1991, two crucial issues concerning a political solution and regional autonomy emerged. The first was the claim which the Muslim political leadership began to make arguing that the Muslims should be a direct party to any political solution to the ethnic conflict. Muslims were the second ethnic minority in Sri Lanka, representing about 7 per cent of the country's population. Although Tamil speaking, the Sri Lankan Muslims consider themselves a distinct ethnic group, with a separate cultural identity defined by Islam. They have also been careful to chart their political aspirations distinctly away from the Tamil community. In the Muslim argument, the Sinhalese and Tamil communities should not be the only stakeholders to a peace settlement. As conceptualized with clarity a few years later, the Muslim leadership, organized newly in the form of Sri Lanka Muslim Congress (SLMC), pointed out that although the war was between two parties — Sri Lankan state and the Tamil rebels — a political solution based on regional autonomy had to be a tripartite one, involving the Sinhalese, Tamil and Muslim communities. The Muslim participation in the process towards a solution as well as in the solution itself was justified on the argument that the Muslims were direct victims of war and violence. This argument challenged and undermined the position held by all Tamil nationalists, moderates and militants alike, that the Sri Lankan Muslims and Tamils were members of one "Tamil-speaking nationality". The second crucial issue to emerge during the deliberations of the Moonesinghe Select Committee was about the extent of devolution and the unit of devolution. By the early 1990s there had developed a general consensus among most of the political parties in parliament that "devolution" was necessary for a political solution to the ethnic conflict. But, there was no consensus over the question of the quantum of powers that the periphery should enjoy. The Tamil parties demanded more powers to provincial councils than were given in the 13th Amendment. This idea for more powers for the provincial councils came to be known in Sri Lanka's policy debate as "Thirteenth Amendment Plus".

Almost all the Sinhalese political parties were not in favour such an expansion of the scope of regional autonomy.

Meanwhile, the question of the "unit of devolution" emerged primarily as a part of the intense debate between Tamil and Muslim parties. The Tamil parties held the view that the continuing merger of the Northern and Eastern provinces as a single politico-administrative unit was not to be subjected to negotiation. The Muslim leaders opposed this argument vehemently. In a context where the LTTE as well as other Tamil rebel groups had used a great deal of violence against the Muslims in the North and the East, including massacres and mass expulsion, the SLMC also demanded a unit of autonomy for Muslims. In the argument developed during this period, regional self-rule for the Muslim community was the best guarantee to prevent Tamil hegemony over the Muslims in a framework of devolution and ensure their protection and security.[5] The SLMC's proposal was to establish a non-contiguous Muslim autonomy unit, combining Muslim-majority administrative units in the Eastern province. This claim, tactically backed by some Sinhalese parties, radically undermined the Tamil claim to an "undivided homeland" in the North and East.

The issue of the unit of devolution, which remained intractable for nearly twenty years, has now being partially resolved through the intervention of the judiciary. In October 2006, the Supreme Court, giving its ruling on a petition filed by the JVP, determined that the merger affected by the President in 1987 under emergency regulations, was illegal. According to the Supreme Court, only Parliament had the legal authority to merge the two provinces. With this de-merger verdict, the Sri Lankan government was able to handle one of the politically most volatile issues in the regional autonomy debate in Sri Lanka. Having successfully pushed the LTTE's military presence out of the Eastern Province in a series of battles that lasted for about a year in 2006–07, the government politically consolidated its military gains by holding the elections for the Eastern Provincial Council. Meanwhile, opinion among the Tamil political parties was divided on the de-merger issue. The Tamil parties, who were aligned with the government, expressed their displeasure over the de-merger, but they accepted it as a new political reality.

LIMITS OF UNILATERAL REFORM INITIATIVES

Engaging the LTTE in a sustainable manner to negotiate a political solution to the ethnic conflict has been one of the most difficult challenges confronted by successive governments in Sri Lanka. This issue came to the centre of the policy debate on peace building in Sri Lanka in 1994–95, 2002–03 as well as in 2005–06. Repeated negotiation failures had also led governments to experiment with unilateral political solutions through a process that excluded the LTTE. The devolution initiative made by the People's Alliance government of President Chandrika Kumaratunga in 1995–2000 was one such major instance of a failed state reform process that excluded the LTTE as a participant.

The background to the People's Alliance (PA) government's move to initiate a constitutional reform process as a prelude to a political settlement to the ethnic conflict was the collapse of peace negotiations between the PA government and the LTTE in April 1995.[6] The government initiated peace negotiations with the LTTE in late 1994 on the premise that a set of proposals for extensive devolution was being prepared by the government. The government also created the impression that those "devolution proposals" would eventually constitute the basis for a peace agreement with the LTTE. However, during the peace talks with the LTTE, the PA government did not present to the LTTE any such reform proposals.

Eventually, in August 1995, four months after the negotiations came to an end, the PA government made public its devolution proposals. The new devolution proposals were quite substantial in terms of the scope of regional autonomy envisaged. For example, the August 1995 devolution proposals sought to strengthen the powers of the Regional Councils, which were to replace the Provincial Councils, by granting to regions most of the powers that were in the concurrent list under the existing 13th amendment. The concurrent powers included those to be jointly exercised by the central government and the Provincial Councils. There were also provisions to further ensure regional autonomy by restricting the powers of the Central Government to control the proposed Regional Councils. The Constitution was also to be amended to give enhanced devolution greater constitutional recognition by describing the Republic of Sri Lanka a "Union of Regions". President Kumaratunga and her government thought that a unilateral offer of an extensive devolution framework would act as a credible incentive for the LTTE to return to the negotiation table. In case the LTTE refused to participate, the government leaders thought that other Tamil and Muslim parties would accept the new framework of devolution, eventually isolating the LTTE politically. The government also thought that such political isolation of the LTTE would in turn help the government's war effort to defeat the LTTE.

Contrary to the government's expectations, the LTTE rejected the devolution proposals of August 1995, calling them "inadequate" to address Tamil aspirations. However, a major reason for the LTTE's rejection of the devolution proposals was that the LTTE saw them as a unilateral exercise by the government without its participation. For the LTTE, these unilateral reform proposals were a part of what it saw as the government's "peace trap for a long-term war" (Balasingham 2004, p. 196). Incidentally, almost all the non-LTTE Tamil parties actively took part in negotiations with the government to work out the devolution proposals of 1995. Some members of the Tamil United Liberation Front (TULF), the main Tamil parliamentary party, played an active role in conceptualizing and even drafting the Devolution Proposals of 1995. In a way, these proposals were "unilateral" in the limited sense of the LTTE being excluded from the process through which they were drafted. The LTTE also interpreted the government's offer of a "unilateral" political package as a covert attempt to win over the Tamil people by politically isolating the LTTE. The LTTE's rejection of the devolution proposals of August 1995 provided the context for President Kumaratunga to adopt a new strategy with a dual track of war and peace. Indeed, the government called this approach as "war for peace". It combined a large-scale and high-intensity military assault on the LTTE and a political appeal to the Tamil people that the government was willing and ready to constitutionalize an extensive autonomy package with or without the LTTE's participation. The military plank of the strategy initially appeared to succeed when the government's armed forces captured in December 1995 the Jaffna peninsula, which had functioned as the LTTE's military and political headquarters. Without resistance, in the face of a massive military offensive by the government, the LTTE retreated to the jungles in the Vanni region, located south of the Jaffna peninsula. However, in the protracted war, the LTTE managed to survive and proved its resilience by returning an offensive with greater strength. By 2000–01, the LTTE could say with confidence that they had restored the military balance of power through a series of successes in the battlefront. The PA government failed on the constitutional reform front as well. Its 1995 devolution proposals and the draft Constitution of 2000 were abandoned because of the lack of cooperation by the main opposition party, the United National Party (UNP).

Events that followed the PA government's strategy of war for peace in 1996–2000 demonstrated three important dynamics in Sri Lanka's conflict. The first is that even a partially unilateral initiative by the government for political reform, with the cooperation of non-LTTE Tamil parties but without the participation of the LTTE, the second principal party to the civil war, had little or no chance to succeed as long as the LTTE remained an efficient military force capable of engaging the state in a long-drawn out war. The second is that a militarily weakened LTTE was unlikely to return to the negotiation table from a position of weakness in order to sign a peace agreement. If at all, the LTTE's tendency has been to return to the negotiation table under conditions of military setbacks, not to negotiate a peace deal, but to re-consolidate itself militarily. The third is that a government could conduct a war, even a costly war, against the LTTE without the support of other political parties, but no government could successfully pursue a political solution through either negotiations or constitutional reform single-handedly, without the support of the opposition political parties. In the absence of such broad support among all the major parliamentary parties, no state reform measure or a peace initiative could succeed.

REFORM-WEARINESS AND ITS CONSEQUENCES

To what extent could an unsuccessful peace process sustain the argument for negotiated peace and regional autonomy in a context when the protagonists to the conflict fail to work out joint settlements to end the conflict? Do such setbacks make the polity reform-weary? Is the tendency for reform negation, like a counter-revolution, an outcome of the polity's reform weariness? Questions of this sort surfaced in Sri Lanka's conflict trajectory in 2003 when failed negotiations and failed state reform initiatives seemed to have re-activated the dynamics of reform negation and relapsing to war.[7] The background to this transition to reform-negation was the abrupt end to the negotiations started in 2002 between the United National Front (UNF) government and the LTTE. The story of this episode very briefly is as follows. The UNF government, which came into office in December 2001, signed a ceasefire agreement with the LTTE in February 2002 as a prelude to direct negotiations. Negotiations began in September 2002 with the Royal Norwegian government providing facilitation. Leading international actors — particularly the U.S., the European Union, Japan, the World Bank, and the Asian Development Bank — backed this negotiation initiative. This was the most "internationalized" of all the peace attempts made in Sri Lanka to end the civil war. The government and the LTTE agreed in their Oslo talks in December 2002 to "explore" a federal solution to the conflict. However, negotiations came to a standstill in March–April 2003 when the LTTE decided to suspend their participation in talks, citing as the reason the non-fulfilment of the commitments made by the UNF government during the negotiations. When the negotiations remained suspended, violations of the ceasefire agreement, particularly by the LTTE, began to rise, eventually creating a condition of "undeclared" and low intensity war between the government's security forces and the LTTE's military cadres.

Two developments that occurred during this period placed the debate on the political solution to the ethnic conflict through regional autonomy in a new context. The first was the willingness demonstrated by the UNF government to move towards a federal framework as the basis of a negotiated ending of the war with the LTTE. The Oslo Communiqué of December 2002 encapsulated a new movement by the government as well as the LTTE towards what appeared at the time as a path-breaking compromise. The Oslo Communiqué stated that "the parties agreed to explore a solution" that was to be "based on a federal structure within a united Sri Lanka" (cited in Uyangoda and Perera 2003, p. 180). The second was the LTTE's own proposals for an Interim Self-Governing Authority (ISGA), submitted to the government in October 2003. The LTTE had developed these proposals within a conceptual framework which could be described as a form of unconventional federalism. The ISGA as envisioned by the LTTE went far beyond what the Sri Lankan government was ready to consider even for a "final" settlement.[8] The crucial point that emerged in this context with regard to the problem of regional autonomy in Sri Lanka was that a vast gulf continued to exist between the Sri Lankan government and the LTTE on the nature, extent and the depth of the actual autonomy framework that should constitute an interim or a final peace settlement. Against that backdrop, the LTTE's proposals went far beyond what the UNF government, which had a federalist idea for a final settlement agreement, could even consider as regional autonomy. It was not surprising at all for this process to reach a deadlock, without producing any interim arrangement in any form. However, the political consequences of the failure of this attempt towards an "interim solution" were far reaching. They marked the beginning of the end of Sri Lanka's regional autonomy debate in federalist terms.

How did the above developments lead to the emergence of an argument against pro-autonomy reforms? The new political context of state reform negation emerged to a considerable degree in response to the government's "federalist" commitment in December 2002 and the LTTE's ISGA proposals in October 2003. The terms of the new argument contra state reform were also shaped by the Sinhalese nationalist fear that the LTTE was implementing a hidden agenda of secession through a federalist deal with the UNF government and with the overt and covert "backing" of the "Western" powers. The fact that the LTTE had by this time remained militarily strong — in the LTTE's own words, this was a period of "military balance of power" between the two sides — also contributed to the Sinhalese nationalist fear of any federalist deal which critics saw as a form of "creeping separatism". Neither the Ceasefire Agreement of February 2002, nor the five rounds of negotiations had provided for de-militarization or surrender of weapons by the LTTE. It became quite clear that the LTTE was seeking regional autonomy while maintaining its weapons and guerrilla units. The LTTE's ISGA proposals that sought interim power even beyond a conventional federalist solution added greater salience to these apprehensions. The main opposition party, the SLFP, described the ISGA proposals as laying down the "legal foundation for a future, separate, sovereign state" by the LTTE.

The real highpoint of the new tendency towards state reform negation was the collapse of the agreement signed by the new United People's Freedom Alliance (UPFA) government and the LTTE for a joint administrative mechanism with regard to post-Tsunami reconstruction work. The Memorandum of Understanding (MoU) signed by the UPFA government and the LTTE envisaged the setting up of an "integrated operational management structure" for the purpose of "planning, implementing and coordinating post-tsunami work". This was called Post-Tsunami Operational and Management Structure (P-TOMS). On paper, the P-TOMS agreement was not a terribly radical one. It was to operate for an initial period of one year, subjected to extension through consensus. The proposed administrative mechanism was to cover only a limited geographical area of two kilometres landwards from the sea in the six districts in the Northern and Eastern provinces.

The MoU for the P-TOMs was signed on 24 June 2005. A few days later, the JVP, which had been leading the Sinhalese nationalist resistance to any peace deal with the LTTE, challenged it before the Supreme Court through a fundamental rights application. The Supreme Court judgment was delivered on 15 July 2005. The Court struck down three of the MoU's minor features. The first was about the location in the LTTE-held Kilinochchi of the office of the proposed Regional Committee to cover six tsunami-hit districts in the Northern and Eastern provinces. The Court suggested re-locating the office outside Kilinochchi in order to ensure free access to it for all affected citizens. The second concerned the powers of the proposed Regional Committee. The Supreme Court determined that certain government functions should not be delegated or transferred to the Regional Committee. Thirdly, the Court decided that all funds, foreign and local, deposited in the Regional Fund should be dealt through the government Treasury. On these three counts, the Supreme Court granted the petitioners an interim stay order of the MoU, advised the government to alter the relevant clauses as instructed in the determination and come back to the Courts on 12 September 2005 for a final determination. When the case was taken up on that day, it was postponed. Meanwhile, the country's political agenda changed totally with the impending Presidential Election in November that year. Without judicial sanction and political support, the agreement for the P-TOMs became effectively null and void. The Supreme Court's decision also reflected the extent to which the state institutions, including the higher judiciary, reflected the re-emergence of the argument for preserving the unitary character of the Sri Lankan state, a stance, spearheaded by the JVP and JHU. The collapse of the P-TOMs also marked the failure of Sri Lanka to seize the humanitarian disaster caused by the tsunami as an opportunity to advance the peace process.

AUTONOMY IN CIVIL WAR?

Sri Lanka's ethnic civil war began earnestly in mid-1983 in the aftermath of the anti-Tamil riots in July that year. During the first phase of the war, there was no political space within Sri Lanka to propose an effective alternative to war. Only human rights and civil society organizations were making the argument that the ethnic conflict needed a political solution based on regional autonomy to the Tamil minority. However, it was an outside actor, the Indian government, which took the idea of political solution through regional autonomy as a serious policy option. The Indian government had been a partial sponsor of the Tamil ethnic insurgency. While playing that role, the Indian government had also begun, as early as 1984, to engage with the Sri Lankan government and the Tamil nationalist groups in search for a constitutional solution. The reason for the Indian government's giving priority to a negotiated constitutional solution has been extensively debated by scholars (Muni 1993; Ganguly 1998; Krishna 1998; Sahdevan and de Votta 2006). One simple reason perhaps was the realization shared by the Indian political and bureaucratic establishments that political instability in the neighbourhood, that had opened up the space for extra-regional powers (particularly the U.S. and Israel) to intervene, was not conducive for India's own security and political interests. Through this engagement, the Indian policy-makers introduced to Sri Lanka's political debate the concept of "devolution" as opposed to decentralization. Until this change, the Sinhalese political class knew only about administrative decentralization. The devolving of state power was quite new to their political world view.

India's early efforts led to the first round of direct talks between the representatives of the Sri Lankan government and the Tamil nationalist groups. The talks were held in August 1984 in Thimpu, the capital city of Bhutan, The Thimpu talks, though failed to produce a tangible political outcome, were important in the development of the Tamil nationalist conceptualization of a political solution to the ethnic conflict. The so-called Thimpu Principles, put forward by the Tamil insurgent groups organized under a common banner, contained what the Tamil nationalists considered at the time as the "four cardinal principles" on which an acceptable political solution should be based. They were (i) recognition of the Tamils as a distinct nationality in Sri Lanka, (ii) recognition of a Tamil homeland, (iii) recognition of the right of the Tamil people for self-determination, and (iv) recognition of the right to full citizenship of all Tamils living in the island (Loganathan 1996, pp. 104–5).

What did these Thimpu principles mean in concrete terms in relation to the regional autonomy debate? It has had minimalist and maximalist interpretations. The provincial council system, introduced in 1987 through the intervention of the Indian government, was a minimalist, albeit pragmatic, construction of the first three Thimpu principles. The Indo-Lanka accord "acknowledged" that Sri Lanka was a "multi-ethnic and multi-lingual plural society" and "recognized" that each ethnic group — Sinhalese, Tamils, Muslims and Burghers — had a "distinct cultural and linguistic identity." Quite crucially, the Accord also "recognized" that the Northern and Eastern provinces of the island had been "areas of historical habitation of Sri Lankan Tamil speaking peoples." The maximalist interpretation of the Thimpu principles has had two constructions: separation, and falling short of separation, power-sharing in a confederal framework.

NEGOTIATING REGIONAL AUTONOMY WITH THE LTTE?

What options could governments with limited visions for autonomy pursue in negotiating a political solution with the LTTE which was committed to secession and maintaining a regime of unrecognized regional autonomy? This was a major problem surfaced in Sri Lanka's autonomy debate during the civil war. The LTTE's conceptualization of regional autonomy went far beyond the normal understanding of federalism. It approximated on the confederal model of autonomy. Often the LTTE had been thinking and acting like a regional or sub-state in Sri Lanka, to the great annoyance of governments. In protocol arrangements during negotiations with the Sri Lankan government, the LTTE had also demanded "parity of status" with the Sri Lankan state. This claim was largely based on the LTTE's self-representation as the ruling class of the emerging state of the Sri Lankan Tamil "nation". This divergence of approach was a fundamental issue that had spread to the way in which various Sri Lankan governments and the LTTE conceptualized regional autonomy. One major occasion when this potentially unbridgeable gulf in conceptualizations was demonstrated was in June–October, 2003 when the UNF government and the LTTE traded their positions on an interim administration for the North and East. The following discussion sets out briefly the developments around the debate on an interim administration which indicated, quite clearly, the way in which the LTTE constructed its vision of power-sharing.

On 17 May 2003, the UNF government, in response to the LTTE's request, produced a set of proposals for an interim administration. The LTTE, dissatisfied with the limited scope of powers, authority and competence envisaged in these proposals, asked the UNF government to formulate a fresh set of proposals. When the new proposals were announced in the last week of May 2003 there was only a marginal improvement in the autonomy frameworks already contained in the UNF government's previous proposals. The LTTE's main grievance against the two sets of proposals of the UNF government for an interim administrative set up was that they ignored what the LTTE perceived as the "stark reality" of a "de-facto administration" run by the LTTE "of its own in vast tracts of territories under its control in the Northeast" (Balasingham 2004, p. 453). Eventually, the LTTE volunteered to prepare its own proposals for an interim administration. After consulting the Tamil diaspora constituencies, the LTTE on 3 October 2003 submitted to the government a set of proposals for an Interim Self-Governing Authority (ISGA).

One key feature of the LTTE's ISGA proposals was that they contained provisions envisaging an extreme measure of regional autonomy. Some of the proposals were within the existing constitution while some others had been conceptualized outside the Sri Lankan constitution. For example, the ISGA proposals stipulated that the interim body would have "plenary powers" for the governance of the two provinces, including "all powers and functions in relation to regional administration exercised by the GOSL [Government of Sri Lanka] in and for the Northeast." It also proposed the establishment of "separate institutions for the administration of justice." The ISGA was to have "powers to borrow internally and externally" and to engage in internal and external trade. In claiming the right to control the access to the sea, the LTTE's proposals suggested that the ISGA should have "control over the marine and offshore resources of the adjacent seas and the power to regulate the access" to the sea (Balasingham 2004, pp. 503–14). It also appeared that the LTTE expected the new interim mechanism to reflect the existence of what it called the "de facto administration" it maintained and eventually formalize it. During this period, the LTTE was quite keen to make the point that it was not just a non-state entity or an armed group, but a "liberation organization" maintaining a "de facto civil administration" to manage a civilian population. Thus, the LTTE's vision of an interim body was to create a structure that would be more than a mere administrative entity. It was to be an entity for self-governance which would be independent of parliamentary control, the control of the central government and not subjected to the framework of the existing Constitution. In short, the ISGA was a proposal for regional statehood. It went beyond the understanding of regional autonomy shared by all other political actors in Sri Lanka.

Looking at this controversy surrounding the issue of interim administration from the perspective of regional autonomy as a solution to the ethnic conflict, a few significant points can be observed. First, the gulf between the minimalist and maximalist positions concerning even an interim autonomy framework held respectively by the Sinhalese ruling parties and the LTTE was extremely wide. Secondly, the UNF government, which acknowledged the idea of an interim solution, was also careful to conceive it well within the legal framework of the existing constitution. In contrast, the LTTE held the view that even an interim framework should go beyond the limits of Sri Lanka's existing constitution. Thirdly, the LTTE believed that for an interim administrative structure to be meaningful, it should have the political features of extensive regional autonomy, approximating on a confederal framework. Fourthly, the position concerning regional autonomy that the LTTE thought would provide a basis for negotiations proved to be far beyond the framework that the Sinhalese political establishment could even acknowledge. It was not a position to promote a negotiated settlement to the conflict.

This backdrop, then, leads to the following two questions: Was the LTTE prepared to negotiate a solution based on regional autonomy? Could a negotiated regional autonomy constitute a viable basis for a political solution? The answer suggested in the discussion above is not a direct "Yes" or "No". Regional autonomy has been an intensely contested idea in Sri Lanka before and during the civil war. While Tamil nationalists campaigned for a maximalist interpretation of regional autonomy even including separation, the governments have stayed within a framework of minimalist federalism. These were incompatible constructions of autonomy. No common ground could be worked out between the two extremes.

AUTONOMY AFTER CIVIL WAR?

When the civil war came to an end in May 2009 with the military defeat of the LTTE, there were expectations that the Sri Lankan government would proceed in the direction of constitutionalizing a political solution to the ethnic conflict. The government had earlier given indications that it was committed to a political solution after the war ended. In fact, the government's position appeared credible in a context where a strong argument had appeared to claim that the LTTE was the main obstacle to a political solution to the conflict. This was the position shared by external actors, particularly India, the U.S., Japan and the EU countries, who were engaged in Sri Lanka's peace process. Well-wishers of Sri Lanka's post-civil war political reforms also expected Sri Lanka's president to take steps to implement a new regional autonomy package incorporating elements to expand the pre-existing framework of devolution. Subsequent events have belied all these political expectations. Years after the end of the war, the government has not taken any concrete step in the direction of institutionalizing a political solution to the conflict. The framework of autonomy continues to remain within the old framework of provincial councils, with no improvements to it.

The reluctance of the Sri Lankan government to return to the path of political solution to the ethnic conflict raises a fundamental question about post-civil war political process in Sri Lanka: is post-civil war peace building possible without political reconstruction of the state in order to address political grievances of ethnic minorities? Sri Lanka's government seems to believe so. The present approach to post-civil war peace-building of the government appears to rest on four key positions. They are: (i) the Sri Lankan state has successfully defeated LTTE terrorism by military means and the state has the will and capacity to thwart the resurgence of any insurgent threat to the state; (ii) the Tamil rebellion was a terrorist threat to the state and there was no "political problem" as such for the government to address politically, (iii) granting regional autonomy to ethnic minorities will endanger the national unity, sovereignty and the territorial integrity of the state in Sri Lanka; and (iv) minorities do have genuine grievances, but they are due to economic underdevelopment of their regions and the devastation brought out by the protracted war. Rapid economic and infrastructure development in the war-torn areas is considered the most effective strategy to address minority grievances and lay a stronger foundation to integrate the minorities with the nation. Seen from this perspective, economic integration should constitute the basis of post-civil war nation-building.

This de-emphasis on, and rejection of, regional autonomy as the basis of a political solution to the ethnic conflict is also linked to the new political context in which minority rights issues are being re-defined in Sri Lanka. The theme of autonomy was at the centre of the political debate when there was an active armed insurgency for minority secession. Though the war has now ended, the conflict remains; yet the political balance of power between the state and the ethnic minorities has been drastically altered. In the new political equilibrium, the discourse of power-sharing and autonomy has been replaced by a discourse of greater centralization of state power.

CONCLUSION

To return to the questions posed at the beginning of this chapter, the discussion in the chapter developed suggests the following: Autonomy offers are necessary to mitigate an ethnic conflict, but may not necessarily be adequate as incentives to persuade the rebels from advancing the secessionist war if the proposed autonomy fails to offer an extensive measure of self-rule. Moreover, as the Sri Lankan experience shows, incomplete and half-hearted autonomy offers ran the risk of further legitimizing the separatist project of the minority community. At the same time, the secessionist armed struggle was not the most effective strategic asset available to the minority community to negotiate regional autonomy. Paradoxically, it created doubts at the level of the government and among other ethnic communities that extensive regional autonomy would lead to early secession. In fact, the relative success of the LTTE's war against the state itself became an impediment to achieving autonomy goals of the Tamil community. This is the major dilemma emerged in Sri Lanka in relation to the LTTE's strategic position of negotiating confederal autonomy from a position of military balance of power. The government too was confronted with a similar dilemma in a context of the protracted civil war with a series of failed peace attempts and inconclusive peace negotiations. The temptation on the part of the government leadership has been either try to impose a political settlement by military means ("war for peace" in 1996–2000) or exclude the LTTE from pragmatic peace deals arranged with other Tamil stakeholders.

To move on to the other set of questions I posed in addressing the autonomy-separation problematic, the discussion in this chapter suggests the following: The ethnic conflict strengthened Sri Lankan state's tendency towards greater centralization and weak pluralization, with the possibility of periodic re-communalization of the state and its institutions. The protracted civil war also made the Sri Lankan state unreformable. It became unreformable in two ways. First, the Sinhalese political establishment's commitment to state reform for regional autonomy has been weak and unsustainable. Second, the Tamil armed struggle for separation was not concerned with reforming the Sri Lankan state, but seceding from it. As a result, the Tamil struggle did not provide a positive impetus as such for state reform in Sinhalese society, but largely, an impetus for reform resistance. That explains why the pressure for state reform came from outside, from India as in the mid-1980s and from the Western powers subsequently. In this rather unenviable context, the possibilities for a solution to the ethnic conflict, based on regional autonomy, are not in the realm of possibilities even after the end of the civil war. A unilateral military victory for the state has failed to provide any political incentives for state reform. While the protracted civil war prevented autonomy, the absence of war has produced new dynamics to negate the relevance of autonomy.

Notes

1. Junius (J.R.) Jayewardene was Sri Lanka's President from 1978 to 1988. The ethnic civil war began during his tenure in office. He is largely blamed for mismanaging the ethnic conflict and pushing it towards violence and war. It is also Jayewardene who paradoxically took the initial steps in 1987 to settle the conflict by political and constitutional means.
2. The UNP and SLFP are Sri Lanka's two main political parties. The UNP was formed in 1947, one year before Sri Lanka's political independence, and the SLFP in 1952. These have also been the country's two main ruling parties, alternating power in cycles of roughly ten years.
3. The JVP is a radical Sinhalese nationalist movement that staged two armed insurgencies, one in 1971 and the other in 1988–89 to capture state power. In the mid-1990s, it became a parliamentary party with just one MP. At the parliamentary elections of April 2004, the JVP managed to get thirty-nine of its members elected to parliament, thereby becoming the third largest single political party in Sri Lanka's parliament. Projecting a militant Sinhalese-nationalist agenda, the JVP has been in the forefront of the campaigns to resist any negotiations with the LTTE, to undermine any extensive regional autonomy for minorities and to oppose any scaling down of the war against the LTTE.
4. In Sri Lanka, Parliamentary Select Committees are usually appointed to produce policy options to complex and controversial public issues, based on maximum consensus among diverse political perspectives. The Mangala Moonesinghe Select Committee's mandate was to produce a framework of a solution to the ethnic conflict based on a broadest possible consensus among political parties and ethnic groups. Moonesinghe was an opposition MP who commanded the respect of the minority parties.
5. One of the unstated, yet overriding concerns among the Muslim political parties about Tamil regional autonomy in the Northern and Eastern provinces was the fear of the Muslim community being reduced to the status of a disempowered regional minority under the Tamils. This in a way illustrates one of the key weaknesses in the conventional federal model in an ethnically plural polity where there are regional ethnic minorities as well. The conventional federalism

through territorial autonomy empowers a national minority to become a regional majority, by becoming a regional ruling entity. But it does not address the concerns and fears of regional minorities like the Muslims and the Sinhalese in Sri Lanka's Northern and Eastern provinces. The Muslim demand for a separate regional unit of autonomy encapsulates this dilemma of conventional federalism.

6   The PA government came into power in 1994 and continued in office till late 2001. The Alliance was led by the SLFP. It had six junior partners. Headed by President Chandrika Kumaratunga, the PA regime promised negotiated peace and constitutional reform, but eventually failed to deliver its key promises.

7   Resistance to state reform on the basis of ethnic pluralism and equality has been a recurrent tendency in Sri Lanka's post-colonial politics. I have developed this thesis of "reform resistance" in Uyangoda (1999).

8   The debate and events surrounding the LTTE's ISGA proposals will be further elaborated later in this chapter.

References

Bachler, Gunter. "Conflict Transformation through State Reform". In *Transforming Ethnopolitical Conflict*, edited by Alex Austin, Martina Fischer, and Norbert Ropers. *The Berghof Handbook* (2004): 273–94.

Balasingham, Anton. *War and Peace in Sri Lanka: Armed Struggle and Peace Efforts of Liberation Tigers*. Mitcham, England: Fairmax Publishing Ltd., 2004.

Edrisinha, Rohan. "A Critical Overview: Constitutionalism, Conflict Resolution, and the Limits of the Draft Constitution". In *The Draft Constitution of Sri Lanka: Critical Aspects*, edited by D. Panditaratne and P. Ratnam. Colombo: Law and Society Trust, 1998.

Ganguly, Rajat. *Kin State Intervention in Ethnic Conflicts: Lessons from South Asia*. New Delhi and London: SAGE, 1998.

Krishna, Sankaran. *Postcolonial Insecurities: India, Sri Lanka and the Question of Nationhood*. Minneapolis: University of Minnesota Press, 1999.

Loganathan, Keteshwaran. *Sri Lanka, Lost Opportunities: Past Attempts at Resolving Ethnic Conflict*. Colombo: University of Colombo, 1996.

Muni, S.D. *Pangs of Proximity: India and Sri Lanka's Ethnic Crisis*. New Delhi: SAGE, 1993.

Peiris, G.L. "Towards Effective Devolution". In *Sri Lanka: The Devolution Debate*. Colombo: International Center for Ethnic Studies, 1996.

Sahadevan, P. and N. deVotta, eds. *Politics of Conflict and Peace in Sri Lanka*. New Delhi: MANAK Publications Ltd., 2006.

Steadman, S.J. *Peacemaking in Civil War: International Mediation in Zimbabwe, 1974–1980*. Boulder and London: Lynne Rienner Publishers, 1991.

Tiruchelvam, N. "The Politics of Federalism and Diversity in Sri Lanka". In *Autonomy and Ethnicity: Negotiating Competing Claims in Multi-ethnic Societies*, edited by Yash Ghai. Cambridge: Cambridge University Press, 2000.

Uyangoda, J. "A State of Desire? Some Reflections on the Unreformablity of Sri Lanka's Post-colonial State". In *Sri Lanka at Cross Roads*, edited by Marucs Meyer and Siri Hettige. Colombo: University of Colombo, 1999.

———. *Ethnic Conflict in Sri Lanka: Changing Dynamics*. Policy Studies 32. Washington, D.C.: East-West Center, 2007.

Uyangoda, J. and M. Perera, eds. *Sri Lanka's Peace Process 2002: Critical Perspectives*. Colombo: Social Scientists' Association, 2003.

Wilson, A.J. *The Break-up of Sri Lanka: The Sinhalese-Tamil Conflict*. Honolulu: University of Hawaii Press, 1988.

9

UNITARIANISM, SEPARATISM AND FEDERALISM: COMPETING GOALS AND PROBLEMS OF COMPROMISE IN SRI LANKA

P. Sahadevan

Negotiating peace in an armed separatist conflict centres on finding an autonomy solution under which ethnic contestants are granted wide-ranging powers to control their affairs within an ethnically defined region (Lapidoth 1996; Ghai 2000). For both the state and the separatists, such a solution denotes compromise on their extreme positions. Realizing the futility of using violence in pursuit of their ethnic goals they participate as stakeholders in autonomy talks — an indication of change in their perception, attitudes and goals. Yet the road to peace tends to be bumpy and tortuous. Difficulties arise not only in initiating a peace process but also making it a success. In reaching a peace accord, both contestants work towards overcoming their structural constraints so that their decision to compromise on their original goals is acceptable to their constituencies. Concluding an ethnic peace accord does not guarantee resolution of conflict. It is possible that a peace process breaks down even while a negotiated political settlement is implemented, leading to the resumption of violence aimed at achieving the original goals of the warring parties. This marks the beginning of a new cycle in the conflict process (Sahadevan 2006).

This latter phenomenon typified Sri Lanka's secessionist conflict involving the Sri Lankan Tamil minority and the Sinhalese dominated Sri Lankan state. It began in 1956 when Sinhalese Buddhist nationalism triumphed and consequently a sense of alienation among the minorities grew due to the electoral interest-driven chauvinistic policies of the Sri Lanka Freedom Party (SLFP)-led government of S.W.R.D. Bandaranaike. Since then, the dynamics have changed to make the conflict in Sri Lanka one of the most protracted in South Asia. Importantly, the history of peace-overtures is as old as the conflict. However, permanent peace remains elusive despite the military success in May 2009 of the government against the Liberation Tigers of Tamil Eelam (LTTE). The Sri Lankan civil war involved two protagonists who had shown great resoluteness in employing violence in pursuit of their goals and, at the same time, displayed stiff resistance to a negotiated solution. The protracted nature of the conflict has produced three distinct forces with strong competing ethnic interests; they are the unitarianists, the separatists and the federalists. The unitarianists are those Sinhalese nationalists who are committed to the principle of the centralized unitary state system; separatists who represent Sri Lankan Tamil nationalism advocate an Eelam (Tamil name for envisaged state in north-east Sri Lanka); federalists are those who, cutting across the country's ethnic divide, firmly believe in a compromise solution based on autonomy and power-sharing. While centralization, in a historical sense, has created the separatists, the extreme positions and uncompromising attitude of both the unitarianists and separatists alike in the wake of death and destruction, has paved the way for the emergence of federalists as a potential force for moderation. The pattern and nature of relations between all three groups are determined by their mutually competing goals. Though the unitarianists and the separatists consider themselves as ethnic enemies, they share in common an opposition to the federalists who advocate an autonomy solution. Thus, while the ethnic enemies seek to annihilate each other, they jointly seek to destroy their common adversary, the federalists.

The competing goals in Sri Lanka's ethnic conflict raise some questions that this chapter seeks to address. What are the ideological bases of these competing forces and how are they sustained to deny lasting peace and frustrate conflict resolution efforts? What are the problems in reaching a compromise solution among all the competing forces? I argue that an entrenched ethnic ideological position influencing the goals and behavior of the unitarianists and the separatists tends to attain greater salience if it is backed by their relative capabilities defined in terms of their power to exert political and military pressure. The assumption is that the greater the ideological entrenchment in unitarianism or separatism in a deeply ethnicized polity like Sri Lanka, the stronger is its resistance to any political compromise. Three critical factors that emerge for discussion from this hypothesis are ideology, power and politics. Compromise requires moderation in the ideological positions of the competitors, changes to their power bases and capabilities and, finally, ending of the politics of ethnic outbidding.

CHARACTERISTICS OF POLITY AND SOCIETY

The ideological positions, programmes and popularity of the competing ethnic forces are located in the structure of Sri Lanka's polity and society. In Sri Lanka's lopsided multiethnic structure, the Sinhalese are the permanent national majority and others (Sri Lankan Tamils, Muslims, Indian Tamils, Malays and Burghers) are permanent minorities. The combined strength of all Sri Lanka's minorities is about one-fourth of the total population. However, the Sinhalese majority is a regional minority in the north and the east where Sri Lankan Tamils constitute an assertive regional majority. Caught in between the Sinhalese-Sri Lankan Tamil conflict are the Sri Lankan Muslims, who are concentrated in the east and are seen as a buffer minority. The Sri Lankan Muslims are directly affected by ethnic violence and also influenced by the ethnic goals and aspirations of both major conflicting parties. Their own demand for the creation of a Muslim province in the east poses a challenge to the Sri Lankan Tamils' comprehensive ethnic agenda, such as their claim to the northern and eastern provinces as their "traditional homeland". This crosscutting of goals has structured the ethnic conflict into a triangular contest involving all three ethnic groups. However, the Indian Tamils remain at the periphery in the sense that though they are affected by the conflict, they do not articulate their own ethnic goals. Thus, ethnic rivalry involves two sets of groups operating at two levels. In one set, at the national level, the Sinhalese majority are pitted against a regional majority, the Sri Lankan Tamils, who otherwise constitute a national minority. The second set, at the regional level, involves a contest between the regional majority of Sri Lankan Tamils and a regional minority of Sri Lankan Muslims. The status of majority or minority has a distinct geographical context. While both these contests are intertwined and as such influence each other's outcome, cumulatively they determine the prospects of peace. In fact, the triangular nature of ethnic competition and intransigent ethnic positions of the parties have made lasting conflict resolution in Sri Lanka a daunting task.

Sri Lanka's ethnic divisions have had a spatial dimension to them, as seen in the readily made distinction between the southern (Sinhalese dominated) and northern (Sri Lankan Tamil concentrated) polities. The Sri Lankan

Tamil dominated northern polity constitutes the strongest single challenge to the south's attempt to maintain its majoritarian national ideology and enjoy the power that is concentrated in the Sinhalese community. Finding that ideology and power are inextricably linked, the northern forces see in the weakening of one, the decline of the other. Like in the south, ethnicity in the north remains the single most important source of electoral mobilization. Electoral issues centre around the ethnic interests of groups and the forces contesting for power primarily belong to the same polity. Importantly, while the northern forces, by and large, keep their activities confined to their polity, their counterparts from the south always seek to expand their operational domain to cover the north by contesting elections sometimes in alliance with the northern parties.

Structural cleavages along ethnic lines have had an abiding impact on interethnic relations. In an atmosphere of sharp ethnic schisms and heightened ethnic consciousness, the competition for power between the unrelenting Sinhalese and Sri Lankan Tamil ethnonationalist forces has become endemic. In perception as well as in behavior, both forces consider themselves as ethnic enemies within the same contested state structure. The enemy image, buttressed by their fear of extinction as ethnic groups, has prompted a strategy of being unrelenting towards each other; the aim is to emerge as survivors, victorious in what is perceived as a zero-sum game. It is in this context that the competing goals — unitarianism versus separatism — of both the Sinhalese and Tamil nationalists and their total opposition to a federal autonomy solution should be analyzed.

UNITARIANISTS

Centralization as a national goal of the Sinhalese majority is propounded and fostered by all political factions in the southern polity. In so far as differences between them exist, this is merely in terms of style and strategies for articulating their sensitivity to the concerns and interests of the ethnic minorities. Mainstream moderate parties such as the United National Party (UNP), the SLFP and scores of leftists have openly adopted hard-line positions on issues of power-sharing, state reform and minority rights while presenting a pro-peace image to the world. Both the UNP and SLFP have blatantly used ethnicity to advance their electoral prospects and to ensure regime survival at the cost of ethnic peace and development. It was the SLFP leadership that launched, in 1956, the dangerous politics of majority appeasement which the UNP leaders have simply adopted. The competitive manner in which both the rival party leaders have taken up the Sinhalese cause by pursuing flagrantly anti-minority and pro-majority policies signaled the breakdown of normal politics (Zartman 1995, p. 5), characterized by the government's inability or unwillingness to redress grievances of the minority and the institutionalization of violence. Almost all political formations in Sri Lanka are forced to accept the framework of ethnic politics and, in the process, even those belonging to the left have made compromises in their socialist ideology to become chauvinists. Their compulsion to join the bandwagon in support of lopsided and undemocratic ethnic policies of both the UNP and SLFP governments has mainly arisen from a fear of electoral extinction in the south.

On the issue of centralized unitary state power as desired by Sinhalese nationalism, there discreetly exists a unanimous view amongst Sri Lanka's ruling elite, irrespective of their political and ideological differences. Leftists, rightists and centrists think alike in favour of maintaining the status quo of the state structure, rejecting the demands by ethnic minorities for comprehensive reform. Although British colonialism laid the juridical foundation for the centralized state project (Moore 1990), it was post-colonial elites representing both the UNP and SLFP who built the super structure to placate the Sinhalese Buddhist nationalists. Both rival parties, therefore, share the credit for creating an ethnic partisan, exclusive and majoritarian state sanctified by three constitutions (1948, 1972 and 1978) that have effectively ensured concentration of powers at the centre while denying their dispersal to the local units. Grounded in a primordial ethnic historical narrative of myths and legends embodied in the *Mahavamsa* (Great Chronicle), the centralized state project has a strong ethnic nationalist goal of creating an exclusive Sri Lankan society wherein the Sinhalese identity is totalized as one that embraces all people who speak the Sinhalese language and practice Buddhism whilst completely ignoring those with minority identities (Pfaffenberger 1994, p. 21). In the hard-line Sinhalese nationalists' view, sharing power with ethnic minorities amounts to compromising the historical integrity of Sinhalese Buddhist civilization by passing the legacy over power to aliens with no legitimate claims to the island.

Thus, there is an intimate link between the unitary political system, historicity and perception of the Sinhalese and the political construction of their ethnic nationalism. If the mythical history has formed an influential factor in creating a sense of insecurity and fear in the minds of many Sinhalese, it has also cemented their desire for cultural superiority and perpetual political hegemony. The unfounded fear of ethnic extinction is articulated as a political justification for the majority's demand for power to be concentrated at the centre within a unitary state framework. A centralized power structure is considered to be an essential source of security and a unitary system is an offensive political weapon to deter threats from minorities and preserve the island's status as a seat of Buddhist faith and civilization chosen by the Lord Buddha (DeVotta 2007, pp. 13–24).

In their defense of the entrenched unitary state system, the unitarianists have rejected a federal solution but some have shown a willingness to develop a system of limited decentralization. In other words, they have resisted any proposal that would prescribe broad autonomy to ethnic minorities in a different state structure, but are prepared to grant limited autonomy within the existing unitary system. The rationale for this approach is that if separatists are granted limited political and economic concessions within the existing state structure then they are more likely to be co-opted into it. More frequently, however, the unitarianists have sought to weaken the socioeconomic fabric of both the Sri Lankan Tamil and Muslim societies in the northern and eastern provinces to increase their dependency upon the contested Sri Lankan State. The calculated policy of selective ethnic suffering to which the minorities are subjected has the agenda of weaning ordinary civilians away from the separatists and increasing the state's territorial control and legitimacy. The war-generated internal displacement of people, curtailment of their normal economic activities as part of stringent national security measures, denial of democratic political benefits and privileges, and systematic neglect of their economic development are all methods employed by the Sri Lankan State to subjugate ethnic minorities. Consequently, successive governments have failed to adopt a coherent and sincere policy of wining hearts and minds of people in the northern and eastern provinces.

Finally, the unitarianists emphasized recapturing territories from the separatists and restoring political processes in "liberated" areas. The war therefore had the grand design of a territorial conquest to end the truncated territorial status of the state and consolidate the Sri Lankan unitary state's position as an unchallenged sovereign entity with complete monopoly over state power. The eastern province has always been the principal target of its policies, and its liberation in 2007 by Sri Lankan security forces enormously boosted the state's morale to completely destroy all traces of Tamil separatism in the north.

SEPARATISTS

Sri Lankan Tamil nationalism is strongly embedded in secessionism. Indeed, it is a reaction against Sinhalese nationalism and a countermeasure to what the latter has sought to advocate and achieve (Wilson 2000). The separatists had enjoyed varying levels of leadership representation and constituency support at different phases of their movement. At their inception in the mid-1970s, they were a conglomerate of moderate and militant formations operating in the northern polity, sharing the same goal of Tamil Eelam amidst inherent differences on the *modus operandi* of achieving it. At the forefront of the secessionist movement was the moderate Tamil United Liberation Front (TULF), which galvanized Sri Lankan Tamil society against the centralized state and kindled its passion for a separate Eelam (Thangarajah 2004). Set against the TULF were another half-dozen major militant organizations, which advocated sustained armed struggle as an alternative to the non-violent agitation launched by the TULF (Rajanayagam 1994, pp. 169–77). Of these, the LTTE had emerged by the 1980s as the most powerful militant organization with an unwavering commitment to Tamil nationalism and separatism (Swamy 1994). A turning point in the history of the Tamil Eelam movement occurred when the India-Sri Lanka peace accord of 1987 combined a strategy of coercion, persuasion and promises to convert almost all separatists, except the LTTE, into potential supporters of an autonomy solution. Yet while this externally induced split in the movement generated considerable confusion and divided Tamil society in the north, it cemented the LTTE's determination to fight militarily for its nationalist cause and to stake a claim as the sole legitimate representative of Sri Lankan Tamils.

The LTTE's emergence as a formidable separatist organization was facilitated by its successful mobilization of hardline Tamil nationalists. Yet while the LTTE leadership made a conscious decision to fight militarily for a separate state through voluntary recruitment (willing separatists), many of its "supporters" only backed the movement under compulsion (reluctant separatists). Through this and other practices, the LTTE acquired a ruthless character, which manifested into a systematic campaign of terror, not only against the Sri Lankan State, but also against other Sri Lankan Tamils (Sahadevan 1995; Bose 1994).

Ideologically, the LTTE justified their Eelam demand by refuting the claims of Sinhalese nationalists, with a view to legitimating their own nationalist cause in the eyes of the world. Rejecting their Sinhalese counterpart's hegemonic sons-of-soil theory, the Sri Lankan Tamil nationalists argued that as both ethnic groups are natives of Sri Lanka, they are therefore its co-owners. The LTTE was convinced of this interpretation and asserted the Sri Lankan Tamil identity to create a division of identities, as opposed to the overarching position and recognition given to the Sinhalese identity (Dissanayake 1995, p. 113). For Sri Lankan Tamil nationalists, numbers do not determine a community's political status. During the British colonial period (1796–1948) they considered themselves not as a minority, but as one of the two equal majority communities. In the post-colonial period they have changed their self-image from "a majority to a nationality", viewing themselves as a separate nation in a contested majoritarian state. Like their Sinhalese counterparts, they attach a skewed meaning to the terms multi-ethnicity and pluralism in the Sri Lankan context. The country, in their view, is multiethnic only to the extent that it accommodates two dominant nations representing the Sinhalese and the Sri Lankan Tamil communities. Thus, the identities of other ethnic groups are ignored or not recognized. Consequently, the conflict is seen in a bi-nation and bi-polar framework between two nationalities, in which other ethnic groups are nonentities or non-actors.

The separatists justify the Sri Lankan Tamil nation's desire for statehood in two ways. First, they consider their state-making project as an unfinished agenda of colonialism. In their view, the establishment of Tamil Eelam signifies restoration of their lost sovereignty, since the Sri Lankan Tamils dominate the northern and eastern provinces. This "Tamil traditional homeland" constituted an independent polity with Jaffna as its capital until it was annexed by the Portuguese in 1619. Second, they insist that as an "oppressed nation", the Sri Lankan Tamils enjoy an inalienable right of self-determination which they want to exercise via secession to save their nation from the destructive polices of the Sinhalese majority (Rajanayagam 1994, pp. 177–80). Thus, their sense of state-ness is deeply rooted in historical experience. Instead of making a generic interpretation of their right to self-determination so as to exclude separatism from their purview, the LTTE preferred to take an extremely rigid legal position buttressed by political arguments to drive home a point that the Tamil nation has already enjoyed sovereignty and all it requires is the international community's recognition (Ignatieff 2000, p. 8).

Clearly, the LTTE's thinking and activities were like a sub-national quasi-state (Uyangoda 2007, p. 40), seeking a parity of status with the Sri Lankan government at the negotiating table and a solution based on the principle of sovereign equality. It did not accept the terrorist tag affixed to it by many countries and considered itself to be a national liberation organization. By establishing shadow state administrative structures and institutions in the north and demanding an interim administrative system in October 2003, the LTTE sought to legalize its state-like functions as part of its agenda of state-making and consolidation. In this context war and peace talks constituted its prominent strategies. In fighting against the centralized Sinhalese-dominated Sri Lankan State, the LTTE had sought to create a Tamil state modeled on its adversary's. In its flawed national vision, the Tamil state was designed as Sri Lankan Tamil hegemonic, ethnic-exclusivist and centralized, in which minorities like the Muslims would be denied equal treatment. This demonstrates the typical majoritarian mindset of a minority seeking to subjugate other minority identities in the same way its own ethnic identity is marginalized by the majority Sinhalese.

If the greatest strength of the separatists has been their unwavering commitment to their nationalist cause then their biggest weakness has been their idealism. Though born as a realistic goal, Eelam has been lost in the 2009 military campaign against the LTTE, which saw the Sri Lankan State regain complete control over the northern and eastern provinces. Though the seeds of Sri Lankan Tamil discontent have not been entirely annihilated by the large-scale military offensive against them, Eelam has become a mere mirage for the foreseeable future. Like many militant nationalists, what little remains of the LTTE leadership have found it difficult to accept the bitter reality of its lost state-building project. Often, ethnic nationalist fantasies make seemingly rational conflict resolution choices absolutely irrational.

FEDERALISTS

In Sri Lanka, the entrenched ideological positions of ethnic groups and the prolonged use of violence in their defense have gradually created intermediary forces of moderation. Sri Lankan federalists are largely the byproduct of violent ethnic confrontation between the unitarianists and the separatists. However, as aspiring intermediaries who seek a meaningful compromise solution, the federalists are the weakest and most vulnerable actors in the conflict. They have been an easy target of the warring parties, who, opposing notions of compromise and reconciliation, have subjected them to death, injury, intimidation, arrest, detention without trial and hate campaigns. Yet, risking their lives, some proponents of a federal solution to the conflict have continued to articulate their views and champion the cause for a democratic, peaceful, pluralist and just Sri Lanka.

Cutting across Sri Lanka's ethnic divide, the federalists have emerged from across the entire political spectrum of Sri Lankan society. They thus constitute members of a multiethnic group who have nonetheless retained their individual identity as members of different ethnic groups. Regarding the Sri Lankan State as the principal source of the conflict they have advocated state reform as their major agenda. This central issue has generated inherent differences among them on the nature, extent and processes of reforming the state.

Sri Lanka's federalists lack cohesion and a common political platform. However, on the basis of their reform proposals to accommodate the minorities in a power-sharing arrangement, they could be loosely divided into three subgroups: confederalists, liberal federalists and quasi-federalists. Confederalists generally comprise hardcore Tamil nationalists who have expressed a willingness to renounce their larger Tamil Eelam goal in favour of a confederal arrangement. This idea was rejected by the LTTE leadership, but promoted by people who were often associated with the LTTE as advisors, campaigners or sympathizers in the Sri Lankan Tamil diasporic populations largely settled in the U.S., Canada, the United Kingdom and Australia. Perhaps, this constituted an unofficial peace policy of the separatist group while fighting for its declared goal. Sornarajah, a Sri Lankan Tamil academic based in Singapore, echoes such thinking: "The Tigers are for secession. They may agree to a confederation in which the aspirations of the Tamil people for pursuing their own cultural and political life can be achieved" (2006, pp. 264–65). In Sornarajah's scheme of confederation, one central government would be responsible for defense and finance, there would be a common foreign policy and all remaining powers would be vested in the confederal units. Interestingly, in December 1995, a confederal style framework document was submitted to President Kumaratunga and LTTE leader V. Prabhakaran. It was prepared by a British firm of solicitors (Bates, Wells and Braithwaite) on behalf of the Sri Lanka Peace Support Group which has as its members Tamil intellectuals and human rights activists from the international community (Edrisinha 2008, pp. 94–96). Later in December 2002, during negotiations with the Sri Lankan government in Oslo, the LTTE also expressed its readiness to explore a federal political solution based on the principle of internal self-determination without abandoning its Eelam goal. This suggests that the LTTE's chief negotiator, Anton Balasingham, who made this commitment, was at least willing to explore confederalism, even though he was subsequently forced to backtrack (Sahadevan 2006; Liyanage 2008). For the LTTE, confederation was an interim option but not a goal. A confederal arrangement would have partially satisfied the LTTE's demand for the Sri Lankan Tamils' right to self-determination and potentially evolved into a political system based on shared sovereignty (with the majority Sinhalese).

Unlike the confederalists who are primarily based outside Sri Lanka, the liberal federalists form part of Sri Lankan civil society and seek to change the political system from within. The liberal federalists tend to emphasize the "shared rule dimension of federalism, pluralism [and] individual rights" and the need to create a "new overarching rainbow nation vision for a new Sri Lanka" (Edrisinha 2008, p. 106). While criticizing the LTTE's conception of federal rule, which is basically confederal and majoritarian in nature, they equally reject Sinhalese nationalist constructions of majoritarianism and unitary statehood. For liberal nationalists, a logical compromise should be based on the notion of shared-rule and not self-rule via the devolution of substantive powers (Edrisinha and Welikala 2008, p. 308). Because their campaign for state reform along federal lines is seen by the unitarianists as corresponding closely with Sri Lankan Tamil nationalist aspirations, the liberal federalists are often portrayed as being national traitors and supporters of terrorism.

The third category of quasi-federalists comprises moderate Tamil politicians who opposed the LTTE and maintain close links with the Sri Lankan government. They are joined by a small group of non-chauvinist Sinhalese politicians who consider a quasi-federal solution (perhaps without using the word "federal") as the most practical way of addressing the minority's autonomy aspirations while allaying the majority's fears about national disintegration. For instance, Tamil United Liberation Front (TULF) leader V. Anandasangaree is a staunch advocate of the Indian quasi-federal model of power-sharing and believes that if the LTTE were to accept a similar model then it would be widely accepted by all parties to the conflict (*The Hindu,* 17 January 2007). However, many Sri Lankan Tamil moderates oppose quasi-federalism because in their view such an arrangement would limit powers to provinces and render them dependent on the central government.

In seeking to limit the excesses of both the Sri Lankan State and the LTTE, the voices of federalists have been emasculated. Hardline governments like the one currently led by President Mahinda Rajapakse are hostile to federal campaigns. This is contrary to the situation that existed during the People's Alliance regime of Kumaratunaga (1994–2000) and under the United National Front government headed by Ranil Wickremasinghe (2002–03). While both of those governments allowed people to articulate their views on decentralization and autonomy as a solution to the conflict, the window of opportunity that once existed for civil society to flourish in Sri Lanka has since been closed.

STRENGTHENING UNITARIANISM: A POST-WAR PROJECT

The government's decisive victory in the Eelam war signifies not just an end of Tamil separatism but also a success of unitarianism. In the post-LTTE period marked by absence of any serious threat or challenges to the state, the current regime of Mahinda Rajapaksa has set an agenda of consolidating unitarianism as an inviolable majoritarian state ideology. Reforming the state is not any more in its agenda; nor is the government willing to consider the moderate Sri Lankan Tamils nationalists' demand for greater power-sharing. The federal autonomists feel threatened since the government shows intolerance *even* to articulation of their demand. Equating federalism with separatism, it seeks to dub such goals as a bid to revive the LTTE's agenda and, on this ground, has threatened to ban the Tamil National Alliance (TNA) for advocating a federal solution to the conflict based on "shared sovereignty and right to self-determination" of the Tamil speaking people (Sahadevan 2010, pp. 17–19).

The unitarian nationalists have now forged a strong bond with the state to strengthen the latter's majoritarian identity and character. The state is emerging as a full-blown ethnocratic entity under which the principles of ethnic centralism, majoritarianism and illiberalism are recognized as its ideological attributes. Both the nationalists and state share the view that any talk of a political solution to the ethnic conflict is an anathema in the post-war context. Yet the government has not made its stand forthright: The President wants to appear before the Sinhalese nationalists as if he is not in favour of strengthening the limited power-sharing arrangement viz., Provincial Council system set up under the Thirteen Amendment. But he has made vague promises to the international community in general and India in particular, to introduce a constitutional reform to achieve peace and reconciliation. In this context, he insists on a home-grown solution and rejects any form of external interference. This emboldened position of the government stems from its military victory. Realistically speaking, instead of negotiating a new post-war political structure, the regime is merely interested in continuing with the existing level and framework of devolution under the partially implemented Thirteen Amendment. Even achieving its full implementation seems to be a difficult proposition now.

The Sri Lankan Tamil nationalists appear fragile and fragmented to the advantage of the post-war regime, which is averse to the emergence of a strong political leadership to demand greater autonomy. In this context, it has been successful in its policy of divide and rule because some of the Tamil leaders have easily succumbed to its pressure and accepted its machinations to reap personal political benefits and positions. Thus, while their people remain thoroughly battered, weak and vulnerable, the pro-government leaders have gained power by being part of the post-war regime. This has weakened the minority's ethnic goals. The counter-ethnic elites like to interpret rather in narrow terms that securing cabinet positions for themselves at the centre is itself a way of power-sharing to empower their community. In the process they are willing to advance the agenda of the regime and, at the same time, work against their ethnic group's deep desire for a permanent political solution based on greater autonomy and multilevel power-sharing.

CONCLUSION

This chapter has examined the incompatible goals of Sri Lanka's nationalist forces and their intricate relations defined, largely, in terms of violence. Competitive interests have complicated interethnic relations while locking ethnic communities into a protracted cycle of conflict. Violence in Sri Lanka was not only confined to the northern and eastern provinces; it engulfed the whole country. Thus, all communities regardless of their ethnicity are victims of the conflict. While bitterly fighting for their cause the ethnonationalists have been unable to find an honorable exit from the conflict. Negotiated peace agreements incorporating a federal autonomy solution offer a desirable end point and would likely satisfy the majority of the Sri Lankan Tamil community. But the reality is that while the unitarianists have been successful and the militant separatists have been defeated, federal autonomy is the option for conflict resolution that has met with the strongest opposition. In order to promote a federal autonomy solution in Sri Lanka, the ethnic nationalist ideologies of both the Sinhalese and Sri Lankan Tamils require far greater moderation.

Intertwined with the beliefs and values of the Sinhalese and the Sri Lankan Tamils is their fear of ethnic extinction. Believing that one ethnic group's survival is linked to the denial of power to the other, both the Sri Lankan government and LTTE accepted the inevitability of the conflict by showing their determination to pursue their irreconcilable end goals despite the heavy cost. This fear of ethnic group extinction is so strong that it is not amenable to any rational moderation strategies.

The desire for peace has always been high in Sri Lanka, but to date violent means have prevailed and "peace" has been enforced rather than mutually agreed upon. Having invested heavily in terms of men and materials, both the communities feel that they have come too far to turn back. Yet the Sri Lankan Tamils have sought to achieve an outcome that is commensurable with what they have invested since the outbreak of conflict in 1956. Such an outcome can only be achieved through the de-politicization of peace as the most fundamental requirement in Sri Lanka, and by replacing the emphasis on real-term investments in pursuit of irreconcilable end goals with a new commitment towards compromise, negotiation and moderation. Such an approach will not be possible for a long time to come.

References

Bose, Sumatra. *States, Nations, Sovereignty: Sri Lanka, India and the Tamil Eelam Movement.* New Delhi: Sage, 1994.

DeVotta, Neil. "From Ethnic Outbidding to Ethnic Conflict: The Institutional Bases for Sri Lanka's Separatist War". In *Politics of Conflict and Peace in Sri Lanka*, edited by P. Sahadevan and Neil DeVotta. New Delhi: Manak Publications, 2006.

———. *Sinhalese Buddhist Nationalist Ideology: Implications for Politics and Conflict Resolution in Sri Lanka.* Policy Studies 40. Washington: East-West Center, 2007.

Dissanayake, T.D.S.A. *War or Peace in Sri Lanka.* Colombo: Swastika (Private) Ltd., 1995.

Edrisinha, Rohan. "Federalism: Myths and Realities". In *Essays on Federalism in Sri Lanka*, edited by Rohan Edrisinha and Asanga Welikala. Colombo: Center for Policy Alternatives, 2008.

Edrisinha, Rohan and Asanga Welikala. "The Interim Self Governing Authority Proposals: A Federal Critique". In *Essays on Federalism in Sri Lanka*, edited by Rohan Edrisinha and Asanga Welikala. Colombo: Center for Policy Alternatives, 2008.

Ghai, Yash. *Autonomy and Ethnicity: Negotiating Competing Claims in Multi-ethnic States.* Cambridge: Cambridge University Press, 2000.

Ignatieff, Michael. *Nationalism and Self-Determination: Is There an Alternative to Violence.* Colombo: ICES, 2000.

Lapidoth, Ruth. *Autonomy: Flexible Solutions to Ethnic Conflicts.* Washington: United States Institute of Peace Press, 1996.

Liyanage, Sumanasiri. *One Step at a Time: Reflections on the Peace Process in Sri Lanka 2001–2005.* Colombo: South Asia Peace Institute, 2008.

Moore, Mick. "Sri Lanka: The Contradictions of the Social Democratic State". In *The Post-Colonial State in Asia: Dialectics of Politics and Culture*, edited by Subrata Kumar Mitra. New York: Wheatsheaf, 1990.

Motherland at Crossroads. Colombo: Niyamuwa Publications, 2007.

Pfaffenberger, Bryan. "Introduction: The Sri Lankan Tamils". In *The Sri Lankan Tamils: Ethnicity and Identity*, edited by Chelvadurai Manogaran and Bryan Pfaffenberger. Boulder: Westview Press, 1994.

Pruitt, Dean G. and Jefrey Z. Rubin. *Social Conflict: Escalation, Stalemate, and Settlement.* New York: Random House, 1986.

Rajanayagam, Dagmar-Hellmann. "The 'Groups' and the Rise of Militant Secessionism". In *The Sri Lankan Tamils: Ethnicity and Identity*, edited by Chelvadurai Manogaran and Bryan Pfaffenberger. Boulder: Westview Press, 1994.

Rajasingham-Senanayake, Darini. "Democracy and the Problem of Representation: The Making of Bi-polar Ethnic Identity in Post/Colonial Sri Lanka". In *Ethnic*

Futures: The State and Identity Politics in Asia, edited by Joanna Pfaff-Czarnecka et al. New Delhi: Sage Publications, 1999.

Rudrakumaran, Viswanathan. "LTTE's Flexibility in the Current Peace Process". In *Envisioning New Trajectories for Peace in Sri Lanka*. Luzern: Center for Just Peace and Democracy (CJPD), 2006.

Sahadevan, P. "On Not Becoming a Democrat: The LTTE's Commitment to Armed Struggle". *International Studies* (New Delhi) 32, no. 3 (1995): 249–81.

———. "Negotiating Peace with the LTTE". In *Politics of Conflict and Peace in Sri Lanka*, edited by P. Sahadevan and Neil DeVotta. New Delhi: Manak Publications, 2006.

———. "Negotiating Peace in Ethnic Wars". *International Studies* 43, no. 3 (2006): 239–66.

———. "Political Trends in Post-War Sri Lanka". In *Ethnic Reconciliation and Nation Building in Sri Lanka: Indian Perspectives*, edited by V. Suryanarayan and Sukumar Nambiar. Chennai: T.R. Publications, 2010.

Sornarajah, M. "Envisioning Sri Lanka". In *Envisioning New Trajectories for Peace in Sri Lanka*. Luzern: Center for Just Peace and Democracy (CJPD), 2006.

Swamy, M.R. Narayan. *Tigers of Lanka: From Boys to Guerrillas*. Delhi: Konark Publishers Pvt. Ltd., 1994.

Thangarajah, C. Yuvi. "The Tamil United Liberation Front: Ethnic Hegemony, Unitary State Democracy and the Dilemma of a Minority Party". In *Political Parties in South Asia*, edited by Subrata Kumar Mitra et al. Westport, Connecticut: Praeger, 2004.

Uyangoda, Jayadeva. "The State and the Process of Devolution". In *Devolution and Development in Sri Lanka*, edited by Sunil Bastian. New Delhi: Konark Publishers Pvt. Ltd., 1994.

———. *Ethnic Conflict in Sri Lanka: Changing Dynamics*. Policy Studies 32. Washington: East West Center, 2007.

Wilson, A.J. "Ethnic Strife in Sri Lanka: The Politics of Space". In *The Territorial Management of Ethnic Conflict*, edited by John Coakley. London: Frank Cass & Co., 1993.

———. *Sri Lankan Tamil Nationalism: Its Origin and Development in the Nineteenth and Twentieth Centuries*. London: Hurst and Company, 2000.

Zartman, I.W. "Dynamics and Constraints in Negotiations in Internal Conflicts". In *Elusive Peace: Negotiating an End to Civil Wars*, edited by I.W. Zartman. Washington, D.C.: Brookings Institution, 1995.

10

AUTONOMY AND ARMED SEPARATISM IN JAMMU AND KASHMIR

Bibhu Prasad Routray

The craving for autonomy in the Indian federal unit (hereafter called the "State") of Jammu & Kashmir (J&K) has as much to do with the special circumstances in which the State acceded to the Indian union, as to the alleged manner in which the autonomy provided by the latter's constitution to the former (as a condition for the initial accession) has gradually diminished over the years. With an overzealous objective to integrate the State with India, and, more importantly, not to cede it to Pakistan, successive political parties/dispensations have tended to resist policies that sought to provide more powers to this State, sometimes disregarding popular aspirations in the region. The net result of this undermining of popular aspirations has been a home grown militancy since the 1980s, which, subsequently, has been sustained by neighbouring Pakistan. Even when there is some degree of realization in New Delhi that autonomy for J&K might be a good idea to address the problem of alienation among the people, the actual devolution of power remains a distant prospect on account of the complexity of political dynamics on the ground.

SPECIAL STATUS OF KASHMIR OVER TIME

J&K is no stranger to formal autonomy. At the time of India's independence from British rule in 1947, the predominantly Muslim J&K (according to some count, Muslims constituted 77 per cent of Kashmir's population), which was being ruled by a Hindu king Maharaja Hari Singh, was given the option of choosing to join Pakistan or India. The Maharaja chose to be with Hindu India. However, the terms of his joining clearly specified that he was surrendering only a limited jurisdiction of J&K to the Union of India. He put it on record that his government will not be bound by nor committed to any future constitutional changes in the Center-State sharing of jurisdiction beyond that which had been specified in the "Instrument of Accession". Thus, Article 370 of the Indian Constitution bestowed a special status on J&K. If autonomy is understood to be a "device to allow ethnic and other groups claiming a distinct identity to exercise direct control over affairs of special concern to them, while allowing the larger entity those powers which cover common interests",[1] Article 370 provided autonomy for J&K in the following ways. It exempted J&K from the provisions of the Constitution that applied to federal units of India. J&K was allowed to have its own Constitution. The Union Parliament's legislative power over the J&K was restricted to three subjects — defence, external affairs and communications. The Indian President was empowered to extend this power over matters specified in the Instrument of Accession after consultation with the J&K government. But, if other constitutional provisions or other Union powers were to be extended to Kashmir, the prior concurrence of the J&K government was required. Such concurrence had to be ratified by the J&K's Constituent Assembly.

By all means, the grant of "special status" came in form of a range of constitutional benefits for J&K and its people. However, in the subsequent years, notwithstanding New Delhi's attempts of making J&K an integral part of the country, the Instrument of Accession became a permanent instrument of division between union and state, to be exploited by forces, both pro and anti-India.

The tussle over autonomy started soon after the political situation began to stabilize, following the United Nations (UN) sponsored ceasefire between Indian and Pakistani forces, in Kashmir in 1949. In elections held for the J&K legislative assembly in 1951, the National Conference (NC) political party led by Sheikh Abdullah won an overwhelming mandate. J&K's autonomy appeared to have been further bolstered by the Delhi Agreement of July 1952 between Indian Prime Minister Jawaharlal Nehru and Sheikh Abdullah. Agreement was reached on a series of points: "the people of Jammu and Kashmir were to be considered Indian citizens; the Constituent Assembly would retain its special powers; non-Kashmiri Indian citizens would be denied property rights in Jammu and Kashmir; and the emergency powers of India's President would be contingent upon approval by the Jammu and Kashmir government".²

However, in what was a turning point in union/state relations, Sheikh Abdullah, sought a guarantee of the perpetual nature of Article 370 and began making open calls for J&K's separation from India, a stand which was in direct conflict with the roadmap Indian rulers had built for the J&K's integration with the country. This led to Sheikh Abdullah's arrest in 1953 and NC got a new ruler, Bakshi Ghulam Mohammed, who advocated a closer union with India. In 1954, India announced that Kashmir's accession to India was final and in 1956, the J&K Constituent Assembly approved the merger with India. The Constitution of J&K was finalized and came into effect on 26 January 1957.

The legal provisions keeping J&K distinct from the rest of India began to be ironed out and the pre-1953 autonomous powers of the State were slowly whittled down. The intentions of the Indian government are evident in the writings of Prime Minister Nehru. He wrote, "I say with all respect to our Constitution that it just does not matter what your Constitution says; if the people of Kashmir do not want it, it will not go there. Because what is the alternative? The alternative is compulsion and coercion".³ Policies framed accordingly meant that "by the middle of the 1950s, any substantive autonomy Kashmir had managed to carry over from its earlier princely statehood had largely vanished".⁴ On November 24, 1966, the head of State elected by the J&K legislature was replaced by a governor nominated by the central government. In a further transgression of autonomy arrangements, President's Rule was imposed despite provision in J&K's Constitution for Governor's rule. B.K. Nehru, who was Governor of Kashmir from 1981 to 1984, was later to write in his memoirs, "From 1953 to 1975, Chief Ministers of that State had been nominees of Delhi. Their appointment to that post was legitimised by the holding of farcical and totally rigged elections in which the Congress party led by Delhi's nominee was elected by huge majorities".⁵

In 1974, representatives of New Delhi and Sheikh Abdullah (who had been released in early 1968) began negotiations which led to the finalization of an Accord on 24 February 1975 affirming the continued relevance of Article 370. The Accord had no place for Sheikh Abdullah's demand that the jurisdiction of the Supreme Court and Election Commission (EC) over J&K be curtailed. Subsequently, Sheikh Abdullah was sworn in as Chief Minister of J&K and he asserted that the "future of the State (J&K) lies with India". On 23 July 1975 an Order was passed debarring the J&K legislature from amending its Constitution on matters in respect of the Governor, the

EC and even the composition of the Legislative Council (Upper House in the J&K Assembly). By the early 1980s, Sheikh's relations with New Delhi had soured.

Another phase of undermining of Article 370 started in the mid 1980s. On 30 July 1986, the President promulgated an order under Article 370, extending Article 249 of the Indian Constitution to J&K. The order empowered Indian Parliament to legislate even on a matter in the State List (the list of powers over which states of the Indian Union have jurisdiction) on the strength of a *Rajya Sabha* (upper house of Indian parliament) resolution. New Delhi, thus, acquired the power to legislate on all matters in the State List.[6] Further, J&K was placed under President's rule from 1990 to 1996.

MILITANCY AND AUTONOMY

Official counts in 2008 put the total fatalities in militancy related violence in J&K over 47,000 in the last two decades.[7] In the four subsequent years, 2008 to 2011, a further 1,406 fatalities have been recorded.[8] Armed conflict, which had begun as a movement from within and, later, transformed into a Pakistani sponsored and sustained movement, was a by product of popular dissent within J&K against the gradual subversion of its autonomy and moves by India to fully integrate with the Union. As mentioned, starting from the early 1980s, the Congress government at the centre adopted a policy of subverting the electoral process in J&K. New Delhi dismissed the legitimately elected NC government of Farooq Abdullah in 1984. Both parties, however, were to rediscover their affinity towards each other within a couple of years. Both entered into an electoral alliance and rigged the J&K elections of 1987 to ensure a win for the NC, with the result that there was an "almost total alienation of the local population from the Indian state".[9]

Among the militant groups, who started operating in the early 1990s, the Jammu and Kashmir Liberation Front (JKLF) advocated the creation of an "independent" Kashmir consisting of the Indian part of the state as well as Pakistan occupied Kashmir (PoK).[10] In fact, the JKLF and the People's League were two notable militant fronts that were in existence even before militancy began actively in 1989. Of these, the JKLF, originally established in 1964, was more active and took the initiative to propound separatist claim in J&K. With slogans like *Hum Kya Chahtey-Azadi* (What do we want, Freedom) and *Chhen key lengey-Azadi* (We will snatch freedom), the JKLF "ignited the militancy in the State over which the ISI (Inter-Services Intelligence, Pakistan's external intelligence agency) assumed total control in the subsequent years".[11] The JKLF, consisting of home-grown cadres, was convinced that the changes in the erstwhile Soviet Union would eventually affect India. One of the commanders of the outfit once said, "India will disintegrate like the Soviet Union. India's Balkanization is inevitable. Only six people were killed in the Baltic Republics and they were given their independence. In Kashmir we have given 21,000 lives".[12] According to one account, 8000 to 10,000 youths had crossed over to Pakistan by 1990 to receive training and arms. They returned fully armed to J&K to launch a liberation struggle and the security forces were to recover about 1,700 Kalashnikovs, 150 rocket launchers, 400 rockets, 100 anti-tank mines and 1000 anti-personnel mines from them[13] in subsequent years.

Pakistan's logistic and military support to groups like the JKLF corresponded to a phase when the country was being increasingly remoulded along Islamic lines. Supporting Kashmiri insurgency was an extension of the internal project of Islamization, taking "paramount position in Pakistani foreign policy"[14] after the Soviet Union's withdrawal from Afghanistan. The JKLF, however, was not an appropriate vehicle for Pakistan's larger objectives in J&K. In fact, "Pakistan discovered a surprising and determined grass-roots resistance by Kashmiri youth to its attempts to transform it into an Islamic crusade."[15] The ISI's renewed strategy of marginalizing the pro-autonomy elements in J&K and promoting radical elements within and outside the JKLF led to the birth of smaller outfits such as the Jammu and Kashmir Students Liberation Front and the Al Badr (established in 1989 and different from the present Al Badr formed in late 1998 by foreign militants). Al Badr was subsequently renamed as Hizb-ul Mujahideen (HM).[16] Other notable outfits targeted by the ISI included the Ikhwan-ul Muslimeen (the Islamized nomenclature adopted in April 1991 by the militant faction of Jammu and Kashmir Students' League) and Al Umar (established in early 1990).

Contrary to the JKLF's objective of seeking J&K's independence, Muslim fundamentalist groups and religious elites in the Valley (including the pro-Pakistan All Parties Hurriyat Conference (APHC)) wanted to make J&K either a part of Pakistan or, at the very least, an independent Islamic state with close ties with Pakistan. Emergence and the growth of such groups coincided with the gradual decline of the JKLF,[17] which had dominated militancy in the beginning years. As a result, the character of militancy in J&K underwent complete transformation. Along with the training and support that it provided to the Kashmiri militants, the ISI also encouraged Afghan war guerrillas to infiltrate into Kashmir to carry out a *jihad* (holy war) against India. By 1996, the JKLF had completely withered as a potent armed movement. Foreigners from several countries, including Pakistan, started participating in the militant activities. Militants were drawn from countries that included Central Asian states, Africa, China etc. These militants were primarily participating in a Pakistan sponsored-*jihad* (holy war) against Hindu India and had little concern for the autonomy aspirations of the people of J&K. The percentage of foreign militants of the total militants killed in J&K grew from a mere 5.7 per cent in 1995 to 53.9 in 2000 and a further 69.38 in 2003. Since then, it has gradually declined. In 2007, out of the 223 militants killed in J&K, 53 were described as "foreign terrorists" by the Indian government.[18]

With a view to creating an Islamic hard-line militant organization, the ISI helped to establish the Harkat-ul Ansar (HuA) (established in October 1993). Two militant formations that actively waged jihad in Afghanistan, the Harkat ul-Jihad al-Islami (HuJI) and Harkat-ul Mujahideen (HuM, a splinter organization of the former) were to be merged into this front. While the merger of these militant formations in Pakistan was accomplished, the arrest of HuA General Secretary Maulana Masood Azhar (who was released from an Indian prison after the hijacking of an Indian Airlines flight in December 19)[19] in February 1994 kept the merger plans incomplete.

Further, sustained anti-militancy operations led to the decline of HuA and formation of the Al-Faran, in an attempt to revive the HuA. However, the attempt failed to take off as the United States banned HUA forcing the latter to adopt the name, Harkat-ul Mujahideen (HuM) which, incidentally, was one of its original factions in the HuA: The ISI is also believed to have promoted the Lashkar-e-Toiba (LeT) which has been active in J&K since 1993. The LeT, along with Jaish-e-Mohammad Mujahideen E-Tanzeem (JeM), established in February 2000, is one of the most active militant organization in J&K.

Besides these major groups, numerous smaller militant formations, locally referred to as *tanzeems*, had functioned in J&K. Among them are the Muslim Janbaz Force (established in May 1990), the Kashmir Jihad Force and the Al Jihad Force. Most of these outfits, however, have ceased to function since long. Essentially, militancy in J&K has moved through different phases[20] classified as the popular *intifada* (rebellion) phase (1990–95) to a demoralization phase (1996–98) and thence to the *fidayeen* (suicide) phase (1999–2002) driven by the militancy's "Talibanization". In effect, since 2002, the character of militancy has remained more or less in the *fidayeen* phase. All militants, both Kashmiri and foreign, continue to be trained and armed in the militant training camps in Pakistan and are systematically pushed into the J&K to carry out their activities.[21] Thus, they mostly serve the interests of the Islamic *ummah* (brotherhood) and/or Pakistan and not so much the aspirations to autonomy of the people in J&K.

THE AUTONOMY DEBATE

In spite of the fact that militancy never spread beyond 31 per cent of J&K's territory,[22] it posed a major challenge to the Indian government. New Delhi's initial response to militancy was to induct armed forces into J&K, preceded by a declaration of President's rule, a constitutional provision by which New Delhi assumed the functions of the J&K government. Along with the militants, common people too bore the brunt of the security force action leading to their further alienation and, a consequent strengthening, of secessionist demands. Negotiating with the militant factions was not an option that New Delhi was interested in pursuing, a strategy which has been described as "completely lacking in direction" by some analysts.[23]

Militancy had support both from inside J&K and outside. Thus, while it was important to garner troops to foil the attempts of the externally promoted militancy, it was equally critical to address the factors that caused local Kashmiris to rally behind the militants. Political rulers in New Delhi, especially in the mid-1990s tried to secure a solution to the Kashmir tangle through assuaging popular apprehensions. The Government tried to engage the separatist APHC, an umbrella organization of the secessionist parties and leaders[24] in a dialogue process, while trying to improve the security scenario. Throughout 1995 till early 1996 the Indian government prepared the ground to hold elections in J&K. In May 1996, elections for the Indian National Parliament were held in which 35–45 per cent voters turned out to cast their votes. Election to the J&K assembly was held in September 1996 in which the voter turnout was around 53 per cent, significantly amidst a call for boycott by the militant groups.[25] The victory of NC political party under Farooq Abdullah provided an opportunity to restart the process of reconciliation. In fact, NC's assuming power was important, simply due to the reason that the party had campaigned extensively on the autonomy issue.

In New Delhi's discourse, any further concession on autonomy to J&K would constitute a step that would loosen central control over the state. While successive central governments have only paid lip service to their "commitment" of devolving powers to the state, the political parties assuming power in J&K, too, have not helped the cause of autonomy by failing to put up a viable power sharing formula acceptable to all concerned. A position that has resonance within autonomy debates in J&K has demanded the restoration of its relationship with India to the pre-1953 period. But the suggested manner in which this has to be achieved has remained unacceptable to New Delhi.

Following his 1996 victory, the NC government headed by Farooq Abdullah appointed two state-level committees to examine the issue of J&K's autonomy.[26] While the State Autonomy Committee (SAC) was to deal with the relationship between J&K and the Union Government in New Delhi, the Regional Autonomy Committee (RAC) was to report on the relationships between J&K's three regions: Jammu, Ladakh and the Kashmir valley.

The SAC report, tabled in the State Legislative Assembly on 13 April 1999, referred to the "mess created by the 40 years of unconstitutional practices" and asked for an immediate restoration of the pre-1953 position of the state within the Union, "if popular sentiment is to be respected and resentments assuaged." The Report suggested invocation of Article 258 of the Constitution for entrusting to the state "functions in relation to any matter to which the executive power of the Union extends." It also claimed that the situation had deteriorated to the extent that Article 370 has acquired a dangerously ambiguous aspect. "Designed to protect the state's autonomy, it has been used systematically to destroy it", the report said.[27] Further, it called for the full enforcement of the 1952 Accord and urged that the Center's writ in J&K be confined to the three subjects of defence, foreign affairs and communications. It called on the President of India to repeal all orders, which are not in conformity with the Constitution (Application to Jammu & Kashmir) Order 1950 and the terms of the Delhi Agreement 1952. The report identified 42 such constitution orders needing review.[28] Also, it was recommended that J&K have its own Prime Minister and Parliament, while remaining a part of the Indian Union; and that all India Service officers not be posted to the state (J&K will raise its own cadres). The Report suggested a fresh accord between J&K and the Union, "to restore the unconstitutionally eroded autonomy of the state and to remove the debris of an unhappy past and build a new relationship reflecting mutual trust and respect".

The RAC report, on the other hand, called "for a major reorganisation of J&K's internal boundaries, with religious identity as the obvious, albeit strictly implicit, criterion for the exercise".[29] It called for breaking the three divisions within the state into eight new regions or provinces, five going to the (Sunni) Muslims and the rest going to the Shias, Buddhists and Hindus. In short, according to an analyst, the report, "designed to serve the narrow political ends of the ruling elite and the larger interests of the majority community".[30] Evidently, while the SAC's findings were rather secular and examined the constitutionality of J&K's relationship with India, the RAC was rather communal. It was clear that the Chief Minister Farooq Abdullah had "armed himself with two reports catering to two different constituencies".[31]

Neither report, however, found any favour with the Hindu population in the State. The Hindus (called *Pandits*) had constituted over 20 per cent of J&K's four million population in 1941, inhabiting, primarily, the Jammu region. Even though their presence in J&K has declined to negligible numbers, owing mostly to an ethnic cleansing by the militants, which lead to a steady and quick outward migration from the valley,[32] they remain crucial stakeholders in the conflict and its resolution. In fact, they, being adamant supporters of J&K's full fledged merger with the Indian union, remain a critical link that any government in New Delhi would ignore at its peril. It was the *Pandits* in 1950s, who, expressing their opposition to the policies and programmes of Sheikh Abdullah, had questioned J&K's "special status" under the Indian Constitution and demanded the full and irrevocable integration of Kashmir with India. The rise of Hindu nationalism in Kashmir became a major source of friction between the Indian government and the Abdullah administration.[33] Similarly, the Hindus and the minority Buddhists in Ladakh who have opposed ideas of an independent J&K, fearing that, in an independent J&K, it is the Muslims who, on account of their numerical strength will, dominate.

On 19 January 2000, the J&K cabinet endorsed the SAC report and forwarded it to New Delhi for consideration. Notwithstanding the national criticism and refusal of the right-wing Bharatiya Janata Party (BJP)-led National Democratic Alliance (NDA) government to accept the proposals, a resolution was passed in the state assembly on June 26 approving the SAC report's recommendations and demanding positive and effective steps for its implementation. Law Minister of J&K, P.L. Handoo, said that the people "want nothing more than what they had in 1953". On 4 July, however, the Indian Government asserted "that the acceptance of this resolution would set the clock back and reverse the natural process of harmonising the aspirations of the people of Jammu & Kashmir with the integrity of the nation".[34] The Indian Law Ministry opposing the 30-point autonomy resolution[35] passed in the J&K assembly made it clear that these would "impinge on the sovereignty of the country".

Another report issued in January 2000 by the Kashmir Study Group (KSG), consisting of legislators of the United States and a committee of academics and foreign policy specialists, recommended a "sovereign status" for J&K, "without an international personality". The report included three versions of J&K's status, with detailed recommendations as well as general concepts that could be the basis for serious negotiations between India and Pakistan. The three versions are:

1. Two Kashmiri entities, each with its own government and special relationships with India and Pakistan
2. One Kashmir "straddling" the LoC,[36] with its own government and special relationships with India and Pakistan
3. One entity on the Indian side of the LoC, composed of areas that chose to join it.[37]

The KSG continues to make recommendations (including on confidence building measures) for the resolution the conflict. However, these have not found favours either with India or Pakistan.

There have been recent attempts to link the issue of autonomy in Indian Kashmir, with that in areas that are under the Pakistan's control (PoK and the Northern areas). While Pakistan has continued to raise the issue of self-governance for the Kashmiris on the Indian side, areas that are under Pakistan's control have no autonomy and are virtual colonies of Pakistan.[38] The condition within the Northern Areas with a population of around 2.8 million is even worse than in the PoK. The population has no fundamental legal, political or civil rights and there are no empowered representative institutions in the area.[39] However, New Delhi's highlighting of the lack of autonomy in PoK and the Northern Areas is rather muted and limited. The virtual absence of expressions of desire by the people of PoK and the Northern Areas to join India after breaking free from Pakistan could be a possible reason. People in these areas are mostly in favour of total independence.

FRACTURED OPINIONS ON AUTONOMY

Opinions in J&K are fractured over its future. While groups such as the JKLF, All Parties National Alliance (APNA), and Gilgit-Baltistan National Alliance (GBNA), are in favour of unity and independence of the entire J&K, the ruling party in PoK, the Muslim Conference, and local branches of national parties such as Pakistan Muslim League and People's Party are in favour of belonging to Pakistan, with autonomy. The PDP in J&K, the NC, Panthers' Party and local branches of national parties such as Congress and BJP are in favour of belonging to India, with autonomy. Some parties on the Pakistani side (e.g. Balawaristan National Front) are in favour of integration of the entire J&K with India, while parties including section within the APHC on the Indian side are in favour of accession with Pakistan. The APHC has split into several factions over the years. The faction headed by Mirwaiz Umar Farooq, a religious leader in the Indian part of J&K, remains overtly supportive of the former Pakistani President General Parvez Musharraf's

2006 proposal of "internal autonomy, self-rule and self-governance." It remains opposed to the independence of J&K and demonstrates little faith in existing autonomy proposals for the state.[40] Such fractured opinion among the stakeholders in the conflict has led to a stalemate.

It needs to be emphasized that there has been a significant realization among the mainstream political parties in India regarding the necessity of introducing measures of autonomy in J&K. Such realization, however, continues to be fairly tentative and limited by the overall objective of retaining the state with India and not disrupting the process of the region's integration with the country. As a result, public statements by political parties and the follow up actions have been divergent. There were indeed few takers of Farooq Abdullah's stand that autonomy need not be construed as a factor that would weaken India's ties with J&K, rather it would pave the way for greater integration of the region with the country.[41]

Similarly, little progress was achieved even after the United Front government's minimum programme, published on 5 June 1996, said "respecting Article 370 of the Constitution as well as the wishes of the people, the problems of Jammu and Kashmir will be resolved through giving the people of that State the maximum degree of autonomy." In 2000, opening up the autonomy debate, Home Minister L.K. Advani of the BJP said his government is willing to consider J&K's demand for autonomy with an open mind. "There is a clear case for devolution of greater powers in favour of the states, though in the case of Jammu and Kashmir there is already a greater autonomy than in the other states", he said.[42] However, the BJP remained in favour of the abolition of Article 370, which it says prevents the full integration of J&K with the rest of India. The Common Minimum Programme of the Congress Party led-United Progressive Alliance (UPA) Government in New Delhi promised maximum autonomy for J&K. The UPA Government's 1st term ended in 2009 without any substantial progress towards the resolution of the problem.

HEALING WOUNDS

As mentioned before, since the mid-1990s and, especially, since the beginning of 2000, Indian government has initiated a wide range of measures to address the concerns of the J&K population. In 2010, New Delhi appointed a group of interlocutors, consisting of a journalist, an academician and a retired bureaucrat to hold wide-ranging discussions with the stakeholders in J&K with a bid to generate suggestions for a political solution to the conflict.[43] There also has been a gradual rethink in New Delhi about its approach to the issue of autonomy for J&K. However, any progress on the ground, corresponding to this rethink, remains inhibited on account of a fractured opinion in J&K as well as among the mainstream national parties and continuing externally sponsored militancy.

The successful and fair elections to the J&K Legislative assembly in 2002[44] and 2008 were landmark events that went a long way in strengthening India's attempts at legitimising its claim over J&K. During the 2002 elections, the Indian government had committed to take the autonomy proposals forward by engaging the new state government and this was a move that resulted in a drastic reduction in the support base of the pro-Pakistan APHC. Being positive of the Indian government's attempts to solve the Kashmir problem, the international community too had backed the elections. Amidst boycott calls by the militant outfits and the APHC, a large majority of Kashmiris exercised their franchise. The violence prone electoral process witnessed the killing of the Kashmir Minister for Law and Parliamentary Affairs and Abdul Gani Lone, a veteran APHC leader belonging to the moderate faction who had turned into a bitter critic of the role of the foreign militants in the state. Over forty political candidates and party activists were also killed. The conclusion of the electoral process and the constitution of the Congress and People's Democratic Party (PDP) coalition government, however, did little further to promote the cause of the state's autonomy.

What it otherwise initiated was a long series of confidence building measures between India and Pakistan including bilateral visits, cultural and political exchanges and resumption of bus and train services between the countries etc. In December 2003, Pakistani President Parvez Musharraf and Indian Prime Minister Atal Behari Vajpayee started a peace process with their meeting in Islamabad, which was followed by subsequent meetings of high level officials in 2004. Such measures continued even after a regime change in New Delhi, where the Congress-led United Progressive Alliance (UPA) replaced the BJP-led National Democratic Alliance (NDA). However, such measures were independent of and were unable to provide any solution to the militancy (or, autonomy) problems in J&K.

The seven phase 2008 elections to the J&K Legislative Assembly were held in the backdrop of the protests that broke out against the J&K State Government's decision of grant of 39.88 hectares of land to the Shrine Board managing the pilgrimage to the Hindu God Amarnath in Kashmir to build temporary prefabricated housing and restrooms for the pilgrims. Separatist groups in Kashmir opposed the land transfer forcing the J&K government to reverse the decision, which in turn infuriated the Hindu population in the Jammu region. Violence, primarily between the police and the civilian population that lasted over twenty days in August and September 2008 resulted in the death of over ten persons. It led to a breakdown of the Congress and PDP coalition government in J&K, necessitating fresh elections. Despite immediate concerns about the viability of the elections in an atmosphere vitiated by violence, the situation normalized fast, indicating a desire among the J&K's population for peace.

The United Jihad Council (UJC), a conglomerate of seventeen terrorist groups headquartered at Muzzafarabad in PoK, and headed by terrorist formation Hizb-ul-Mujahideen (HM) chief Syed Salahuddin, had called for a boycott of the elections.[45] The Pakistan Foreign Office spokesman Muhammad Sadiq had also said that polls in J&K do not reflect the "authentic" aspirations of the people of the State[46] However, the fact that polls were held with high percentage of popular participation[47] underlined the declining influence of the separatists, or, at least a yearning for peace and stability among the civilian population in J&K. Prominent separatist leader Syed Ali Shah Geelani admitted that such a high voter turnout was something he had never thought would happen. "Our people have shown a weak resolve and this voting has pushed us far back in our struggle for freedom", he said.[48]

CONCLUSION

Any solution to the Kashmir conflict continues to remain hostage to the swings in Indo-Pakistan relations. In spite of the attempts made by both countries to introduce elements of sanity into their relationships, the issue of what India considers to be Pakistan's sponsorship of terrorism in J&K, remains a thorn in the issues. Incidents like the 26 November 2008 terrorist attacks in India's financial capital, Mumbai by LeT cadres from Pakistan[49] and Pakistan's reluctance to act against them led to a dip in the relations between the two countries. India unilaterally stalled all bilateral meetings and the peace process suffered a setback. Bilateral high level visits and meetings thereafter have taken place between the two countries have remained bereft of any progress towards stabilization. The conflict between these two nuclear powers has had its impact on the entire South Asian region, including J&K.

Declining terrorist violence in J&K[50] might still herald a glimmer of hope for the autonomy aspirations in the state. Even while relations between India and Pakistan continue to violate the realm of normalcy, New Delhi still might consider granting some additional level of autonomy to the state as a strategy to reach out to its people and to stabilize the region and promote a favourable pro-India atmosphere. The ruling Congress Party in New Delhi on a number of occasions has hinted at the possibility of considering autonomy for the state within the ambit of the Indian constitution.[51] Any progress on this front would, however, remain subject to a convergence of opinions among the various stakeholders both on the scale and parameters of the autonomy provisions — a hard possibility by any means. Until that happens, J&K continues to stand at the crossroads.

Notes

[1] Yash Ghai, "Autonomy and Ethnicity: A Framework for Analysis", in *Autonomy and Ethnicity: Negotiating Competing Claims in Multi-ethnic States*, edited by Yash Ghai (Cambridge: Cambridge University Press, 2000), p. 8.
[2] "Kashmir: The View from Srinagar", International Crisis Group (Brussels), 21 November 2002, p. 6.
[3] *Selected Works of Jawaharlal Nehru*, Second Series, vol. 18, 1 April–15 July 1952 (New Delhi: Oxford University Press for the Jawaharlal Nehru Memorial Fund, 1996), p. 418.
[4] Robert G. Wirsing, *Kashmir in the Shadow of War: Regional Rivalries in a Nuclear Age* (New York: M.E. Sharpe, 2003), p. 203.
[5] B.K. Nehru, *Nice Guys Finish Second* (New Delhi: Penguin Books, 1997), pp. 614–15.
[6] A.G. Noorani, "Article 370: Law and Politics", *Frontline*, vol. 17, no. 9 (September 2000): 16–29.
[7] This includes over 20,000 civilians, 20,000 terrorists and 7,000 security force personnel. "Over 47,000 killed in two decades of terrorism in J&K", *Times of India*, 22 November 2008. Unofficial counts, however, are much higher. For example, the separatist All Parties Hurriyat Conference (APHC) says more than 100,000 people have died since the insurgency broke out in 1989. See "India revises Kashmir death toll to 47,000", *Reuters*, 21 November 2008.
[8] Annual Report 2011–12, Ministry of Home Affairs, Government of India, p. 7 and South Asia Terrorism Portal, <http://www.satp.org/satporgtp/countries/india/states/jandk/data_sheets/annual_casualties.htm>.
[9] Šumit Ganguly, Larry Jay Diamond, and Marc F. Plattner, eds., *The state of India's democracy* (Baltimore, Maryland: Johns Hopkins University Press, 2007), p. 54.
[10] According to the official JKLF website "the best solution of the issue is to reunite the divided Jammu Kashmir State and make it a fully independent and truly democratic sovereign State". See "JKLF-Ideology", <http://www.jklfuk.co.uk/Ideology.php>.

11 "Jammu & Kashmir: Militant Groups: An Overview", South Asia Terrorism Portal, <http://satp.org/satporgtp/countries/india/states/jandk/militant_outfits/index.html>.
12 Quoted in Tavleen Singh, *Kashmir: A Tragedy of Errors* (New Delhi: Penguin, 1996), p. 189.
13 Ibid., p. 176.
14 Thomas A. Marks, "Jammu & Kashmir: State Response to Insurgency, The Case of Jammu", *Faultlines: Writings on Conflict & Resolution*, no. 16 (January 2005): 4.
15 Christopher Thomas, *Faultline Kashmir* (Middlesex: Brunel Academic Publishers Ltd., 2000), p. 273.
16 Nicholas Howenstein, "The Jihadi Terrain in Pakistan: An Introduction to the Sunni Jihadi Groups in Pakistan and Kashmir", Pakistan Security Research Unit (PSRU), Research Report 1, University of Bradford, 5 February 2008, p. 16.
17 Currently, JKLF functions as a non-violent organization in the PoK, Pakistan, various European countries and the United States.
18 Status Paper on Internal Security Situation, Ministry of Home Affairs, Government of India, 1 September 2008, p. 4.
19 Maulana Masood Azhar was freed from an Indian prison in exchange for passengers on a hijacked Indian Airlines jet. His brother, Ibrahim, is thought to have been one of the hijackers. Maulana Azhar set up Jaish-e-Mohammad in early 2000, shortly after being set free by India. See "Profile: Maulana Masood Azhar", *BBC*, 16 December 2002, <http://news.bbc.co.uk/2/hi/south_asia/578369.stm>.
20 Sumantra Bose, *Kashmir: Roots of Conflict, Paths to Peace* (New Delhi: Vistaar Publications, 2003).
21 The Indian claims regarding the existence of such militant training camps have been backed up by the local politicians in Pakistan occupied Kashmir (PoK). For example Arif Shahid, secretary general of the All Parties National Alliance (APNA) told the BBC in May 2010, "Jihadi activities have been restarted during the last few weeks. Most of the activities are concentrated in the Neelum Valley along the LoC." Shahid, who visited the region with other APNA leaders, said that militants were based there in large numbers and have set up camps in the area. "The men are not locals — they have long hair and beards. Most do not speak the local language. We can make out from their appearances and languages they are not from any part of Kashmir. They have set up camps in the region and many are crossing the border", he said. See "Kashmir militants 'regrouping' in Pakistan", *BBC*, 24 May 2010, <http://news.bbc.co.uk/2/hi/south_asia/8683367.stm>.
22 It never affected Ladakh, lying in the eastern part of the State and sharing the border with China. Ladakh consists of 69 per cent of J&K's landmass.

23 Tavleen Singh writes, "When making excuses for why there were never any attempts at a political solution the government has a stock reason: there were so many groups that it was never clear who to talk to. This is only part of the truth; the other part which nobody likes to talk about is that an almost deliberate attempt was made to keep the right people away from Kashmir." See *Kashmir: A Tragedy of Errors*, p. 192.

24 APHC's website is available at <http://www.hurriyat.net/>. For a profile of APHC, also see "All Parties Hurriyat Conference", <http://satp.org/satporgtp/countries/india/states/jandk/terrorist_outfits/Hurriyat.htm>.

25 Urmila Phadnis and Rajat Ganguly, *Ethnicity and nation-building in South Asia* (New Delhi: Sage Publications, 2001), p. 205.

26 Sanjay Chaturvedi, "The Ethno and the Geo: A New Look into the Issue of Kashmir's Autonomy", in *The Politics of Autonomy: Indian Experiences*, edited by Ranabir Samaddar (New Delhi: Sage Publications, 2005), p. 148.

27 Muzamil Jaleel, "The state of J&K's autonomy", *Indian Express* (New Delhi), 31 August 1999.

28 Robert G. Wirsing, *Kashmir in the Shadow of War: Regional Rivalries in a Nuclear Age*, p. 208.

29 Ibid., p. 205.

30 Navnita Chadha Behera, *State, Identity and Violence: Jammu, Kashmir & Ladakh* (New Delhi: Manohar, 2000), p. 265.

31 Aijaz Ahmad, "Kashmir Conundrum: India, Pakistan, the United States and the Question of 'Autonomy'", *Frontline*, vol. 17, no. 15 (22 July–August 2000).

32 Official figures reveal around 59,542 families had migrated from Kashmir after the onset of militancy. Of these, 34,202 went to Jammu. Around 21,684 families are registered as migrants outside J&K. In May 2010, the J&K Government initiated a move to facilitate the return of the migrant *pandits*. Office of the J&K Relief Commissioner said, "We have received applications from over 4,400 families who are ready to come back. We have asked them to furnish details of their plans so that the government can make necessary arrangements." See Ishfaq-ul-Hassan, "Process for Kashmiri pandits' return begins", 31 May 2010, <http://www.dnaindia.com/india/report_jammu-and-kashmir-govt-begins-process-of-kashmiri-pandits-return-to-valley_1390159>.

33 Rajat Ganguly, "India, Pakistan and the Kashmir Dispute", Asian Studies Institute & Center for Strategic Studies, <http://www.victoria.ac.nz/asianstudies/publications/other/India%20Pakistan%20and%20the%20Kashmir%20Dispute.pdf>.

34 Quoted in Robert G. Wirsing, *Kashmir in the Shadow of War: Regional rivalries in a Nuclear Age*, p. 209.

35 "Law ministry opposes J&K autonomy resolution", 18 July 2000, <http://www.rediff.com/news/2000/jul/18auto.htm>.

36 LoC or the Line of Control, is a 720-kilometre long non-linear boundary over rugged terrain near Jammu in the southwest up to glacial heights of

the Himalayas near China's Sinkiang province in the northeast, is the actual boundary between the Indian part of Kashmir and the Pakistani-occupied Kashmir (PoK). It came into existence after the Shimla agreement between India and Pakistan in 1972.

37. Paul Wallace, "Countering Militant Movements in India: Kashmir and Khalistan", in *Democracy and Countermilitancy: Lessons from the Past*, edited by Robert J. Art and Louise Richardson (Washington, D.C.: United States Institute of Peace Press, 2007), p. 459.

38. While PoK ostensibly has an elected Legislative Assembly, real power is wielded by the "*Azad* (Independent) Jammu and Kashmir Council" presided over by the Prime Minister of Pakistan, who nominates five of the thirteen members of the Council. The rules made by the Council are not subject to judicial review. The PoK Government merely implements decisions of the Council. See G. Parthasarathy, "Demilitarisation and autonomy in J&K", *Hindu Business Line*, 13 January 2006.

39. Ibid.

40. Hurriyat leader Mirwaiz Omar Farooq has said the separatist conglomerate would consider "an alternative negotiated settlement" of the Jammu and Kashmir problem providing greater autonomy to the Kashmiri people even if it did not lead to an independent state. See "Hurriyat may accept greater autonomy for Jammu and Kashmir", *Hindustan Times*, 23 September 2002.

41. Farooq in a message on the eve of 50th year of India's independence said, "The concept of autonomy is not to weaken the ties of the state with the rest of the country but it will go a long way in greater integration by meeting the regional aspirations of the people." He also said, accession of Jammu and Kashmir with Indian union was a "historic reality which no power on earth can undo". "Autonomy will not sever J&K from nation: Farooq", *Indian Express*, 16 August 1997.

42. India open on Kashmir autonomy, 23 June 2000, <http://news.bbc.co.uk/1/hi/world/south_asia/803473.stm>.

43. By February 2011, the interlocutors had submitted four reports to the Government and the recommendations of these confidential reports were under study by the Government till the writing of the paper. See "Role of Interlocutors for J&K", Press Release, Ministry of Home Affairs, Govenrment of India, 23 February 2011, <http://pib.nic.in/newsite/erelease.aspx?relid=70063>.

44. For a detail analysis of the 2002 elections, see Radha Kumar, "The Kashmir Election and After", *The Hindu*, 16 September 2002.

45. Ajaat Jamwal, "J&K: A Peaceful Poll?", *South Asia Intelligence Review*, vol. 7, no. 19 (17 November 2008), <http://satp.org/satporgtp/sair/Archives/7_19.htm#assessment2>.

46. "India slams Pakistan's comments on Jammu and Kashmir polls", 21 November 2008, <http://www.rediff.com/news/2008/nov/21indpak-india-slams-pak-comments-on-jk-polls.htm>.

47 An estimated 63 per cent of voters (around three million out of the 4.8 million eligible voters) cast their votes, which was by far the highest turnout recorded in the Valley in the past twenty years. See Riyaz Wani, "Kashmir's democratic catharsis", 24 July 2009, <http://www.opendemocracy.net/article/email/kashmirs-democratic-catharsis>.

48 Balraj Puri, "Lessons from the Jammu and Kashmir Elections", *Mainstream*, vol. 47, no. 2 (24 January 2009).

49 A group of ten Lashkar-e-Toiba terrorists carried out simultaneous raids on several locations in Mumbai on 26 November. The raid on two hotels, Taj and Trident and the Jew inhabited Nariman House lasted till 28 November. A total of nine terrorists involved in the attack were killed and one was arrested. A total of 195 persons including twenty-two foreign nationals were killed in the attacks.

50 J&K Police figures indicates that in 2010, the militancy parameters like number of incidents, death of civilians, security forces and militants was the lowest, since the inception of militancy in 1990. See "New Year Message-2011", Statement of the Director General of Police, website of the J&K Police, <http://jandkpolice.org/message_dgp_2011.htm>. The year 2011 witnessed a further 30 per cent decrease in the number of terrorist incidents and 34 per cent and 52 per cent decrease in civilian and SFs fatalities respectively compared to the year 2010. See Annual Report 2011–12, Ministry of Home Affairs, Government of India, p. 7.

51 Prime Minister Manmohan Singh told a meeting of representatives of various political parties from J&K that if there was a consensus between them on autonomy, the Center would consider it within the ambit of the Constitution.

References

Behera, Navnita Chadha. "State, Identity and Violence: Jammu, Kashmir & Ladakh". New Delhi: Manohar, 2000.

Bose, Sumantra. "The Challenge in Kashmir: Democracy, Self Determination and a Just Peace". New Delhi: Sage Publications, 1997.

———. "Kashmir: Roots of Conflict, Paths to Peace". New Delhi: Vistaar Publications, 2003.

Chibber, Lt. Gen. M.L. "Criminal Folly in Kashmir". New Delhi: Manas Publications, 1998.

Gauhar, G.N. "Elections in Jammu and Kashmir: India's Success, Pakistan's Defeat". New Delhi: Manas Publications, 2000.

Grover, Verinder, ed. *The Story of Kashmir: Yesterday and Today*. New Delhi: Deep and Deep Publications, 1995.

Hewitt, V. *Reclaiming the Past: The Search for Political and Cultural Unity in Contemporary Jammu and Kashmir*. London: Portland Books, 1996.

Koul, M.L. *Kashmir: Wail of a Valley*. Delhi: Gyan Sagar Publications, 1999.

Ray, Maj. Gen. Arjun. *Kashmir Diary: Psychology of Militancy*. New Delhi: Manas Publications, 1997.
Roy, Sekhar Basu. *New Approach Kashmir: Violence in Paradise*. Calcutta: Deep Prakashan, 1999.
Schofield, Victoria. *Kashmir in the Crossfire*. London: I.B. Tauris Publishers, 1996.
Swami, Praveen. *India, Pakistan and the Secret Jihad: The Covert War in Kashmir, 1947–2004*. New Delhi: Routledge, 2006.
Tavleen Singh. *Kashmir: A Tragedy of Errors*. New Delhi: Penguin, 1996.
Wirsing, Robert G. *Kashmir in the Shadow of War: Regional Rivalries in a Nuclear Age*. New York: M.E. Sharpe, 2003.

11

ARMED CONFLICTS AND MOVEMENTS FOR AUTONOMY IN INDIA'S NORTHEAST

Shanthie Mariet D'Souza

The little known North East region of India, which comprises seven federal units[1] (referred to hereafter as "states") and connects to the Indian mainland by a narrow 22 kilometre land corridor, has been a theatre of prolonged armed conflicts. Beginning with India's independence in 1947, several armed insurgent movements have emerged in each of these states with wide ranging demands. While some of the insurgencies have demanded outright secession from India, others have asked for greater self-governing rights, still others insist on the partitioning of existing states into new administrative units as also on various forms of autonomy to preserve their unique identity and gain greater control over their lives and resources. Most of these insurgencies, exploiting the prevalent alienation and grievances among the people against what they refer to as an "apathetic and distant" New Delhi, have spanned over decades without being resolved. Each of these insurgencies has also been accompanied by lesser known non-armed movements by ethnic groups, clamouring for greater administrative powers. These multiple movements have generated a specter of instability in the region, which has continued irrespective of the government's limited success at establishing peace and improving governance through the existing provisions for autonomy under the Indian constitution.

OFFICIAL APPROACH TOWARDS THE "EXCLUDED NORTHEAST"

The British, during their rule in India, annexed the Assam plains in 1826. It was the beginning of a process of domination over the North Eastern region, which culminated in the control over the Mizo Hills in 1890.[2] All these areas formed parts of Assam Province of British India. Under the Government of India Act, 1935, the hill areas of Assam were divided into two categories — "excluded" and "partially excluded areas". Areas such as Lushai Hills (now Mizoram), the Naga Hills (now Nagaland) and the North Cachar Hills (now part of Assam) were declared as "excluded areas". No federal or provincial legislation extended to the districts automatically. Areas such as the Khasi and Jaintia Hills, the Garo Hills (now all part of the state of Meghalaya), and the Mikir Hills (in Assam) were declared as "partially excluded areas". These areas were administered by the state government subject to the special powers of the Governor. In effect, the 1935 Constitution did not accord local self government or political autonomy to the hill tribes of the excluded and partially excluded areas to manage their local affairs".[3]

In 1873, the British introduced the Inner Line Regulation to prevent the entry of outsiders into the area without valid permit.[4] This permit system also debarred the hill people from interaction with the peoples from the Indian mainland and kept them away from the socio-political influence of the outside world. Manipur, Tripura and Khasi States (presently the Khasi Hills in the state of Meghalaya) continued to remain as "princely states" under British control till India's independence.

Most tribal communities inhabiting the hills in the region, thus, remained cut off from social and political developments taking place in mainland India. While it served the interests of the British by preventing the pro-independence movement from engulfing the region, it created a sense of "independence" among the tribals, which was, later, to be used by the insurgencies as a plank for their secessionist demands.

Contrary to the British policy of insulating the North East, the official approach of independent India towards the region was radically different. A new India, eager to maintain control over the entire territory of the country preferred to assume a unitary character and the British policy of maintaining status quo and isolation was replaced by a policy of development and integration. This ran against the demands of several tribes in the North East for whom the departure of the British had opened up windows for complete independence. As a part of the process of integration, the

Constituent Assembly of India set up an Advisory Committee to deal with matters relating to the minorities and the tribals. A sub-Committee, under the chairmanship of Gopinath Bordoloi, the first Chief Minister of Assam state, was formed to advise the Constituent Assembly on the tribal affairs in the North Eastern region. Following the Sub-Committee's suggestion, a certain amount of autonomy was enshrined in the Six Schedule of the Constitution. The Committee recommended for a "simple and inexpensive set up (District Councils) of the tribal areas", a "regional council for the tribes other than the main tribe". The idea was to build up autonomous administration in the hill areas of Assam so that the tribal people could preserve their traditional way of life, and safeguard their customs, and cultures. The Committee also recommended the abolition of the excluded and the partially excluded areas.[5] In the subsequent years, the government set up autonomous district councils, carved out union territories out of Assam and, even later, provided them with independent state status acceding to popular demands.

MULTIPLE INSURGENCIES IN THE NORTH EAST

The nature and number of insurgencies in the North East is complex and mind boggling. The *South Asia Terrorism Portal* lists more than 120 insurgent outfits operating in the seven states of the North East.[6] Many of these insurgencies have been, however, largely inactive, after a few years of existence. A number of them have negotiated peace agreements with the government. At present, there are about 20 active armed militant movements in the region. For the sake of analysis, this chapter takes into consideration only the major insurgencies. Occasional reference, however, is made to the peripheral insurgencies with limited areas of influence, to explain the dynamics of the nature of the armed movements.

Available official data indicates that between 1992 and 2009, North Eastern Indian states recorded at least 19,225 fatalities, with an average of 1,068 deaths per year. Maximum fatalities, within the said period, have been recorded in Assam. This state, ravaged by about 37 insurgencies (at present, about eight are active) recorded at least 7,340 fatalities between 1992 and 2009. Assam was followed by Manipur, where 39 insurgencies (at present, about 15 are active) accounted for at least 5,569 fatalities.[7] Official data for 2010 indicates that the northeast region recorded 773 incidents accounting for the death of 94 civilians and 20 security forces. In addition, 3,306 insurgents were neutralized (arrested, killed or surrendered).[8]

Table 11.1
Major Insurgent Groups in North East[9]

Outfit	Affected State	Founding Year	Purported Objective	Status
ULFA	Assam	1979	Secession	One faction in ceasefire and another faction active
NDFB	Assam	1986	Secession	Ceasefire
NSCN-IM	Nagaland & Manipur	1987	Secession	Ceasefire
NSCN-K	Nagaland & Manipur	1987	Secession	Ceasefire
UNLF	Manipur	1964	Secession	Active
PLA	Manipur	1978	Secession	Active
PREPAK	Manipur	1977	Secession	Active
NLFT	Tripura	1989	Secession	Active
ATTF	Tripura	1990	Secession	Active

Table 11.2
Security Situation in the North East

Year	2003	2004	2005	2006	2007	2008	2009
Incidents	1,332	1,234	1,332	1,366	1,489	1,561	1,297
Security Forces killed[10]	90	110	70	76	79	46	42
Civilians Killed	494	414	393	309	498	466	264
Insurgents Killed	523	404	406	395	514	640	571
Total Fatalities	1117	928	869	708	1091	1052	877

Source: Ministry of Home Affairs, Government of India.

Table 11.3
State-wise Fatalities in the North East

Year	Assam		Manipur		Nagaland		Tripura	
	Incidents	Fatalities	Incidents	Fatalities	Incidents	Fatalities	Incidents	Fatalities
2003	358	401	243	205	199	86	394	296
2004	267	315	320	258	186	97	212	164
2005	398	254	554	410	192	99	115	61
2006	413	242	498	311	309	147	87	50
2007	474	436	584	388	272	154	94	39
2008	387	373	740	517	321	213	68	26
2009	424	368	659	436	129	31	19	10

Source: Ministry of Home Affairs, Government of India.

NAGA MOVEMENT: SOVEREIGNTY OR AUTONOMY?

The Naga National Council (NNC) that raised the banner of revolt against the Indian state in the 1950s, nwas the first organized, armed movement in the North East.[11] The NNC, under the leadership of Angami Zapu Phizo, of the Angami Naga tribe, argued that the Nagas were independent before the British subjugated them and hence, after the British left, their independent status should be restored. Since India's leaders were disinclined to grant such favours to the NNC, the outfit started an armed campaign, declaring that the movement enjoyed the support of the Naga population. As evidence, it cited a referendum held by the outfit in the Naga hills. According to the outfit, an incredible 99 per cent people voted in favour of independence for Nagaland. NNC's armed campaign lasted till 1975, when it signed an Accord with the Indian government.[12] However, a group of cadres, dissatisfied with the Accord, broke away to form the National Socialist Council of Nagaland (NSCN) in 1980. The NSCN, however, further split along tribal lines, in 1987, giving origin to the National Socialist Council of Nagaland-Isak-Muivah (NSCN-IM), led by Chairman Isak Chisi Swu and the National Socialist Council of Nagaland-Khaplang (NSCN-K) led by chairman S.S. Khaplang.[13] The IM faction commanded the loyalty of, primarily, the Tangkhul Nagas where as the Khaplang faction was seen as representing the Sema and Ao Naga tribes. The NSCN is believed to have been responsible for a rapid escalation in the level of insurgency in the region and is aptly referred to as the "mother of all insurgencies" in the North East. Both the NSCN-IM and the NSCN-K carried out armed campaigns against the Indian state as also against each other. The objective of both movements is roughly the same, i.e. to carve out an independent state of Nagaland. In 1997, the NSCN-IM signed a ceasefire agreement with the Indian Government. In 2000, the NSCN-K followed suit. Since then, there has been a noticeable reduction in the encounters between security forces and insurgents in the state although inter factional warfare has continued unabated, resulting in high levels of civilian killings. This has led observers to term the present state of affairs as "negative peace".

What is noticeable, however, is the gradual softening of the independence related stand of the outfit in the recent years. The NSCN-IM, during its protracted negotiations with the Indian government since 1997, is seen to have diluted of its demand for total independence from India. The outfit, in its public postures, however, maintains a rigid stand. Its demand of creating a *Nagalim* (greater Nagaland)[14] comprising of contiguous territories in neighbouring states of Assam, Manipur, Nagaland and Arunachal Pradesh, which the outfit claims, are inhabited by the Naga tribes has run into problems too. Since most of these states are unwilling to part with their territories, the idea of Nagalim remains just that: an idea.

Starting with the declaration of Nagaland as an independent state, Indian government's position has been of consolidation in Nagaland. The authorities have held free and fair elections regularly, in which a large voter turnout has, invariably, been recorded.[15] The militant outfits, on the other hand, have, equally invariably, called for a boycott of the electoral process. But such calls have had little impact on public perception in the recent years. Even though the insurgencies in the state retain considerable amount of firepower, their ability to obstruct the process of integration of Nagaland with the Union of India has been vastly eroded.

As a consequence, negotiations with the Government have led to a further dilution of the range and scope of demands by the NSCN-IM. Instead of pursuing a highly unlikely goal of integrating the Naga-inhabited areas of neighbouring states, the outfit is considering the idea of rehabilitating the Naga tribes from different states within Nagaland. Such a process, however, is not free from opposition. Initial relocation of some of the Tangkhul Nagas, who are mostly residents in the neighbouring State of Manipur, within Nagaland has led to a backlash from several Naga tribes, already residents in Nagaland. Such a policy, which is seen as promoting the interests of a Naga tribe, not belonging to the State of Nagaland, has led to a section of the NSCN-IM cadres to breakaway from the outfit and form the NSCN-Unification (NSCN-U).[16] The NSCN-IM, is bargaining with the Government of India for a separate constitution, a separate flag and legislative powers regarding the affairs of Nagaland. The Indian Government, however, is unwilling to make such concessions, apprehensive of setting a precedent that would encourage for other militant formations fighting the Indian State. Being aware of the dwindling support base of the NSCN-IM and the possibility of a further downgrading of demands, the Indian government is willing to drag its foot on a final agreement. It is highly possible that the NSCN-IM would eventually settle on a much watered down set of demands, a far cry from the original demand of an independent Nagaland.

The bitter factional rivalry between the NSCN-IM and the NSCN-K has remained a major obstacle to peace in Nagaland, although in 2010 incidents of violence between the two factions were drastically reduced. The NSCN-K has expressed in clear terms that any agreement between the NSCN-IM and the Indian government would not be acceptable to it.

SUCCESS STORIES OF COUNTER INSURGENCY (COIN) IN THE NORTHEAST

The proposition that armed movements for autonomy are mainly demands for better governance rings true in the context of three successful cases of resolution of conflicts in the North East. Interestingly, the Indian government has not been able to replicate the success stories, in the region, beyond Mizoram, the Bodo insurgency in Assam and the recent counter-insurgency successes in Tripura. Each of these cases indicate that the grievances motivating most of the insurgency movements concern governance issues, grievances which can be redressed through the existing administrative structures. This renders the demand for autonomous powers redundant.

Insurgency in the state of Mizoram (then, part of the state of Assam) started with a famine, termed as "Mautam" (literally, "bamboo dying"), in 1959. As the Government of Assam dithered in sending relief to the people, alienation among the people grew and a prolonged insurgency was launched by the Mizo National Front (MNF), earlier known as the Mizo National Famine Front (MNFF). Laldenga, a former bank clerk who went on to lead the MNF, demanded the "sovereign independence of Greater Mizoram".[17] Induction of the army into the state by the Indian government led the rebel leadership to seek refuge in neighbouring countries and continue fighting till 1986, when an Accord was signed between the MNF and the Indian Government. The grant of "[S]tatehood was a prerequisite to the implementing of the accord signed between the MNF and the Union Government."[18] Accordingly, Mizoram was declared a full-fledged state within the Indian union. As per a compromise, the ruling Congress party in the State paved way for the rebel leadership to take over political power in Mizoram. Even though the Mizo Accord did not fulfil MNF's original demand of sovereignty for Mizoram, the process of political inclusion for the insurgent leadership led to the culmination of the insurgency. The state, since then, has remained peaceful. MNF continues as a political party that contests periodic elections in the state and it has emerged victorious on most occasions.

The resolution of the Bodo insurgency in the state of Assam is another instance of a raging insurgency reaching its end without achieving its original demand of carving out an independent state from Assam. The insurgency movement of the Bodos, the largest plains tribes in the state of Assam, has generally been described as an identity movement by an ethnic group against the dominance by the mainstream Assamese. The All Bodo Students Union (ABSU) launched its movement in March 1987 on the basis of a 92-point charter of demands submitted to the Assam government. The original charter of demands was soon whittled down to consist of just three "political" demands: (a) the creation of a separate state of "Bodoland"; (b) the setting up of district councils in the tribal areas on the south bank of Brahmaputra; and (c) the inclusion of the Bodo-Kacharis of Karbi Anglong in the Sixth Schedule of the Constitution.[19] The political demands of the students' body, however, were subsequently appropriated by two insurgencies, the National Democratic Front of Bodoland (NDFB) and the Bodo Liberation Tigers (BLT). While the BLT wanted a state within the Indian union, the NDFB had a secessionist demand.[20]

After seven years of insurgency, on 6 December 2003, 2,641 cadres of the BLT renounced violence and surrendered along with arms and ammunition.[21] The BLT, prior to its en-masse surrender, had been observing a ceasefire with the Government since 14 July 1999. The deal with the Government of India and the Government of Assam resulted in the creation of a Bodoland Territorial Council (BTC) that overlooks the affairs of the Bodos in separate districts of the state.[22] The BTC experiment is a repetition of a similar attempt in 1993 that had created the Bodoland Autonomous Council (BAC). Infighting among the Bodo groups had led to a collapse of the experiment and the dissolution of the BAC. Following the creation of the BTC, the BLT was dissolved to form a political party, which has contested, won seats in the Assam legislative assembly elections in 2007 and went on to become a coalition partner of the ruling Congress Party in the state.

Even though the BLT managed to secure an autonomous council (and not its original demands of a separate state), the NDFB clearly fell short of its secessionist demands. Following nearly two decades of insurgency, the NDFB on October 8, 2004, announced a six-month long unilateral ceasefire.[23] The decision followed a reversal of its fortunes in the aftermath of the December 2003 onslaught by the Bhutanese army targeting the insurgent camps of the United Liberation Front of Assam (ULFA), the NDFB and the Kamtapur Liberation Organisation (KLO). The NDFB is believed to have suffered huge losses in the operations and was compelled to opt for peace with the Indian government. Following several rounds of parleys, the group's leadership, representatives of the Union Government and the Government of Assam signed a ceasefire agreement on 25 May 2005, at New Delhi.[24] Since then, majority of the NDFB cadres have been settled in designated camps. NDFB chief Ranjan Daimary who chose to stay put in Bangladesh and did not become a part of the ceasefire agreement, was arrested and handed over to India by the Bangaldesh authorities on 30 April 2010.[25] Even though a formal process of dialogue is yet to start between the outfit and the government, it can safely be assumed that the Bodo insurgency in Assam has reached its end.

The most recent case of counter-insurgency success has been achieved in Tripura. Insurgency in the state of Tripura, which is flanked on three sides by Bangladesh, had started as a reaction to the unrestricted migration of Hindu Bengali population from East Bengal (which subsequently became Bangladesh) to the state of Tripura. This population movement reduced the ethnic tribal population of the state to a state of minority. As these tribals retreated towards the hill and forest areas, the Bengalis dominated every sphere of society and government. Insurgent groups consisting of tribals, including the National Liberation Front of Tripura (NLFT) and the All Tripura Tiger Force (ATTF) raised a campaign to restore the tribals' primacy. Initially, the movement received significant popular support from the tribal population. Widespread economic backwardness among the tribal population (roughly one third in the state) and their lack of access to development initiatives of the government, essentially dominated by the Bengalis, provided the impetus for the insurgency. The fact that insurgents had established their camps and safe havens in neighbouring Bangladesh and were carrying out attacks through the porous international borders had crippled the state response to the developing insurgency. For over a decade, insurgency movements pushed the state of Tripura to the brink of collapse. There was little challenge to their routine of massacres, abductions, extortions etc. In 2001, Tripura was designated by the National Crime Records Bureau (NCRB) of the Government of India as one of the most crime prone states of the country.[26] Gradually the insurgencies had tuned into criminal enterprises and had even targeted their own constituency of tribals for extortion and killings. Nonetheless, security forces' response to their activities remained adhoc and mostly reactive.

Recent years, however, witnessed a turnaround. Building on a model of a police-led response to insurgency, Tripura's Police managed to reverse the trajectory of insurgent violence and mobilization despite continued support provided to such groups in Bangladesh.[27] The core of the police strategy was to establish a strong presence in the most remote areas of the State, in order to minimize the reaction time for counter-insurgents operations. In addition, police stations, posts and camps were upgraded infrastructurally to bolster its capacity for response. There was also a visible augmentation of the police intelligence network. The improved geographical dominance of

Table 11.4
Counter-insurgency success in Tripura

Year	2003	2004	2005	2006	2007	2008	2009	2010
Incidents	394	212	115	87	94	68	19	30
Insurgents killed/arrested/surrendered	654	608	212	196	303	382	308	155
SFs killed	39	46	11	14	06	03	01	2
Civilians killed	207	67	28	14	14	10	08	2

Source: Annual Report 2010–11, Ministry of Home Affairs, Government of India, Annexure III, p. 286.

the security forces resulted in increasing flows of information from even the tribal population, who have long borne the brunt of insurgents' excesses, but had been too terrorized to extend cooperation to the police in the past.

To complement the police-led counter insurgency campaign, the Government of Tripura took a number of steps to bridge the ethnic divide between the tribals and the Bengalis. Improvement in the overall security situation allowed the government to take a number of its development initiatives to the farthest and inaccessible corners of the state, further sinking the popular support for the insurgents. In some cases, the state government also initiated a village reorganization scheme, enabling the tribals located in the remote forest and hill areas to relocate to newly constructed villages along the national and state highways. This allowed the state to deliver medical and educational benefits to the tribals and effectively isolate them from insurgent attacks.

Insurgency in Tripura, however, is by no means over. Insurgents have not entirely lost their operational capacities and spheres of influence. However, gradual loss of their safe houses in Bangladesh continues to make their revival difficult. Significant reduction in their influence over political and administrative process in the state and a steady decline of their support base among the ethnic tribal populace underlines that armed movements can be resolved through a mixture of politico-security measures, without acceding to the demands of the insurgents or even addressing the autonomy concerns that tend to surface every now and then.

INTER-TRIBAL RIVALRY AND COMPETITION FOR RESOURCES

Autonomy demands in the North East are mostly linked with livelihood issues and hence, it is argued that such concerns can be addressed through good governance, and not necessarily through drastic makeovers in the existing administrative arrangements. It is competition over available resources that have been a major source of acrimony between various marginalized tribes. As a result, the tribes are just not in a constant war of attrition with the "non-tribal outsiders",[28] but also with their fellow tribal groups who are seen as a threat to their existence since they source their livelihood from the same resource set.

The clashes between Naga-Kuki ethnic groups in Manipur and the hostility between Khasi and Garo ethnic groups in Meghalaya in the 1990s are some examples of inter-tribe conflict. Similarly, the clashes between the ethnic Karbis and the Dimasas, the Karbis and the Kukis in Assam also corroborate the view that such conflicts show an increasing trend. The insurgents have taken advantage of such conflict to widen/deepen their popular support and mass base. For example, the KLNLF carried out a campaign targeting the Kuki population in the Karbi Anglong district in 2004.[29]

EXISTING AUTONOMY ARRANGEMENTS: THE WORKINGS AND DYNAMICS

After India gained independence, "a new scheme of simple and inexpensive administration for the tribesmen of certain hills districts of the then state of Assam, based on the recommendations of the North-East Frontier Tribal and Excluded Areas Sub-Committee of the Constituent Assembly known as the Bordoloi Sub-Committee was incorporated in the Sixth Schedule to the Constitution of India.[30] This provided for constitution of Autonomous District Councils (ADCs) for major tribesmen and Autonomous Regional Councils for minor tribesmen other than the major tribal people within a district."[31] With these arrangements the Sixth Schedule offered a fair degree of self-government to the tribal people "by providing for autonomous districts and the creation of district and regional councils, which would exercise some of the legislative and judicial functions within the overall jurisdiction of the Assam legislature and the parliament."[32] Over the years, a number of autonomous district councils have been set up in various states under the provision of the Sixth schedule. However, autonomy and immunity to insurgency need not go hand in hand.

The hypothesis that the demands for autonomy are mere demands for better governance and not just aspirations for the creation of autonomous structures of governance is illustrated in the following anecdotes. The Karbi Anglong district in southern Assam, the largest in the state, is one of the Autonomous hill districts of the state. An Autonomous Council in the district constituted under the provision of the Sixth schedule (namely, Karbi Anglong Autonomous Council (KAAC)) controls all the development departments in the district.[33] A similar administrative arrangement in the neighbouring North Cachar Hills district known as The North Cachar Hills Autonomous District Council (NCHADC) has three wings of administration: Legislature, Judiciary, and Executive. Apart from the subjects enshrined in the sixth schedule, the Goverment of Assam has transferred almost all executive power to the Council except for those pertaining to general administration, police, treasury, elections and the judiciary.[34] The NCHADC is in charge of the revenue administration in the state. It collects and fixes land revenue, and handles overall management in regard to land — private and public. However, the objective of providing better governance through the District councils has remained unfulfilled in case of both the NCHADC and the KAAC. The councils have, instead, turned into a theatre of bitter politicking. The ruling Congress Party in the Assam and local parties like the Autonomous State Demand Committee (ASDC) have fought intensely to control the affairs in the Council. The utter failure of the ADCs has, in fact, given rise to a demand for formation of autonomous states in these districts.

Moreover, in spite of the existing provisions of autonomy, both districts have witnessed a significant surge in insurgent activities. The United People's Democratic Solidarity (UPDS) was formed in March 1999 with an objective of securing a homeland for the Karbi tribals within the framework of the Indian constitution by expanding the geographical limit of the present district of Karbi Anglong to include all the contiguous Karbi inhabited areas. After three years of armed movement, specially targeting the non-Karbi population, the outfit signed a ceasefire agreement on 23 May 2002. However, this led to a split in the outfit with a section of cadres forming another outfit, the Karbi Longri North Cachar Hills Liberation Front (KLNLF). While UPDS continues to negotiate with the government at the time of writing, 422 cadres of the KLNLF surrendered and entered into a ceasefire agreement in February 2010.[35]

Similarly, in the North Cachar Hills district, the Dima Halim Daogah (DHD) was formed in 1995, with an objective of forming a separate homeland for the Dimasa tribe. The outfit entered into a ceasefire agreement with the Indian government on January 1, 2003. However, differences over the negotiations led to the formation of a splinter group, the Black Widow on June 24, 2004. After a violent stint spanning over five years, the Black Widow entered into a ceasefire agreement in October 2009.[36]

Autonomy, however, continues to be the state's preferred strategy to deter separatist movements from assuming violent overtones. The Assam government appears to have taken an extremely liberal stand on granting Autonomous District Councils to the tribes in Assam, without ascertaining the rationale behind such demands. This, despite the fact that the ADC experiment has been one of the most colossal failures in the experiment of granting autonomy to the tribes in the North East.

The incumbent Chief Minister of Assam is on record saying that his government would provide ADCs to any tribe demanding them. By forming the ADCs, the state government has been able to evade the responsibility of providing good administration for the entire territory of the state. At the same time, the non-release of funds by the state government, combined with a reluctance to part with significant legislative and administrative powers has made the ADCs mere tools to serve the personal and political interests of the tribal elites.

In marked contrast to the stand of the Assam government, other states of the North Eastern region have a rather unfavourable approach towards the existing ADCs within their geographical area, which are viewed as structures that undermine the authority of the state. The Mizoram government is in favour of dissolving the ADCs for the Chakma, Hmar, Lakher and Pawi tribes in the state. It has opposed, for years, the demand to create an ADC for the Reang tribes. Similarly, in Manipur, both the Manipur North Autonomous District Council and the Sadar Hill Autonomous District Council continue to function with very limited powers.

DEGENERATION OF INSURGENCIES

Another noticeable aspect of the separatist movements in the region is the gradual degeneration of the major insurgencies in the region to mere criminal and terrorist entities. To start with, many of the insurgencies in the North East had a reasonable set of demands that sought to address the alienation and deprivation pervasive among the tribals of the region. However, over the years, the insurgents' manifestos have shifted from insisting on the realization of those demands to concentrating more on receiving pecuniary benefits. Armed insurgency, thus, has been increasingly used with the latter end in mind.

For example, the ULFA highlighted a genuine popular concern in Assam against the illegal migration of Bangladeshi population into the state. It also spoke of the exploitation of Assam's natural resources (like oil) by "colonial" India for which Assam received little financial remuneration. The vastly popular Assam agitation in the 1980s, helped the cause of the outfit, which established a parallel government in the state. In the subsequent years, however, the outfit took refuge in Bangladesh and altered its position on the illegal migrants.[37] ULFA leadership in Bangladesh operated under the patronage of the Pakistani external intelligence agency, the Inter-Services Intelligence (ISI), which generously funded and armed the outfit.[38] Insurgent outfits like the ULFA had been turned into instruments of ISI's anti-India activities. In addition, the ULFA top leadership also invested in profit-making ventures in Bangladesh such as travel agencies, private schools, leather industry. In addition, large scale extortion activity in Assam contributed substantially to the outfit's coffers.

It attacked the non-Assamese Hindi speaking population to express its opposition to "Indian" presence in the state. It targeted the oil pipelines to highlight the "wrongful" exploitation of the state's natural resources by India. However, at the same time, it filled its coffers through extortion from the oil companies and the non-Assamese businessmen. Several of its bomb explosions killed Assamese school children. As a result, its popularity plummeted and only a few today support its demand for an independent Assam. In November and December 2009, Bangladesh handed four top ULFA leaders including its chairman Arabinda Rajkhowa to the Indian authorities.[39] The outfit's Commander-in-Chief Paresh Barua, however, continues to evade arrest and still speaks of securing an independent Assam, free from India's "subjugation".[40] In February 2011, the ULFA faction led by Arabinda Rajkhowa, started a peace dialogue with New Delhi.

Insurgencies in the region arose to fill up the vacuum created by dysfunctional administrative and political institutions. In the early stages of the insurgency movements, they benefited from the disenchantment prevalent among the exploited segments of the populace by promising an alternative and better system of governance. With time, some of these insurgencies have identified the prevalent chaos as excellent opportunities for financial windfall. Protracted conflicts in the region have led to the growth of an extremely opportunistic and corrupt bureaucrat-politician-contractor nexus in many of the states and the insurgencies have benefited immensely from such symbiotic relationships. Endemic violence and the states' inability to restore normalcy, have been chronic in states like Manipur, which has been ruled for years by weak and corrupt governments. This has helped the insurgencies to start and continue a highly lucrative extortion regime which spares not even the politicians and the bureaucrats. Popular narrative in Manipur indicates that every government official is made to part with a percentage of his salary by the insurgents. A few years back, the Indian Army Chief even accused the Chief Minister of Manipur of funding two insurgencies. On numerous occasions, hospitals, insurance agencies, business establishments, schools, transport agencies in the state have shutdown as a result of monetary demands of the insurgents. Civilians and government officials have been abducted and killed for failing to fulfil such demands.

The growing criminalization of the insurgencies is further evident from the rise of multiple organizations claiming to represent the same constituency. Apart from the two factions of the NSCN in Nagaland, several states of the region are also witnesses to such phenomena. For example, in Manipur, at least 15 insurgencies claim to represent the Kuki tribals. In Tripura, both the NLFT and the ATTF claim to speak for the indigenous tribal population. With limited avenues to increase their war chest, these insurgencies often fight each other (a practice reminiscent of gang wars) in bitter area domination exercises. In the economically impoverished and industrially backward North East, insurgency has often been referred to as the most thriving industry. The ability of the state to generate employment for its vast unemployed population remains, at best, limited. Insurgency movements have, thus, managed to attract a section of the youth, by their elaborate system of salary and ex-gratia payment for the deceased cadres.

CONCLUSION

India's success in resolving the insurgency movements in the North East has been limited. Although there has been significant progress in Tripura and Meghalaya in reducing insurgency related incidents and fatalities, states like Manipur, Assam and Nagaland continue to be trouble spots, without a solution in sight. Several scholars have argued that the approach of the Indian government towards the armed insurgencies in the region has ended up promoting the rise of such movements. Be it the military means through which New Delhi has tried to crush these movements or the tactic of protracted negotiations with the insurgencies with an objective of wearing them down, New Delhi's role has been a matter of intense debate among the analysts. Authors argue that such a policy is an outcome of the "weak federalism" enshrined in the constitution that provides enormous powers to a Central government engaged in the "twin projects of nation-building and national development."[41] However, it is also true that under the present circumstances, the option of using autonomy to resolve the armed conflicts has ceased to be a viable formula. Given the state of disarray and degeneration that the armed movements in the region are in, better governance through the existing structures of administration alone promises to be a more reliable pathway to peace and stability in the region.

Notes

1. Traditionally India's northeast comprises of seven states: Arunachal Pradesh, Assam, Manipur, Nagaland, Meghalaya, Tripura and Mizoram. In 2003, the state of Sikkim too has been included in the northeast. This chapter, however, limits itself to analysing the affairs in the seven states.
2. The sequence of British annexation was as following: Assam plains (1826), Cachar plains (1830), Khasi Hills (1833), Jaintia plains (1835), Karbi Anglong or Mikir Hills (1838), North Cachar Hills (1854), Naga Hills (1866–1904), Garo Hills (1872–73) and Mizo Hills (1890). See P.S. Datta, "Autonomy Movements in Assam — Documents", 1993, pp. 5–6.
3. R.N. Prasad, "Sixth Schedule and Working of the District Councils in North-Eastern States", *Dialogue* (New Delhi), vol. 6, no. 2 (October–December 2004).
4. The inner line permit system is still prevalent. For example, to visit states such as Mizoram, Arunachal Pradesh and Nagaland, Indian nationals require a permit from the state governments of the respective states which is valid for about fifteen days and can be extended further. For foreign nationals, states such as Manipur in addition to the three mentioned states, require Restricted Area Permits.
5. R.N. Prasad, "Sixth Schedule and Working of the District Councils in North-Eastern States".
6. "India — Terrorist, Insurgent and Extremist Groups", South Asia Terrorism Portal, <http://www.satp.org/satporgtp/countries/india/terroristoutfits/index.html>.
7. Insurgency related incident and figures have been collated from Annual Report, Ministry of Home Affairs, Government of India, various years.
8. Annual Report 2010–11, Ministry of Home Affairs, Government of India, p. 13.
9. ULFA is an acronym for United Liberation Front of Asom, NDFB for National Democratic Front of Bodoland, NSCN-IM for National Socialist Council of Nagaland-Isak-Muivah, NSCN-K for National Socialist Council of Nagaland-Khaplang, UNLF for United National Liberation Front, PLA for People's Liberation Army, PREPAK for People's Revolutionary Party of Kengleipak, NLFT for National Liberation Front of Tripura and ATTF for All Tripura Tiger Force. Fairly detail profiles of these insurgencies in the northeast are available at the South Asia Terrorism Portal, <www.satp.org>.
10. Counter-insurgency operations in the Northeast are conducted by the Army, Police and the para-military forces. The category "Security Forces" include all three.

11. For a detailed analysis of the Naga insurgency, see Udayon Misra, *The Periphery Strikes Back: Challenges to the Nation-State in Assam and Nagaland* (Shimla: IIAS, 2000). A shorter analysis by the same author is available in Udoyan Misra, "Naga Peace Talks: New Parameters, Fresh Challenges: The Issue of Sovereignty vs, Autonomy", in *Problems of Ethnicity in the North-East India*, edited by B.B. Kumar (Delhi: Astha Bharati, 2007).
12. The Shillong Accord was signed between the Government of India and the NNC cadres whereby the outfit accepted the primacy of the Indian constitution.
13. Isak Chisi Swu is the Chairman of the NSCN-IM and Thungaleng Muivah, its General Secretary. Khaplang is the Chief of the NSCN-K.
14. The NSCN-IM defines Nagalim as "a nation occupying an area of 120,000 sq. km of the Patkai Range at the tri-junction of China, India and Burma. Nagalim was apportioned between India and Burma. The part which India claims is subdivided and placed under four different administrative units: Assam, Arunachal Pradesh, Manipur and Nagaland states. The eastern part which Burma claims is placed under two administrative units: Kachin State and Sagaing Division (formerly known as the Naga Hills)", <http://www.nagalim.us/>.
15. For example, over 90 per cent voters exercised their franchise in the 2009 Parliamentary elections, <http://ceonagaland.nic.in/LokSabha2009/VoterTurnout.htm>.
16. For a profile of NSCN-U, see "National Socialist Council of Nagaland-Unification", South Asia Terrorism Portal, <http://www.satp.org/satporgtp/countries/india/states/nagaland/terrorist_outfits/NSCN_U.HTM>.
17. "About Mizoram", website of the Mizoram State Government, <http://mizoram.nic.in/about/history.htm>.
18. Ibid.
19. Monoj Kumar Nath, "Bodo Insurgency in Assam: New Accord and New Problems", *Strategic Analysis* (New Delhi), vol. 27, no. 4 (October–December 2003): 536.
20. The NDFB manifesto reads, "The Indian occupation of the territories of the Boro people in defiance to latter's prerogative to live as a free and independent people followed by the aggression of the Indian civilians as well as the illegal migrants of the neighbouring countries practically pushed the Boro people into a stateless people — both physically and spiritually. But no other than the Boro people have the right to rule over their ancestral territories. The NDFB is born to liberate our ancestral land, the land where our forefathers settled and started our civilization with hardship since time immemorial where their bones are still lying. It may not be viable, practicable or based on reality to liberate all the territories that once Boro people ruled. However, the NDFB shall fight to liberate every inch of our ancestral land", Manifesto of the National Democratic Front of Bodoland, undated, <http://www.geocities.com/ndfb2001/manifesto.htm>.

21. "2,641 militants surrender in Assam", 6 December 2003, <http://www.rediff.com/news/2003/dec/06assam.htm>.
22. A Memorandum of Settlement (MoS) for the creation of the BTC was reached at a tripartite meeting held in New Delhi on 10 February 2003, between the representatives of Union Government, Assam Government and a BLT delegation. The main provisions of the MoS relate "to creation of the BTC, an autonomous self governing body within the State of Assam and under the provisions of the Sixth Schedule of the Constitution of India to fulfil economic, educational and linguistic aspirations, socio-cultural and ethnic identity of the Bodos; and to speed up the infrastructure development in BTC area."
23. Manjula Bhattacharyya, "Safe passage offered to NDFB chief", *The Tribune*, 19 October 2004.
24. "India in truce with Bodo rebels", 25 May 2005, <http://news.bbc.co.uk/2/hi/south_asia/4578703.stm>.
25. Sushanta Talukdar, "Daimary held, handed over to BSF", *Hindu*, 2 May 2010.
26. Bibhu Prasad Routray, "Tripura: Creating An Unenviable Record", *South Asia Intelligence Review*, vol. 2, no. 14 (20 October 2003).
27. The remarkable counter-insurgency success in Tripura is yet to be documented and analysed in any serious manner. For a short assessment of the police effort see Ajai Sahni and Bibhu Prasad Routray, "Counter-insurgency Success", *South Asia Intelligence Review*, vol. 4, no. 7 (29 August 2005), <http://www.satp.org/satporgtp/sair/Archives/4_7.htm#assessment1>.
28. An "outsider" in the Northeast can be a fellow Indian who does not belong to the State, or can also be an illegal migrant who has entered into the State from countries like Bangladesh or Myanmar.
29. Wasbir Hussain, "Turf War in a Time of Truce", 17 October 2005, <http://www.outlookindia.com/article.aspx?228968>.
30. The Sixth Schedule of the Indian Constitution [Articles 224(2) and 275 (1)] deals with provisions relating to the administration of tribal areas in the states of Assam, Meghalaya, Tripura and Mizoram.
31. R.N. Prasad, "Panchayati Raj System in Mizoram", in *Decentralized Planning and Development*, edited by Amalesh Banerjee (New Delhi: Kanishka, 2004), p. 147.
32. Political Union of North-Eastern India, <http://www.indiansaga.info/history/postindependence/north_east.html>.
33. Official website of the Karbi Anglong district, Assam, <http://karbianglong.nic.in/>.
34. Official website of the North Cachar Hills district, Assam, <http://nchills.gov.in/NCHILLS-ADMIN.htm>.
35. "KLNLF Cadres Surrender in Karbi Anglong", 11 February 2010, <http://www.demotix.com/news/245989/klnlf-cadres-surrender-karbi-anglong>.
36. "Black Widow rebels surrender in Assam", 2 October 2009, <http://ibnlive.in.com/news/black-widow-rebels-surrender-in-assam/102569-3.html>.

37 Army operations within Assam forced the ULFA to relocate its camps and leadership to Bangladesh. In the early 1990s, in a publication, ULFA asked the people of Assam to appreciate the contribution made by the Bangladeshi migrants to the State. Such a stand led to a decline in its support base.
38 "Ex-Bangla spy chief confirms ISI-Ulfa link", <http://www.defence.pk/forums/bangladesh-defence/27606-ex-bangla-spy-chief-confirms-isi-ulfa-link.html>.
39 "ULFA chairman Arabinda Rajkhowa handed over to Delhi", 2 December 2009, <http://www.ndtv.com/news/india/ulfa_chairman_flown_to_delhi.php>.
40 "ULFA sticks to sovereignty demand", *Hindu*, 9 December 2009.
41 Sanjib Baruah, *India Against Itself: Assam and the Politics of Nationality* (New Delhi: Oxford University Press, 1999), p. 201.

References

Baruah, Sanjib. *India Against Itself: Assam and the Politics of Nationality*. New Delhi: Oxford University Press, 1999.

Bhaumik, Subir. *Insurgent Cross Fire: North-East India*. New Delhi: Lancer Publishers, 1996.

Chaube, S.K. *Hill Politics in Northeast India*. Patna: Orient Longman Limited, 1973.

Das, Samir Kumar. *Regionalism in Power*. New Delhi: Omsons Publications, 1997.

Datta, P.S., ed. *North East and the Indian State: Paradoxes of a Periphery*. New Delhi: Vikas Publishing House, 1995.

Dutta, N.C., ed. *Politics of Identity and Nation Building in North-East India*. New Delhi: South Asian Press, 1997.

Gohain, Hiren. *Assam: A Burning Question*. Guwahati: Spectrum Publications, 1985.

Hazarika, Sanjoy. *Strangers of the Mist: Tales of War & Peace from India's Northeast*. New Delhi: Penguin Books, 1995.

———. *Rites Passage: Border Crossings, Imagined Homelands, India's East and Bangladesh*. New Delhi: Penguin Books, 2000.

Kamei, Gangmumei. *Ethnicity and Social Change: An Anthology of Essays*. Imphal: Pouganglu Gangmei, 2002.

Maitra, Kiranshankar. *The Noxious Web: Insurgency in the Northeast*. New Delhi: Kanishka Publishers, Distributors, 2002.

Marwah, Ved. *Uncivil Wars: Pathology of Terrorism in India*. New Delhi: Harper Collins Publishers India, 1995.

Misra, Udayon. *The Periphery Strikes Back: Challenges to the Nation-State in Assam and Nagaalnd*. Shimla: Indian Institute of Advanced Study, 2000.

Nuh, V.K. *Struggle for Identity in North-east India: A Theological Response*. Guwahati, New Delhi: Spectrum Publications, 2001.

Nibedon, Nirmal. *North-East India: The Ethnic Explosion*. New Delhi: Lancers Publishers, 1981.

Nag, Sajal. *Contesting Marginality: Ethnicity, Insurgency and Subnationalism in North-East India*. New Delhi: Manohar, 2002.

Sachdeva, Gulshan. *Economy of the North-East: Policy, Present Conditions and Future Possibilities*. Delhi: Konark Publishers, 2000.
Sarin, V.I.K. *India's North-East in Flames*. Uttar Pradesh: Vikash Publishing House, 1982.
Singh, Bhupinder. *Autonomy Movements and Federal India*. Jaipur and New Delhi: Rawar Publications, 2002.
Singh, Rajkumar Manisana. *Customs of Manipuri Hindus*. Manipur: Smt Usha Devi, 2001.
Singh, Prakash. *Kohima to Kashmir: On the Terrorist Trail*. New Delhi: Rupa & Co., 2001.
Tucker, Shelby. *Among Insurgents: Walking Through Burma*. New Delhi: Penguin Books, 2000.
Verghese, B.G. *India's North East Resurgent: Ethnicity, Insurgency, Governance, and Development*. New Delhi: Konark Publishers, 1997.

12

SOUTHERN THAILAND: THE TROUBLE WITH AUTONOMY

Duncan McCargo

To the casual observer, the Southern Thai conflict looks like a classic case of autonomy waiting to happen. A minority population is conveniently located close to one of the country's borders; and assimilation policies have been incompletely successful, leaving residues of bitterness, resentment and violence. Rather than continue to run the minority region from Bangkok, why not simply give the Malay Muslims of the far South some form of autonomy? Why would a solution that seems to have "worked" (or at least to have reduced violence and improved matters greatly) in comparable conflicts ranging from Northern Ireland to Aceh not be worth exploring in the context of Southern Thailand? Unfortunately, it is not quite that simple.

Thailand's national identity, summarized in the ubiquitous shibboleth "Nation, Religion, King", is predicated upon a set of national myths about the country's origins. These include a belief that Siam was never colonized; that colonization was averted through the genius of King Chulalongkorn and the Chakri dynasty; and that Siam successfully adopted various features of a modern western nation, in order to demonstrate a high level of "civilization" that would provide a vaccine against colonization.[1] The models adopted by Siam were those of the two dominant colonial powers in Southeast Asia, Britain and France, both unitary states. In expanding Bangkok's territorial reach to include Lao, Khmer and Malay populations, Siam consistently favoured assimilation and centralization over federalist alternatives. Over time, traditional rulers were replaced by career bureaucrats appointed from Bangkok, in a process often dubbed "internal colonialism".

While leading civilian statesman Pridi Phanomyong did advance alternative ideas for governing Thailand (as the nation became) during the period following the 1932 end of absolute monarchy, by the 1950s Pridi was in exile, and the Chakri dynasty was once more in the ascendant. The long reign of King Bhumibol Adulyadej (since 1946) has seen the collapse of the communist threat in Thailand, remarkable economic growth, and the emergence of a more democratic politics. For most Thais, King Bhumibol deserves immense personal credit for guiding Thailand through an extraordinary period of transformation. Internal colonialism, assimilation, and the vigorous suppression of local identities have all been part of a winning formula for governing Thailand. To tinker with this formula is tantamount to questioning the legitimacy of the Chakri dynasty's preferred mode of rule. To introduce any form of autonomy in the far South would be to cede Thai territory to the enemy; worse still, it would tarnish the *barami* (charisma, merit, standing) of a great King whose time on the throne must be soon drawing to an end. As such, for many Thais (even quite liberal ones, let alone conservative bureaucrats and military officers), openly discussing ideas of autonomy for the far South actually borders on treason.

THE CONFLICT

Rebellion and violent conflict characterized the region intermittently for much of the twentieth century, though unrest declined considerably after the early 1980s. Since late 2001, however, Thailand's southern border has been the focus of renewed political violence.[2] The three provinces of Pattani, Yala and Narathiwat (plus four districts in neighbouring Songkhla) contain a Malay Muslim population of around 1.3 million people, or roughly 80 per cent of the population. Most speak Pattani Malay as their first language; while they hold Thai identity documents, they enjoy an ambiguous relationship with the Thai state (and some are dual Thai-Malaysian nationals). At the same time, Malay Muslims comprise less than 3 per cent of Thailand's population, and so constitute a very marginal group within the country as a whole, despite their numerical dominance in the deep South.

Between January 2004 and February 2011, 4,621 people were killed and 7,505 injured in the southern Thai insurgency.[3] The renewed violence reflected a reinvigorated and highly aggressive militant movement; it also illustrated the persistent failures of the Thaksin administrations (2001–06) in developing strategies to counter the violence. Thaksin's attempts to politicize security arrangements in the South, and his preoccupation with reshuffling senior police and military commanders, as well as relevant ministers, all contributed to major security failures such as the 28 April 2004 Kru-Ze mosque siege (in which thirty-two men were killed at point-blank range), and the deaths of 78 unarmed demonstrators in military custody on 25 October 2004.

Thaksin's attitude to the South reflected his frustrations with the political solution brokered by his predecessors in response to early waves of violent insurgency in the region from the early 1960s to the early 1980s. Thaksin believed that the social compact created by his predecessors had favoured the Democrat Party, the Fourth Army,[4] and their allies in the palace. The Prem Tinsulanond government (1980–88) had brokered an elite pact that dramatically reduced violence in the region. Members of the Islamic religious elite in the South received generous state subsidies to convert their pondok[5] into private Islamic schools offering both a religious and secular curriculum. At the same time, Malay Muslim politicians were encouraged to seek election to parliament in their own right, and some were able eventually to assume ministerial positions. Local government reforms in the 1990s allowed Malay Muslims to assume elected office as the heads and members of provincial, municipal and sub-district organizations. While these changes appeared to open up greater political space for Malay Muslim communities, in practice this space was tightly delimited.[6] Local authorities had limited budgets and were subject to constant monitoring and interference by district officers and provincial governors, all of whom were centrally appointed by Bangkok's Ministry of Interior. Representative politics was firmly subordinated to rule from the centre. During the Thaksin period, the limitations of representative politics under Thai rules became increasingly apparent: Malay Muslim politicians who had joined Thaksin's Thai Rak Thai Party[7] found themselves captured by Bangkok, and unable to speak out against the government's repressive security policies. Thaksin's administration successfully delegitimated Malay Muslim politicians in the eyes of their voters, thus undermining the basis of Thai rule in the deep South.

AUTONOMY IN HISTORICAL PERSPECTIVE

A central claim of the militant movement in Pattani is that the Malay sultanate was autonomous for centuries, until it was colonized by Siam in the early 1900s. Thai nationalist historians led by Prince Damrong Rachanuphap, by contrast, contend that Pattani paid tribute to Thai rulers from the Sukhothai period (1238–1438) onwards, and was, effectively, a tributary state of Siam for hundreds of years. In practice, however, a wide range of readings are possible, along a continuum stretching from the hard-line "Pattani has always been part of Thailand" to the equally doctrinaire "Pattani has always been independent". In a thoughtful recent paper on Pattani historiography, Davisakd Puaksom observed that "accepting tributary status as a survival policy in order to gain 'protection' is one thing, but 'belonging' to Siam is another".[8] Davisakd's argument is that Bangkok's grip on Pattani has never been really strong; Siam has faced repeated resistance and rebellion from a locale that has never accepted its *de facto* subordination to Thai dominance. Yet neither side in the conflict is willing to accept the complexity and ambiguity of their historical relationship. For the militant movement in Pattani, demands for absolute independence have become a relentless mantra.[9] In much the same way, Bangkok has long persisted in asserting a right to absolute control over the region. Any talk of renegotiating the relationship between centre and periphery smacked of treachery, and was tantamount to the humiliating "surrender" of Thai territory.

Prominent Pattani Islamic teacher Haji Sulong had proposed a form of self-government for the three provinces in March 1947, in a seven-point submission to a government committee. The seven proposals were: the four provinces (including Satun) should be governed together, by a local Muslim governor empowered to appoint and dismiss officials; Malay should be used as a language of instruction in primary schools; taxes collected in the area should be spent there; 80 per cent of the government officials should be local Malays; Malay and Thai should both be official languages; provincial Islamic committees should have authority to issue regulations concerning Islamic affairs; and Islamic courts should be separated from the provincial courts.[10] Conservatives were outraged by these proposals, which Sulong submitted to a Pridi Phanomyong-backed government (1946–47) that had expressed a willingness to consider alternative governance arrangements.[11]

Over the next six decades, intolerance towards such ideas only grew, since they appeared to threaten royalist understandings of Thai history that grew increasingly hegemonic during the Ninth Reign (1946–present). A series of constitutions declared Thailand to be one indivisible kingdom; the country was governed by a cadre of career bureaucrats based on standard principles that did not acknowledge regional, ethnic or cultural differences. Such assimilation policies worked relatively well in other parts of Thailand, including Satun,[12] but were deeply resented by Malay Muslims, who believed that their own region had a distinct and legitimate identity of long historical antecedence. While Haji Sulong's calls for a special form of governance in the region were quite different from the separatist stance supported by former

Malay ruler Tengku Abdulqadir, and his son Tengku Mahmud Mahayiddin, the Thai authorities were apparently incapable of understanding the difference between demands for autonomy and the quest for a separate state.[13] Jim Ockey has argued that Sulong's support for autonomy drew him into Thai politics on the side of Pridi Phanomyong, which later turned out to be the losing side: "Ironically, it was his involvement in Thai politics, rather than any attempt to separate from it, that would lead to his untimely death."[14] Sulong was arrested in 1954 and was apparently murdered by the police shortly afterwards, along with one of his sons.

While many educated Malay Muslims today personally support some form of autonomy, such arguments are normally expressed indirectly: to speak out in favour of autonomy is still to risk being branded a separatist, since there has been no intellectual space or political space for a moderate, reformist position. At one academic workshop I attended concerning options for governance reform in the area, the Malay-Muslim chair opened the session by declaring that all the day's discussions would be framed by the constitutional stipulation that Thailand was a unitary kingdom.[15] In an act of calculated naivety, a Bangkok-based academic participant then asked why more radical options could not be discussed in a closed-door academic forum, but no one replied. Our hosts were desperate to avoid any suggestion that they were promoting — or even tolerating — disloyal or separatist ideas. A serious discussion of the principles and practicalities of different modes of self-governance, let alone a separate Pattani state, simply could not be held in public, and precious few Malay Muslims would explore these topics very far with outsiders, even in private conversations. The oppressive ideology of the unitary kingdom remains remarkably hegemonic throughout Thailand. Buddhist government officials in the three provinces are usually uncomfortable with any talk of decentralization, seeing it as a potential "thin end of the wedge", a prelude to separatism.[16] Such concerns mirrored the views of officials elsewhere in the country, who had a considerable vested interest in preserving the current system: if governors ever ceased to be appointed, for example, the promotion and incentive structure of the Interior Ministry would collapse. A culture of resistance to virtually any form of decentralization was widespread among Interior Ministry officials and their allies: following the 2006 military coup, the highly conservative National Legislative Assembly abolished regular elections for village headmen, giving all incumbents the right to remain in office until the age of 60. A major political breakthrough of the 1990s was overturned at a stroke, with virtually no public protest. Given the prevailing climate, Malay Muslims were loath to put their heads above the parapet to press for decentralization measures. During the formal sessions of one workshop on options for decentralization, all the Malay Muslim participants advocated making modest amendments to the existing system of local government. But over dinner later that day, one participant remarked that he fully expected some sort of special administrative zone in the deep South before long, and other participants nodded in agreement.[17]

Sulong's 1947 petition continues to offer a useful set of starting points for options and debates around forms of autonomy in the South. The first of these concerns the scope of the region. Sulong envisaged a large region covering four provinces, including Satun. Sixty years on, Satun seems far more integrated into the rest of Thailand, and the case for including it as part of a special administrative region is rather problematic. There is a much stronger case for including four Malay-majority districts across the provincial border in Songkhla: Chana, Thepha, Nathwai and Saba Yoi. If some version of autonomy for the deep South is to be seriously explored, how would the "special zone" be defined and delimited? The second starting part is the notion of a "local governor". Sulong envisaged one governor for the whole region; but since Bangkok already elects its own governor, and recent constitutions envisage the possibility of other provinces doing the same, might Pattani, Yala and Narathiwat also elect their provincial governors? Electing governors in each of the three provinces would not be the same as creating a regional autonomous zone, but could offer a compromise solution that remains entirely consonant with the idea of Thailand as a unitary state. A third starting point is the idea that 80 per cent of government officials in the region should be local Malays, a notion that has been termed "representative bureaucracy".[18] Might localizing the bureaucracy go a long way towards alleviating Malay Muslim resentment of the Thai state? Such localization could take more or less radical forms. In conservative readings, localization might be carried out without any fundamental change in governance structures, or in the administrative relationship between Bangkok and far South. Unfortunately, even such relatively mild policy options were not actually mentioned — let alone proposed — by the only official body to have undertaken a systematic study of policy options for the South, the National Reconciliation Commission of 2005–06.

DEFINITIONS AND DISCOURSE

A language barrier makes autonomy hard to discuss in Thailand. Former premier Anand Panyarachun told the Foreign Correspondent's Club of Thailand that there was "no word" for autonomy in Thai, implying that the lack of a widely accepted direct translation rendered such political demands moot, simply for cultural and linguistic reasons.[19] The Thai word *ekkarat*, which might be rendered as "self-government", is most commonly translated as "independence"; this partly explains why Malay Muslims who call for the border provinces to be given more control over their own affairs have been routinely branded "separatists". Similarly, calls for a special zone (*khet phiset*) in the region raise hackles, and lead to objections that Malay Muslims are asking for privileges denied to other parts of the country. The term "self-governing area" (*khet pokkhrong ton eng*) is similarly hard for most Thais to swallow.

Singapore-based Thai academic Ora-orn Poocharoen has suggested that some new Thai vocabulary is needed in order to create the necessary discursive space to debate alternative governance arrangements for the deep South.[20] She suggests using the word *isara* to capture the meaning of the word "autonomy" (as already used in *ongkon isara*, or "autonomous organization", which has a positive connotation in Thai). Thus the border region might be granted "administrative autonomy" (*hai isara nai kanborihan pheun thi*), and be termed *khet isara, pheun thi isara* (autonomous zone or area), or *klum jangwat isara* (group of autonomous provinces). These terms could suggest a sharing of the burden of governance, rather than simply shifting it away from Bangkok. While some Thais will no doubt also find fault with these proposed terms, they offer a useful heuristic device for thinking beyond the boxes of existing linguistic choices. Another option is simply to render into Thai the English word "autonomy", thereby removing the emotional connotations of the various alternative Thai terms.

AUTONOMY AND THE NRC

At the beginning of March 2005, newly re-elected Prime Minister Thaksin Shinawatra established the National Reconciliation Commission (NRC), chaired by former prime minister Anand Panyarachun (1991–92). The fifty-member NRC was charged with exploring policy options to address the Southern conflict, and reflected criticism of Thaksin's hardline, security-oriented policies by senior figures close to the palace. After more than a year of deliberations, the NRC published its report in June 2006. The NRC's recommendations were largely ignored by Thaksin and by subsequent administrations. The modest recommendations focused mainly on issues of justice, identity and economic development, and none involved innovative proposals for the reform of governance in the region.[21]

In a presentation in Pattani on 30 October 2006, one former NRC member argued that the Commission had faced a fundamental choice between two different directions, determined by two different views of the conflict: was the conflict fundamentally a struggle over issues of justice, or was the conflict an expression of political aspirations by the Malay Muslim community?[22] Talking about justice was much easier than talking about governance, since the justice agenda allowed for a focus on implementation, and the cataloguing of specific grievances, while blurring core questions about how power was organized. Justice thus became the lowest common denominator upon which everyone could agree.

There was some early hope that the National Reconciliation Commission would broach ideas of autonomy in its report, that Thai Buddhist NRC members might say things that Malay Muslims dared not utter: the desirability of giving local people genuine political control of an area that differed greatly from the rest of Thailand in terms of culture, language and religion. Some Malay Muslim NRC members apparently hoped that their Buddhist colleagues would be willing to broach autonomy directly in the Commission's recommendations. But while a number of NRC members — primarily Bangkokians — sought to advance the idea of some form of substantive decentralization — it soon emerged that NRC chair Anand Panyarachun was not willing to pursue the idea. Some speculated that Anand had been given a "red light" from the palace, an indication that the King was implacably opposed to any kind of decentralization. One member explained that Anand and deputy chairman Prawase Wasi had tested the waters back in April 2005 with a proposal for a "Pattani Metropolitan Authority", and backed off when they met with hostile reaction from the press.[23] All talk of autonomy or a "special administrative zone" in the South was subsequently off-limits for discussion, even at closed-door NRC meetings.[24]

> The idea of autonomy or a special zone became a taboo in the meetings. They would limit that as much as possible. Anand or Prawase would immediately intervene when this was brought up. I have the feeling that they already fixed on that idea.[25]

Some Malay Muslim NRC members had hoped that Anand and Prawase — whose loyalty to the monarchy and the Thai state was beyond question — might have assisted them by articulating such proposals. Yet a number of NRC members believed that Anand was acting on instructions "from above" to ensure that these ideas did not find their way into the Commission's report.[26]

The NRC report mentions "decentralization" five times; four of the usages refer in very general terms to the remit of two proposed new bodies, the Southern Border Provinces Peace Strategy Administration Center (SBPSAC) and Council for the Development of the Southern Border Provinces Area.[27] The appropriate form of decentralization is not discussed in the report, but the policy is left to these new bodies to "promote" (SBPPASC) and "provide recommendations" (CDSBPA). The word "autonomy" does not appear once in the report, while there is a single reference to "special administrative zone", as something the militants were said to have opposed.[28] Nor does the NRC report mention the option of elected provincial governors, or the idea of representative bureaucracy. The failure of the NRC report to make a bold proposal for reforming the mode of governance in the three provinces meant that there was little prospect of undercutting the militant movement through a political offensive. From this perspective, the NRC report had simply failed the test; its proposals were worthy, but too dull to have any real impact. *The Nation* newspaper journalist Supalak Ganjanakhundee, co-author of an invaluable book on the conflict,[29] accused the NRC of not going far enough — the recommendations were simply insufficiently bold,[30] since the Commission failed to propose a special set of governance arrangements for the three provinces.

Many local politicians favoured building upon the creation of TAOs by further decentralizing power structures in the deep South. One Malay Muslim *nayok* TAO[31] argued that the existing bureaucratic structure should be dismantled, and gubernatorial elections introduced:

> I support elections for the governor and *nayok* TAO. We can abolish *kamnan*, because we already have TAOs in place. We now have two systems running in parallel ... the people sent down here by the government to solve the problems don't know anything about it. None of them ever ask for my advice. I cannot rely on those people.[32]

Informants who expressed these sorts of ideas often pointed out that Bangkok and Pattaya had their own distinctive governance arrangements, and that the constitution allowed for the election of provincial governors.[33] Bangkok Thais had elected their own governors from 1985 onwards, but withheld the same rights from people with a strong historical and cultural claim to oversee their own affairs. The failure of the NRC even to consider elected governors as an option for the three provinces illustrated the difficulties surrounding discursive progress, let alone serious policy initiatives — and had the effect of legitimating violent struggle against an apparently intractable Thai state. A further difficulty concerned fears of a "contagion effect": would granting some form of decentralization in the South lead to parallel demands in the Northeast, the North, and other parts of Thailand, both of which also have strong regional identities? Given the essentially arbitrary nature of the modern Thai state, which includes large populations who might claim Malay, Khmer, Chinese or Lao ethnicity, conservatives feared that granting greater autonomy to the southern border provinces could lead to the unraveling of Thailand as presently understood.

VIEWS ON THE GROUND

The question of what Malay Muslims in the region really want is a vexed one. Conducting accurate surveys of popular sentiment in the area remains extremely difficulty, since ordinary informants are equally fearful of both Thai state agencies and militant groups. The militants themselves persistently decline to claim responsibility for their actions or to advance a formal set of demands. Many analysts have suggested that the militant movement constitutes a form of "leaderless rebellion", a "network without a core", rather than a conventional top-down insurgency.[34] "Hassam" a self-proclaimed militant leader cited in *Time* magazine, appeared vague about the demands of the movement, telling interviewers that he did not want an independent Islamic state, just a boost in representative politics — "more Muslims in local government" — coupled with reductions in the level of Thai security forces.[35] Leaflets apparently produced by the movement were also sketchy about militant demands; this main focus was on demonizing the Thai state and the *munafik* who supported it, and on regaining Pattani from Siamese oppression.[36] Only a handful of leaflets went further. One directly stated "Our effort is to create an Islamic kingdom in the land of Pattani",[37] while another asserted "we will construct the Pattani state as a righteous palace, and make it safe and peaceful in the desirable way in the sight of God".[38] Former Narathiwat MP Najmuddin Umar believed that in practice, over time two core demands would emerge: negotiations for autonomy, and a referendum on the question of independence.[39] Najmuddin predicted that if such a referendum ever took place, those advocating independence might win by a margin of around 2: 1. While those actively involved in militant activity constituted only a tiny minority of the region's population, large numbers of Malay Muslims were clearly ready to support militant activity by joining demonstrations, peopling barricades, or refusing to provide information to the authorities. The real political views of these Malay Muslims remained unknown: how far was their cooperation with the militants the result of fear, and how far did it reflect opposition to the Thai state?

The only detailed elaboration of post-independence political arrangements appears in the appendices to *Berjihad di Pattani*, a controversial booklet found on the body of one of the militants killed inside the Kru-Ze mosque on 28 April 2004. The document proposes creating a body known as the "Council for Constitution and Traditional Customs of the State of Pattani". This *ulama* Council would then appoint a King, a ruler descended from the old Pattani sultans. The Council would be empowered to remove the King if he behaved unjustly. The *ulama* Council would also appoint a lower council, comprising educated professionals selected by the people, which would serve as a kind of cabinet to oversee the running of the Pattani state. The elaborate political structures envisaged in *Berjihad di Pattani*, which combine a just monarch, the rule of *ulama*, and modern notions of managerial rule by popularly selected technocrats, ask more questions than they answer, drawing on multiple competing sources of legitimacy. But calling for the restoration of the old Pattani sultanate was calculated to infuriate conservative Thais: the proposal went straight to the heart of the problem, the Chakri dynasty's legitimacy deficit in the far South.

In practice, independence for a tiny Pattani state sandwiched between Thailand and Malaysia seems a deeply unrealistic prospect, and there are reasons to believe that the militants would settle for some form of autonomy. Drawing on his participation in informal talks on the conflict brokered by former Malaysian prime minister Mahathir Mohamad (1981–2003) on the island of Langkawi in early 2006, Anand Panyarachun insisted to me that no one supported autonomy, not even the separatist groups.[40] But others involved in the Langkawi talks have suggested that the discussions never got down to brass tacks. PULO foreign affairs spokesman Kasturi Makota strongly intimated that the militant movement would be interested in discussing such possibilities, if the Thai authorities had a serious proposal to make.[41] He claimed that BRN-C[42] would also be ready to join such talks, which PULO would be happy to facilitate. Only a liberalization in the wider political climate would make popular discourse about new governance arrangements possible, and only under such changed conditions could the degree of public support for some form of autonomy readily be ascertained.

AUTONOMY REVISITED

Perhaps the most interesting recent contribution to the autonomy debate was an intervention by former NRC Vice-Chair Dr Prawase Wasi in late 2007, shortly before the general election. Speaking at a Bangkok seminar on 8 November, Prawase cut to the chase, declaring that talking about autonomy for the region was not an expression of disloyalty to the monarchy. Given Prawase's standing as a senior figure in Thai society, and a key member of the liberal wing of "network monarchy",[43] this was a remarkable statement, and marked a significant step forward from the public positions espoused by the NRC. Using a medical analogy, he suggested that different organs of the body might need different forms of treatment in order to save a patient from dying, so different parts of a state should be able to retain their identity:

> But we tend to forbid talking about this, because it can't be mentioned, we are afraid of touching on royal powers or something, but I think we should talk about it. Having autonomy does not mean we don't love the King. If there was no democracy, his Majesty would not be happy at all.[44]

Prawase's carefully chosen words were significant in various ways. He explicitly suggested that self-governance was linked to the preservation of identity, a very different position from the NRC view that "Malay Muslims of Thai nationality" could retain their identity within the existing centralized power structures of the Thai state. He explicitly linked the idea of self-governance to democracy, suggesting that real democracy might require the granting of autonomy to groups with a strong sense of identity. He also stated that the King was a supporter of democracy (an apparent response to those commentators, such as American journalist and unauthorized royal biographer Paul Handley, who had suggested that the King advocated anti-democratic ideas);[45] by implication, the King ought to have no problem accepting some form of autonomy for the South. Perhaps most importantly, Prawase's use of his medical metaphors pointed to a clear prognosis: a new form of governance in the South was now potentially a matter of life or death. Thailand had to adapt, or the nation might cease to exist in its current form. While surgery on the Thai body politic might prove painful, there was no realistic alternative.

Dr Prawase's public statements are always thoughtful, deliberate, and calculated to bring his ideas media exposure.[46] As the architect of the 1997 constitution and many subsequent projects of social and political reform, Prawase is Thailand's leading social entrepreneur, a master at provoking public debate and sowing the seeds of policy change. An apparently casual Prawase seminar comment often bears significant fruit within three to five years, as he gradually mobilizes his formidable networks of bureaucratic and civil society supporters to develop new initiatives.

Perhaps the first sign that Prawase's efforts to mainstream the discussion of autonomy as an option for the South was having an impact came in February 2008, when newly-appointed Interior Minister Chalerm Yubamrung expressed support for exploring autonomy as an option for the far South.[47] Apparently influenced by his advisors, the outspoken and often controversial minister may have been hoping to upgrade his image from "godfather" to that of political heavyweight, by advocating a major policy initiative. In the event, the idea was quickly slapped down as potentially dangerous by prime minister Samak Sundaravej; Chalerm was ousted in a cabinet reshuffle a few months later. But Chalerm's raising the idea at all testified to the fact that such talk was no longer taboo. Ideas of autonomy were at last becoming thinkable, if not yet actionable. Something was stirring among Bangkok's public intellectuals and politicians. The point was further illustrated when Samak himself returned from a visit to Indonesia and suggested to Cabinet that the "Aceh model" might offer a solution to the problems of Southern Thailand.[48] At the end of June 2008, a team of academics led by Srisompob Jitpiromsri of Prince of Songkhla University, Pattani, published a lengthy report advocating the creation of a new Ministry to oversee the Southern border provinces.[49]

CONCLUSION

Autonomy for Thailand's southern border region remains a surprisingly difficult policy option to explore, for a range of historical, emotional and political reasons that have been outlined here. To express support for (or even a passing interest in) ideas of autonomy has been seen as taking the side of the old Malay sultans, Haji Sulong, and Pridi Phanomyong against the Chakri dynasty, the palace, and the military-bureaucratic establishment of Thailand. As such, a reasoned debate about options for substantive decentralization of power in the region is almost impossible. The issues are simply too bound up with national mythology and popular emotions to be discussed on their other merits. To date, there has been no public forum at which a range of options for autonomy in the South have been directly discussed, or any published policy document in which alternative possibilities are systematically outlined.

Despite Thailand's apparently strong and unitary state, intense conflicts between Thaksin supporters and loyal monarchists since 2006 have demonstrated that the country is characterized by deep social and political divides. As the royal succession grows ever nearer, these divides are becoming more and more acute. The darkest fear of the Bangkok elite is that autonomy for the deep South, accompanied by a succession crisis, might help trigger the dismemberment of modern Thailand, unraveling the great nation-building achievements of Chulalongkorn and Bhumibol: as part of this process, a Malay sultan could be restored in Pattani. While such fears are extremely far-fetched, they testify to the level of national anxiety that currently afflicts Thailand.

Nevertheless, there is now real hope for a more open and productive debate about governance options for the far South that will move beyond hysteria and anxiety. The recent intervention by no less a figure than Prawase Wasi, urging his fellow Thais not to equate discussing autonomy with disloyalty to the palace, was an important step forward. So was former Interior Minister Chalerm Yubamrung's public statement of support for exploring these issues. The problem remains the rather glacial pace at which a change in elite thinking is taking place, at a time when the violence in the South demands urgent attention. Further acts of boldness are needed from those who dare to push the envelope on these possibilities. Autonomy proposals may or may not hold the key to resolving the Southern Thai conflict, but an open debate about policy alternatives and possible new forms of governance would be an important step forward.

Notes

The research presented here was funded by the Economic and Social Research Council, grant number RES-000-22-1344. Research assistance drawn upon was provided by Bhatchara Aramsri and Kaneeworn Opetagon. Many thanks are due to Srisompob Jitpiromsri and his colleagues at Prince of Songkhla University, Pattani, for hosting my fieldwork from September 2005 to September 2006; and to Thomas Parks and Ora-orn Poocharoen for their very useful comments on an earlier version of this chapter.

1. On more discussion of the historical background to the Southern Thai issue, see the chapter by Thomas Parks in this volume.
2. For background analysis of the Southern Thai conflict, see International Crisis Group, "Southern Thailand: Insurgency, Not Jihad", *Asia Report* 98 (May 2005), <http://www.crisisgroup.org>, and other ICG reports at the same site; Human Rights Watch, "No One is Safe: Insurgent Violence against Civilians in Thailand's Southern Border provinces", *Human Rights Watch Report*, vol. 19, no. 13(C) (August 2007); Marc Askew, *Conspiracy, Politics and a Disorderly Border: The Struggle to Represent Insurgency in Thailand's Deep South* (Washington, D.C.: East West Center, 2007); Duncan McCargo, ed., *Rethinking Thailand's Southern Violence* (Singapore: NUS Press, 2007) (a revised version of the March 2006 special issue of *Critical Asian Studies*, vol. 38, no. 1); and Duncan McCargo, *Tearing Apart the Land: Islam and Legitimacy in Southern Thailand* (Ithaca, NY: Cornell University Press, 2008).
3. Personal communication from Srisompob Jitpiromsri, 22 March 2011. While the Joh-Ai-Rong army base attack of 4 January 2004 is generally seen as the

symbolic starting point of the renewed violence, serious attacks on the security forces had begun as early as December 2001, less than a year after the first Thaksin Shinawatra government took office.

4   The Army region covering the South.
5   Traditional Islamic boarding schools.
6   For a detailed elaboration of these arguments, see McCargo, *Tearing Apart the Land*.
7   Literally, "Thais love Thais" party.
8   Davisakd Puaksom, "Patani historiography in contention", in *Thai South and Malay North: Ethnic Interactions on a Plural Peninsula*, edited by Michael Montesano and Patrick Jory (Singapore: NUS Press, 2008), p. 76.
9   Davisakd, "Patani historiography", p. 88.
10 Chalermkiat Khunthongpetch, *Hayi Sulong Abdul Kade: kabot ru wiraburut haeng si jangwat phak tai* [Haji Sulong Abdul Gade: Rebel or Hero of the Four Southern Provinces], (Bangkok: Matichon Publishing, 2005), p. 87.
11 See James Ockey, "The religio-nationalist pilgrimages of Haji Sulong Abdulkadir al Fattani", p. 25, unpublished, undated paper. Ockey argues that Sulong's political goals were inseparable from his aspiration to revitalize and purify local Islam.
12 On the case of Satun, see chapter by Thomas Parks in this volume.
13 For a discussion, see James Ockey, "Elections, Political Integration and Cultural Pluralism in the Lower South of Thailand", in *Thai South and Malay North*, edited by Montesano and Jory.
14 James Ockey, "The religio-nationalist pilgrimages", p. 32
15 Workshop in the lower South, 9 March 2006.
16 Ockey, "Elections, Political Integration and Cultural Pluralism".
17 Workshop discussion, Pattani, December 2005.
18 See Ora-orn Poocharoen, "Representative Bureaucracy: An Alternative for Bridging the Gap between the State and Citizen", draft research paper, Faculty of Political Science, Chulalongkorn University, 24 December 2006.
19 Anand Panyarachun speech to Foreign Correspondents' Club of Thailand, 18 May 2005, recorded on DVD issued by the National Reconciliation Commission, 2005.
20 Dr Ora-orn Poocharoen, LKY School of Public Policy, National University of Singapore, e-mail communications of 9 and 27 June 2008.
21 National Reconciliation Commission, *Overcoming Violence Through the Power of Reconciliation*, English version (Bangkok: NRC, 2006).
22 Presentation at EWC and IDSS workshop on Southern conflict, CS Pattani Hotel, 30–31 October 2006.
23 NRC member interview, 21 May 2006.
24 Anand recounted to me that when he met militant leaders at talks in Langkawi, Malaysia, brokered by former Malaysian premier Mahathir Mohammed, they informed him that autonomy was not one of their demands. Conversation,

7 September 2006. He told an interviewer that following two or three meetings with "this group" he did not believe separatism or an independent state was the aim of the movement either. *Post Today*, 24 July 2006.

25 NRC member interview, 21 May 2006.
26 This point draws on several interviews and conversations with NRC members. It is also equally possible to argue that Anand received no actual instructions "from above", but sought nevertheless to ensure that the NRC report accorded with the known or assumed preferences of the palace.
27 NRC Report, pp. 104–7.
28 NRC Report, p. 58.
29 Supalak Ganjanakhundee and Don Pathan (with the Nation Group news team), *Santhiphap nai plaew phleung* [Peace in Flames] (Bangkok: Nation Books, 2004).
30 *Samphat Supalak Ganjanakhundee: kor or sor mai lomlaeo, kae sunplao thaonan eng* [Interview with Supalak Ganajanakhundee: The NRC was Not a Failure, It was just Pointless], <www.prachatai.com>, 19 June 2006.
31 TAO is an abbreviation for "Tambon (Sub-district) Administrative Organization"; TAOs are led by nayok, elected heads.
32 Nayok TAO, 28 November 2005. Kamnan are the chief headmen of each subdistrict.
33 For example, TAO nayok interview, 13 December 2005.
34 For a detailed discussion of the debate concerning the nature of the militant movement in the South, see Duncan McCargo, *Tearing Apart the Land*, pp. 168–81.
35 Andrew Marshall with Don Pathan, "In death's shadow", *Time* (Asia), 26 November 2006.
36 *Munafik* are "traitors" to the Islamic religion.
37 Leaflet 34, found inserted into the journal of Thamma Withaya Foundation, 28 September 2004.
38 Leaflet 53, fax dated 4 August 2005.
39 Najmuddin Umar interview, 18 August 2006.
40 Conversation with Anand Panyarachun, 7 September 2006.
41 Kasturi Makota, Patani United Liberation Organization (PULO) Foreign Affairs chief, interview in Sweden, 10 May 2007.
42 Barisan Revolusi Nasional Coordinate.
43 On the idea of "network monarchy", see Duncan McCargo, "Network monarchy and legitimacy crises in Thailand", *The Pacific Review*, vol. 18, no. 4 (2005): 499–519.
44 Prachatai On-Line "'Prawase': non tai pokkhrong ton eng yan mai krathop phrarachamnat lae mai chai mai rak 'nai luang'" [Prawase: insists self governance for South does not affect royal powers and does not suggest lack of love for the King], <www.prachatai.com> (accessed 10 November 2007).
45 See Paul Handley, *The King Never Smiles: An Unauthorized Biography of King Bhumibol Adulyadej* (New Haven CT: Yale University Press, 2006), pp. 430–31.

⁴⁶ For a revealing discussion of the mechanisms by which Prawase helped create the 1997 constitution, see Prawase Wasi, "An overview of political reform", in *Reforming Thai Politics*, edited by Duncan McCargo (Copenhagen: NIAS, 2002), pp. 21–27.
⁴⁷ *Financial Times*, 12 February 2008.
⁴⁸ See "Aceh model to be studied, adopted for quelling strife", *Bangkok Post*, 4 June 2008. Precisely what Samak meant by the "Aceh model" remains unclear, but the term seems to hold open the possibility of reviewing governance arrangements.
⁴⁹ Srisompob Jitpiromsri and Sukri Langputeh, *Kanpokkhrong thongthin baep phiset nai jangwat chaidaen phaktai, raingan khrongkan wijai kanpokkhrong thongthin nai jangwat thi mi khwam laklai chatiphan* [Special arrangements for local government in the Southern border provinces: Research report on local government in ethnically diverse provinces], Center for Peace and Development Studies, Mahidol University, 30 June 2008.

References

Anand Panyarachun, speech to Foreign Correspondents' Club of Thailand, 18 May 2005, recorded on DVD issued by the National Reconciliation Commission, 2005.

Andrew Marshall with Don Pathan. "In death's shadow", *Time* (Asia), 26 November 2006.

Askew, Marc. *Conspiracy, Politics and a Disorderly Border: The Struggle to Represent Insurgency in Thailand's Deep South*. Washington, D.C.: East West Center, 2007.

Chalermkiat Khunthongpetch. *Hayi Sulong Abdul Kade: kabot ru wiraburut haeng si jangwat phak tai* [Haji Sulong Abdul Gade: Rebel or Hero of the Four Southern Provinces]. Bangkok: Matichon Publishing, 2005.

Davisakd Puaksom. "Pattani Historiography in Contention". In *Thai South and Malay North: Ethnic Interactions on a Plural Peninsula*, edited by Michael Montesano and Patrick Jory. Singapore: NUS Press, 2008.

Human Rights Watch. "No One is Safe: Insurgent Violence against Civilians in Thailand's Southern Border provinces". *Human Rights Watch Report*, vol. 19, no. 13 (C) (August 2007).

International Crisis Group. "Southern Thailand: Insurgency, Not Jihad". Asia Report 98, May 2005. <http://www.crisisgroup.org>.

McCargo, Duncan. "Network monarchy and legitimacy crises in Thailand". *The Pacific Review*, vol. 18, no. 4 (2005): 499–519.

———., ed. *Rethinking Thailand's Southern Violence*. A revised version of the March 2006 special issue of *Critical Asian Studies*, vol. 38, no. 1. Singapore: NUS Press, 2007.

———. *Tearing Apart the Land: Islam and Legitimacy in Southern Thailand*. Ithaca NY: Cornell University Press, 2008.

National Reconciliation Commission. *Overcoming Violence Through the Power of Reconciliation*. English version. Bangkok: NRC, 2006.

Ockey, James. "Elections, Political Integration and Cultural Pluralism in the Lower South of Thailand". In *Thai South and Malay North: Ethnic Interactions on a Plural Peninsula*, edited by Michael Montesano and Patrick Jory. Singapore: NUS Press, 2008.

———. "The religio-nationalist pilgrimages of Haji Sulong Abdulkadir al Fattani". Unpublished, undated paper, p. 25.

Ora-orn Poocharoen. "Representative Bureaucracy: An Alternative for Bridging the Gap between the State and Citizen". Draft research paper, Faculty of Political Science, Chulalongkorn University, 24 December 2006.

Paul Handley. *The King Never Smiles: An Unauthorized Biography of King Bhumibol Adulyadej*. New Haven CT: Yale University Press, 2006.

Prachatai On-line "'Prawase': non tai pokkhrong ton eng yan mai krathop phrarachamnat lae mai chai mai rak 'nai luang'" [Prawase: insists self governance for South does not affect royal powers and does not suggest lack of love for the King]. <www.prachatai.com> (accessed 10 November 2007).

Prawase Wasi. "An overview of political reform". In *Reforming Thai Politics*, edited by Duncan McCargo. Copenhagen: NIAS, 2002.

Srisompob Jitpiromsri and Sukri Langputeh. *Kanpokkhrong thongthin baep phiset nai jangwat chaidaen phaktai, raingan khrongkan wijai kanpokkhrong thongthin nai jangwat thi mi khwam laklai chatiphan* [Special arrangements for local government in the Southern border provinces: Research report on local government in ethnically diverse provinces]. Center for Peace and Development Studies, Mahidol University, 30 June 2008.

Supalak Ganajanakhundee. *Samphat Supalak Ganjanakhundee: kor or sor mai lomlaeo, kae sunplao thaonan eng* [Interview with Supalak Ganjanakhundee: the NRC was not a failure, it was just pointless]. <www.prachatai.com> (accessed 19 June 2006).

Supalak Ganjanakhundee and Don Pathan (with the Nation Group news team). *Santhiphap nai plaew phleung* [Peace in Flames]. (Bangkok: Nation Books, 2004).

13

THE LAST HOLDOUT OF AN INTEGRATED STATE: A CENTURY OF RESISTANCE TO STATE PENETRATION IN SOUTHERN THAILAND

Thomas Parks

Similar to other countries in Southeast Asia, Thailand has been affected by internal conflicts for much of the post-colonial era. The resurgence of violence in southern Thailand is the latest episode of an ongoing centre-periphery conflict that has its roots in the consolidation of the Thai state beginning in the early twentieth century. Contrary to the Philippines and Indonesia, however, Thailand has never seriously considered decentralization of state authority as a response to insurgent grievances. While other countries in South and Southeast Asia have recently experimented with autonomy arrangements as response to long-running separatist conflicts, the concept of autonomy has long been anathema to the Thai body politic.

There have, however, been periods of relaxed centralization, increased restraint by Thailand's security forces, and the expansion of political space for conflict-affected minority populations that have been instrumental in fostering a détente between the state and separatist insurgents, leading to significant periods of calm. In most cases, actually, Thailand's minority populations have been peacefully integrated into the nation-state, especially in regions where the extension of the state happened gradually, with limited intrusion into local communities. In the Thai context, the critical policy dialogue on the causes and responses to insurgency does not consider autonomy *per se*, but rather the degree to which centralization of authority is applied over time and the level of state coercion used to enforce this authority.

This chapter will analyze the historical ebb and flow of centralization and coercion by the Thai state in conflict-affected peripheral regions. In particular, why have some ethnic minorities been peacefully integrated into the state, while others have resisted state control for decades? We will use a simple model, designed for this analysis, to compare different state approaches for consolidating control in minority regions and corresponding patterns of resistance to state authority. The model will be used to compare the history of centre-periphery relations in Satun province (located at the western end of the border with Malaysia) and the northeastern region (usually referred to as Isaan), as a contrast to the conflict-affected southern border provinces of Pattani, Yala and Narathiwat. While these regions share many similar characteristics — including relatively recent incorporation into the Thai state; a high concentration of non-Thai minority groups; and the deterioration of local autonomy as the state consolidated its power in the early twentieth century — the level of violent resistance to the state has varied considerably between them.

If coercive methods of state penetration tend to alienate minority populations, mobilize resistance to the state and exacerbate conflict, why has the Thai government continued to rely on this approach in the south? Furthermore, if the policies and structures of state penetration are widely recognized as irritants to the conflict, why have these policies continued to exist even during periods of calm? This chapter will argue that the core problem in the perpetuation of the conflict lies in the apparatus of state penetration that, now, has deep roots in the southern provinces, and is defended by powerful interests that have heavily invested in the status quo. Ending the conflict in southern Thailand will require a major re-alignment of political interests to allow for a relaxation of central control and the passage of controversial reforms. These are unlikely to occur in the current political environment.

STATE PENETRATION AND THE ORIGINS OF ARMED INSURGENCY

In South and Southeast Asia, the consolidation of state control in peripheral regions has been a defining challenge for many countries in the post-colonial era, and has provided the impetus for several long-running armed insurgencies.

The nation-building process has usually entailed rapid centralization of state authority and control over local resources, which has shifted the locus of power in the peripheral regions from local elites to central state actors. In many cases, this power shift has engendered centre-periphery conflicts between central state actors and peripheral resistance movements organized by displaced local elites.

Broadly speaking, the story of state-building and integration of ethnic minorities has been largely a successful one in Thailand. Compared to other multi-ethnic states in Southeast Asia, Thailand has managed to integrate large populations of ethnic minority groups into the national political and economic mainstream with a high degree of success. Many of Thailand's most powerful people today originate from assimilated minority populations, including several recent prime ministers.

The case of the southern provinces, however, illuminates the unpleasant face of state-building in Thailand. The Malay Muslim[1] population in the southern provinces is arguably the last major unintegrated non-Thai ethnic group. While there are other cases, these southern provinces are unique in terms of the longevity and resilience of their local resistance to political integration by the state. Forced assimilation efforts by the state have only served to strengthen local resistance, and the population remains largely unassimilated.[2] Why have integration and assimilation efforts failed in the southernmost provinces?

One important explanation for this failure can be found in the history of poor governance and mismanaged state efforts to integrate the local population. Over the past 100 years, the Thai government has sought to consolidate its control over the Malay Muslim population in the southern provinces through a combination of state penetration policies and a heavy security presence. State penetration can be defined as the imposition of state control in peripheral regions by centralizing control of local affairs, displacing traditional local power structures, and undermining (or suppressing) local identities that compete with the national identity as defined by the state. The policies of penetration also often include manipulation of local politics through the marginalization of local leaders, stifling of local political dissent, and allocation of positions and privileges to non resident newcomers that are loyal to the state. These policies are usually intended to accelerate integration and assimilation, and correspondingly reduce support for resistance movements. In southern Thailand, however, these measures have had the opposite effect, and have prolonged violent confrontation by alienating the local population and strengthening local support for resistance movements.

The history of political relations between the centre and peripheral regions in Thailand can be summarized as a gradual, long-term decline of local autonomy in peripheral regions. Today Thailand is one of the most centralized states in Southeast Asia. Prior to 1900, however, the Government of Siam had very little control over the daily affairs in its peripheral regions. Much of the territory along today's international borders once belonged to independent city-states that enjoyed substantial autonomy from Siam and other neighbouring power centres. Power-centres would use coercion, co-optation, and other means to extend their influence into the periphery. This arrangement allowed for significant local autonomy in the peripheral regions. According to Thongchai, the outlying tributary regions "were regarded as separate kingdoms;" the ruler of the tributary "had his own court, administrative and financial system, tax collection, army, and judicial system."[3]

The drawing of international borders and the formation of the modern nation-state led to the breakdown of this traditional arrangement between elites in the centre and the periphery. In the late eighteenth century, Siam was surrounded by expansionist colonial powers including British Malaya and Burma, and French Indochina. Concerned by increasing pressure for territorial concessions, and an increasingly belligerent tone from some Western traders in the area, the Royal Government of King Chulalongkorn took steps to consolidate its weak control over the border regions that separated Siam from neighbouring colonial territories. From 1890 to 1909, the government undertook a series of mapping initiatives and negotiated treaties with the Western powers to demarcate international boundaries.[4]

These new territorial borders were an entirely new phenomenon in Southeast Asia, and in many cases, cut right through the traditional territories of ethnic minorities in the regions lying along the border. This process effectively divided populations with shared ethnic identities on both sides of the border, and in many cases, divided families and long-established kinship networks. The Anglo-Siamese treaty of 1909, for example, divided the population and territories of the Malay sultanate of Pattani[5] and the northernmost province of Kedah (including the modern Thai province of Satun) from the rest of the ethnic Malay homeland.[6]

Beginning in the 1880s, the Siamese government initiated a series of reforms that fundamentally changed the state and dramatically altered the relationship between centre and periphery. The reforms affected revenue, local administration, religious hierarchy, and education in the outlying areas. By controlling the flow of resources and revenue, the government could increase its wealth and capacity, while weakening potential rivals including the aristocracy, provincial rulers, and the Europeans.[7] Traditionally, provincial nobles had controlled the local labor force and economy through corvée labor and local taxes. The reforms allowed the central government to control revenue in the provincial areas, removing the source of wealth and power from local rulers and establishing direct economic relationships with the rural population.

Under the newly formed Ministry of the Interior, the government enacted a series of sweeping administrative reforms led by the king's half-brother Prince Damrong Rajanubhab.[8] From the late 1870s, the government stationed commissioners in the outlying tributary states with a predominantly military role. These commissioners gradually wrested control over local affairs from the hereditary local elites, through a combination of coercion and co-optation.[9] After 1893, the government began to further dismantle the traditional structure of local rule by turning local rulers into civil servants, and forcing them to draw their salaries from the government instead of revenue from local sources.[10] In most cases, provincial elites continued to live a comfortable existence, though their control over local affairs rapidly diminished leaving them to perform a mostly symbolic role. As the old provincial governors from the traditional local elites began to die off, they were usually replaced by Thai officials from Bangkok with strong loyalties to the monarchy. According to Keyes, "The centralizing of the bureaucracy, thus, had the effect of endowing the separation between the rulers and ruled with an ethnic overtone", leading outlying minority populations to feel that "political power was the prerogative of the 'Thai' rather than of themselves".[11]

The state also sought to extend its control over the regions by creating a new Buddhist hierarchy that integrated the various Buddhist traditions in the provinces into a single religious structure controlled by the government. The new rules and hierarchy were designed to weaken provincial Buddhist traditions and create a dominant central Thai Buddhist tradition.[12] While, prior to this policy, all honors and positions for local monks had been determined by the local elites or local population, the new system created powerful incentives for monks to comply with central control by ensuring that advancement within the Sangha and access to resources was awarded only to those monks who cooperated with the state.[13]

The most pervasive and successful mechanism of state penetration has been Thailand's system of standardized education. Education in the provinces had traditionally been through local religious institutions, and generally conducted in Buddhist temples or local Islamic schools (*pondok*). State-sponsored education down to the village level was first introduced in 1889 with the creation of the Ministry of Education, and later accelerated with the Primary Education Act of 1921 that required all children to attend at least five years of state-sponsored education. By the 1930s village schools were being built in even the most remote regions.[14] In most of the provinces, especially the more remote minority regions, these were the first schools in the area and were generally seen as important symbols of development and patronage of the state. By teaching Thai history and geography, and respect for the Thai monarchy, all in the Central Thai dialect, the education system was very effective in instilling a sense of Thai identity and loyalty to the state. Furthermore, there is some evidence that the national education system led to a dilution of regional and local non-Thai identity, by not allowing the use of non-Thai language curriculum, and limiting the number of locally hired teachers. The education system has been so effective at instilling Thai identity, in fact, that the public schools have become the front line of the separatist conflict in the southernmost provinces. Malay Muslim resistance leaders have long decried the school system as a state effort to destroy local identity and traditions. In the latest round of violence, the school system has been regularly targeted.[15]

UNCONSOLIDATED PERIPHERIES: COMPARING STATE APPROACHES

While state penetration has affected many peripheral regions in Thailand, not every region has received the same level of attention. The troubled southern provinces have long been a focal point of state penetration efforts, based on the perception among central Thai political, bureaucratic, and military elites that the region was a threat to national security. In other regions, where the level of perceived threat has been much lower, or where the local population's resistance to state penetration has been less pronounced, the state's efforts have been much more gradual and generally less coercive and disruptive.

To analyze this process, we will use the following model (Relationship between State Coercion and Minority Integration) (see Figure 13.1) to compare the experience of state penetration in different peripheral regions in Thailand.[16] The diagram below illustrates the relationship between the level of non-military coercion used by the state in a particular region, and the level of integration over time. The arrows represent the use of the state's capacity to manipulate local conditions in order to move the minority population towards full integration with the state.

The first scenario is *de facto autonomy*, where the state applies very little, if any, effort to integrate the peripheral region, and instead allows the local indigenous or traditional elites[17] to maintain control over local affairs

Figure 13.1
Relationship between State Coercion and Minority Integration

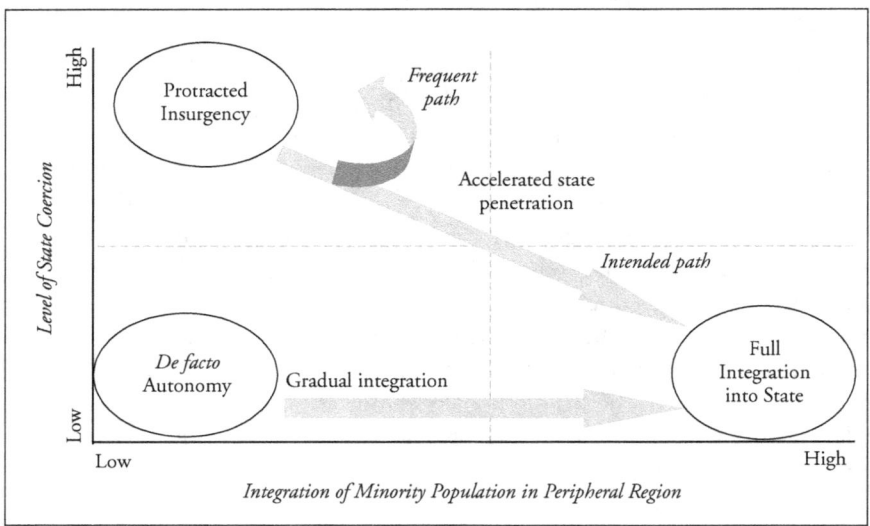

with minimal interference by the central state. The regions where the state allowed *de facto autonomy* were considered non-threatening and too remote to justify the high cost of increasing the state's presence. This scenario can be understood as maintaining the status quo arrangement from the period before the penetration of the state into the peripheral region (pre-1900 for Thailand). Governing arrangements between centre and periphery were mostly unchanged, as peripheral territories were generally left alone, and the state's presence remained very remote.

The second scenario is gradual integration. Instead of remaining outside of the state system, these regions have been gradually integrated into the economic and political mainstream of the country, usually in response to political and financial incentives from the state. These regions have experienced some degree of growing state presence and assimilation efforts, often with the concurrence of local elites. While national state penetration policies have had some impact on the local population, the level of coercion was very low, as was the intensity of enforcement. As a result, the integration of the local minority population has been more gradual and less disruptive. In this scenario, local elites have generally been non-resistant to state integration, and the state typically allowed them some degree of continuing authority during the transition period. These local elites were eventually absorbed into national structures, including the civil service and the military, allowing them to maintain their privileged status. This process would often take decades, but was generally successful at integrating the local region with minimal resistance, and at low cost to the state. Local customs were allowed to remain, as long as the loyalty of the local ethnic minority population to the state was not in question.

In the accelerated state penetration scenario, state capacity is exercised to force ethnic and religious minority populations to integrate into the state, and accelerate the assimilation of the national language, religion, and culture. This scenario is highly coercive, as it usually entails forced assimilation, denigration of local traditions and identities, and removal of local elites from any position of authority. This scenario typically occurs in regions where there is a perceived threat to national security, and some resistance to state penetration among the local population. The most intensive periods of accelerated state penetration have occurred during authoritarian regimes, when all channels for political dissent have been cut off. To quickly consolidate administrative control of the region, the state typically sent officials from the centre to take over local governance and exert greater control over the local economy. The government encouraged transmigration to these regions by other ethnic groups in the country, including central Thai and other ethnic minorities, by creating incentives and offering privileged status or access to state power and resources. In some cases, the government transferred underperforming civil servants to these regions as a means of punishment. This scenario tended to generate enormous resentment among the local population, leading to organized resistance against the state.

Protracted insurgent conflict is usually the outcome of a failed attempt at accelerated state penetration. In such cases, the government has often continued to use heavy-handed state penetration measures despite the fact that they tend to generate more violent resistance to the state. This scenario typically produces a protracted cycle of violence as the government uses high levels of coercion to suppress local dissent which strengthens local resistance, leading to greater support for the insurgency among the local minority population.

The final category, full integration into the state, is the intended outcome of state policy. This scenario entails local participation in national politics, full recognition of the authority of the state, and widespread acknowledgement of the state's legitimacy in the peripheral region. For the vast majority of Thailand's minority groups, political integration with the Thai state has reached very advanced levels, where almost all members of the groups recognize the legitimacy and authority of the state.

COMPARISON OF THREE REGIONS: STATE PENETRATION AND PATTERNS OF RESISTANCE

To assess the impact of the different methods of state penetration, we will compare the southern provinces to two other regions in Thailand. Satun province offers a useful comparison because it shares ethnic, religious, and cultural origins with the southernmost provinces, but has followed a remarkably different path in terms of national integration. Satun lies along the border with Malaysia, on the western edge of southern Thailand. It was formerly part of the Malay Sultanate of Kedah. Similar to the other provinces, the Anglo-Siamese treaty of 1909 incorporated Satun into the Thai state, separating it from the rest of Kedah. The population is more than 70 per cent Muslim, and its history and geographic proximity indicate that most of the local population can trace its origins to Kedah and northern Malay lineage.

Despite these similarities to the other southern provinces, there has never been any separatist related violence in Satun, and the level of support for separatism is extremely low.[18] Today, Satun is highly integrated into the Thai state, and anecdotal evidence indicates that Thai identity is widespread there. Recent research indicates that more than 99 per cent of the local population speaks Thai and very few can speak Malay.

The lack of separatism in Satun and the high level of integration can be explained by the non-coercive process of integration with Thailand and largely cooperative centre-periphery relations. A quiet backwater that presented little threat to the state, Satun was mostly left alone during the early years of state penetration (1900–32). Since the end of the absolute monarchy in 1932, Satun has been through a long process of gradual, peaceful integration with the Thai state.

The second region for comparison is Isaan. From 1965 to 1985, the Thai government fought an armed insurgency by the Communist Party of Thailand (CPT), based in the northeastern border provinces. While the Thai government and international observers have generally characterized the conflict in Isaan as the epicentre of a wider ideological conflict playing out across mainland Southeast Asia, this explanation is contested by many Isaan residents and historians of the region. In fact, the origins of the conflict in Isaan can be attributed to centre-periphery tensions and the local experience of state penetration. According to McCargo and Hongladarom, Bangkok's efforts to subordinate Isaan has "long generated considerable resistance", leading to "frequent rebellion" and a "challenge to the power of the Thai state."[19] Somchai Phatharathananunth links the CPT insurgency

Table 13.1
Historical Comparison of State Approaches and Local Response

	De Facto Autonomy	Gradual Integration	Accelerated State Penetration	Protracted Insurgency
Occurrence	Satun (1900–32) Isaan (1900–32)	Satun (1932–present) Isaan (pre-1947, post-1985)	Southern provinces (since 1900); Isaan (1948–82)	Southern provinces (1903, 1922–23, 1947–48, late 1960's, 1975, 1979–81, and 2004–present); Isaan conflict-affected provinces (1948–82)
Management of local elites	Local elites maintain control, recognize sovereignty of state	Co-opted into state service or institutions; temporarily retain local authority during transition	Removal from local authority, and marginalized under centralized rule	Local elites frequently become insurgent leaders, and enemies of the state
Local receptivity to state presence	Mixed	High	Low	Low
Perceived threat from non-consolidation	Very Low	Low	High	Very High
Presence/resilience of local, non-Thai identity	Mixed	Low	High	High
State method for compelling integration	Deferred	Incentives	Coercive policies	Coercive force and coercive policies
Likelihood of violent resistance in response to state policy	Low	Low	High	Very High

with a long tradition of Isaan resistance to the Thai state, driven by political marginalization, economic deprivation, and the suppression of regional identity.[20] After the 1958 military coup, when "peaceful channels for airing their grievances were closed, the Isan activists turned to the armed struggle of the CPT." Somchai argues that the political activism of the past 30 years in Isaan can be understood as a continuation of this once violent struggle through more open political channels.

While the early years of state penetration were relatively quiet in Isaan compared to the southern provinces,[21] the process created a great deal of disruption in local communities and the displacement of local elites, which sowed the seeds of local resistance that began to appear during the early democratic periods in the 1930s and 1940s.[22] In the late 1940s and 1950s, as the level of state coercion grew and channels for political dissent closed, the growing alienation of the Isaan population created an environment that was fertile for organized resistance to the state.

The divide between the centre and periphery in the case of Isaan is partly an ethnic one. Similar to southern Thailand, the grievances that gave rise to conflict in Isaan can largely be attributed to discrimination from the various processes of state penetration by the central Thai-dominated government, especially from 1947 to 1973. While the population of Isaan is primarily Buddhist, most of the population is ethnically distinct from the Central Thai, tracing their ethnic origins back to the former Lao Kingdoms along the Mekong River that declined in the early nineteenth century. While Isaan has become much more integrated into the Thai state during the economic expansion of the past 30 years, prior to 1973 the level of integration remained very low.[23] During the most intensive period of state penetration, the great majority of Isaan residents perceived themselves as distinct from the Central Thais and collectively discriminated against by the government. In the early 1980s, the insurgency began to wane after a major shift in the government's approach towards a more responsive policy to provide redress for local grievances. This change of policy, combined with the introduction of incentives to lure insurgents to demobilize, created new space for local politics and greater focus on local community development, eventually leading to the restoration of stability in the region.

DISPLACEMENT OF LOCAL ELITES

In the southern provinces, the local nobility were quickly removed from positions of local authority and replaced with officials sent by the Ministry of Interior. These officials were predominantly ethnic Thai from the central region. In his influential study of the southern provinces, Surin Pitsuwan describes the early years of state penetration into the southern provinces and the implications of that process for the next 100 years of centre-periphery relations. "Beginning in 1902, the nobility (in Pattani) was stripped of its power and all functions of the provinces were gradually transferred to the bureaucrats from the capital or provinces in the north."[24] In the decades after this abrupt shift in local authority, the state turned its attention towards "integrating the sons of the former Malay nobility into the system by offering them opportunities for on-the-job training with the Thai governor-general."

The central Thai officials sent by the Ministry of the Interior invariably did not speak the local dialect or understand local customs. Despite guidance from King Chulalongkorn to enact the reforms with sensitivity to local customs, the officials responsible for administering the reforms showed little regard for Islamic beliefs and local customs, leading to a rapid deterioration of relations with the local population and elites. Pitsuwan argues that the animosity of the Malay Muslims against the Central Thai bureaucrats was extremely intense, and that this animosity remains today.[25]

Once removed from power and denied many of the privileges they had previously enjoyed, the Pattani nobility found little incentive to cooperate with Siam. Instead, they found new legitimacy and influence in mobilizing local resistance to Thai rule, planting the seeds of separatism and armed revolt.[26] Many of the former nobility, including the former Sultan of Pattani Abdul Kadir, formed the core of the early resistance movement that has inspired many of the subsequent insurgent movements in southern Thailand.

By contrast, this period of transition in Satun province was mostly non-coercive and far less disruptive. The tiny circle of Malay nobles in Satun had little reason to resist Siam. Satun was a minor sultanate for much of the eighteenth century and most of the sultans were sent from the court of Kedah with the blessing of the Siamese King. The last sultan of Satun, Tengku Baharuddin, who formally took power in 1900, was a former administrator for the previous sultan, and not a descendant from royalty. After a battle of succession with a relative of the previous sultan, he was awarded the position after the intervention of King Chulalongkorn. Therefore, before the administrative reforms had even begun, Satun had a local ruler that was favourable to Siam.

Throughout the early decades of administrative reforms, Satun was allowed to maintain a high level of local autonomy and Muslim elites remained in power. The first two governors of Satun, Tengku Baharuddin (1902–14) and Tui bin Abdullah (1914–32), were ethnic Malay on good terms with the

Siamese government. Instead of encouraging resistance to the growing state presence in Satun, they encouraged the local population to learn Thai and accept Siamese authority. In return, this backwater benefited from state-funded development projects, including the first public schools in the province. After 1932, de facto local autonomy moved towards gradual integration as Satun's local elites became involved in national politics. According to Sukree Longputeh, a Thai-Muslim scholar from Satun, the political elites from Satun are remembered best for their pragmatism and ability to work within the Thai political system to get concessions, development assistance, and to overturn policies that discriminated against Muslims.[27]

In Isaan, the displacement of local elites in the early stages of administrative reforms precipitated the rise of political dissent in the 1930s and left-wing movements in the 1950s and 1960s. The administrative reforms were generally carried out in Isaan without much resistance. According to Charles Keyes, the process was allowed to unfold gradually, as the local elites would become governors or occupy other official positions, and be incorporated into the civil service. It is likely that "many of the traditional *cao muang* leaders with their local roots and local bases of power were replaced by central Thai officials with more ties to Bangkok than to the provinces and districts to which they were posted. To the extent that this practice was followed, Northeasterners experienced, for the first time, the subordination of local political interests to the Central Thai objective."[28]

The discontent from this process resurfaced later as local elites sought other means of reestablishing themselves in local politics. In the brief parliamentary period of the 1930s, many of the early parliamentarians from Isaan were from traditional Isaan elite families. Keyes argues that this trend indicates that these elites were seeking to regain positions of power through a new means, and can be interpreted as "manifestations of political discontent" that can be "traced to the thwarting of the political ambitions of the local Isaan leaders as a consequence of the extension of Thai control".[29] The MPs from Isaan were some of the most vocal in opposition to right-wing governments, including the pre-war government of Phibun Songkhram.

As anti-communist activities increased in the late 1940s, after Phibun Songkhram returned to power in a military coup, several of these MPs were targeted under dubious circumstances. In the "Kilo 11" incident in 1949, four prominent Isaan MPs were killed by police, leading to public outrage in Isaan.[30] Two other MPs were brought to trial on charges of separatism, though the trial ended inconclusively. Keyes argues that these events had "lasting repercussions in the Isaan region."[31] Considered local heroes for their accomplishments in national politics, these attacks inflamed local anger in particular because of the impression that they were targeted primarily because they were from the northeast. In the aftermath of these incidents, a strong sense of Isaan regional identity and alienation from the Thai state began to emerge, based on a shared experience of discrimination and a realization of the loss of local control over politics.

SUPPRESSION OF NON-THAI LOCAL IDENTITY

State penetration has included several measures to promote Thai identity among ethnic minorities and suppress any vestigial non-Thai identities. Common measures have included laws prohibiting minority languages in schools or the courts, discriminatory policies against local customs or beliefs, teaching of the Thai language and promotion of a pro-Thai curriculum in public schools, and insisting on the display of Thai symbols in all public buildings, schools, and religious institutions.

In the southern provinces, Malay Muslim communities continue to maintain a strong identification with Malay ethnicity, traditions, and history. The majority of the population in these southern provinces continues to speak the local dialect of Malay instead of Thai. The resilience of the ethnic Malay identity can partly be explained by the shared sense of history and nostalgia for an independent past that unites the Malay Muslims of Southern Thailand. Emerging at the beginning of the sixteenth century, the Pattani Sultanate was a thriving kingdom for almost 300 years, enjoying substantial economic relations with Chinese, European and Arab traders, as well as substantial military power. Several authors have argued that Pattani was an important religious centre in Southeast Asia, where Islamic scholarship and teaching had thrived for centuries.[32]

Thai government efforts to subdue and integrate the Malay Muslim population through forced assimilation have created a deeply felt animosity towards the Thai state. The ultra-nationalist regimes of Phibun Songkhram (1938–44, 1948–57) sought to build a modern, Thai-centric, unified nation, through a series of "Cultural Mandates", that regulated language, dress, cultural practices, and religion. By restricting the use of Islamic law, introducing Thai-Buddhist values and symbols in schools, and forbidding the use of the local Pattani Malay dialect in local government, the Thai government became a direct threat to the local Malay Muslim way of life. In response to the Thai nationalistic fervour of the time, a group of Malay Muslim leaders organized a political resistance movement, led by Haji Sulong. Sulong, a local Islamic leader from Pattani, was a leading advocate for a semi-independent state who led negotiations with the Thai government of Pridi Bhanomyong in the post-World War II period. In 1947, the group submitted a set of seven demands to the Thai Government that sought to reverse the process of state penetration and forced assimilation. Despite some limited reforms, the Thai Government did not address their fundamental grievances, and later arrested Haji Sulong and many of the other local leaders. In early 1948, tensions escalated dramatically, culminating in the disastrous Dusung Nyior incident, in which government forces attacked a Malay Muslim village that was accused of supporting separatists. These events became a defining moment in the separatist movement and served as rallying point for the separatist movements that were to emerge in the 1950s and 1960s.

In contrast, local identity among Satun's Muslims has never been a point of friction in centre-periphery relations. While Satun was also subjected to many of the assimilationist policies of past Thai governments, the level of coercion in Satun was negligible compared to the other southern provinces. Without significant resistance from the local population, the Thai government had no reason to use serious coercion against the local population to accelerate assimilation.

Based on a series of interviews conducted by the author in 2005, there is strong evidence to suggest that most Satun Muslims have lost their sense of Malay identity, indicating an advanced stage of integration into the Thai state. In the vast majority of cases, Muslims in Satun consider themselves to be Thai and do not hold any sentimental attachment to the historical connections with Kedah, Malaysia, or Pattani.[33] Satun Muslims, particularly those in rural areas, have had little exposure to the ideas and debates within the wider Malay Muslim community and separatist movements.[34] For example, for most Muslims in southern Thailand, the term "Thai Muslim" is associated with the government's attempts to assimilate the Malay Muslim communities of Thailand into the central Thai mainstream, and to separate Malay identity from Islam. Yet in Satun, the term is widely used by the local Muslim community to describe themselves. Satun Muslims are either not cognizant of this political interpretation of the term, or they are unconvinced.

In Isaan, the process of state penetration played an instrumental role in the creation of a regional identity that later became central to an ethno-regional armed insurgency against the state.[35] Prior to 1948, Keyes argues that there was very little sense of shared identity among Isaan residents, either amongst themselves or with the Lao across the border. As the region became more integrated into Thailand, and the local economy shifted to a cash economy, thousands of Isaan residents migrated to the major cities of Central Thailand. The shared experiences of economic deprivation, political marginalization and discrimination led to a growing political consciousness among these Isaan migrants.[36] The early class of Isaan political leaders, with links to the former local nobility, was a focal point of this new regional identity. After these leaders were targeted in the late 1940s and 1950s for their leftist political inclinations, Isaan regionalism took on a new prominence and became a mobilizing force for anti-government groups.

The politics of local identity continue to be an issue of centre-periphery tension today in the northeastern region. According to Somchai, after decades of state efforts to disconnect Isaan identity from Lao identity, the result is a "split identity" for many natives of this region.[37] Many residents of Isaan still consider themselves ethnic Lao, and speak the local Lao dialect, though usually in private. As a result, local identity remains a source of centre-periphery tension for many people in Isaan.[38]

CAN STATE PENETRATION BE UNDONE?

Despite more than a century of centrally-driven state penetration efforts in Thailand's southern provinces, the level of integration of the Malay Muslim minority population is extremely low and violent resistance to the state remains a continuing challenge to the central government. There is substantial evidence to conclude that coercive state penetration efforts have been ineffective at best, and have most likely exacerbated the conflict. Despite this, there is very little support in Thai political circles for adopting a new approach in the south. Recent governments have continued to use an accelerated state penetration approach. Even the coup government of General Surayut Chulanont made very little progress in changing course in the south, despite public promises to take a softer, more constructive approach.

One critical problem is that state penetration cannot be undone overnight, and may actually be irreversible. After more than a century of state penetration efforts, the apparatus of state penetration now has deep roots in the southern provinces, and is defended by powerful interests that have heavily invested in the status quo in Bangkok. Any attempt to change course will directly threaten the institutions that have been charged with administering state policy in the south and the state's allies in the south that have relied on state privileges and protection.

The politics of overturning state penetration requires a major realignment of interests. To reach agreement on the decentralization of central state authority and undoing the discriminatory measures, the government would have to overcome the resistance of those actors who have invested in the centralized state apparatus. In Thailand, this set of interests is very powerful, making the prospects for change especially daunting. There are a number of economic and political interests, licit and illicit, that have invested heavily in the southern provinces, and would stand to lose should the presence of the central government diminish. The ethnic Thai Buddhist population living in the three southern provinces relies heavily on central state protection and services, and would feel threatened by any significant withdrawal of central state power and authority from the region. Several analysts have argued that the security forces benefit from their continued heavy presence in the southern provinces. Even if these competing interests lose the argument in the centre, it will be difficult to dislodge them from their position in the southern provinces.

Bureaucratic inertia is another major impediment. The Thai bureaucracy and judicial system benefit from the current system of centralized governance, based on Thai-Buddhist norms. Any decentralization of authority would threaten the power of Bangkok's bureaucratic elites by limiting their control over local governance and reducing their share of the national budget. Decentralization of authority as a means to placate local grievances in the south could also be perceived as a major loss of face for the Bangkok bureaucracy. In addition, sections of Thailand's political and military elite argue that decentralization for the southern provinces could precipitate similar requests for decentralized authority in other parts of Thailand, a nightmarish scenario for many in the Thai bureaucracy. As a result, even if an elected government made significant reforms in the south, many of these changes would be resisted by the ministries charged with implementing the changes.

As recent elections have demonstrated, Thai electoral politics seems to have ensured the continuation of the status quo. The popularity of hard line approaches among the majority of Thai voters makes special compromises for the south unlikely in the current political climate. For example, the Thaksin and Samak governments had ample political incentives to maintain the old approach in the south, based on the strong support for a hard line approach by the electoral strongholds for these governments in the north and northeast regions. The Democrat Party has greater incentive to appeal to the population of the southern provinces, but despite this, there was little change in government policy towards the south during the Abhisit government's tenure.

There are some signs, however, that the political climate may be changing. During the 2012 parliamentary elections, the Peau Thai Party, led by Prime Minister Yingluck Shinawatra (sister of former Prime Minister Thaksin) campaigned for greater local autonomy in the southern provinces through establishment of a special administrative zone, or "Meung Pattani". Despite this, Peau Thai did not win a single seat in three southernmost provinces. After the election, this proposal was quietly dropped.

Finally, the lingering resentment and alienation felt by the ethnic Malay Muslim population in the south from the past coercion and harsh state penetration policies will not be easily reversed. For the state to re-establish confidence with this population, the process of reform and decentralization would have to be sustained over a long period of time and lead to sweeping changes in local governance.

To date, the violence has remained entirely in the southern provinces, with the exception of a few attacks in Hat Yai less than 100 km to the northwest. As long as the violence in the southern provinces does not directly threaten security in the centre, it is unlikely that there will be major changes in the administration of the southern provinces of Thailand. In the case of Isaan, the very real threat of a Vietnamese invasion provided the necessary impetus for a dramatic shift in the government's approach towards a more accommodative pragmatic strategy, responding to local grievances, that was instrumental in reducing the level of support for the CPT insurgents. A similar change of course will be necessary in southern Thailand to permanently restore stability in the south.

The vestiges of a century of state penetration continue to exacerbate the situation in southern Thailand. Without addressing these irritants, the Thai Government risks further inflaming local grievances, leading to greater support for the insurgents, and undermining cooperation between the Malay Muslim population and the state. Many of the lingering tensions from state penetration could be reduced through incremental reforms that would not require a major overhaul of the current centralized system of governance in Thailand. Unfortunately, even the most modest of reforms are unlikely in the current political climate.

Notes

[1] "Malay Muslim" refers to the majority population in Pattani, Yala, and Narathiwat provinces. While they are citizens of Thailand (with a few exceptions), this group is generally considered ethnic Malay, and can trace their origins to former Malays sultanates in the region. They primarily speak a local Malay dialect called "Pattani Malay" as their first language. The Thai government typically refers to this population as "Thai-Muslim" or "Thai-Islam", and does not distinguish this group from other Muslim populations in the country.

[2] Even among Muslim minority groups in Thailand, most have reached a high level of integration. Omar Farouk's study, "The Muslims of Thailand", recognized

thirteen different groups of "assimilated" Muslim ethnic groups, while only the Malay Muslim population in the southern border provinces remained "unassimilated". Omar Farouk, "The Muslims of Thailand: A Survey", in Omar Farouk, *The Muslims of Thailand, Volume 1: Historical and Cultural Studies* (Bihar, India: Center for Southeast Asian Studies, 1989).

3 Thongchai Winichakul, *Siam Mapped: A History of the Geo-Body of a Nation* (Chiang Mai, Thailand: Silkworm Books, 1994), p. 82.

4 Thongchai, p. 128.

5 The common transliterated spelling from the local Malay dialect is *Patani*. The transliterated spelling from Thai is *Pattani*. For the purposes of this chapter, the term *Patani* is used to describe the pre-1909 sultanate of Patani, and the current Thai spelling is used to describe the Thai province of *Pattani* in post-1909.

6 Clive Christie, "Ethnicity, Islam and Irredentism: The Malays of Patani", in *A Modern History of South East Asia: Decolonization, Nationalism and Separatism*, by Clive Christie (London: I.B. Tauris, 1996), p. 174.

7 Pasuk Phonpaichit and Chris Baker, *Thailand: Economy and Politics*, 2nd ed. (New York: Oxford University Press, 2002), p. 235.

8 David Wyatt, *Thailand: A Short History*, 2nd ed. (New Haven: Yale University Press, 2003), pp. 192–97.

9 Pasuk and Baker, pp. 239–40.

10 Charles F. Keyes, "Isan: Regionalism in Northeastern Thailand", Cornell Thailand Project, Interim Reports Series, Number 10, Southeast Asia Program, Cornell University, March 1967, pp. 16–17.

11 Keyes, p. 18.

12 Kamala Tiyavanich, *Forest Recollections: Wandering Monks in Twentieth Century Thailand* (Chiang Mai, Thailand: Silkworm Books, 1997).

13 Somchai Phatharathananunth, *Civil Society and Democratization: Social Movements in Northeast Thailand* (Copenhagen, Denmark: Nordic Institute of Asian Studies Press, 2006), p. 33.

14 Keyes, p. 19.

15 While the attacks on public schools are usually blamed on insurgents, some observers have argued that some of the attacks on schools may be orchestrated by other groups as a means of instigating unrest.

16 This model has been developed by the author for this analysis.

17 Local traditional elites include those local leaders that exercised political authority before the advent of state authority. In most cases, peripheral regions were governed by village headmen, religious leaders, or powerful local families that maintained authority through a combination of religious prowess and inherited position.

18 For further explanation, see Thomas Parks, "Maintaining Peace in a Neighborhood Torn by Separatism: The Case of Satun Province in Southern Thailand", paper presented at Thailand Development Research Institute (TDRI) annual conference, Pattaya, Thailand, 11 November 2005.

19 Duncan McCargo and Krisadawan Hongladarom, "Contesting Isan-ness: Discourses of Politics and Identity in Northeast Thailand", *Asian Ethnicity*, vol. 5, no. 2 (June 2004): 221.
20 Somchai, pp. 46–52.
21 One notable exception was the Holy Man Revolt of 1902, a popular movement against the state that affected most parts of Isaan and mobilized thousands of local people. The movement was defeated by a Siamese military expedition in February 1902 that left hundreds dead. According to Somchai, the revolt was directly linked to state efforts to centralize power, and resulted in a decision to slow down the pace of centralization. Somchai, p. 31.
22 Keyes, pp. 17, 21.
23 Keyes, p. 2
24 Surin Pitsuwan, *Islam and Malay Nationalism: A Case Study of the Malay Muslims of Southern Thailand* (Bangkok: Thai Khadi Research Institute, Thammasat University, 1985), pp. 22, 32.
25 Pitsuwan, p. 32.
26 Parks, p. 21.
27 Interview with Sukree Longputeh, Dean of the Faculty of Liberal Arts and Social Services, Yala Islamic College, Pattani, 25 July 2005.
28 Keyes, p. 17.
29 Keyes, p 17.
30 This incident occurred along a quiet stretch of highway, where the nearest landmark was a sign marking kilometer 11. As a result, the media referred to this event as the "Kilo 11".
31 Keyes, p. 34.
32 Ibrahim Syukri, *History of The Malay Kingdom of Patani*, translated from *Yawi* by Conner Bailey and John Miksic (Chiang Mai, Thailand: Silkworm Books, 1985).
33 Parks, p. 14.
34 On issues of identity, Satun Muslims seem to be unaware of the political sensitivities felt by other Muslims in Thailand. Parks, p. 15.
35 Keyes.
36 Keyes, pp. 36–38.
37 Somchai, p. 45.
38 McCargo and Hongladarom, p. 222.

References

Christie, Clive. "Ethnicity, Islam and Irredentism: The Malays of Pattani". In *A Modern History of South East Asia: Decolonization, Nationalism and Separatism*, edited by Clive Christie. London: I.B. Tauris, 1996.

Farouk, Omar. "The Muslims of Thailand: A Survey". In *The Muslims of Thailand, Volume 1: Historical and Cultural Studies*, edited by Omar Farouk. Bihar, India: Center for Southeast Asian Studies, 1989.

International Crisis Group. "Southern Thailand: Insurgency, Not Jihad". *Asia Report* No. 98 (18 May 2005).

Keyes, Charles F. "Isan: Regionalism in Northeastern Thailand". Cornell Thailand Project, Interim Reports Series, Number 10, Southeast Asia Program, Cornell University, March 1967.

Mahakanjana, Chandra-nuj. "Decentalization, Local Government, and Socio-political Conflict in Southern Thailand". East-West Center Working Paper no. 5 (August 2006).

McCargo, Duncan, ed. *Rethinking Thailand's Southern Violence*. Singapore: NUS Press, 2007.

McCargo, Duncan and Krisadawan Hongladarom. "Contesting Isan-ness: Discourses of Politics and Identity in Northeast Thailand". *Asian Ethnicity*, vol. 5, no. 2 (June 2004).

Parks, Thomas. "Maintaining Peace in a Neighborhood Torn by Separatism: The Case of Satun Province in Southern Thailand". Paper presented at Thailand Development Research Institute, Annual Conference 2005, "Towards Social Harmony", 11 November 2005.

Phatharathananunth, Somchai. *Civil Society and Democratization: Social Movements in Northeast Thailand*. Copenhagen, Denmark: Nordic Institute of Asian Studies Press, 2006.

Phongpaichit Pasuk and Chris Baker. *Thailand: Economy and Politics*. 2nd ed. New York: Oxford University Press, 2002.

———. *Thaksin: The Business of Politics in Thailand*. Chiang Mai, Thailand: Silkworm Books, 2004.

Pitsuwan, Surin. *Islam and Malay Nationalism: A Case Study of the Malay Muslims of Southern Thailand*. Bangkok, Thailand: Thai Khadi Research Institute, Thammasat University, 1985.

Syukri, Ibrahim. *History of The Malay Kingdom of Pattani*, translated from *Yawi* by Conner Bailey and John Miksic. Chiang Mai, Thailand: Silkworm Books, 1985.

Tiyavanich, Kamala. *Forest Recollections: Wandering Monks in Twentieth Century Thailand*. Chiang Mai, Thailand: Silkworm Books, 1997.

Vaddhanaphuti, Chayan. "The Thai State and Ethnic Minorities: From Assimilation to Selective Integration". In *Ethnic Conflicts in Southeast Asia*, edited by Kusuma Snitwongse and W. Scott Thompson. Singapore, Institute of Southeast Asian Studies, 2005.

Winichakul, Thongchai. *Siam Mapped: A History of the Geo-Body of a Nation*. Chiang Mai, Thailand: Silkworm Books, 1994.

Wolters, O.W. *History, Culture, and Region in Southeast Asian Perspectives*. Singapore, Institute of Southeast Asian Studies, 1982.

Wyatt, David. *Thailand: A Short History*. 2nd ed. New Haven: Yale University Press, 2003.

14

INTERLOCKING AUTONOMY: MANILA AND MUSLIM MINDANAO

Steven Rood

For more than thirty years there have been a variety of "autonomous governments" in areas of Mindanao. Over the course of six national administrations, numerous regional administrations, and varying intensities of separatist armed conflict, there is general agreement that "autonomy" has not resolved the issues plaguing Muslim Mindanao. Explanations for such systematic failure must go beyond accusations of bad faith or incompetence. This paper examines the multifaceted incentives faced by factions on both sides — Mindanao Muslims and Manila elites — which shape forms of autonomy in Mindanao and limit their effectiveness in addressing grievances which drive separatist sentiment. It concludes with suggestions for ways forward that might satisfy both sides in the interaction.

The current period of armed conflict between Muslims in the Philippines and the central state in Manila has now lasted over thirty-five years. In 1968 two events occurred that stirred rebellion. In the "Jabidah massacre" Muslims who had been recruited into the military in order to invade Sabah were slain by their officers when the operation was shut down (one survived to tell the tale) (Dañguilan and Gloria 2000, pp. 2–23). In the same year, a "Muslim Independence Movement" (MIM) was organized by former Governor of Cotabato Province, Datu Udtog Matalam who was disappointed by his role within Manila-centric politics (Abinales 2000, pp. 140–41, 167–68). The movement acquired an armed component with the founding of the Moro[1] National Liberation Front (MNLF) in the early 1970s.

Reasons that have been adduced for the length of this confrontation range from the insincerity of the national government in addressing grievances, to the self-interest of the actors (the Armed Forces of the Philippines or the local warlords who profit from the war's continuance), to divisions within the Muslim community (within and among revolutionary movements, traditional leaders and elected politicians) whose inability to unite hampers the achievement of their goals. One attempt at resolving the conflict has involved instituting "autonomous governments" in areas of Mindanao, with new varieties being instituted in 1977, 1990, and 2001. While decentralization (ranging from increased autonomy for local governments to changing the nature of the Philippine state from a unitary one to a federation) has long been, and continues to be, a feature in discourses about governance in the Philippines, "autonomy" in Mindanao has been a special case — not available to the rest of the Philippines.[2]

The 1976 Tripoli Agreement between the Philippine government and the MNLF called for autonomy to be granted to 13 provinces in Mindanao and Palawan. But in the implementation, Ferdinand Marcos, in 1977, used his martial law powers to institute, instead, two autonomous regions (the pre-existing administrative regions IX and XII) in Muslim Mindanao covering 10 provinces,[3] with regional legislative assembly elections for the two regions conducted in 1979 and 1982. After the fall of Marcos in 1986, the autonomy arrangement was re-worked under the 1987 Constitution — there was a Regional Consultative Commission, following which Congress passed an Organic Law (Republic Act 6734) and in a 1989 plebiscite, four provinces (Sulu, Tawi-Tawi, Maguindanao, and Lanao del Sur) voted to join an Autonomous Region in Muslim Mindanao (ARMM) that began operations in 1990. Then in the 1996 "Final Peace Agreement" between the government and the MNLF (entitled "Final Agreement on the Implementation of the Tripoli Agreement"), revisions of the Organic Act for the ARMM were mandated, and after the January 2001 overthrow of Joseph ("Erap") Estrada, the revised version was allowed to become law (Republic Act 9054) by President Gloria Macapagal-Arroyo in mid-2001. In an August 2001 plebiscite the Islamic City of Marawi (in Lanao del Sur) and the province of Basilan (though not its capital, Isabela City) voted to join the ARMM.

Table 14.1
Outline of Autonomy in Mindano Through the Years

President	Framework	"Autonomy"
Marcos (1967–86)	1976 Tripoli Agreement with MNLF	Autonomous Regions 9 and 12
Aquino (1986–92)	1987 Constitution	Republic Act 6734 (1989) Autonomous Region in Muslim MIndandao (ARMM) — Sulu, Tawi, Maguindanao, Lanao del Sur
Ramos (1992–98)	1996 Final Peace Agreement with MNLF	
Estrada (1998–2001)		
Arroyo (2001–2010)		Republic Act 9054 (2001) added to ARMM — Basilan (except Isabela City); Islamic City of Marawi

From the very beginning in 1977, the MNLF branded Marcos' moves towards two autonomous regions covering 10 provinces in Mindanao as violating the Tripoli Agreement and refused to participate in those administrations. Again, despite overtures from the new Aquino administration, in 1988–90 the MNLF did not participate in the establishment of the ARMM as provided by the 1987 constitution, and two majority Muslim areas (Marawi City and the province of Basilan) voted not to join the Autonomous Region. The 1996 Final Peace Agreement with the MNLF included provisions for a new Organic Act for the Autonomous Region after a transition period, but in 2001 all factions of the MNLF were dissatisfied with Republic Act 9054 and elements associated with Chairman Nur Misuari briefly engaged in armed rebellion (leading to Misuari's flight to Malaysia, and subsequent repatriation to arrest in the Philippines). And, finally, the Moro Islamic Liberation Front (MILF) has repeatedly rejected "autonomy" as a solution to the "*Bangsamoro* (Moro Nation) Problem" so that current (on-again/off-again) negotiations use such vague terms as "Bangsamoro Juridical Entity" (BJE).

After eleven, twenty-two or thirty-five years of "autonomy" (depending on how one counts) elections were held as scheduled in August 2008 for another term for the Governor, Vice-Governor, and members of the Regional Legislative Assembly. Some advocated postponement of the elections so that negotiations with the MILF could be finalized first (and the relation between the ARMM and the BJE clarified); others argued that fulfilling the 1996 Final Peace Agreement requires the continued operation of the ARMM (with perhaps some amendments to the Organic Act, currently being discussed by the MNLF, the government, and the Organization of the Islamic Conference). In the end, the election was held as scheduled, and, while the incumbent governor won more than 90 per cent of the vote, the peace process ground to a halt. There was an upsurge in the fighting, the government dissolved its peace panel while pursuing "rogue" MILF commanders, and the Philippine Supreme Court declared "unconstitutional" the most recent draft agreement, the Memorandum of Agreement on Ancestral Domain. The issue of "autonomy" within the peace process thus remains unsettled but the current ARMM officials state their willingness to step down in the event that a peace agreement would require them to do so (e.g., if a "provisional" BJE superseded the ARMM).

In this chapter I will not try to document or discuss the alleged dysfunctions of governance in the Autonomous Region in Muslim Mindanao, nor debate whether the 2001 version of the Organic Act (Republic Act 9054) adequately fulfils the requirements of the 1996 Final Peace Agreement with the MNLF. The fate or shape of "autonomy" under a future peace agreement with the MILF is still the subject of negotiation. Rather, in this chapter, the question is posed: why has "autonomy" remained central to discussions of Muslim Mindanao for decades, and why do actors in both Manila and Mindanao persist in achieving a solution within the ambit of "autonomy."

FROM THE VIEWPOINT OF MANILA

In a sense, it might seem obvious why policy-makers in Manila would want to work within "autonomy" — it appears to be an arrangement that would allow meeting legitimate demands of Muslims in the Philippines — now often referred to as the *Bangsamoro* (or Moro nation) without sundering the territorial integrity of the Philippines. Of course, the content of "autonomy" would still need to be specified, but in the abstract, while connoting some degree of self-rule, autonomy does not mean independence.

In fact, however, satisfying the legitimate demands of ethnic minorities in the Philippines have not required "autonomy". Conversely, grants of "autonomy" have not, in fact, satisfied the demands of the Muslims. Let us take each of these two points in turn.

That "autonomy" is not necessary is shown by the experience of Northern Philippines. In the 1987 Constitution, formulated after the overthrow of Ferdinand Marcos, both the Cordillera (the mountainous region of northern Luzon, with indigenous people who are a mixture of Catholics, Protestants, and animists) and Muslim Mindanao were mandated (under Article X) to have autonomous regions. This was despite the constitutional commission having voted down a proposal for all regions of the country to be constituted as separate states in a federal union on account of its divisive potential. Nonetheless, those two regions which seemed to be demanding autonomy were granted this asymmetrical arrangement.

The fact that the Cordillera has twice voted not to institute such a region demonstrates that "autonomy" is not necessarily needed to meet legitimate demands of unhispanized Filipinos. For Cordillerans, it seems (to this observer, at least) that the demands were largely met by a combination of the 1991 Local Government Code (which allows more power to the local governments as elected by majority Cordilleran localities) and the 1997 Indigenous Peoples Rights Act (which provides for control over natural resources in delineated local ancestral domains). In a sense, "village" is the largest unit for which an ordinary Cordilleran can imagine the need for autonomy, so region-wide autonomy was not necessary.

The other problem with the idea that the Manila elite might be resorting to "autonomy" as a way to meet legitimate demands of Muslims in the Philippines, is that "autonomy" might not be sufficient. There is widespread agreement that such demands have not, in fact, despite "autonomy" provisions, been met (Rasul 2007). Whether one believes the Philippine state has been unwilling to satisfy demands, or merely unable, the fact remains that there has been a reluctance to look beyond "autonomy" measures for solutions to the struggle. What might be the motives for the Manila elite to frame their answer to "the Mindanao problem" in this fashion?

SHIFTING MAJORITIES

One way of viewing the question is to look at the internal dynamics of decision-making about peace and conflict in Manila that leads to long periods of policy stasis. Paul Oquist (2002) writes about how three positions seem to be roughly equally balanced among national policy-makers:

- "victory" or the belief that military force can prevail over separatist forces;
- "pacification" or sufficient concessions to cease open hostilities; and
- "developmentalist" policies to address the roots of the conflict.

Oquist is describing the protracted nature of peace talks which have been taking place for more than twenty-five years as different thrusts are pursued and policies debated. But this can also provide a framework for understanding moves by the national government to institute "autonomy" for Muslim Mindanao. As explained below, "autonomy" based solutions provide common ground for at least two of the three camps of policy-makers described by Oquist above, during those periods when a "victory" strategy is not being pursued.

It is the multifarious semantics of "autonomy" that generates stable outcomes even though national policy coalitions supporting "autonomy" might shift. Any sort of autonomy is within the territorial integrity of the Philippines, so both the victory and pacification camps can support a minimalist definition (though the developmental camp would want more). These two camps are united in wanting the "Mindanao Problem" to stop

Table 14.2
Shifting Manila Coalitions on "Autonomy" over Time

Developmentalist	Pacification	Victory
		Martial Law early 1970s
1976 Tripoli Agreement		
	"Autonomous Regions" 9 & 12	
1987 Constitution		
RA 6734 Autonomous Region in Muslim Mindanao (1989)		
1996 Final Peace Agreement		
		Estrada's 2000 "All Out War"
RA 9054 Autonomous Region in Muslim Mindanao (2001)		

resulting in violent conflict, without a real interest in solving basic problems. The developmentalist camp would be dissatisfied with a minimalist definition, since it leaves festering problems in the relation of Muslims to the Philippine state.

On the other hand, the design of "autonomy" could aim at meeting demands of secessionists, leading to support from both pacification and developmental camps (though, in this case, the victory camp may balk at the changes — e.g., to the Constitution — needed to implement fuller autonomy). In this case, treating root causes is the aim of developmentalists, and as long as violence subsides the pacification camp would be satisfied. Thus, "autonomy" as an abstract strategy is always capable of gaining 2/3 support among policy elites — a stable reliable answer, centred on "pacification" but leaning towards either "victory" or "developmentalist." A brief chronological review of the narrative of autonomy in this light can illustrate what such an analysis means.

Ferdinand Marcos declared Martial Law in September 1971, in the midst of fierce clashes with both communist and Muslim separatist insurgents. Both conflicts had been increasing in intensity, with a revived "New People's Army" (NPA) under the direction of the Maoist Communist Party of the Philippines growing in strength nationwide, and the MNLF stepping up its attacks in Mindanao.

At the beginning, the Martial Law administration was clearly aiming for victory. However, starting in October 1973, President Marcos was faced by the Arab Oil Embargo, launched to punish those countries which had supported Israel in the Yom Kippur war. Marcos immediately made statements calling for the restoration of the rights of the Palestinians and full Israeli withdrawal to the 1967 borders — so the Philippines won exemption from the boycott. However, in 1974, the Organization of the Islamic Conference (OIC) passed a Resolution calling for the "just solution to the plight of Filipino Muslims within the framework of the national sovereignty and territorial integrity of the Philippines." The flurry of Philippine diplomacy continued, with peace talks in Jeddah in early 1975, and in early 1976 the Tripoli Agreement was reached. This agreement between the MNLF and the Philippine government was negotiated under the auspices of the OIC, hosted by Libya's Mohamar Qadaffi, with President Marcos' wife Imelda spearheading the Philippine effort.

"Autonomy" in the Tripoli Agreement was explicitly not "independence" so it appealed to those in the Philippine government interested in "victory" over the separatists — but its implementation in two separate pre-existing regions was clearly part of a strategy of "divide and rule".

Thus, any "developmentalist" faction would not support the policy. Still, by promising a subsidence of violence, it could rely on support from those in the "pacification" camp. From the beginning President Marcos relied on the wording of the Tripoli Agreement that referred to "constitutional processes" to manoeuvre for two separate regions (instead of one) — an idea that was rejected by the MNLF. The MNLF as an organization remained in opposition, reverted to its rhetorical stance for independence, and was recognized by the OIC as the "sole and legitimate representative of the Bangsamoro people." At the same time, government policy encouraged members of the MNLF to revert to allegiance to the government, and in 1979 even members of the "original 90" (the first batch of MNLF trainees) participated in the elections for legislative councils in the two regions. As a "pacification" strategy, this seemed to have worked, as indicated by the fact that for a number of years there was a relative lull in the fighting.

After the fall of President Marcos, the 1987 Constitution (Article X) clearly voiced the concerns of developmentalists as it specified "geographical areas sharing common and distinctive historical and cultural heritage, economic and social structures" to be a basis for "autonomy" and gave the region autonomous powers over (among others):

> Section 20 (3) Ancestral domain and natural resources; Section 20 (4) Personal, family, and property relations; Section 20 (7) Educational policies; Section 20 (8) Preservation and development of the cultural heritage

However, the Aquino coalition shifted to the right as peace talks with both the MNLF and the communist New People's Army began to get bogged down, and the actual implementation of the autonomy provisions was more on the "pacification" side. The appointed Regional Consultative Commission did not complete a unified draft Organic Act, leaving the Philippine Congress relatively free to mould the final version that was subjected to the plebiscite. Pacification seemed to have been achieved, as the lull in the fighting continued but without any peace agreement with the MNLF (much less with the MILF, which had, by now, formally split off from the MNLF).

Interestingly enough, it was former Armed Forces of the Philippines general Fidel V. Ramos who launched an explicitly developmentalist approach to peace making after assuming the presidency in 1992. As I have described elsewhere (Rood 2005), drawing on Ferrer (2002), there was a "bottom-up" approach to an overall peace process:

A long series of workshops and meetings was held to arrive at positions in all peace negotiations—with the National Democratic Front, the Moro National Liberation Front, and the Reform the Armed Forces Movement (RAM). In the end, settlements were arrived at for the latter two groups (and progress was made with the National Democratic Front).

The result was the 1996 Final Peace Agreement (FPA),[4] which included such "developmentalist" aspects as the Southern Philippine Council for Peace and Development (SPCPD) and the Special Zone of Peace and Development (SZOPAD). Again, developmentalist implementation of the FPA was hampered by a number of factors — local settler opposition to inclusion in the SZOPAD (and thus coverage in a subsequent plebiscite on joining the ARMM), SPCPD's dependence on the office of the President, the onset of the 1997 Asian Economic Crisis that deprived the Philippine government of funds, and the election in 1998 of Joseph ("Erap") Estrada as the President of the Philippines.

Estrada's assumption of office marked a definite shift towards the "victory" position, most clearly in relation to the Moro Islamic Liberation Front, with which the government had been in preliminary talks since 1997. In the first half of 2000, the "All-Out War" against the MILF resulted in government forces overrunning the fixed positions of the MILF, particularly their main community Camp Abubakar in Maguindanao (where President Estrada subsequently joined military men in a celebratory feast that included alcohol and pork). The lasting effects of these tactics (at least from the viewpoint of decision-makers in Manila) cannot really be assessed because of the political turmoil that began in October 2000, caused by accusations of corruption related to illegal gambling, that resulted in the impeachment trial of President Estrada. "People Power II" when crowds once again thronged to the EDSA highway, as they had in 1986 to overthrow President Marcos, resulted in a premature end to President Estrada's term in January 2001.

Newly installed President Gloria Macapagal-Arroyo pledged to pursue peace and development with the Moro Islamic Liberation Front, opening peace talks and negotiating a cessation of hostilities. However, with respect to the Moro National Liberation Front (and thus, with respect to the Autonomous Region, which the MILF has thus far studiously shunned), the policy seemed considerably less "developmentalist" than with the MILF. With Manila's encouragement, internal movements within the MNLF led to attempts to promote Nur Misuari to "Chairman Emeritus" (which he resisted). Similarly, Republic Act 9054, the new Organic Act that supposedly fulfilled the 1996 FPA, was allowed to lapse into law without the President's signature despite the protests of all factions of the MNLF that this version of the organic act betrayed the FPA. When the August 2001 plebiscite on the Organic Act went ahead nonetheless, elements of the MNLF engaged in armed action against Philippine government security forces (particularly in Sulu) and Misuari fled to Malaysia only to be detained (and returned to house arrest in the Philippines). It was only in late 2007 that the government and the MNLF began to negotiate once again, in "tripartite" meetings with the Organization of the Islamic Conference. Misuari was acquitted of all charges in late 2009, and the government signed an MOU with the MNLF in early 2010 to review the current version of "autonomy" (RA 9054), among other things.

By the end of 2008, the peace process with the MILF was at a standstill. In August 2008 a scheduled signing of a "Memorandum of Agreement on Ancestral Domain" (MOA-AD) was derailed by politicians (both Christian and Muslim) from Mindanao who obtained a Temporary Restraining Order from the Philippine Supreme Court. The MOA-AD was the Philippine government's agreement with the MILF on some of the most contentious issues of territorial expansion additions to the ARMM that would then comprise the Bangsamoro Juridical Entity (BJE), along the lines of preliminary agreements on the scope of powers over the ancestral domain. The mayors of the cities of Iligan and Zamboanga, along with the vice-Governor of Cotabato province, objected to the lack of consultation, before the agreement, on the scope of geographic coverage, and the powers being offered. In the end, the Supreme Court declared the MOA-AD unconstitutional, elements of the MILF attacked a number of areas in and outside the ARMM, the government dissolved its peace panel, and in November 2008, the International Monitoring Team (led by the Malaysian contingent) was withdrawn.[5]

Here, once again, we can see the effects of coalitional dynamics among victory (in this instance, led by Mindanao politicians but joined by politicians in Manila), pacification, and developmentalist perspectives. However, with respect to the MILF, "autonomy" is not the rhetorical central point as it has been with the MNLF for 30 years — the MILF reject "autonomy" based on the MNLF's experience with it, and so negotiation is couched in such deliberately vague concepts as "Bangsamoro Juridical Entity."

SELECTION ELECTIONS

Thus far it has been argued that "autonomy" was a stable policy outcome of factional manoeuvring in Manila as the Philippine government strove to solve problems of peace and development in Muslim Mindanao. But beyond being useful as coalitional glue, the Autonomous Region in Muslim Mindanao has some positive benefits for elites in Manila. In this paper, we are not discussing some of the more contentious issues such as individuals profiting from a wartime situation ("unpeace" as civil society activists dub it) — either monetarily or in terms of careerism (e.g., the notion that service in the Mindanao conflict is necessary to fast track promotion within the Armed Forces). Nor is it really possible to discuss the theory that control over natural resources motivates policy-making in Manila since such motivation would be indistinguishable from the more generalized defence of the territorial integrity of the Republic of the Philippines. Neither class of motivation seems to explain the persistence of "autonomy" as a policy option favoured by Manila.

Rather, the benefit to Manila elites (in general) from having "autonomous" regions in Muslim Mindanao, that I wish to draw attention to, are those in the electoral arena. Throughout the postwar era, Muslim Mindanao was notorious for being vulnerable to electoral manipulations (Coronel 2005):

> In 1949, by all accounts a fraudulent election, it was said that "the birds and the bees" voting in Lanao enabled Elpidio Quirino to bag the presidency. During the Marcos era, the joke was that after every voting, Ali Dimaporo, the Maranao strongman who was a staunch ally of the dictator, would call up Malacañang and ask his patron, "Apo, how many more votes do you need?" Decades later, not much seemed to have changed ….

This commentary was written as part of an analysis of how, in May 2004, Gloria Macapagal-Arroyo won overwhelmingly in the Mindanao province of Lanao del Sur despite the popularity of movie actor Fernando Poe, Jr. (who had played various roles of heroic Muslims in the movies). In fact, the "Hello Garci" scandal that broke in June 2005, about alleged 2004 conversations between the President and Commission on Elections (COMELEC) Commissioner Garcillano, centred on leaked recordings of cellular phone discussions of activities in Muslim Mindanao.

Rather than trace the details of that incident in 2004, we can briefly relate the most blatant episode, that of the May 2007 elections for the nationally-elected Senate in the province of Maguindanao in the ARMM.

For the 12 available slots, the Government fared badly in nationwide tallies, with 7 members of the "Genuine Opposition" winning, two independents, and three from the administration's Team Unity, winning. The 12th place finish was by Team Unity candidate Juan Miguel Zubiri, winning by a 20,000 vote margin (11,004,099 to 10,984,807) over Aquilino Pimentel III.

This margin of victory appeared at the last moment, relying on the vote tallies in the province of Maguindanao. Factional manoeuvring led by Maguindanao Provincial Governor Datu Andal Ampatuan (father of ARMM Regional Governor Datu Zaldy Ampatuan) had arranged for 20 of the 22 races for municipal mayor to be uncontested, and the provincial results showed a 12–0 outcome in the Senate for the administration. A train of events had the Commission on Election's provincial election supervisor saying that the municipal returns (on which provincial results are based) had been stolen, and then that they had merely gone missing and had been found. Then the election supervisor himself went missing, finally to be arrested and brought to Manila. The provincial results were duly counted, and had a margin of over 120,000 votes for Zubiri over Pimentel, enough to allow Zubiri (over protests that continue) to claim the twelfth slot.[6]

As noted above, this problem pre-dates the institution of "autonomy" but blame for its continuation in such blatant form into the twenty-first century can be laid, partially, on a perception that Muslim Mindanao is different, as the candidate himself proclaimed:

> When asked about this statistical improbability, Zubiri said that unlike in Bukidnon [his home province elsewhere in Mindanao], where the voters have varied ethnic and religious affiliations, voters in Maguindanao follow a "bloc voting" scheme.
> "The tribal leaders give an order and people follow," Zubiri said.

In short, "autonomy" is the institutional face of a continued "distinctive historical and cultural heritage" (to use the language of the 1987 Constitution). The acknowledgement of this distinction allows the party in power in Manila more scope for manipulation of electoral returns. Accordingly, consider a pithy summary by a [pseudonymous] source sympathetic to the MILF:

> As a Philippine colony, the Moro homeland also serves as the source of manufactured votes and 'ghost voters' to ensure the poll victory of the ruling regime. This has, in fact, brought notoriety to the so-called ARMM, which is noted for the 'swing votes' that have invariably guaranteed the perpetuation in power of any ruling regime in the Philippine government (or its favored candidates) through these farcical

elections. Hence, 'failure of elections' — which necessitate holding of post-election 'special elections' — in many provinces of the ARMM has become a 'normal' practice in every political exercise in the ARMM. Moro leaders in government are duty-bound to deliver their 'votes'. This should also explain why no Moro politician ever became head of the so-called Muslim autonomous region — from the time of Marcos to the present dispensation — without the anointment and/or blessings of the regime in power.[7]

FROM THE VIEWPOINT OF MUSLIM MINDANAO

While we have explicated why Manila has repeatedly looked to "autonomy" as an arrangement in Muslim Mindanao, it remains to account for why participation by Muslims in such an arrangement has also persisted over the decades. I do not wish to treat here the question of why revolutionary movements such as the MNLF and the MILF might drop a demand for independence, or at least put it in abeyance. That would depend on internal dynamics (about which we know little, particularly for the MILF), assessments of the possibility of achieving victory by force of arms, and relations with international actors – these are aspects that lie beyond the subject of the relationship between Manila and Muslim Mindanao.

For ordinary Muslims and Muslim leaders, it might seem that the vision of the 1987 Constitution (Article X, Section 15) of a special region covering "areas sharing common and distinctive historical and cultural heritage, economic and social structures" with an elected government would be attractive. And, indeed, there was considerable excitement in 1990 and 1996 when, first, a post-dictatorship Autonomous Region in Muslim Mindanao was instituted, and, then, a post-Peace Agreement accommodation paved the way for the MNLF leadership to take many positions (including Chairman Nur Misuari as Governor) in the regional government.

Still, in the face of disappointment after 1990, and after 1996, persistent engagement with "autonomy" needs to be examined. There is popular disenchantment with the autonomous government, as seen in a household survey conducted by the Asia Foundation in 2002 (see Table 14.3):

We can see that the regional government is more trusted than the national government only in Maguindanao (the seat of the ARMM is Cotabato City, not technically part of ARMM but geographically within the province). In the rest of the ARMM, it is the least trusted level of government.

Table 14.3
Household Survey undertaken late 2002 in ARMM

	Marawi City	Lanao del Sur	Maguin-danao	Sulu	Tawi-tawi
Net trust* on levels of government					
Provincial government	+68	+74	+61	+62	+70
National government	+20	+12	+43	+24	+60
ARMM government	+17	+1	+48	+19	+34

* Net Trust Ratings = %Very much/Much Trust minus %Little/Very Little Trust

Such lack of trust by the average voter is not easily translatable into political action — given the problems with elections described above. The answer to the persistence of "autonomy" in the face of failures and disenchantment by average Muslim residents of the Autonomous Region lies, I believe, in the scope that an "autonomous" region gives the elites of political clans for pursuing their own local interests.

Philippine politics has generally been very locally-based (McCoy 1993; Hutchcroft and Rocamora 2003). The rise of a national media has weakened the link between locally-based politicians and the election of Presidents and Senators, and the proliferation of possible candidates at the local level has in many areas led to the rise of reform politicians, but change has been slow to come to conflict-torn Muslim Mindanao. In fact, the use of "family" as an organizing principle remains even more important in Muslim Mindanao (Beckett 1993, pp. 304–5):

> The fact remains that most Maguindanaoan politicians were members of family coalitions, and that the public viewed them as such, even when they were divided. Kinship and lineage were central elements in the precolonial social structure, and they persisted both as cultural codes and in the persons of such long established families as the Sinsuats and Masturas ... the explanation for this survival seems to be the lack of other bases for differentiation, factors such as ideology, class, or sectional interest. Although this pattern could be observed in much of the Philippines between 1946 and 1972, it particularly held true for the Maguindanaoan....

As Marcos engaged in his victory/pacification strategy against the Moro National Liberation Front in the late 1970s, he particularly encouraged members of traditional ruling families who had joined the MNLF to revert to allegiance to the government. It was relatively easy for datus and traditional leaders to surrender and join in the government's efforts. As noted, following the elections for the two regional autonomous governments in 1979 many of the "Top 90" who had been trained in Malaysia beginning in 1969 and who had formed the MNLF, joined the government in the two autonomous regions (Castro 2005, p. 108). Thus, while the revolutionary movement had hoped to organize politics in new ways, reality quickly reverted to the status quo.

SYMPTOMS OF CLAN DOMINANCE

There are a number of consequences of the dominance of political clans — the most obvious of which is electoral violence. Many of the pathologies of Philippine elections are pronounced in Muslim Mindanao, but are not unique to that region (Rood 2007):

> What is unique to ARMM, and ought not be glossed over, is the fact that conflict among clans for political power regularly overwhelms the electoral system. The overwhelming majority of voters in areas with "failed elections" are in the ARMM.

Election violence is one manifestation of a more general problem of persistent clan conflict (known as *rido* among the Maranao and by other terms in other ethnolinguistic groups) (Torres 2007). This problem is not unknown in the rest of the Philippines but is worse in ARMM. Surveys have shown that conflict among clans is the form of violence that most affects the day-to-day lives of residents of the ARMM.

Election rivalry is one of the main causes of rido, but land is an equally important cause of persistent conflict between clans. Even honor and pride are motivating factors, as there is an incentive to demonstrating a capacity for violent defence of the family's interests. In general, in the absence of the rule of law, clans are the functional structures that protect individuals, assert claims to resources and respect, and allow a modicum of certainty instead of a Hobbesian state of nature where there is a war of all against all.

One of the more interesting symptoms of clan dominance is the subdivision of local governments into smaller segments so that clans do not clash over dominance. In the rest of the Philippines, changing the boundaries of a local government unit requires an Act of Congress, but the Regional Legislative Assembly of the ARMM does have the power to divide municipalities.[8] This is undertaken explicitly to keep the peace (Llanto 2008). There is popular recognition of this problem — in a Social Weather Stations Survey in early 2008, 62 per cent of respondents in the ARMM felt that it was good to have an unopposed candidate, to reduce violence.

The persistence of clan politics in the ARMM, even as it weakens elsewhere in the Philippines, of course has a lot to do with almost forty years of on-again/off-again separatist violence in the region. Not only does the conflict reinforce the necessity for the capacity for violent self-defense by family, but it stifles investment and economic growth thus weakening the middle classes who might demand reform. Beyond the effects of violence, "autonomy" provides rhetorical cover to traditional clan-based leaders in two ways. First, it can be asserted that Muslims, having a distinct historical and cultural heritage, are more inclined to follow these traditional leaders. Secondly, being part of the governance of an autonomous region allows clan leaders to assert they are serving the Bangsamoro, thus reducing the attraction of revolutionary movements such as the MNLF and MILF.

In short, having an Autonomous Region in Muslim Mindanao allows clan leaders to exercise their political options with more freedom. Hence, from the early Marcosian Regions IX and XII — with the partial exception of Nur Misuri's (1996–2001) and Parouk Hussin's (2001–05) governorships of the ARMM — the traditional leaders rather than leaders of the MNLF have found the regional government a convenient mechanism for exercising considerable latitude in their political activities.

CONCLUSION: THE WAY FORWARD

This discussion of the interests that "autonomy" serves among Manila and Muslim Mindanao traditional clan elites ought not to be taken as implying that there are no legitimate demands of Muslims in the Philippines. Living in what has often been described as "the only Christian country in Asia", in the poorest parts of the archipelago, amidst the destruction of decades of intermittent war — the grievances of Muslims in the Philippines are no mystery. And, some "entity" is needed to address the common interests of the Bangsamoro — negotiations with the MILF use terms like "Bangsamoro Juridical Entity" as a way to avoid labelling the result "autonomy."

The political dynamic of "autonomy" becomes more difficult as the government negotiates simultaneously with the MILF and different factions of the MNLF. All these groupings now maintain that the current ARMM under Republic Act 9054 is unhelpful. For the MNLF factions, RA 9054 does not fulfil the Final Peace Agreement, while for the MILF, "autonomy" is a failure. At the same time there are divisions, with MNLF Chairman Nur Misuari publicly calling the government's peace talks with the MILF "illegal" (since there is already a Final Peace Agreement) while sympathizers of the MILF call the MNLF a "spent force."

My argument is that solutions to the Bangsamoro problem will have to take interests of elites into account. And, perhaps surprisingly, based on the analysis of interlocking autonomy, this author is quite optimistic that such a solution can be reached.[9] The insights of the preceding analysis can be summarized as follows. "Autonomy" serves as coalitional convenience among Manila policy elites. Muslim Mindanao traditional elites also find it convenient. In both cases, the interests that are served are political. Finally, electoral manipulation is the key mechanism by which these mutual political interests are serviced.

Put this way, the solution is simple — that the policy stasis can be broken by a definitive shift of momentum to the pacification/developmentalist end of the spectrum (overwhelmingly rejecting the "victory" option), and the simultaneous reform of the system of elections in the Philippines. Depending on one's state of optimism these are either two quite simple things, or are tremendously difficult. This author's view is that these are fairly simple policy initiatives that can be initiated by a Manila administration with political capital, such as in the "honeymoon" period at the beginning of a President's six-year political term, and the initiatives can be designed in such a way that they are implementable.

President Ramos, as noted above, demonstrated in 1992–96 that it is possible decisively to shift momentum on peace processes towards developmentalism. However, with respect to the MNLF's 1996 Final Peace Agreement (FPA), the crucial mechanism of a free, fair, peaceful, and honest system of elections was not pursued. At the regional level, Nur Misuari was the anointed administration candidate for governor after the FPA was signed, and at the national level little progress was made in instituting better elections. Thus, post 1996 the incentive of electoral manipulation remained, thus maintaining the old nexus between Manila and the ARMM.

Filipinos are beginning to see the benefits of electoral modernization as carried out in the May 2010 national elections. The August 11, 2008 ARMM elections were viewed by both the Commission on Elections and nongovernment organizations interested in electoral reform as a pilot test for the broader implementation of various forms of mechanization and transparency. The subsequent May 2010 general elections saw a continuation of the upsurge in citizen activism for that began in the 2007 elections (arising in reaction to the election scandals of 2004 and 2005). Electoral reform is a crucial piece in the peace jigsaw. Should the "autonomous" region cease its function as a vote bank for (largely, administration) candidates, then a crucial reason would be eliminated for Manila elites to back the traditional clan leaders who actually facilitate the manipulations.[10] And, without such backing, the ability of such leaders to maintain dominance in the midst of other Muslim elites (a growing educated middle class, a civil society growing in density, a private sector with aspirations of economic growth, and — perhaps most crucially — revolutionary movements) would weaken. In short, the argument is that a peace agreement of suitable shape can be sustained if combined with electoral reform.

Given the analysis of the transactional nature of interlocking autonomy in the past, with both Manila and Muslim Mindanao elites having incentives to maintain the current status quo, what would enable any new arrangement to be in equilibrium and implementable?

With respect to communities just outside of the current ARMM, both Muslim and Christian, the issue is relatively clear. There need to be adjustments to current boundaries at the margins of the Autonomous Region in Muslim Mindanao — but only for those more-or-less contiguous areas that are majority Muslim. The mid-2008 uproar over the Memorandum of Agreement on Ancestral Domain (MOA-AD) was triggered by the inclusion in the list of areas of the proposed Bangsamoro Juridical Entity (BJE) of barangays that were not, in fact, majority Muslim. Prior consultation with affected communities (the lack of which was another grievance raised by oppositors to the Supreme Court) can ensure that territorial redrawings are limited to those areas that are indeed majority Muslim. The citizens in these areas need to be consulted directly — even the MOA-AD envisioned a plebiscite. And, for plebiscite results to be credible, electoral reform is crucial.

Once adjacent areas have been informed of these changes, and consent given, there are accommodations that could be made to encourage the assent of local governments losing territory. For instance, the governments of the "mother" municipalities and provinces could be guaranteed the same level of Internal Revenue Allotments (block grants from the national government) instead of reductions caused by reduced population and geographic area as parts of their local government units are transferred to a Bangsamoro Juridical Entity.

There are some areas that are not contiguous to the current boundaries of the ARMM, and for these the relations with the BJE need to be clear and non-threatening. A prospective example is the ongoing set of activities of the Bangsamoro Development Agency, set up by the government and the MILF to undertake development projects. Such projects have ranged widely in geographic scope, sometimes well outside the current ARMM, and local government leaders have learned to appreciate such efforts. In short, relations of local Muslim villages with the BJE will be acceptable to surrounding settler communities if the thrust of the settlement is economic development at the local level.

At the local level within Muslim Mindanao, one of the stumbling blocks to a sustainable peace agreement with the MILF lies with traditional leaders. Note that the basis of power being asserted by revolutionary movements such as the MNLF or MILF — the interests of the entire Bangsamoro people — is quite different from the particularistic clan-based power structure of traditional politicians. The optimism expressed above also assumes that the Muslim middle class — increasingly engaged — become forces for local voting reform while nationwide reform also blocks up avenues for electoral fraud.

In the longer term, there need to be political parties within Muslim Mindanao that can accommodate both clans and revolutionaries in competition for the votes of the citizenry. Healthy development of such politics would require a sustained peace, something which has not been available for decades in Muslim Mindanao.

Notes

[1] When the Spanish colonized the Philippines in the sixteenth century, they called the Muslims that they encountered "Moro" after the Muslims they had recently ejected from the Iberian Peninsula. In the late 1960s, Muslims in the Philippines began to re-appropriate the term, making what had once been a pejorative epithet into a positively valued self-description.

[2] While the Cordillera in northern Luzon could also achieve autonomy under the 1987 Constitution, the region has twice (in 1990 and 1998) failed to ratify proposed Organic Acts. Thus, the Cordillera Administrative Region has now the same status as all other administrative regions of the country. It is only the Autonomous Region in Muslim Mindanao that has an elected regional government.

[3] Leaving out Davao del Sur, South Cotabato, and Palawan — as per the results of the April 1977 Referendum-Plebiscite

[4] <http://www.c-r.org/our-work/accord/philippines-mindanao/peace-agreement.php>. "The final agreement on the implementation of the 1976 Tripoli Agreement between the Government of the Republic of the Philippines (GRP) and the Moro National Liberation Front (MNLF) with the participation of

the organization of Islamic Conference Ministerial Committee of Six and the Secretary General of the organization of Islamic Conference."
5. In mid-2009 fighting died down again and by the end of 2009 negotiations between the government and the MILF had resumed. However, by June 2010, as the term of President Arroyo was coming to an end, the parties managed to sign a sketchy "Declaration on the Continuity of Peace Negotiation" in anticipation of the July 2010 changeover to the new administration of President Benigno S. (Noynoy) Aquino III.
6. The Philippine Center for Investigative Journalism (PCIJ) covered this issue and all its aspects in a number of posts, for instance: <http://www.pcij.org/blog/?p=1810>; <http://i-site.ph/blog/?p=219#more-219>; <http://i-site.ph/blog/?p=221#more-221>.
7. Ibrahim Canana, "What Election?", e-mail in circulation.
8. The Regional Legislative Assembly created in, 2007, a new province, Sharif Kabunsuan, carved out of the province of Maguindanao. The Vice-Governor of Maguindanao, Sinsuat was appointed officer-in-charge and ran for election in 2007. While the election outcome was being disputed, the Philippine Supreme Court ruled that the Regional Legislative Assembly did not have the power to create a province since that implies creating a new Congressional District, which requires an Act of the Philippine Congress. In late 2008 the Court finally ruled that the new province must be dissolved back into the original Maguindanao.
9. It is worth noting here that this paper does not deal with the perceptions of "autonomy" that the predominantly Christian "settler community" in Mindanao has. This community has been left out of the negotiations and dialogue, and has rejected participation in "autonomy" in every forum possible (from public demonstrations, to local government resolutions, to plebiscites). In point of fact, as noted in the body of the conclusion, this ought not be an insurmountable problem for a lasting solution, as long as the interests of the settler community are taken into account, and are seen to be taken into account.
10. The worst example of this problem was seen in 23 November 2009, when some fifty-eight people were killed, allegedly by forces loyal to the Ampatuan clan of supporters of a political opponent (Wilson 2009). For how that provincial-level incident relates to governance in the ARMM and relations with Manila, see Arguillas (2011).

References

Abinales, Patricio N. *Making Mindanao: Cotabato and Davao in the Formation of the Philippine Nation-State*. Quezon City: Ateneo de Manila University Press, 2000.

Arguillas, Carolyn O. "Maguindanao: The Long Shadow of the Ampatuans". In *Democracy at Gunpoint: Election Related Violence in the Philippines*, edited by

Yvonne T. Chua and Luz R. Rimban. Quezon City: Vera Files Incorporated and the Asia Foundation, 2011.

Beckett, Jeremy. "Political Familes and Family Politics among the Muslim Maguindanaoan of Cotabato". In *An Anarchy of Families: State and Family in the Philippines*, edited by Alfred W. McCoy. Madison: University of Wisconsin Center for Southeast Asian Studies, 1993.

Castro, Delfin. *A Mindanao Story: Troubled Decades in the Eye of the Storm*. Manila: Delfin Castro, 2005.

Coronel, Sheila S. "Ate Glo in Hot Water. Lanao's Dirty Secret". *I Report*, Issue no. 4, November 2005. <http://www.pcij.org/i-report/4/lanao.html>.

Danguilan Vitug, Marites and Glenda Gloria. *Under the Crescent Moon*. Quezon City: Institute for Popular Democracy, 2000.

Ferrer, Miriam Coronel. "Philippines National Unification Commissions: National Consultation and the 'Six Paths to Peace'". In *Owning the Process: Public Participation in Peacemaking*, edited by Catherine Barnes. *Accord* 13. London: Conciliation Resources, 2002. <www.c-r.org/accord/peace/accord13/phi.htm>.

Hutchcroft, Paul D. and Joel Rocamora. "Strong Demands and Weak Institutions: The Origins and Evolution of the Democratic Deficit in the Philippines". *Journal of East Asian Studies 3* (2003): 259–92. <http://www.tni.org/archives/rocamora/demands.pdf>.

Llanto, Jesus. "Creating More LGUs Prevents Conflicts in ARMM". *Newsbreak*, 28 March 2008. <http://newsbreak.com.ph/index.php?option=com_content&task=view&id=4314&Itemid=88889051>.

McCoy, Alfred W., ed. *An Anarchy of Families: State and Family in the Philippines*. Madison, Wisconsin and Quezon City: Center for Southeast Asian Studies and Ateneo de Manila University Press, 1993 and 1994, respectively.

Olarte, Avigail. "Why you should doubt the Maguindanao election results — 5". i-site's 2007 election files, 12 July 2007. <http://i-site.ph/blog/?p=221#more-221>.

Oquist, Paul. *Mindanao and Beyond: Competing Policies, Protracted Peace Process, and Human Security*. Multidonor Program for Peace and Development in Mindanao Fifth Assessment (Peace and Development Learning Experiences in Asia. UNDP PARAGON Regional Governance Program) Manila, 23 October 2002. <www.undp-paragon.org/rgp/data/5th_mission_report.pdf>.

Rasul, Amina. *Broken Peace? Assessing the 1996 GRP-MNLF Final Peace Agreement*. Manila: Philippine Council for Islam and Democracy, Konrad Adenauer Stiftung, and Magbassa Kita Foundation, Inc., 2007.

Rood, Steven. *Forging Sustainable Peace in Mindanao: The Role of Civil Society*. Washington Policy Studies no. 17. Washington, D.C.: East-West Center, 2005.

―――. "In the Philippines: Elections in Mindanao". <http://asiafoundation.org/in-asia/2007/05/16/in-the-philippines-elections-in-mindanao/>.

Torres, Wilfredo Magno III, ed. *Rido: Clan Feuding and Conflict Management in Mindanao.* Makati City: The Asia Foundation, 2007.

Vitug, Marites Dañguilan and Glenda M. Gloria. *Under the Crescent Moon: Rebellion in Mindanao.* Quezon City: Ateneo Center for Social Policy and Public Affairs, Institute for Popular Democracy, 2000.

Wilson, Karl. "Violent deaths lay bare Philippines' politics", 25 November 2009. <http://www.thenational.ae/apps/pbcs.dll/article?AID=/20091125/FOREIGN/711249893/1138>.

15

HISTORY, DEMOGRAPHY AND FACTIONALISM: OBSTACLES TO CONFLICT RESOLUTION THROUGH AUTONOMY IN THE SOUTHERN PHILIPPINES

Ronald J. May

The conflict between the government of the Philippines and the Moro separatists in the southern Philippines has become one of the longest running, and most intractable, internal conflicts in Southeast Asia. This is so despite attempts by successive Philippine governments to negotiate some form of autonomy arrangements with the separatists. This paper briefly reviews the Philippines experiments with Muslim autonomy and addresses the question: why have the autonomy negotiations between the Philippine government and the Moros proved so intractable? It suggests that the answers lie primarily in three features of the Philippines situation: first, longstanding historical circumstances which have left a legacy of antipathy and distrust between important elements of the Muslim and Christian Filipino communities; secondly, a pattern of internal migration, encouraged by national governments throughout the twentieth century, which has changed the ethnic demography of Mindanao and Sulu, locking both sides into a position from which it has been difficult to progress to a settlement; and thirdly, the factionalization of Philippine Muslim society, which has made negotiation difficult.

THE LONG VIEW: A BRIEF HISTORY OF MORO SEPARATISM

The origins of Moro identity

The basis for the Muslim claims to a separate identity, and arrangements for recognizing the special status of Philippine Muslims, have a long history. When the Spanish colonizers came to the Philippine islands in 1565 and encountered Islamic communities, they effectively resumed the crusades against those they identified as the "Moro", using the Christianized "indios" as their footsoldiers. But although they defeated Muslim forces in the north, and encouraged Christianized Filipinos to settle on the northern and eastern coasts of Mindanao, the Spaniards never did achieve effective sovereignty over the Muslim (or over much of the tribal/*lumad*[1]) communities in Mindanao and Sulu.[2]

In 1898, following the Spanish-American War, the United States took possession of the islands of Mindanao and Sulu. Under American colonial rule, once "pacification" had been achieved a general policy of "benevolent assimilation" was extended to the Muslim population, though this was resisted by Muslim communities, as well as by some of the more enlightened American administrators. From 1903 to 1920 the then predominantly Muslim districts of Mindanao and Sulu were administered first through a separate Moro Province and then through a Department of Mindanao and Sulu. Following the creation of the Philippine Commonwealth in 1935 a group of Moro leaders from Lanao petitioned the U.S. president not to include Mindanao and Sulu in an independent Philippines, arguing that Christian Filipinos discriminated against Moros and treated them abusively. Confirming these forebodings, the Commonwealth swiftly moved to repeal the *Administrative Code for Mindanao and Sulu*, which had allowed some leeway in the application of national laws in the Moro provinces, and refused official recognition of traditional Moro civil titles (see Gowing 1979, pp. 168–79).

An inflow of migrants from the populous provinces of Luzon and the Visayas began early in the twentieth century, spontaneously and as part of a policy of the American administration, and later the Philippines Commonwealth, to develop Mindanao as a new frontier by encouraging cattle ranching, plantations, and smallholder resettlement. Although migration ceased during the Second World War, the immediate postwar years saw a rapid increase in inmigration. By 1980, the proportion of Muslims in the population of Mindanao, which had been estimated at 76 per cent in 1903, had fallen to 23 per cent.[3] This demographic change brought conflicts over land and threatened the authority of traditional Muslim political leaders.

The emergence of the MNLF and creation of an Autonomous Region of Muslim Mindanao

During the latter part of the 1960s and the early 1970s, tensions amongst Muslim, *lumad* and Christian Filipino communities in Mindanao heightened, culminating in the creation of the Moro National Liberation Front (MNLF) under the leadership of Nur Misuari. The MNLF's core demand was for a "free and independent state for the Bangsa Moro people", comprising the 25 provinces of Mindanao, Sulu and Palawan. Organizationally, the MNLF was loosely structured, dominated by a few strong personalities and frequently divided by factional squabbles.

The growing conflict in the south was cited by President Marcos in declaring martial law in 1972. Following the declaration, fighting escalated, with thousands killed and tens of thousands displaced, many seeking refuge in the neighbouring Malaysian state of Sabah. The MNLF received both moral and material support from Muslim states and organizations in the Middle East, North Africa and Southeast Asia, and from the Organization of Islamic Conference (OIC) (see Che Man 1987).

In 1976, negotiations conducted under the auspices of Libya's President Gaddafi resulted in the signing of the Tripoli Agreement, which promised Muslim autonomy in the 13 Philippine provinces of historical Muslim influence.[4] The scaling down of demands from 25 to 13 provinces came as a result of pressure from the OIC. However, by 1976, as a result of inmgration, only five of these provinces (and on Mindanao only two) still had a majority Muslim population.

Discussions over the details of implementation of the Tripoli Agreement quickly broke down, with both sides accusing the other of violating the conditions of the Agreement. President Marcos nevertheless went ahead to conduct a referendum on Muslim autonomy, which was boycotted by the MNLF and its supporters. The outcome was that two autonomous regional governments were established in those parts of Mindanao-Sulu (Region IX, Western Mindanao and Region XII, Central Mindanao) which voted for autonomy, though they lacked popular legitimacy and had limited effectiveness.

Around this time the MNLF split. Misuari's leadership was challenged in 1977 by Hashim Salamat, then the Cairo-based chairman of the foreign affairs bureau. Salamat accused Misuari of autocratic leadership, communist sympathies and corruption, and sought to persuade the OIC to recognize him (Salamat) as new chairman of the MNLF. Unsuccessful in this, Salamat set up a rival organization, the Moro Islamic Liberation Front (MILF), which drew its support primarily from the Maguindanao-speaking areas of Mindanao. Five years later a further split occurred when a MNLF-Reformist Group (MNLF-RG) was formed, mostly from among members of the Maranao elite, with headquarters in Jeddah. During the late 1970s and early 1980s several attempts were made to unite the various factions but reconciliation proved elusive.

In the lead-up to the "People Power revolution" of 1986, the mainstream anti-Marcos forces courted Misuari, and following the demise of President Marcos, the Aquino government pursued negotiations with the MNLF. A new constitution, ratified in 1987, made specific provision for an Autonomous Region of Muslim Mindanao (ARMM) (and for an autonomous region in the Cordilleras of Luzon, home to a number of cultural communities or "tribal" groups), and set in motion procedures for its creation, including the creation of a regional consultative commission (RCC) to draft an organic act and provision for another plebiscite to determine its adoption. After a difficult start (see Basman, Lalanto and Madale 1989), the process of drafting legislation for the ARMM was completed and in 1989 the proposal was put to the people in the thirteen provinces and nine cities listed in the Tripoli Agreement on the basis that only those provinces and cities voting to do so would become part of the ARMM. In the event, only four provinces (Maguindanao, Lanao del Sur, Tawi-Tawi and Sulu) and no cities voted to be included in the ARMM, and again the main Moro factions rejected the exercise, though an ARMM was established.

The 1996 Agreement

When President Aquino's term in office came to an end in 1992, she was succeeded by former Philippines Constabulary commander, General Fidel Ramos. Ramos promptly reopened negotiations with Misuari. Ramos' initiative came as an unwelcome surprise to many in Mindanao, who believed that the move gave a new lease of life to Misuari and the MNLF, whose influence seemed to have diminished after their rejection of the ARMM.

The new round of negotiations, carried out mostly through a ministerial committee of the OIC, chaired by Indonesia, culminated in a new agreement, signed by President Ramos and Chairman Misuari in 1996. The 1996 agreement was widely acclaimed as a settlement of the long-running conflict in the south. But while the 1996 agreement was an achievement, in that it brought Misuari and his faction of the MNLF "back into the fold" (to use a phrase in common currency at the time), perceptions of it as a long-term settlement were unrealistic, for reasons spelled out below.

The agreement signed by Ramos and Misuari, which was described as "The Final Agreement on the Implementation of the 1976 Tripoli Agreement", provided for the creation of a Special Zone of Peace and Development (SZOPAD) corresponding to the provinces and cities covered by the Tripoli Agreement, which was to "be the focus of intense peace and development efforts" over the next three years, and of a Southern Philippines Council for Peace and Development (SPCPD) which was to have powers to "control and/or supervise … appropriate agencies of the government that are engaged in peace and development activities in the area [of the SZOPAD]". Such agencies included the Southern Philippines Development Authority, set up by the Marcos administration to promote development in Mindanao (but which in practice almost certainly did more for the Christian areas of Mindanao than for Muslim Mindanao), regional offices of the Office of Muslim Affairs and Office of Southern Cultural Communities, and the Special Development Planning Group, an *ad hoc* body of government officials from the Department of Trade and Industry, the National Economic and Development Authority, the Department of Public Works and Housing, and other agencies. Local government units in the area, including the ARMM, were to remain subject to existing (national) legislation.

Provision was also made for a Consultative Assembly of 81 members (44 of them from the MNLF), headed by the chair of the SPCPD. Its functions were to serve as a forum for consultation and provide appropriate advice to the SPCPD, and to recommend policies to the president through the chairman of the SPCPD. The SPCPD was also to be assisted by a *Darul Iftah* (religious advisory council) appointed by the SPCPD chair. Misuari was appointed to chair the SPCPD. The MNLF's military wing, the Bangsa Moro Army (BMA), was to be disbanded, and the agreement provided that 7,500 BMA troops were to be recruited into the Armed Forces of the Philippines (AFP) and the Philippine National Police (PNP). Additionally, a special socio-economic, cultural and educational programme was to be developed for members of the MNLF not absorbed into the AFP/PNP, to help them and their families acquire education, technical skills and livelihood training.

The SPCPD was to come under the Office of the President and to receive funding through a presidential vote. The OIC was requested to support the implementation of the agreement. Potential jurisdictional problems between the existing ARMM and the larger SZOPAD/SPCPD were largely avoided by Misuari's election in 1996 as governor of the ARMM.

The 1996 Peace Agreement was to be implemented in two phases. Phase 1 was to cover three years, during which legislation was to be drawn up to replace the organic act (RA6734) under which the ARMM had been set up in 1987, to give effect to the provisions of the Final Peace Agreement and expand the geographical coverage of the ARMM. Such legislation, after being passed by Congress and approved by the president, was to be submitted to a plebiscite in the SZOPAD within two years from the establishment of the SPCPD (i.e. by September 1998). Phase 2 was to see the creation of an executive council, legislative assembly and administration with legislative powers in the area of autonomy. The head of the autonomous region was to be an *ex officio* member of the National Security Council on all matters affecting the autonomous region. Phase 2 was also to see the establishment of Special Regional Security Forces (SRSF) — in practice, a PNP regional command — in the Autonomous Region. Detailed provisions were included for an integrated system of education, which would perpetuate "Filipino and Islamic ideals and aspirations". *Madaris* (Islamic schools) were to be included under the Regional Autonomous Government education system, and Arabic recognized as a medium of instruction in *madaris* and other Islamic institutions. Economic and fiscal autonomy arrangements in Phase 2 included the right of the autonomous region government to contract foreign and domestic loans.

Among non-Muslim communities in Mindanao the 1996 Peace Agreement generated considerable anxiety. Christian community leaders, led by Congresswoman Maria Clara Lobregat, organized demonstrations against the agreement, and there were threats that the Christian vigilante groups which had been active during the conflicts of the early 1970s would be revived. In Congress, there was opposition to the granting of autonomy and accusations that President Ramos had "sold out" to the militant Muslims. In the Senate, there were demands for the withdrawal of powers from the SPCPD and Consultative Assembly, and for the exclusion of local government units from SPCPD control; six of the twenty-four senators voted against a resolution supporting the peace agreement. In the House of Representatives, the House Appropriations Committee threatened to block funding for the SPCPD and Consultative Assembly. Just prior to the signing of the final agreement a group of congressional representatives and a provincial governor filed a petition in the Supreme Court seeking the invalidation of the agreement (see *Accord* 1999).

Against this background, when the implementing executive order (EO 371) was signed in October 1996, it was a significantly weakened version of the final agreement. As one commentator wrote in 1999:

> ... the transitional structures [the SPCPD and Consultative Assembly] ... were too powerless to make an impact. They had very limited funding, no police powers, no control over national projects and programmes that were supposed to be within their remit, and no jurisdiction over significant sections of the bureaucracy in the region (Gutierrez, in *Accord* 1999, pp. 66–67).

Among other things, the provision in the agreement for forty-four MNLF members in the Consultative Assembly was dropped, and the provisions of the agreement which placed specified government agencies under the control and/or supervision of the SPCPD were deleted. In fact, the SPCPD was given little scope for policy action except through the Office of the President.

There were, moreover, substantial limitations to the agreement. First, since Misuari and the MNLF were recognized as the leadership of the Moro movement by the OIC, the Philippine government was effectively locked into negotiating with Misuari. However, by 1996 the MILF was probably the stronger of the two main factions and it was not party to the 1996 agreement; indeed in 1993 MILF chairman Salamat said the MILF would reject any attempt by the Philippine government to open separate negotiations with the MILF unless the GRP-MNLF talks were concluded, and the MILF specifically distanced itself from the 1996 agreement, vowing to continue the armed struggle. Secondly, as with earlier attempts at Moro autonomy, the 1996 agreement contained provision for a plebiscite to determine whether the parts of the SZOPAD not included within the ARMM would decide to join, and it was obvious to anyone who had followed the saga of Muslim autonomy arrangements that once the vote was taken, the predominantly non-Muslim provinces and cities would opt to stay out of the ARMM — as they had done in 1977 and 1989 (see May 2001). The plebiscite was put off for as long as possible, but in 2001 it was finally held, and the inevitable happened: of the now 14 provinces and 14 cities canvassed, only five provinces and one city (the addition of Basilan and Marawi City) voted to be part of the ARMM.

Meanwhile, the SPCPD and ARMM under Misuari had fallen well short of people's expectations and there was growing opposition to Misuari's leadership. There were complaints that jobs within the ARMM administration went exclusively to MNLF supporters, and that the administration was rife with corruption. Promises of financial assistance and investment from Muslim countries had for the most part not materialized. Misuari blamed the national government for failing to provide adequate funding and support to the ARMM — and there were certainly grounds for arguing that the government had done little to promote development in the predominantly Muslim provinces, which are still amongst the nation's poorest — and in 1999 threatened that if conditions did not improve he "would return to the hills" (interview with Misuari, Makati, 1999). Already, there were reports of some former MNLF guerrillas joining the MILF or operating as independent units in Sulu.

The breakdown of the 1996 Agreement and the rise of the MILF

In November 2001, on the eve of ARMM elections and having been denied the backing of the governing Lakas-NUCD-UMPD party, Misuari made good his threat, attacking a military post in Sulu and subsequently fleeing to Malaysia. Protesting the alleged failure of the 1996 Agreement, a meeting of the Bangsamoro People's Congress in Zamboanga declared Misuari the inaugural president of the Bangsamoro Republik. He was subsequently arrested and repatriated, and until April 2008 was under house arrest in Manila. In April 2008 it was reported (*Manila Times* 3 April 2008) that Misuari had been deposed from the leadership of the MNLF.

Ramos had also initiated negotiations with the other major Moro faction, the MILF. In the early 1990s the MILF had established a number of permanent camps in Lanao del Sur and Maguindanao, with headquarters at Camp Abubakr on the border between the two provinces. These became, in effect, small municipalities under MILF administration. There were reports that the MILF's military wing was undergoing transition from guerrilla force to a "semi-conventional army". It was later revealed that since 1994 the MILF, through contacts established in Afghanistan in the late 1980s, had also been hosting a Jemaah Islamiya (JI)-run training camp in Mindanao (see ICG 2003, 2008). The Ramos government appears to have tacitly agreed to accept the MILF's influence in the area, provided that it maintained the peace, and initiated a series of peace talks, which produced an Agreement for General Cessation of Hostilities in 1997. When President Ramos' term ended in 1998, however, there were still unresolved issues.

The situation was further complicated by the emergence in the early 1990s of a new Muslim insurgent group, Al-Harakat al-Islamiyah, better known as the Abu Sayyaf group. Abu Sayyaf was established by a former

MNLF member and charismatic preacher, Abdurajak Janjalani. It supported the general demand for a separate Bangsa Moro and voiced other political objectives, but was primarily involved in extortion and kidnapping for ransom. There has been interaction between Abu Sayyaf and hardline MILF and MNLF supporters, but at an official level both the MNLF and the MILF have denounced the group, and the Philippine government has refused to enter negotiations with it.

Ramos' successor, Joseph Estrada, attempted to take up the campaign initiated by his predecessor but quickly became frustrated by the lack of progress in negotiations with the MILF and violations of the General Cessation of Hostilities. In 2000, after MILF attacks on non-Muslim communities in western Mindanao, the Estrada government launched an "all-out war" against the MILF (see *Philippine Daily Inquirer* 17, 19 February 2000). The offensive was highly visible, as AFP forces overran Camp Abubakr and over forty other MILF strongholds, but was largely ineffective: the MILF simply retreated, regrouped and eventually returned to their bases when the AFP had withdrawn.

Estrada's presidency came to a premature end in 2001 when, facing impeachment over charges of corruption, he stepped down from office and Vice President Gloria Macapagal-Arroyo succeeded him. Under president Macapagal-Arroyo, attempts were made to reverse the new militarization of the conflict and negotiations with the MILF, facilitated through the Malaysian government, were revived. An Agreement on the Framework of the Peace Talks was signed in March 2001, a new Tripoli Agreement on Peace in June, and an Agreement on the Guidelines for the Implementation of the Agreement on the General Cessation of Hostilities in August. (Between 1997 and 2006 the Philippine government and the MILF signed 63 agreements on various issues.[5]) A Bangsamoro Development Agency was also created to channel funds, mostly coming from the World Bank and the Japan International Cooperation Agency, to development projects. In 2003 an International Monitoring Team, with personnel from Malaysia, Brunei, Libya and subsequently Japan, was created to oversee the ceasefire (which has been broadly maintained, despite several notable lapses). The International Monitoring Team has worked closely with Philippine government and MILF coordinating committees on cessation of hostilities and local monitoring teams. However, progress towards a settlement has proved tortuous. On several occasions negotiations stalled but recommenced. In April 2008 it was reported that the Malaysian government, frustrated at the lack of progress in the peace talks, was withdrawing from the process, beginning in May 2008 (*Straits Times*, 26 April 2008). Since Malaysia has provided about 70 per cent of the personnel of the International Monitoring Team, its withdrawal would effectively eliminate the international monitoring of the already fragile cessation of hostilities and risk a new escalation of fighting (see Lingga 2008).

A major sticking-point in the negotiations between the Philippine government and the MILF has been the issue of "ancestral domain" — essentially, the area claimed as traditional Muslim homelands as the basis for a Bangsamoro. From around 2004 MILF negotiators sought agreement on a "Bangsamoro Juridical Entity", comprising the present ARMM as core territory, together with 735 municipalities outside the ARMM which were said to have a Muslim-majority population. Provision was to be made also for "special socio-economic and cultural affirmative action" in 1459 conflict-affected areas (or "special intervention areas") outside the Juridical Entity. The Bangsamoro Juridical Entity was to be able to apply its own laws, within the framework of a Basic Law. (See interview with MILF Negotiating Panel chair Mohagher Iqbal, *Bulatlat* 2–8 December 2007; Mastura 2006; Tuminez 2007). The concept of the Bangsamoro Juridical Entity has been developed to overcome the longstanding problems of incompatibility between the territorial claims of the Moros and the demographic reality of the present. In November 2006, a number of "consensus points" on ancestral domain and the Bangsamoro Juridical Entity, including the land and maritime areas to be covered, were agreed between the MILF and Philippine government negotiators. It was also proposed to introduce a form of "Moro self-determination" to address the controversial issue of sovereignty. A final agreement, to be submitted to an internationally-monitored referendum, was anticipated in mid 2008. The Philippine government, however, has insisted that any territorial additions to the ARMM must, as mandated by the constitution (Art. X S.10), be subject to local plebiscite, a condition which is unacceptable to the MILF, which withdrew from the talks in December 2007 (see *Manila Times*, 18 January 2008; *luwaran.com*. 5, 23 May 2008). In announcing the withdrawal of its IMT personnel, Malaysia's chief mediator, Othman Abdul Razak, implicitly accused the Philippine government of not acting cooperatively to find a way out of the impasse, prompting an editorial in the *Philippine Daily Inquirer* (8 May 2008) to accuse Othman of "a gross misunderstanding of both the Philippine position and the limits of constitutional democracy".

A new round of peace talks between the Philippine government and the MILF peace panels, facilitated by Malaysia, began in December 2009 and was concluded in Kuala Lumpur in April 2010. This resulted in agreements to cease hostilities, improve security on the ground, resettle people displaced by the conflict, introduce additional international and local bodies to support the dialogue, and initiate a "final Comprehensive Compact".

Negotiations again broke down in 2010 but were due to resume early in 2011. However, a split within the MILF may lead to a postponement of the proposed talks.

In the late 1990s there was talk of establishing a federal system in the Philippines, a proposal which was taken up from 2003 by the Citizens' Movement for a Federal Philippines. The advocates of federalism specifically argued for federalism as a means of ending the conflict in Mindanao. In her State of the Nation address in 2005 President Macapagal-Arroyo endorsed the idea of federalism and announced her intention to establish a constitutional review to consider a shift from a presidential to a parliamentary system and from a unitary to a federal system. Initially, there was a good deal of support for the federal option among Muslim leaders — though, given the poor record of autonomy arrangements, it is not at all clear why they thought that federalism would be to their advantage. In the event, however, popular support for federalism waned and in December 2005 the proposed federal arrangements were shelved.[6]

Following a visit to the Philippines in mid 2006 by a delegation from the OIC, a long-awaited tripartite review (by the OIC, the Philippine government and the MNLF) of the 1996 Agreement commenced in Jeddah in November 2007. Misuari — still recognized by the OIC as the key Moro spokesman — was prevented from attending, but appointed his legal adviser, Randolph Parcasio, to chair the MNLF panel, and selected chairs for five working groups, on shari'a law, education, political representation, a regional security force, and the economy and natural resources. Misuari's appointment of Misuari-loyalists served to exacerbate the factionalism within the MNLF which culminated in the move against him in April 2008 (see *Mindanao Examiner*, 22 January 2008). Talks were continuing in late 2010 at a meeting hosted by Libya.

OBSTACLES TO RESOLUTION OF THE MINDANAO CONFLICT

The legacy of distrust

Before the arrival of the Europeans, Jolo was a major regional entrepôt, and a link in the trade between the Arab world and China. Slavery was a major component of the regional trade and Muslim slave traders from Mindanao and Sulu undertook regular raids on the barangays of northern Mindanao and the Visayas to support their trade (Warren 1998, 2002). Memories of such raids are preserved in local histories and in the remnants of watchtowers built along the coastlines to provide warning to the local communities. Even today, some older folk in the Visayas and northern Mindanao can recall being told as children that if they did not behave, the "Moros" would take them away.

The Spanish campaigns against the Moro over some 350 years — during which *indio* converts were deployed against the Moro, and Muslims were vilified by Spanish soldiers and priests — entrenched ethnic/religious stereotypes and mutual distrust. The United States substantially inherited the religious-based social and ethnic hierarchy established by their predecessors. However, as administration passed progressively from Americans to Filipinos, many Philippine Muslims feared they were at greater risk of cultural marginalization under a Filipino administration than they were under U.S. colonial rule. Their apprehensions were shared by the American Secretary of the Interior, Dean Worcester, who warned that to hand over control of the non-Christian tribes [including the Moro] to Filipinos "would speedily result in disaster" (*Report of the Philippine Commission, 1909–1911*, cited in Lopez 1976, p. 113).

As inter-communal tensions escalated in the 1960s, and the private armies of political rivals battled for control of political and economic resources, the police were frequently seen to be taking sides against the Muslims. Mosques and churches often became the targets of attack (see May 1992).

In the early 1970s several studies of "ethnic attitudes" revealed a generally negative attitude towards Muslims on the part of Christians, and a somewhat lesser negative attitude towards Christians on the part of Muslims (Lacar and Hunt 1972; Gomez 1973; Bulatao 1974; Filipinas Foundation 1975). In 1979 Gowing wrote:

> [The Spanish and American legacy of] Muslim-Christian hostility contributed heavily to the picture of the Moro in Christian minds as a cunning, ruthless, cruel savage; a pirate; a slaver .... The image includes a perception of the Moros as backward and stubbornly unprogressive ... there is an equally negative "Christian image" in the minds of Muslim Filipinos that is also part of the colonial legacy. The Christian is seen by the Moro as a coward, a cheat, a bully and a land-grabber who, if he could, would destroy Islam (1979, pp. 41–42).

In a more recent study Tolibas-Nuñez has found that such attitudes persist; she concludes: "In a nutshell, the perceptions and understandings that

Muslims and Christians have of each other lack objectivity and are colored by strong biases and prejudices; but especially strong are the biases Christians have of Muslims" (1997, p. 84).

In 1996, the opposition to the agreement between Ramos and Misuari from Christian community spokespeople like Congresswoman Lobregat suggested deep levels of religious and cultural intolerance. Subsequently, the proposed integration of former BMA fighters into the AFP and PC was hampered by resentment on the part of some soldiers that Muslims were being admitted to the AFP even though they did not always meet the required educational standards, and Muslim recruits complained that they were discriminated against and prevented from observing their religious obligations. Many dropped out.

In recent years, there has been a greater degree of sensitivity at senior levels, and the Philippine government has been happy to have the Malaysian government take the leading role in negotiations with the MILF, but longstanding antipathies at the community level underline the difficulties of achieving reconciliation within an expanded ARMM.

THE DEMOGRAPHIC FACTOR

As has been observed above, the changing demography of Mindanao, as a result of heavy immigration of Christian Filipino settlers from the north during the twentieth century, has meant that by the time the Tripoli Agreement was signed in 1976, only 5 of the 13 provinces listed in the agreement still had a majority Muslim population. For this reason alone, the MNLF was opposed to the plebiscites on Muslim autonomy in 1977 and 1989, and the 2001 plebiscite, which attempted to expand the ARMM on the basis of the SZOPAD established in by the 1996 Agreement, was destined to fail.

A breakthrough on this issue seemed to emerging in recent negotiations with the MILF, in the latter's development of the concept of a "Moro Juridical Entity" encompassing Moro ancestral domain (see above). It is not clear, however, whether this concept will prove acceptable to all factions of the Moro movement, let alone to the Philippine government and to non-Muslims within the geographical space of the Juridical Entity.

FACTIONALIZATION

The formation of the MNLF initially brought together a number of mostly young Philippine Muslims from different linguistic/ethnic groups,[7] and from beyond the elite. Chairman Misuari was a Tausug-Samal, of non-aristocratic background, who had been involved in leftist politics at the University of the Philippines in Manila. Vice Chairman Abul Khayr Alonto came from an elite Maranao background, and Salamat, who became a vice chairman, was a Maguindanaon of aristocratic background. The MNLF leadership shared a vision of an independent Bangsa Moro (Moro nation) but the MNLF's 1974 manifesto also declared "That the Revolution of the Bangsa Moro people is revolution with a social conscience"; in the words of a former chairman of the Front's political secretariat: "The Bangsa Moro Revolution does not only seek to liberate our people from the colonial oppression of Filipino colonialism but also from the bondage of traditionalism" (Syed Lingga, quoted in Gowing 1979. p. 241).

As noted above, by the mid 1970s tensions within the MNLF leadership had become strongly apparent. The differences were partly personal (in particular, there were allegations that funds received from foreign supporters had not been used appropriately), partly ideological (Misuari's leftist leanings were not shared by all and some felt that the movement should be more religiously-oriented), and partly strategic (some of the MNLF leadership opposed Misuari's acceptance, under pressure from the OIC, of the shift from demanding Bangsa Moro independence to accepting Muslim autonomy). But the cleavages also tended to follow ethnic/linguistic, and to an extent class, lines. The movement eventually fractured, with the MNLF, under Misuari, and the MILF, under Salamat, vying for recognition as the dominant faction.

The post-1996 arrangements, involving the SPCPD and the ARMM, privileged Misuari and the MNLF. Not only did this exacerbate tensions between MNLF and MILF supporters but, as has happened in other post-conflict situations, Misuari proved to be more competent as a rebel leader than as an administrator and lack of development within the SZOPAD and allegations of corruption within the ARMM tended to undermine Misuari's popularity and authority.

By the late 1990s, Misuari's leadership came under challenge from within the MNLF, initially from a "National Islamic Command Council" and in 2001 from a group calling itself "the (Executive) Council of the 15", led by MNLF Vice Chair Parouk Hussin. The Council of the 15 claimed it had "retired" Misuari, giving him the title "chairman emeritus" and reportedly had support from Indonesia, Malaysia and Libya, and from the presidential adviser on Muslim Mindanao. Misuari responded by dismissing those he described as "traitors", but it was soon after this that he abandoned the post of governor of the ARMM and briefly returned to armed insurgency. He was succeeded as governor by Hussin. Challenges to Misuari's leadership within the MNLF continued while he was under house arrest in Manila and in April 2008 it was reported that Misuari had been ousted by the Central Committee of the MNLF and replaced as chairman by Muslimin Sema, a member of the Council of 15 and mayor of Cotabato City.

Following elections in the ARMM in 2005, the MNLF lost control of the Regional Assembly. This has further complicated the task facing the Philippine government in its attempts to negotiate a settlement of the long-running dispute. With Misuari under challenge within the MNLF and the MNLF marginalized within the ARMM, the MNLF's claim to leadership has been diminished, though it still has the backing of the OIC and argues that the Philippine government must continue to negotiate with the MNLF to fulfill the terms of the Tripoli Agreement. Meanwhile, the MILF, now clearly the most influential element of the Moro movement, has been conducting its own negotiations, unilaterally, with the Philippine government. And to complicate matters, the leadership of the ARMM Assembly, which is now dominated by "traditional politicians" aligned to neither the MNLF nor the MILF, argues, with some justification, that the Philippine government should be negotiating with it. To date, the three Moro parties have shown little propensity to collaborate, and it is unlikely that the Philippine government can sustain three sets of bilateral negotiations.

CONCLUSION

At a workshop at the Australian National University in 2004, scholar and peace activist Fr Eliseo Mercado said of the peace process in the southern Philippines, "We keep thinking we see light at the end of the tunnel. But as we approach the end of the tunnel all we see is another tunnel." After more than thirty years of conflict and negotiation, a resolution of the situation still seems distant, though the level of violence has declined.

Given the geographical concentration of the Moro population, the history of a broadly shared Moro identity, and the willingness of successive Philippine governments to engage in negotiation (albeit within the framework of the national constitution), the Philippines case would seem to offer good prospects for successful autonomy arrangements, but these prospects have not been realized.

What the story of Moro separatism demonstrates is the difficulty of reaching a settlement of separatist demands with an entrenched cultural minority whose traditional territory has been subject to heavy immigration by another, numerically dominant, culturally differentiated, inmigrant group — even when that minority is geographically concentrated and successive national governments (with varying degrees of commitment) have pursued attempts at resolution.

The Philippine government's insistence on a referendum to establish the territory of the ARMM — a policy which has guaranteed that the agreed territory will be less than that claimed by the MNLF and the MILF, and recognized in the Tripoli Agreement — has been a recurrent stumbling block, in 1977, 1989 and 2001. The MILF's innovative concept of the Bangsamoro Juridical Entity seemed to promise a possible way around this problem, but ultimately the Philippine government's position, that any change must be within the framework of the Philippine Constitution — and thus subject to popular vote within the areas affected — has continued to pose an as yet insurmountable obstacle to a settlement.

In the Philipines case, the role played by outside intervention, specifically through the OIC, the Malaysian government and the International Monitoring Team, has been generally positive, both in putting pressure on successive Philippine governments to seek non-military solutions and in mediating negotiations between the two sides. But it has not been sufficient to create a lasting settlement.

The deep-seated historical/cultural/religious differences and mutual distrust between Philippine Muslim society and mainstream Filipino Christian society, and the factionalization of the Moro movement, which means that the Philippine government must now negotiate on multiple fronts — with the OIC-backed MNLF, the MILF and the Malaysian government, and the traditional politicians who now dominate the ARMM assembly — have exacerbated the difficulties of resolving Moro demands.

So long as negotiations continue, armed conflict is unlikely to resume on anything like the scale of the early 1970s, though groups like Abu Sayyaf and opportunistic politicians and criminal gangs will continue to exploit the situation for their own ends. Meanwhile, the light at the end of the tunnel is faint.

Notes

1. In recent times the term "lumad" has been widely used in reference to the people of Mindanao previously referred to as "tribal" or belonging to "cultural communities".
2. Following the common Philippine practice, unless specifically noted otherwise "Mindanao" hereafter refers to the island of Mindanao and the neighbouring islands of the Sulu Archipelago.
3. For an overview of Mindanao's demography in the 1980s, see Costello (1992).

4   These were Basilan, Sulu, Tawi-Tawi, Zamboanga del Sur, Zamboanga del Norte, North Cotabato, Maguindanao, Sultan Kudarat, Lana del Norte, Lanao del Sur, Davao del Sur, South Cotabato, and Palawan; the area was also to include "all the cities and villages situated in the [thirteen provinces]". In 1992 the new province of Sarangani was carved out from South Cotabato. Another new province, Shariff Kabunsuan, was created in 2006 by subdivision of Maguindanao Province; it became a sixth province within the ARMM.
5   See Lingga (2006).
6   For a critical account of the federalism debate see May (2007), Bacani (2004) and Rood (2007).
7   The Muslim population of the Philippines comprises thirteen linguistic groups, of which four — the Maranao-Iranun of Lanao, the Maguindanaon, and the Tausug and Samal of the Sulu Archipelago — together account for over 80 per cent of the Moro population.

References

Bacani, Benedicto R. *Beyond Paper Autonomy: The Challenge in Southern Philippines*. Makati City: Konrad-Adenauer-Stiftung and Center for Autonomy and Governance, NotreDame University College of Law, Cotabato, 2004.

Basman, Taha M., Mama S. Lalanto, and Nagasura T. Madale. *Autonomy for Muslim Mindanao: The RCC Untold Story*. Marawi City: B'lal Publishers, 1989.

Bulatao, Rudolfo A. "Ethnic attitudes in five Philippine cities". *PSSC Social Science Information* 1, no. 3 (1974).

Bulatlat. <http://www.bulatlat.com/>.

Che Man, Wan Kadir bin. *Muslim Separatism: The Moros of Southern Philippines and the Malays of Southern Thailand*. Singapore: Oxford University Press, 1990.

Costello, Michael A. "The demography of Mindanao". In *Mindanao: Land of Unfulfilled Promise*, edited by M. Turner, R.J. May and L.R. Turner. Quezon City: New Day Publishers, 1987.

Filipinas Foundation Inc. *Philippine Majority-Minority Relations and Ethnic Attitudes*. Makati: Filipinas Foundation, 1975.

Gomez, Hilario M. "Muslim-Christian relations". In *The Filipino in the Seventies: An Ecumenical Perspective*, edited by V.R. Gorospe and R.L. Deats. Quezon City: New Day Publishers, 1973.

Gowing, Peter G. *Muslim Filipinos: Heritage and Horizon*. Quezon City: New Day Publishers, 1979.

Gutierrez, Eric. "The politics of transition". In Accord Issue 6, *Compromising on Autonomy: Mindanao in Transition*, edited by Mara Stankavitch. London: Conciliation Resources, 1999.

International Crisis Group (ICG). "Jemaah Islamiyah in South East Asia: Damaged But Still Dangerous". *Asia Report* no. 63 (2003).

———. "The Philippines: Counter-insurgency vs. Counter-terrorism in Mindanao". *Asia Report* no. 152 (2008).
Lacar, Luis Q. and Chester L. Hunt. "Attitudes of Filipino Christian college students toward Filipino Muslims and their implications for national integration". *Solidarity* 7, no. 7 (1972): 3–9.
Lingga, Abhoud Syed M. "Role of Third Parties in Mindanao Peace Process". Institute of Bansamoro Studies Discussion Paper no. 2006–01 (2006).
———. "Malaysia's Pull-out from the International Monitoring Team: Implications to Peace Process in Mindanao". Institute of Bansamoro Studies Discussion Paper no. 2008–01 (2008).
Lopez, Violeta B. *The Mangyans of Mindoro: An Ethnohistory*. Quezon City: University of the Philippines Press, 1976.
Mastura, Datu Michael O. "A Time for Reckoning for the Bangsamoro People. How did we get there? Where do we go next?". Institute of Bansamoro Studies Discussion Paper no. 2006–01 (2006).
May, R.J. "The wild west in the south: a recent political history of Mindanao". In *Mindanao: Land of Unfulfilled Promise*, edited by M. Turner, R.J. May, and L.R. Turner. Quezon City: New Day Publishers, 1992.
———. "Muslim Mindanao: four years after the peace agreement". In *Southeast Asian Affairs 2001*. Singapore: Institute of Southeast Asian Studies, 2001.
———. "Federalism versus autonomy in the Philippines". In *Federalism in Asia*, edited by Baogang He, Brian Galligan, and Takashi Inoguchi. Cheltenham: Edward Elgar, 2007.
Rood, Steven. "Will federalism solve the long-standing conflicts in the Philippines?". Paper prepared for the "Dialogues on Federalism", Center for Local and Regional Governance, National College of Public Administration and Governance, University of the Philippines, 2007.
Stankavitch, Mara, ed. *Compromising on Autonomy: Mindanao in Transition*. Accord Issue 6. London: Conciliation Resources, 1999.
Tolibas-Nuñez, Rosalita. *Roots of Conflict: Muslims, Christians and the Mindanao Struggle*. Makati City: Asian Institute of Management, 1997.
Tuminez, Astrid S. "This land is our land: Moro ancestral domain and its implications for peace and development in the Southern Philippines". SAIS Review 27, no. 2 (2007): 77–91.
Warren, James F. *The Sulu Zone: The World Capitalist Economy and the Historical Imagination*. Amsterdam: VU University Press, 1998.
———. *Iranun and Balingingi: Globalization, Maritime Raiding and the Birth of Ethnicity*. Singapore: Singapore University Press, 2002.

16

CONCLUSION

Michelle Ann Miller

The path to peace and away from armed separatist conflict is never a smooth or linear process. Intense or protracted periods of fighting tend to squeeze out the political middle ground where support for negotiated settlements is most strongly situated. Even when the warring parties agree to participate in peace talks, they often do so without first relinquishing their intransigent nationalist ideologies and zero sum end games. In many cases, the institutional design of the autonomy package is not mutually agreed upon by the key players in the conflict, the implementation of autonomy is only partial or lackluster, and/or the conciliatory spirit of autonomy is subverted by the concurrent enforcement of more repressive and militaristic approaches to conflict resolution.

This book began with the dilemma of how much freedom to grant disenfranchised minorities without releasing control over the parent state's sovereign territories to armed separatist insurgents. Autonomy was presented as a potential compromise solution for the men and women who take up arms as the most extreme means of seeking redress for the real or perceived shortcomings of the parent state by fighting to create their own independent polity. The case studies in this volume explored a range of possible outcomes to the central question of whether autonomy has, or could potentially serve as an effective mechanism for managing armed separatist sentiment and activity in South and Southeast Asian contexts.

Three broad answers to this core question have been borne out by the cases in this volume, although these are marked by a high level of internal differentiation. In general terms, the examples reviewed in this book may be categorized as those which: (a) prove the proposition that autonomy is an effective mechanism for managing armed separatist disputes, (b) refute the claim that autonomy helps to stem the specter of armed separatism, or (c) neither prove nor disprove the argument for or against autonomy in the absence of a decisive military victory or a clear political settlement. Most of the case studies in this book fall into the third category and thus remain explosive laboratories for experimentation in the continuing search for conflict resolution in this long-troubled region.

In the first category, the resolution in 2005 of the three-decade long armed separatist rebellion in Indonesia's westernmost province of Aceh via wide-ranging powers of decentralization in the form of "self-government" attests to the viability of autonomy as a desirable model for conflict resolution. Self-government in Aceh has been nurtured and consolidated by the unwavering commitment to peace by Indonesia's political leadership and former Free Aceh Movement rebels, as well as by the institutionalization of important aspects of democratic procedure with assistance and funding provided by the international community. The strong domestic and international support that this peace process continues to enjoy has led Aceh to be viewed by some as a model for emulation and replication by other countries experiencing territorial disputes. Most nation-states in South and Southeast Asia, however, have been reluctant to devolve any significant authority and resources to their aggrieved minority populations or to grant the international community a mediating role in negotiations. These are factors which were critical to the successful termination of the Aceh conflict and to the subsequent post-conflict peace process there.

In the second category, the cases of Sri Lanka and East Timor provide starkly contrasting examples of how conflicts may be resolved without recourse to an "autonomy solution". Whereas in Sri Lanka the central government militarily defeated the armed separatist Liberation Tigers of Tamil Eelam (LTTE) in 2009 after a number of failed offers of autonomy, in East Timor the opposite occured as East Timorese rebels rejected an Indonesian government offer of broad autonomy in 1999 in favour of national self-determination. In reality, East Timorese resistance to Indonesian rule was less a question of armed separatism (as it was portrayed by Indonesian authorities) than it was an issue of armed resistance against the illegal occupation of an aggressive neighbouring state. For practical purposes, though, Indonesia retained forced sovereignty over East Timor for more than three decades while the rest of the world watched in silence. It was only after 30 August 1999, when the East Timorese people voted in a United Nations-sponsored referendum on independence, that East Timor's sovereign status was restored.

In Sri Lanka, the Sinhalese political establishment engaged in a protracted multi-stage peace process with the LTTE, which included a number of limited offers of autonomy, before militarily defeating the Tamil rebels in May 2009. During the conflict, the Sri Lankan government portrayed the LTTE as the chief obstacle to reaching a political settlement with its Tamil civilian population. In the post-conflict era, however, no definitive steps have been taken to develop a comprehensive autonomy package to provide redress for the root causes of Tamil grievances towards the Sri Lankan state beyond a narrow emphasis on infrastructure and economic development projects. From the Sri Lankan state's perspective, its military victory over once contested Tamil territories has refuted the necessity of autonomy as a tool for post-conflict management. For Sri Lanka's Tamil minorities, however, the state's delegitimization of their grievances through its reductionist focus on economic issues and territoriality underscores their marginality at the fringes of the Sinhalese ethnonationalist project while perpetuating many of the problems that originally gave birth to the conflict. Without initiatives to meaningfully integrate Tamils into the Sri Lankan nation-state there thus remains a high risk that the seeds for future conflict will find fertile ground.

The case of Sri Lanka is set in stark relief against Aceh, where a broadly agreed upon autonomy formula enabled former Acehnese rebels to participate in the Indonesian nation-building project rather than in opposition to it. In Sri Lanka, the state's military defeat of the LTTE may have enhanced its ability to pursue more effective economic policies in its troubled Tamil territories, but it has achieved little in the way of strengthening its popular legitimacy among Tamil minorities. As described in the introductory chapter of this volume, when a state lacks political legitimacy to govern *with* societal consent then it tends to govern *over* society through the use of force or coercion in order to retain a monopoly over the instruments of political power. Similarly, when societal resistance to state authority is high, it reflects a failure of political institutions and their leaders to respond to grievances and to channel societal demands and expectations accordingly. This is what happened in East Timor under Indonesian occupation, when a widespread lack of faith among the East Timorese people in Indonesia's right to rule resulted in the popular rejection of Indonesia's offer of broad autonomy in 1999 in favour of independence.

In other countries in South and Southeast Asia where armed separatist conflicts are ongoing, there is a tendency among states to wield political power through force and coercion in conjunction with limited offers of autonomy to the minority regions and peoples concerned. It is this third category of states with continuing armed separatist disputes where the verdict on autonomy as a viable tool for conflict management remains especially uncertain. In Indonesia's easternmost province of Papua, in southern Thailand and the Philippines, in Jammu, Kashmir and India's northeast, and in the ethnic minority regions of Burma/Myanmar, dual-track policies of repressive forms of governance on the one hand and government offers of autonomy on the other hand have been used concurrently to respond to separatist insurgencies. Put somewhat differently, the experience of nationalist minorities in each of these countries has often been one of a schizophrenic mix of persuasive-repressive state approaches aimed at annihilating armed separatism as a necessary precondition for peace. Of course, these case studies diverge internally on localized contextual conditions such as the nature and complexity of autonomy arrangements, the intensity of fighting between the warring parties at particular junctures in history, and the degree of "ethnic flooding" by the dominant nationalist group into minority territories. Yet all of the above examples illustrate that the manner in which carrot-and-stick policies have thus far been deployed has undermined or eroded whatever sense of goodwill autonomy was originally intended to create amidst ongoing fighting in the field.

What this tells us is that unless autonomy is implemented with an equal concern for the protection and defense of the collective and individual rights of minority peoples then its value as a sustainable pathway to peace will be compromised, often fatally so. Without exception, the South and Southeast Asian cases reviewed in this book have illustrated that when autonomy packages have been inaugurated in the absence of a rights-based approach to conflict management then grassroots support for autonomy has been lacking. This is because the purpose of autonomy is to create political space to pave the way to the consolidation of peace. However, if first order human rights and/or second order civil and political rights are unavailable to the affected minorities during the implementation phase of autonomy then armed separatist movements are more likely to garner grassroots support for their cause and to be perceived locally as defenders of the civilian population against a hostile and predatory state. That is, if statist violence threatens the basic survival of minorities then this aggression is likely to be reciprocated by minority non-state actors. In such cases, whatever space is initially created by an autonomy framework to work towards peace is bound to close and cease to exist amidst deep mutual mistrust, human rights depredations and a lack of confidence in autonomy as a viable model for conflict management.

The state of Burma/Myanmar and its ruling Tatmadaw armed forces offers one of the harshest examples in this book of what happens when the rule of law is repeatedly subverted by a litany of state-driven transgressions against ethnonationalist minorities. With autonomy arrangements in Burma's ethnic minority areas amounting to little more than a ceasefire, the rule of law has become so seriously attenuated that Burma's minorities appear to lack access to any political framework within which to begin to pursue a meaningful negotiated settlement. Moreover, the military junta's tolerance of atrocities against civilians and the abundance of opportunities for personal enrichment that have been created by the thriving war economy attest to a lack of political will by the Tatmadaw to introduce any alternative policies in ethnic minority regions that could threaten the existing socio-economic order.

It is not inconceivable that states could stem the specter of armed separatism through a military approach and still retain political legitimacy if the state's monopoly over the use of physical force and coercion is exercised in a responsible manner aimed at defending rather than violating the rights of ordinary civilians. For this to occur, counterinsurgency operations would have to be highly targeted against armed combatants while protecting the rights and freedoms of minority citizens and prosecuting human rights violators through a functioning and impartial judicial system. Yet in many parts of South and Southeast Asia where national armed forces are poorly paid and where the rule of law is weak or non-existent (especially in war zones), there are few incentives to improve the discipline and professionalism of troops in the field. Furthermore, the guerilla-style military campaigns of armed separatists are usually made possible by strong grassroots backing that allows insurgents to easily blend into the civilian population. This difficulty in identifying and isolating armed combatants further complicates state efforts to win back minority hearts and minds into the dominant nationalist fold, and the human rights violations against civilians that typically accompany such counterinsurgency operations only exacerbate pre-existing grievances against the state.

Nation-states in South and Southeast Asia often rely heavily on their coercive powers to address the problem of armed separatism due to a lack of confidence among central elites that autonomy is an appropriate tool for conflict resolution. Such reservations stem from concerns about a loss of central state control and the belief that nationalist minorities will abuse the devolution of state powers and resources to continue their push for independence, thus threatening the territorial integrity of the nation-state in its existing form. In the case of Thailand, the invocation of historical narratives centred on the reified roles of "nation, king and religion" in Thai nation-building processes have created a powerful political culture of resistance to open discussion about decentralization. As the chapters on Thailand in this book have explained, so sensitive is the subject of autonomy among Thai Buddhist nationalists (who equate autonomy with disloyalty to the monarchy) that reasoned policy debate about a shared-rule solution to the low intensity armed separatist conflicts in the Muslim-majority provinces of Pattani, Yala and Narathiwat has been virtually impossible. While there is hope in some circles that the looming question of Thailand's monarchical succession may encourage a break from the present, the glacial pace of change in myopic government discourses offers little in the way of any immediate hope for a non-military alternative to conflict resolution in the southern border provinces. At the same time, however, Bangkok has been relatively successful in managing centre-periphery relations and ethnic diversity in the western Muslim-majority province of Satun, which has been non-coercively integrated into the Thai nation-state building project with minimal outside interference. In Thailand's northeastern region of Isaan, too, despite a lack of formal autonomy, the once violent struggle against Bangkok's economic neglect and suppression of regional identity has been diverted through political channels since the introduction in the 1980s of more responsive central government policies aimed at providing redress for local grievances through community development programmes and incentives for insurgents to disarm.

This book has also shown how the concerns among central government leaders about the potential for autonomy to strengthen the causes of armed separatists are not always ill-founded. Many armed separatist movements have seized the opportunity presented by a rolling back of central state authority to recruit new members, consolidate their constituencies, and lobby the international community to support their independence agenda. The examples of the Phillipines and Indonesia in particular have highlighted how armed separatist movements there flourished during transitions away from authoritarianism and towards more democratic regimes of governance when central state power was at its weakest and when national political elites were especially vulnerable to societal pressure for reform. Yet the more time that elapsed after the initiation of democratization, the less willing, and, in many cases, the less capable democratizing regimes became to pursue a shared-rule outcome with their disaffected minorities.

The case of Papua in eastern Indonesia illustrates this point well. At the start of Indonesia's democratization process national leaders in Jakarta were willing to grant political concessions to Papuans and to recognize a "special place" for them (along with the Acehnese and East Timorese) within the Indonesian republic. However, as hardline Indonesian nationalist leaders began to claw back some of their former influence over government decision-making, and as the Papuan independence campaign became more strident, the more Jakarta reverted to a repressive Papua policy approach and Indonesian military depredations against Papuan civilians increased. Papuans were further alienated from the Indonesian nationalist cause by Jakarta's unilateral imposition of a "special autonomy" package which split Papua into three separate provinces in what was seen locally as a divide-and-conquer strategy. At the same time, Indonesia's ongoing policy of transmigration (the conspicuous population transfer of mostly ethnic Javanese to Papua) led to the loss of ancestral lands and fuelled feelings among many Papuans that they were being made strangers in their own homeland, particularly in urban coastal areas.

In the Philippines, the saturation of members of the predominantly Christian population into the mainly Muslim area of Mindanao in the south has similarly alarmed many Mindanao Muslims. Yet it must be remembered that Mindanao Muslims- like the Papuans and most of the other separatist minorities described in this book- are not a homogenous entity and have been deeply divided in articulating their demands and expectations. Beyond their broadly shared Moro identity, Mindanao Muslims have been highly factionalized with the result that Manila has had to negotiate the terms of autonomy on multiple fronts, much like Jakarta's fraught attempts to engage the splintered Papuan separatist movement in dialogue.

This factionalism among nationalist minorities has in many cases complicated the task of negotiating a broadly agreed upon autonomy formula that is not prone to sabotage by one or more of the warring parties. In the chapters on India in this book, we have seen how the competing interests of insurgents have destabilized attempts to implement various forms of autonomy in Jammu and Kashmir and in India's narrow northeastern corridor. In the northeast, a bewildering array of armed and unarmed rebel movements have presented New Delhi with wide-ranging demands including outright secession, greater autonomy through various powers of self-governance, and even the partition of existing states into new administrative units. The conflicts in Jammu and Kashmir, too, have attracted a variety of competing rebel groups who claim to represent the interests of indigenous ethnic and religious groups in the contested territories. Some of these groups, however, have been more preoccupied with attempting to influence the precarious balance of power between India and neighbouring Pakistan.

Towards the beginning of this book, mediated constitutionality, or the resolution of armed separatist conflict via a return to and reliance upon the rule of law, was presented as a desirable means of arriving at an autonomy settlement. Via a mediated approach, the state and sub-state rule of law is restituted and its constitutional legitimacy is restored in the eyes of the major parties to the conflict. In this volume, different forms of mediated constitutionality have helped to protect the peace in Aceh, in East Timor after independence, and, less explicitly, in Satun and Isaan in Thailand. The great majority of case studies in this book, however, have so far been unable to move beyond their intransigent competing claims to sovereignty and have squandered valuable opportunities for mediation. In the process, the rule of law has too frequently been sacrificed even as various political arrangements have been partially or half-heartedly implemented.

The answer to the central question underpinning this book, then, is that autonomy can only offer the beginning of a solution to the problem of armed separatism and is not a final solution in itself. What autonomy provides is the skeleton or basic framework to flesh out a mediated settlement that is mutually agreeable to the key parties to the conflict. Ideally, such a negotiated settlement is predicated upon the protection of the collective and individual rights of minorities according to the rule of law. Without such a rights-based approach to conflict resolution it is difficult to see how autonomy can deliver a shared rule outcome that is acceptable to all of the warring parties. If disaffected minorities feel that it is more dangerous to remain within the existing state than to risk attempting to physically remove themselves from its borders then this implies that the autonomy formula does not include a basic guarantee of first order human rights. If the human rights and/or second order civil and political rights of the minority region and its people are suppressed or subordinated to the dominant nationalist group then it follows that autonomy will not provide sufficient space to address the root causes of the conflict and its remedies. And, if transgressions by either state or non-state actors persist while autonomy provisions are being implemented then this indicates that one or more of the parties to the conflict is not seriously committed to the key terms of the political settlement.

While autonomy or some other shared-rule formula would appear to provide the best avenue through which to pursue a rights-based approach to peace, the question remains as to what autonomy solution, if any, would be considered sufficient for minorities who have lost their lives, livelihoods and loved ones through protracted intra-state conflict? Clearly, the issues that give rise to and perpetuate armed separatist conflicts go deeper than claims to territorial sovereignty. While the necessary conditions for conflict resolution vary between individuals, communities and minority regions, most of the armed separatist movements in this book continue to exist because they find the current autonomy arrangements in their regions unacceptable in one form or another.

The final question, then, should work backwards to ask how post-conflict futures might be imagined and framed in the most sustainable way? Any answer to this question should prioritize the scenario within or without the existing state that is most likely to protect public safety, defend minority civil and political rights, and guarantee free and fair elections. These are issues that both separatists and state actors will have to eventually address in the event of any form of conflict resolution that is seen as politically legitimate in the eyes of the minority population, whatever the outcome. The question of how more equal and inclusive individual and collective minority rights can be eventually attained is, or should be, the only compelling case for proceeding with armed separatist conflict in the first place.

INDEX

A

Abdullah, Farooq, 180, 183, 184, 187
Abdullah, Sheikh, 178, 179, 185
Abdulqadir, Tengku, 221
Abdul Razak, Othman, 287
ABRI, 94–97, 99–103, 107n8
ABSU. *See* All Bodo Students Union (ABSU)
Abu Sayyaf group, 285–86
Aceh, 64, 66, 71
    armed separatist conflicts in, 10
    autonomy, 19, 37–39
    challenges of, 52–53
    civil emergency, 47
    conflicts in, 19, 27–28, 41, 46, 47
    Daerah Istimewa, 38
    decentralization, 38, 40, 42, 44, 52
    democratization, 39, 42, 49
    deteriorating security environment, 42
    Helsinki peace agreement in, 36, 37, 45, 47–53
    independence movement, 43
    Islamic law in, 42, 43
    negotiated settlement to, 40–48
    self-government in, 38, 45, 48–51, 297
    separatist insurgency, 41
    special autonomy to, 36, 38, 48
    tsunami in, 27–28, 47, 52
Aceh model, 229
Aceh Monitoring mission, 26
Acehnese NGOs, 49
Acehnese *ulama*, 42, 43
Acheh-Sumatra National Liberation Front (ASNLF). *See Gerakan Acheh Merdeka* (GAM)
Act of Congress, 270
Act of Free Choice (AFC), 61, 62, 74n6
ADCs. *See* Autonomous District Councils (ADCs)
Administrative Code for Mindanao and Sulu, 279
Adulyadej, Bhumibol, 218
Advani, L.K., 187
Advisory Committee, India, 198
AFC. *See* Act of Free Choice (AFC)
AFP. *See* Armed Forces of the Philippines (AFP)

AGAM. *See Angkatan Gerakan Acheh Merdeka* (AGAM)
Ahtisaari, Martti, 19, 46, 48
AIETD. *See* All Inclusive East Timorese Dialogue
Alatas, Ali, 79
Al Badr. *See* Hizb-ul Mujahideen (HM)
Al-Harakat al-Islamiyah group, 285
All Bodo Students Union (ABSU), 203–4
All Inclusive East Timorese Dialogue (AIETD), 79
All Parties Hurriyat Conference (APHC), 181, 183, 186, 188
All Parties National Alliance (APNA), 186, 191n21
All Tripura Tiger Force (ATTF), 205, 211
Alua, Agus, 71
ameliorative policies, 2, 46
American colonial rule, 279
Ampatuan, Andal, 267
Anandasangaree, V., 172
Angami Naga tribe, 201
Angkatan Gerakan Acheh Merdeka (AGAM), 54n5
Anglo-Siamese treaty of 1909, 238, 243
Annan, Kofi, 82
anti-communist activities, 247
APHC. *See* All Parties Hurriyat Conference (APHC)
APNA. *See* All Parties National Alliance (APNA)
armed conflicts, 114
  in J&K, 180
  in Northeast India, 196–212
armed forces
  Indonesia, 39, 41
  of Sri Lankan state, 136, 149
Tatmadaw, 299
Armed Forces for the National Liberation of East Timor, 95
Armed Forces of the Philippines (AFP), 282, 286, 290
armed insurgency in Thailand, 236–40
armed insurgent movements, 196
armed movements, 201, 203
armed rebellion in Srilanka, 137
armed separatism
  specter of, 297, 300
  in Srilanka, 137
armed separatist
  guerilla-style military campaigns of, 300
  perpetuation of, 4
armed separatist conflicts, 2, 7, 9, 11, 24, 29, 36, 256, 296, 298, 303, 304
  in Aceh, 10
  in Asia, 36
  in India, 11
  in Indonesia, 37–38
  management of, 7
  in Muslim-majority provinces, 301
  negotiating peace in, 162
  resolution of, 302
  in South and Southeast Asia, 4, 9, 298
armed separatist minorities, 8
  self-determination for, 2
armed separatist movements, 1, 2, 5, 77, 299, 301
  resurgence of, 4
armed separatist rebellion in Indonesia, 297
ARMM. *See* Autonomous Region in Muslim Mindanao (ARMM)

Index

arms for peace ceasefire agreements, 130
Article 370 of the Indian Constitution, 178–80, 187
ASDC. *See* Autonomous State Demand Committee (ASDC)
Asia
  armed separatist conflicts in, 36
  geopolitical and financial crisis in, 1998, 79
ASNLF. *See* Acheh-Sumatra National Liberation Front (ASNLF)
Assam, 198, 204, 209–11
  Bodo insurgency in, 203, 205
  hill areas, division of, 197
  Karbi Anglong district in, 208
  Karbis and the Kukis in, 207
ATTF. *See* All Tripura Tiger Force (ATTF)
Aung San, 115, 120
Australian Parliamentary delegation in East Timor, 97
authoritarian forms of government, 4
authoritarian regimes, 4, 5
Autonomous District Councils (ADCs), 207–9
Autonomous Regional Councils, 207
Autonomous Region in Muslim Mindanao (ARMM), 267–68, 283–85, 287, 290
  clan politics in, 271
  creation of, 280–81
  elections in, 2005, 292
  Maguindanao in, 266
  Organic Act for, 257–59
  Regional Legislative Assembly of, 270–71

survey in, 2002, 269
Autonomous State Demand Committee (ASDC), 208
autonomy
  Acehnese, 37–39
  after civil war, 156–58
  in civil war, 153–54
  de facto, 240, 241, 247
  defining, 6–8
  desirability of, 8
  establishment of, 25
  for ethnic minority, 113, 118
  forms of, 1, 5
  idea of, 16–17, 19
  inadequate, 139
  initiatives, 8
  institutional design of, 296
  Kachin political struggle for, 127–28
  purpose of, 299
  reform regime capacity for, 140
  regimes, 5
  regional. *See* regional autonomy
  special. *See* special autonomy
  as state reform, Sri Lanka, 140–44
  substantial, 139, 238, 248
  as sub-state model, 19–20
autonomy debate
  in J&K, 183–86
  in Sri Lanka, 137, 144–45, 147, 151, 154
autonomy proposal, 80, 86–87, 89, 230
  Indonesia, 60
  Moroccan, 82
  special, 67–68
autonomy settlements, 130
autonomy trap in Sri Lanka, 138–40

Azhar, Maulana Masood, 182, 191n19

B
BAC. *See* Bodoland Autonomous Council (BAC)
Badan Pemeriksa Keuangan (BPK), 50
Baharuddin, Tengku, 246
Baker, James, 82
Baker Peace Plan, the, 82–84
Balasingham, Anton, 171
Balibo Declaration, 85, 90n25
Bali Declaration, 90n25
balkanization
  India, 181
  Indonesia, 40
bamarization, 115
Bangkok, 220–23, 225, 227, 250, 301
  bureaucratic elites, 251
  internal colonialism, 217–18
Bangladesh, 205
  ULFA leadership in, 210
Bangsa Moro Army (BMA), 282, 290
Bangsamoro, autonomy, 19
Bangsamoro Development Agency, 274, 286
Bangsamoro Juridical Entity (BJE), 258, 265, 271, 273, 274, 287, 293
Bangsa Moro Revolution, 291
Barua, Paresh, 210
benevolent assimilation, Philippines, 279
BGF. *See* Border Guard Forces (BGF)
Bhanomyong, Pridi, 248–49
BJE. *See* Bangsamoro Juridical Entity (BJE)

BLT. *See* Bodo Liberation Tigers (BLT)
BMA. *See* Bangsa Moro Army (BMA)
Bodo insurgency in Assam, 203–4, 205
Bodoland Autonomous Council (BAC), 204
Bodoland Territorial Council (BTC), 204, 214n22
Bodo Liberation Tigers (BLT), 204
Border Guard Forces (BGF), 116
Bordoloi, Gopinath, 198
Bordoloi Sub-Committee, 207
BPK. *See Badan Pemeriksa Keuangan*
British colonialism, 115, 166
BTC. *See* Bodoland Territorial Council (BTC)
Buddhism, 120, 128, 166. *See also* Islam
Buddhists, 184, 185
  in Isaan, 245
  tradition, 239
Bunker Agreement, 61
Bureaucratic inertia, 251
Burma, 299–300
  and KIO/KIA, 120–21

C
Camp Abubakar, 285, 286
  in Maguindanao, 264
campaign and violence in Timor-Leste, 86–88
Camp David Summit, 2000, 48
Carrascalão, Mario, 98, 103
ceasefire
  definition of, 113
  in East Timor, 97, 98, 101, 104
  in Myanmar, 128–30

Index

and political economy of Kachin State, 123–25
ceasefire agreement, 115–16
 between Indian and Pakistani forces, 178
 with LTTE, 150, 151–52
 in Northeast India, 204–5, 208–9
Chakri dynasty, 218, 227
China and KIO territories, 122–23
Christian Filipinos, 279, 280, 290
Christian Kachin community, 120
civic nationalism, 22
civic shortfall of the state, 18
civil emergency in Aceh, 47
civilization, Sinhalese Buddhist, 166
civil war in Sri Lanka, 163
 autonomy after, 156–58
 autonomy in, 153–54
 ethnic, 137, 153–54
 ethno-political, 139
 protracted, 136, 137, 149
 secessionist, 139
 violence in, 162, 163
CMI. *See* Crisis Management Initiative (CMI)
CNRM. *See* Conselho Nacional da Resistencia Maubere (CNRM)
CNRR. *See* National Council of Revolutionary Resistance
CNRT. *See* Concelho National da Resistencia Timorense (CNRT)
colonialism
 British, 115, 166
 Filipino, 291
 internal. *See* internal colonialism
colonization in Thailand, 217
Communist Party of Thailand (CPT), 243, 245

Concelho National da Resistencia Timorense (CNRT). *See* National Council of Timorese Resistance (CNRT)
confederalists, 171
conflict mediation model, 29
conflict resolution, 18–19
 in Myanmar, 128–30
conflicts
 armed separatist, 2, 7, 9, 11, 24, 29, 36, 256, 298, 301, 303, 304
 self-determination, 5
 in Sri Lanka, 163
Conselho Nacional da Resistencia Maubere (CNRM). *See* National Council of Maubere Resistance (CNRM)
conservative nationalists, 40
consolidating control, state approaches for, 236
constitutional authority, 24
constitutionality, mediated, 17, 30, 302–3
constitution-drafting process in Myanmar, 114, 117, 128
contagion effect in Thailand, 225–26
Cordillera, 260, 274n2
Council for the Development of the Southern Border Provinces Area (CDSBPA), 225
counter insurgency
 Jakarta's growing reliance on, 44
 in Northeast India, 203–6, 212n10
 operations, 300
 operations against GAM, 39, 42, 55n10
 in Tripura, 214n27

CPT. *See* Communist Party of Thailand (CPT)
creeping separatism, 151
Crisis Management Initiative (CMI), 46
CRRN, 104

D
Daerah Istimewa, Aceh, 38
Daerah Operasi Militer (DOM), 39, 54n9
Daimary, Ranjan, 204–5
Darul Islam, 38, 42, 54n4, 54n6
Darul Islam Rebellion, 54n6
decentralization
    Aceh, 38, 40, 42, 44, 52
    and autonomy, 172
    in form of self-government, 297
    in Mindanao, 257
    reforms, 8
    in Thailand, 221–22, 235, 250, 251
decolonization process, 78, 83
    conducting, 81
de facto administration, 155–56
de facto autonomy, 11, 240–41, 247
de facto subordination, 220
Democratic Republic of Timor-Leste (RDTL), 94
democrative process
    Indonesia, 84
    Morocco, 84
democratization, 5
    Aceh, 39, 42, 49
    Indonesia, 301
    in Indonesia, 88
    in Myanmar, 117
Democrat Party in Thailand, 251
demographic factor for Mindanao, 290

devolution proposals
    LTTE's rejection of, 148–49
    of PA, 148
DHD. *See* Dima Halim Daogah (DHD)
Dili, 79, 88, 98, 99, 104
    CNRT in, 87, 91n34
    invasion of, 95
Dima Halim Daogah (DHD), 208
disenfranchised minorities, 296
District Development Councils, Sri Lanka, 144
Di Tiro, Hasan Muhammad, 38
divide-and-rule, Myanmar, 115, 119
Djopari, John, 71
do Amaral, Francisco, 103
DOM. *See Daerah Operasi Militer*
Dom Boa Ventura, 78
Dutch, 61
    administration, 71
    colonialists, 59
dynamism, 21

E
earned sovereignty model, 17, 24, 25, 29
East Timor, 25, 27, 43, 297
    Australian Parliamentary delegation in, 97
    broad autonomy for, 100, 101
    campaign and violence in, 86–88
    case study of, 77–80, 81
    ceasefire, 97, 98, 101, 104
    cyclical occupation, 94–101
    independence, 106n1
    Indonesian invasion of, 93
    Indonesian policy in, 94–101
    Indonesian troop strength in, 98, 99

Index

integration in, 20, 85
international law, role of, 84–86
liberation of, 95
military officers in, 97
military operations command in, 99
national identity dispute in, 38
parallels and paradox of, 83–84
peace plan, 104–5
twenty-four year conflict in, 94
violence in, 86–88
East Timorese Popular Representative Assembly, 95
East Timorese rebels, 297
East Timorese resistance, 101–6, 107n2
East Timor Sub-Regional Military Commander, 97
Economic and Social Research Council, 230n1
economic dimension of Papua, 62
economic rationalism, 7
education, 42, 115, 116, 127, 131n6, 238, 288
 Sri Lanka, 141
 in Thailand, 239–40
Eelam People's Revolutionary Front (EPRLF), 143
Eelam, Tamil, 168, 169
Eelam war, 172
election
 in Aceh, 43–44, 49–53
 in East Timor, 101
 in Indonesia, 96, 102–4
 in J&K, 178, 180, 183, 188, 189
 in Myanmar, 114, 117, 118, 128, 130
 in Philippines, 266–68, 270–71
 in Sri Lanka, 142, 147
 in Thai, 251

electoral cycle, Indonesian, 94, 102–4
Electoral reform, 273
endemic violence in Manipur, 210
EPRLF. *See* Eelam People's Revolutionary Front (EPRLF)
Estrada, Joseph, 264, 286
ethnic ceasefire groups, 119
ethnic civil war in Sri Lanka, 137, 153–54
ethnic Malay identity, resilience of, 248
ethnic minorities in Thailand, 237
ethnic minority armed insurgency in Srilanka, 136
ethnic nationalism, 166
ethnic peace accord in Sri Lanka, 162
ethnic Thai Buddhist population, 251
ethnic violence, 164
ethno-symbolic unities, 21
European Union's Election Observation Mission in Aceh (EUEOM), 50–51
Executive Council, 283
external sovereignty, 131n4

F

factionalism, 302
factionalization in Mindanao, 290–92
Falintil forces, 95–96
Falintil leader, 103
Farooq, Mirwaiz Umar, 186, 193n40
FCC. *See* Fretilin Central Committee
federalism, 288
 in Indonesia, 40

in Northeast India, 211
in Sri Lanka, 162–74
federalists, 163, 170–72
 liberal, 171
Filipino colonialism, 291
Filipino Muslims, 262
Filipinos, 272
Final Peace Agreement (FPA), 265
 implementation of, 264
 with MNLF, 257, 258, 272
financial crisis in Asia, 1998, 79
Finland's conversion of autonomy, 20
forced assimilation
 efforts, 237
 policies of, 1
four cardinal principles, 154
FPA. *See* Final Peace Agreement
Free Aceh Movement, 19, 27, 36, 297
Fretilin, 81, 103
 forces, 95–96
 leaders, 95, 102, 103
Fretilin Central Committee (FCC), 102
Fretilin dominated Constituent Assembly, 106n1

G
GAM. *See Gerakan Acheh Merdeka*
Gandhi, Indira, 141
Gandhi, Rajiv, 141
Garo Hills, 197
Geelani, Syed Ali Shah, 189
General Cessation of Hostilities in 1997, 285, 286
Gen Ohn Myint, 128
geopolitical crisi in Asia, 1998, 79
Gerakan Acheh Merdeka (GAM), 28, 36, 38, 39, 41–43, 49–53, 53n1, 54n5, 56n20

administrative officials, 53n3
and Indonesian security forces, 44, 45
military capabilities, 45
peace talks with, 47–48
regeneration, cause of, 37
Gilgit-Baltistan National Alliance (GBNA), 186
government, authoritarian forms of, 4
Government of India Act, 1935, 197
group identity, formalization of, 22
guerilla-style military campaigns of armed separatists, 300
Gusmão, Xanana, 78, 89n4, 97, 99–105

H
Habibie, B. J., 38, 46, 79, 80, 93, 99, 100, 105
Handley, Paul, 228
Hari Singh, Maharaja, 178
Harkat-ul Ansar (HuA), 182
Harkat ul-Jihad al-Islami (HuJI), 182
Harkat-ul Mujahideen (HuM), 182
Helsinki peace agreement in Aceh, 36, 37, 45, 47–53
Hikoyabi, Hana, 71
Hindus in J&K, 184, 185
Hizb-ul Mujahideen (HM), 181, 189
Holy Man Revolt of 1902, 254n21
holy war *(jihad)*, 181, 182
Horta, José Ramos, 78
House Appropriations Committee, 283
Howard, John, 89n10, 100
HuA. *See* Harkat-ul Ansar (HuA)

HuJI. *See* Harkat ul-Jihad al-Islami (HuJI)
Hukawng Valley, 124–25
HuM. *See* Harkat-ul Mujahideen (HuM)

I
Iberian countries, 83
ICG. *See* International Crisis Group (ICG)
ICJ. *See* International Court of Justice
IFES. *See* International Foundation for Election Systems (IFES)
IMF. *See* International Monetary Fund
India
  armed separatist conflicts, 11
  Northeast. *See* Northeast India
  peace enforcement, 142
  in Sri Lankan conflict, 141
Indian Ocean tsunami, 37, 45, 46
Indian Tamils, 163
India-Sri Lanka Accord of 1987, 19, 141, 142, 145, 154, 168
Indigenous Peoples Rights Act, 1997, 260
Indonesia
  armed forces, 39
  armed separatist conflicts, 37–38
  autonomy, 79
  balkanization of, 40
  culture, 61
  cyclical occupation in East Timor, 94–101
  democratization in, 49, 84, 88
  electoral cycle, 94, 102, 103
  federalism in, 40
  invasion of East Timor, 93
  nationalists, 38
  political leadership, 40, 41, 47
  security forces, 37, 44, 45, 50
  state authority, 41
  state power and authority, 39
  violence in, 10
Indonesian Marines, 96
Indonesian military, 38, 60, 69, 80, 87, 95–97, 103, 107n3
  to civilian control, 37
  internal factionalism, 46
  pre-eminent role of, 63
  regime, 78
  violent manner in, 61
Indonesia's special autonomy package in Papua, 63–65, 67–68
Inner Line Regulation permit system, India, 197, 212n2
insurgencies
  counter. *See* counter insurgency
  criminalization of, 211
  in Mizoram, 203
  in Northeast India, 198–200, 209–11
  in Tripura, 205–6
inter-communal tensions, 289
Interim Self-Governing Authority (ISGA), LTTE's proposals for, 151–52, 155
internal colonialism, 114
  in Bangkok, 217–18
internal conflicts, 4, 5, 46
  in Thailand, 235
internal sovereignty, 131n4
International Court of Justice (ICJ), 81
International Crisis Group (ICG), 51
International Foundation for Election Systems (IFES), 51

International law, hope and myth of, 84–86
international legal elements, 77, 89
International Monetary Fund (IMF), 40
International Monitoring Team, 265
 in Mindanao, 286, 287
Inter-Services Intelligence (ISI), 181, 182, 210
Irian Barat, 59
Isaan, 5, 236, 243, 252, 301
 displacement of local elites, 247–48
 identity, 250
 political leaders, 250
 state penetration, 243, 245, 249
ISGA. *See* Interim Self-Governing Authority (ISGA)
ISI. *See* Inter-Services Intelligence (ISI)
Islam, 38, 146, 249. *See also* Darul Islam
 in Aceh, 43
Islamic law, 248
 in Aceh, 42, 43
Islamic religious elite in Southern Thailand, 219
Islamization, 181

J
Jabidah massacre Muslims, 256
Jaffna peninsula, 149
Jaintia Hills, 197
Jaish-e-Mohammad Mujahideen E-Tanzeem (JeM), 182
Jakarta, 80, 93–95, 97–100, 105
 act of integration of, 93
 Papuan challenges to, 62
 policy towards territory, 60, 64
 political leaders in, 38
 regulations, 70
 special autonomy to Aceh, 42
Jammu and Kashmir Liberation Front (JKLF), 180–81, 186, 191n17
Jammu & Kashmir (J&K)
 armed conflict in, 180
 autonomy, 183–86, 186–87
 ceasefire agreement, 178
 conflicts in, 302
 Legislative assembly, 178, 184, 188, 193n38
 militancy and autonomy, 180–82
 separatism in, 177–90
 sovereign status for, 185–86
 special status of, 177–80
Janatha Vimukthi Peramuna (JVP), 142, 147, 152, 159n3
Janjalani, Abdurajak, 286
Japan International Cooperation Agency, 286
Javanese-led Muslim leadership, 62
Jayewardene, Junius, 141, 159n1
JeM. *See* Jaish-e-Mohammad Mujahideen E-Tanzeem (JeM)
jihad (holy war), 181, 182
Jinghpaw Wungpawng, 120
J&K. *See* Jammu & Kashmir (J&K)
JKLF. *See* Jammu and Kashmir Liberation Front (JKLF)
junta, 120–25
 divide-and-rule policy of, 119

K
KAAC. *See* Karbi Anglong Autonomous Council (KAAC)
Kachin Development Networking Group (KDNG), 116, 124, 125, 129, 132n16

Kachin Independence Organization and Army (KIO/KIA), 116, 119, 127–28
  ban of poppy cultivation by, 121
  border checkpoints of, 122–23
  guerilla resistance, 121
Kachin National Consultative Assembly (KNCA), 128
Kachin nationalist movement, 120, 121
Kachin nationalist project, 131n10
Kachin State
  armed struggle in, 120–21
  deforestation in, 124
  geographies of militarization, 121–23
  HIV/AIDS infection in, 127
  political economy of, 123–25
  political struggle, 127–28
  security threats, 126–27
  tribes in, 120
Kachin State Progressive Party (KSPP), 128
Kadir, Pattani Abdul, 246
Kamtapur Liberation Organisation (KLO), 204
Karbi Anglong Autonomous Council (KAAC), 208
Karbi Longri North Cachar Hills Liberation Front (KLNLF), 207, 208
Karbis and the Kukis in Assam, 207
Kashmir Study Group (KSG), 185–86
KDNG. *See* Kachin Development Networking Group (KDNG)
kembali ke Ibu Pertiwi, 59
Keyes, Charles, 247, 249
Khaplang S.S., 201
Khasi Hills, 197

Kilinochchi, 152
kindergarten theory, 40
KIO/KIA. *See* Kachin Independence Organization and Army (KIO/KIA)
Kissinger, Henry, 95
KLNLF. *See* Karbi Longri North Cachar Hills Liberation Front (KLNLF)
KLO. *See* Kamtapur Liberation Organisation (KLO)
Komando Pelaksana Operasi Jaring Merah, 39
Koskeniemmi, Marti, 86
KSG. *See* Kashmir Study Group (KSG)
Kumaratunga, Chandrika, 148, 149

L
Lashkar-e-Toiba (LeT), 182, 189, 194n49. *See also* Liberation Tigers of Tamil Eelam (LTTE)
Latin American countries, 4
Law No. 31/2002, 48
Law No. 44/1999, 42, 43
Law on Governing Aceh (LoGA), 36, 48–53
LeT. *See* Lashkar-e-Toiba (LeT)
liberal federalists, 171
liberalization in Thailand, 227
liberal nationalists, 172
liberation of East Timor, 95
Liberation Tigers of Tamil Eelam (LTTE), 3, 20, 27, 136, 140, 142, 145–46, 159n3, 163, 168–74, 297
  autonomy after civil war, 156–58
  ceasefire agreement with, 150, 151–52

devolution proposals, rejection of, 148–49
federalism and, 151, 154, 156
negotiating regional autonomy with, 154–56
proposals for ISGA, 151–52, 155
Provincial Council system, rejection of, 142–43
reform-weariness, 150–53
unilateral reform initiatives, limits of, 147–50
war for peace, 49
Line of Control (LoC) in Jammu, 186, 192n36
Liquica district, 88
Lobregat, Maria Clara, 283
LoGA. *See* Law on Governing Aceh (LoGA)
Lone, Abdul Gani, 188
Longputeh, Sukree, 247
LTTE. *See* Liberation Tigers of Tamil Eelam (LTTE)
lumad, 280, 293n1
Lushai Hills. *See* Mizoram
Luzon, 279

M
Macapagal-Arroyo, Gloria, 257, 264, 266, 286, 288
Madaris, 283
Madrid Accord, 81
Maguindanao
in ARMM, 266
Camp Abubakar in, 264
Maguindanaoan politicians, 269
Mahayiddin, Tengku Mahmud, 221
Mahmud, Syamsuddin, 42
majoritarian state-formation project, 140
Makota, Kasturi, 227

Malay identity, ethnic, 248
Malay Muslims, 63, 218, 220–23, 246, 252n1
communities, 248, 249
NRC members, 224
politicians, 219
population, 237, 248, 250, 252, 253n2
resistance leaders, 240
Malay sultanate, 219
Mangala Moonesinghe Parliamentary Select Committee, 145, 159n4
Manila
autonomy, 259–60
coalitions on autonomy, 261
developmentalist policies, 261–65
elites, 260, 266
1987 Constitution, 257, 258, 260, 263
pacification policies in, 261–63, 265
peace and conflict in, 260–65
selection elections, 266–68
victory policies in, 261, 262, 264, 265
Manipur, 197, 198, 209, 211
endemic violence in, 210
Naga-Kuki ethnic groups in, 207
Manmohan Singh, 194
Maoist Communist Party of the Philippines, 262
Marcos, Ferdinand, 257, 262, 263, 280–82
Marker, Jamsheed, 100
Martial Law, 45, 257, 262, 280
Marxism-Leninism, 103
Maubere people, 101
Mauritania, 81
Mautam, 203

mediated constitutionality, 17, 30, 302–3
Meghalaya, 197, 211
　Khasi and Garo ethnic groups in, 207
Melanesians, 63
Memorandum of Agreement on Ancestral Domain (MOA-AD), 259, 265, 273
Memorandum of Settlement (MoS), 214n22
Memorandum of Understanding (MoU), 152
　for P-TOMs, 152
Mercado, Fr Eliseo, 292
Mikir Hills, 197
MILF. *See* Moro Islamic Liberation Front (MILF)
militarization
　Kachin, geographies of, 121–23
　in Myanmar, 117
military
　approach, deemphasizing, 2
　in East Timor, 99
　of Fretilin, 95
　Indonesian. *See* Indonesian military
　in J&K, 181–82
　in Myanmar, 116–18
militias, 80, 91n38, 119, 120, 128
　attack of, 87
　Oecussi, 87
　pro-autonomy, 31n7
　violence by, 87
MIM. *See* Muslim Independence Movement (MIM)
Mindanao, 266, 279. *See also* Autonomous Region in Muslim Mindanao (ARMM)
　conflict, obstacles to resolution of, 288–90

decentralization in, 257
demographic factor, 290
factionalization in, 290–92
federalism in, 288
International Monitoring Team in, 286, 287
MILF attacks on non-Muslim communities, 286
pacification in, 279
people power revolution of 1986, 281
Mission for the Referendum in Western Sahara (MINURSO), 81, 82, 84
　establishment of, 86
Misuari, Nur, 258, 272, 280–82, 284, 285, 290, 291
Mizo Hills, 197
Mizo National Famine Front (MNFF), 203
Mizo National Front (MNF), 203
Mizoram, 209
　insurgency in, 203
MLF. *See* Partido Marxista-Leninista Fretilin
MNF. *See* Mizo National Front (MNF)
MNFF. *See* Mizo National Famine Front (MNFF)
MNLF. *See* Moro National Liberation Front (MNLF)
MNLF-RG. *See* Moro National Liberation Front-Reformist Group (MNLF-RG)
MOA-AD. *See* Memorandum of Agreement on Ancestral Domain (MOA-AD)
modernist, 21
Mohamad, Mahathir, 227
Moonesinghe Committee, 146
Moroccan autonomy proposal, 82

Morocco, 81–83
  democrative process in, 84
Moro identity, origins of, 279–80
Moro Islamic Liberation Front (MILF), 258, 264, 267, 281, 284
  breakdown of 1996 Agreement and rise of, 285–88
Moro Juridical Entity, 290
Moro National Liberation Front (MNLF), 20, 263, 282, 284, 285, 292
  "All-Out War", 264
  emergence of, 280–81
  formation of, 290
  FPA with, 257, 258, 272
  leadership, 291
  post-Peace Agreement, 268
  Tripoli Agreement, 262
  victory/pacification strategy, 269–70
Moro National Liberation Front-Reformist Group (MNLF-RG), 281
Moro Province, 279
Moro self-determination, 287
Moro separatism
  ARMM, creation of, 280–81
  Moro identity, origins of, 279–80
  1996 Agreement, 281–85, 283, 285–88
Morrocan regime, 88, 89
MoS. *See* Memorandum of Settlement (MoS)
MRP, 67
  establishment of, 69, 70
Musharraf, Parvez, 186–87, 188
Muslim Independence Movement (MIM), 256
Muslim insurgent group, 285

Muslim-majority provinces, armed separatist conflicts in, 301
Muslim Mindanao
  autonomous Region in. *See* Autonomous Region in Muslim Mindanao (ARMM)
  autonomy in, 256, 268–70
  election violence in, 270
  1987 Constitution, 268
  peace and development in, 266
  political clans, dominance of, 270–71
  rido in, 270
Muslim minoritarian state-formation project, 140
Muslim province, demand for creation of, 164
Muslims
  elites, 246, 273
  Filipino, 262
  Jabidah massacre, 256
  Malay. *See* Malay Muslims
  Mindanao, 302
  in Satun, 249
  in Sri Lanka, 140–41, 146, 149, 164
  Sunni and Shias, 184
  violence against, 147
Myanmar, 299–300
  autonomous spaces in, 118–20
  ceasefire and conflict resolution, 128–30
  consolidation of, 115
  constitution-drafting process in, 114, 117, 128
  democratization in, 117
  divide-and-rule policy, 115
  ethnic states and Bamar divisions, 117

military state building, 116–18
National Convention in 2004, 118
opium cultivation in, 125
political autonomy in, 113, 117
political struggle, 127–28
state consolidation in, 115
Myanmar gates, 122

N
NAD law. *See* Nanggroe Aceh Darussalam (NAD) law
Naga Hills. *See* Nagaland
Naga-Kuki ethnic groups in Manipur, 207
Nagaland movement, sovereignty/autonomy, 201–2
Nagalim, 201–2, 213n14
Naga National Council (NNC), 201
Nanggroe Aceh Darussalam (NAD) law, 43–45, 49, 50
National Council of Maubere Resistance (CNRM), 104, 105
Peace Plan in 1992, 78–79
National Council of Revolutionary Resistance (CNRR), 103
National Council of Timorese Resistance (CNRT), 78, 80, 105
campaigners, training, 87
in Dili, 87, 91n34
National Crime Records Bureau (NCRB), 205
National Democratic Front of Bodoland (NDFB), 204, 213n20
National identity, 21
and citizenship, 22
National Islamic Command Council, 291
nationalists
liberal, 172
unitarian, 173

National League for Democracy (NLD), 114
National Liberation Front of Tripura (NLFT), 205, 211
National political elites, 5, 8
National Reconciliation Commission (NRC) in Thailand, 222, 223–26
National Socialist Council of Nagaland (NSCN), 201, 211
National Socialist Council of Nagaland-Isak-Muivah (NSCN-IM), 201, 202, 213n14
National Socialist Council of Nagaland-Khaplang (NSCN-K), 201
National Socialist Council of Nagaland-Unification (NSCN-U), 202
national state penetration policies, 241
nation-building, 21, 38, 237
NCHADC. *See* North Cachar Hills Autonomous District Council (NCHADC)
NCRB. *See* National Crime Records Bureau (NCRB)
NDA-K. *See* New Democratic Army-Kachin (NDA-K)
NDFB. *See* National Democratic Front of Bodoland (NDFB)
Negara Kesatuan Republic Indonesia (NKRI), 59
negotiated settlement, Aceh, 40–48
Nehru, B. K., 179
Nehru, Jawaharlal, 178, 179
New Delhi, 196, 211
political rulers in, 183
New Democratic Army-Kachin (NDA-K), 115, 128

New Mon State Party (NMSP), 116, 119
New Order's national development project, 38, 54n8
New People's Army (NPA), 262, 263
NGOs, 48–50
nineteen-point proposal, 118
NKRI. *See* Negara Kesatuan Republic Indonesia
NLFT. *See* National Liberation Front of Tripura (NLFT)
NMSP. *See* New Mon State Party (NMSP)
NNC. *See* Naga National Council (NNC)
non-military coercion, 240
non-Muslim communities, MILF attacks on, 286
non-partisan army of national liberation, 104
non-Thai local identity, suppression of, 248–50
North Cachar Hills, 197
North Cachar Hills Autonomous District Council (NCHADC), 208
North Cachar Hills district, 208
Northeast India
  armed conflicts in, 196
  armed insurgent movements in, 196
  armed movements in, 201, 203
  autonomy demands in, 207
  ceasefire agreement, 204–5, 208–9
  conflicts in, protracted, 210
  counter insurgency in, 203–6, 212n10
  degeneration of insurgencies, 209–11
  existing autonomy arrangements in, 207–9
  federalism in, 211
  insurgencies in, multiple, 198–200
  inter-tribal rivalry and competition, 207
  official approach to, 197–98
NPA. *See* New People's Army (NPA)
NRC. *See* National Reconciliation Commission (NRC)
NSCN-K. *See* National Socialist Council of Nagaland-Khaplang (NSCN-K)
NSCN-U. *See* National Socialist Council of Nagaland-Unification (NSCN-U)

O
Ockey, Jim, 221
Oecussi militias, 87
OIC. *See* Organization of Islamic Conference (OIC)
Oquist, Paul, 260–65
Organic Law (Republic Act 6734), 263, 265, 283
  for ARMM, 257–59
Organization of Islamic Conference (OIC), 262, 263, 265, 280–83, 291, 292
Oslo Communiqué, 151

P
PA. *See* People's Alliance (PA)
pacification in Mindanao, 279
Pakistan
  logistic and military support, 181
  militant formations in, 182
Pakistani external intelligence agency, 210

Pakistan occupied Kashmir (PoK), 180, 186, 191n21, 193n38
Pandits. *See* Hindus
Panglong Agreement, 120
Panyarachun, Anand, 222–24, 227
Papua, 301–2
  implementation special autonomy issues in, 68–71
  Indonesia's special autonomy package in, 63–65
  integration of, 63, 67
  powers of, 66
  reintegration of, 59, 63
  separatism in, 59–73
  tribal diversity, 62
Papua Human Rights Commission, 66–68
Papuan Independence Organisation, 63
Papuan People's Representative Council, 67
Papuans
  community, 62
  conflict, causes of, 60–61
  culture, 61, 66
  economic dimension of, 62
  elites, 60, 61
  grievances of, 60–63
  MRP, establishment of, 69, 70
  national identity, 60
  nationalists, 59–60
  pro-independence, 65
  protection of, 66
  self-determination, 61–62
  special autonomy, attitudes to, 65–68
Parcasio, Randolph, 288
Partido Marxista-Leninista Fretilin (MLF), establishment of, 103

Patani United Liberation Organization (PULO), 227
Pattani, 223–24
  militant movement in, 219–20
Pattani Malay, 218, 252n1
Pattani Metropolitan Authority, 224
Pattaya, 225
Paul, Pope John, II's, 104
Peace Plan, 89n6
  CNRM's 1992, 78–79
  stages of, 81
pendatang, 61
People's Alliance (PA), 160n6
  devolution proposals of, 148
  in Sri Lanka, 148, 149
Phanomyong, Pridi, 218, 220, 221
Phatharathananunth, Somchai, 243, 245
Philippine National Police (PNP), 282, 283
Philippines, 301, 302
  Southern. *See* Southern Philippines
  violence in, 271
Philippines Commonwealth, 279
Phizo, Angami Zapu, 201
Pitsuwan, Surin, 246
PNP. *See* Philippine National Police (PNP)
PoK. *See* Pakistan occupied Kashmir (PoK)
Polisario Front, 81–83, 86
political autonomy in Myanmar, 113, 117
political economy of Kachin State military, 123–25
political formations in Sri Lanka, 166
political geography, 2
political struggle in Myanmar, 127–28

political violence, 218
Poocharoen, Ora-orn, 223
Portugal, 100
  autonomy, 79–80
  revolution in, 78
Portuguese Timor, 94
Post-colonial states, 21, 23
  formation of, 16
  people of, 18
Post-Tsunami Operational and Management Structure (P-TOMS), 152, 153
Prabhakaran, V., 171
Premadasa, R., 143
Primary Education Act of 1921, 240
primordialist, 21
pro-autonomy militias, 31
protracted civil war, 136, 137, 149
Protracted insurgent conflict, 242
Provincial Council system in Sri Lanka, 144, 148, 154
  consequences of, 142
  LTTE rejection of, 142–43
  and 13th Amendment, 140, 141
P-TOMS. *See* Post-Tsunami Operational and Management Structure (P-TOMS)
Puaksom, Davisakd, 220
PULO. *See* Patani United Liberation Organization (PULO)
Purwanto, Colonel, 97, 103

Q
Qadaffi, Mohamar, 262
quasi-federalists, 172

R
RAC. *See* Regional Autonomy Committee

Rachanuphap, Damrong, 219
Railaco sub-district, 88
Rajapakse, Mahinda, 172
Rajkhowa, Arabinda, 210
Ramos, Fidel, 263, 272, 281–83, 285, 286, 290
rationalism, economic, 7
RCC. *See* Regional Consultative Commission (RCC)
RDTL. *See* Democratic Republic of Timor-Leste
rebellion conflict in Thailand, 218
Rebellion Resistance Force, 128
reconciling minority, 2
Red Net Operation Implementation Command, establishment of, 39
Reformasi, 64
reform-weariness in Sri Lanka, 150–53
Regional Autonomous Government education system, 283
Regional Autonomy Committee (RAC), 184
regional autonomy in Sri Lanka, 136–37
  negotiating with LTTE, 154–56
  state power sharing, 138–40
  state reform, 140–47
Regional Committee in Sri Lanka, 152
Regional Consultative Commission (RCC), 257, 263
  creation of, 281
Regional Councils in Sri Lanka, 148
Regional Legislative Assembly, 275n8
  of ARMM, 270–71
representative bureaucracy, 222
Republic Act 9054, 258, 259, 265, 271–72

Republic of the United States of
    Indonesia (RUSI), 59
Resolution 1813, 82–83
Revolutionary Front for liberation
    of Timor-Leste, 78
revolution in Portugal, 78
rido in Muslim Mindanao, 270
right to self-determination, 90n26,
    93, 98, 100, 169
Ruak, Taur Matan, 102
Rudy, Frank, 82
RUSI. *See* Republic of the United
    States of Indonesia

S
SAC. *See* State Autonomy
    Committee (SAC)
Sadiq, Muhammad, 189
SADR. *See* Saharawi Arab
    Democratic Republic (SADR)
Saharawi Arab Democratic Republic
    (SADR), 81
Salamat, Hashim, 280, 281, 284
Santa Cruz massacre, 98, 99, 105
SARET. *See* Special Autonomous
    Region of East Timor
    (SARET)
Satun, 5, 220, 222, 243, 246, 247,
    301
  Muslims in, 249
  violence in, 243
Satun province, 236
  lack of separatism in, 243
  state penetration, 243
  transition in, 246
SBPSAC. *See* Southern Border
    Provinces Peace Strategy
    Administration Center
    (SBPSAC)
secessionist civil war, 139

secessionist conflict in Sri Lanka,
    163
Security Council, 82, 83, 86
self-determination, 23, 38, 79, 85,
    86, 89, 90n26, 93, 94, 98,
    100, 143, 169
  act of, 100, 106
  for armed separatist minorities, 2
  claim of, 23–24
  conflicts, 5
  internal, 171
  under international law, 85
  measure of, 144
  mediated solutions for, 24–30
  national, 297
  in Papua, 61–62
  Tamil nationalist agitation for,
    144
  of Timor-Leste, 84, 88
  in UN Charter, 1945, 90n26
  United Nations-monitored
    referendum on, 43
  of Western Sahara, 81
self-government, 19
  in Aceh, 38, 45, 48–51, 297
  challenges of, 52–53
  decentralization in form of, 297
self-identifying bonded political
    group, 20
self-identifying groups, 18
semi-federalist, 144–45
Sentral Informasi Referendum Aceh
    (SIRA), 48, 49, 51
separatism
  in Jammu & Kashmir (J&K),
    177–90
  mediated constitutionality as
    solution to, 16–30
  in Moro, 279–88
  in Papua, 59–73

in Satun, 243
in Sri Lanka, 162–74
separatist armed insurgency in Sri Lanka, 138
separatist claimants, 30
separatist claims, 17, 18, 20, 27, 28
    to nationhood, 21
separatist conflict resolution, 28
separatist disputes, conflict resolution of, 17
separatist insurgency, 38
    Aceh, 41
separatist insurgents, 1
separatist minorities, 1, 8
separatist movements, 18, 28–29
    commitment of, 20
separatists, 163, 167–70
Shillong Accord, 213n12
Shinawatra, Thaksin, 223
    administrations (2001–06), failures of, 218–19
Shinawatra, Yingluck, 251
Siamese authority, 247
Sinhalese, 164–66
Sinhalese Buddhist
    civilization, 166
    nationalism, 163
Sinhalese ethnonationalist project, 298
Sinhalese majority, 27, 164
    national goal of, 165
Sinhalese nationalism, 166, 167
Sinhalese nationalist, 143, 151, 173
    forces, 140
Sinhalese state formation project, 140
Sino-Myanmar border, 122, 130
SIRA. *See Sentral Informasi Referendum Aceh* (SIRA)
SLFP. *See* Sri Lanka Freedom Party (SLFP)

SLMC. *See* Sri Lanka Muslim Congress (SLMC)
socio-cultural differences in Papua and Indonesia, 64
Soeharto president, 37–39, 60, 63, 64, 93–95, 98–102
Solossa, Jaap, 67
Solossa, Jacob, 65
Songkhram, Phibun, 247, 248
South Asia/Southeast Asia, 297
    armed separatist conflicts in, 4, 298
    governments in, 1–2, 3–4
    nation-states in, 300
    states in, 1
South Asia Terrorism Portal, 198
Southern Border Provinces Peace Strategy Administration Center (SBPSAC), 224
Southern Philippines. *See also* Mindanao
    ARMM, creation of, 280–81
    benevolent assimilation, 279
    features of, 278
    Moro identity, origins of, 279–80
    Moro separatism, 279–88
    1996 Agreement, 281–85, 283, 285–88
Southern Philippines Council for Peace and Development (SPCPD), 264, 282–84, 291
Southern Philippines Development Authority, 282
Southern Thailand
    autonomy, 227–29
    colonization in, 217
    conflict in, 218–19
    contagion effect in, 225–26
    decentralization, 221–22

Index

displacement of local elites, 245–48
education in, 239–40
ethnic minorities in, 237
historical autonomy perspective of, 219–22
liberalization in, 227
non-Thai local identity, 248–50
NRC and, 223–26
resurgence of violence in, 235
state authority, 235, 237, 250, 251
state penetration in. *See* state penetration, Thailand
violence in, 218, 235, 252
sovereignty. *See also* earned sovereignty
conditional devolution of, 24
for J&K, 185–86
Naga movement, 201–2
in Westphalian, 22
Spanish-American War, 279
Spanish colonizers, 279
Spanish Sahara, 81
SPCPD. *See* Southern Philippines Council for Peace and Development (SPCPD)
Special Autonomous Region of East Timor (SARET), 80, 87, 100
special autonomy
to Aceh, 38, 42, 48
in Papua, 63–65, 67–68, 68–71, 302
Papuan Attitudes to, 65–67
Special Autonomy Law, 69, 70–71
Special Regional Security Forces (SRSF), 283
special status of J&K, 177–80
Special Zone of Peace and Development (SZOPAD), 264, 282–84, 290

Sri Lanka, 27, 297, 298
armed rebellion in, 137
armed separatism in, 137
autonomy, 19, 137, 138–40, 153–54, 156–58
civil war in. *See* civil war in Sri Lanka
conflict in, 163
ethnic minority armed insurgency in, 136
federalism in, 162–74
federalists, 163, 170–72
Indian peace enforcement, 142
People's Alliance (PA) government in, 148
policy shift, feature of, 141
political formations in, 166
polity and society, 164–65
Provincial Council system in. *See* Provincial Council system in Sri Lanka
reform-weariness in, 150–53
regional autonomy in. *See* regional autonomy in Sri Lanka
secessionist conflict, 163
separatist armed insurgency in, 138
separatists, 163, 167–70
state reform in, 140–47
unilateral reform initiatives, limits of, 147–50
unitarianism, 172–74
unitarianists, 163, 165–66
UNP government in, 142, 149
violence in, 174
Sri Lanka Freedom Party (SLFP), 142, 163, 165
Sri Lanka Monitoring Mission, 25
Sri Lanka Muslim Congress (SLMC), 146, 147

Sri Lankan Tamil ethnonationalist forces, 165
Sri Lankan Tamil nationalism, 167
Sri Lankan Tamil nationalists, 173
Sri Lankan Tamil society, 168
Sri Lanka's Tamil minorities, 298
SRSF. *See* Special Regional Security Forces (SRSF)
State Auditing Agency, 50
state authority
  devolution of, 17
  Indonesian, 41
state authority, Thailand
  decentralization of, 235, 250, 251
  rapid centralization of, 237
State Autonomy Committee (SAC), 184, 185
State Law and Order Restoration Council (SLORC), 114
State Peace and Development Council (SPDC), 117
state penetration
  Isaan, 243, 245, 249
  Satun province, 243
state penetration, Thailand, 236–40, 250–52
  accelerated, 242
  defined, 237
  in different peripheral regions, 240–42
  non-Thai local identity, suppression of, 248–50
  and patterns of resistance, 243–45
  policies of, 237, 241
  protracted insurgency, 242
state reform in Sri Lanka, 140–47
state-secessionist dichotomy, 25
statist violence, 4, 39, 299

substantive autonomy arrangements, 6
sub-state model, autonomy as, 19–20
Suebu, Barnabas, 70
Sukarnoputri, Megawati, 44, 45, 68–69
Sulong, Haji, 220–22, 248, 249
Sulu, 279, 289
Sumule, Agus, 65
Sundaravej, Samak, 229
Sunni Muslims, 184
Suwarya, Endang, 45
SZOPAD. *See* Special Zone of Peace and Development (SZOPAD)

T
Talibanization, 182
Tambon Administrative Organization (TAO), creation of, 225
Tamil Eelam, 168
  establishment of, 169
Tamil ethnic insurgency, 153
Tamil guerilla groups, 142
Tamil minority, 27, 138, 145, 163
Tamil National Alliance (TNA), 173
Tamil nationalism
  ideology of, 141
  Sri Lankan, 167
Tamil nationalist, 156
  groups, 138, 141–44, 153
  project, 145
Tamil rebels, 137, 146, 147, 157, 298
Tamils in Sri Lanka, 164, 165, 168, 169–70, 174
Tamil-speaking people, 140–41
Tamil state-formationists, 140

Tamil state-formation project, 140
Tamil Tigers. *See* Liberation Tigers of Tamil Eelam (LTTE)
Tamil United Liberation Front (TULF), 142, 149, 168, 172
tanda peuturi droe, 53n3
Tangkhul Nagas, 201, 202
tanzeems, 182
Tatmadaw, 116, 126, 127
    armed forces, 299
    atrocities, 128–29
    border checkpoints of, 122
    free-fire zones of, 119
Tavleen Singh, 192n23
Tentara Nasional Indonesia (TNI), 37, 42, 53n2, 96, 107n8
terrorist
    in J&K, 189–90
    in Pakistan, 189
terrorist attacks in India, 189
Thai Buddhist nationalists, 301
Thai Buddhist population, 251
Thai electoral politics, 251
Thai-Islam, 252n1
Thailand, 300–1
    formal colonization, 2–3
    minority populations, 235
    national identity, 217
    Satun and Isaan in, 5
    Southern. *See* Southern Thailand
Thailand's security forces, 235
Thai Muslim, 247, 249, 252n1
Thai nation-building process, 300
Thaksin administrations (2001–06), failures of, 218–19
Thimpu Principles, 153–54
third wave of nationalism, 16
13th Amendment, 140–43, 146, 148, 173
Timorese people, 80
    expression of, 85
    sporadic revolts by, 77–78
Timor-Leste. *See* East Timor
Tinsulanond, Prem, 219
TNA. *See* Tamil National Alliance (TNA)
TNI. *See Tentara Nasional Indonesia*
tribal diversity in Papua, 62
TRIKORA Regional Command, 60
Tripoli Agreement, 1976, 257, 258, 281, 286, 290, 292, 293
    implementation of, 274n4, 280, 282
    in Philippine government and MNLF, 262
Tripura
    insurgencies in, 205–6, 211
    violence in, 205
Truth and Reconciliation Commission, 49
tsunami
    in Aceh, 27–28, 47, 52
    India Ocean, 37, 45, 46

U

UJC. *See* United Jihad Council (UJC)
ulama Council, 227
ULFA. *See* United Liberation Front of Assam (ULFA)
ultra-nationalist regimes, 248
Umar, Najmuddin, 226
UNAMET. *See* United Nations Mission on East Timor (UNAMET)
UN Decolonization Committee, 80, 81, 84
UNF. *See* United National Front (UNF)

UN General Assembly Resolution 3485, 85
UN General Assembly Resolution 37/30, and 23, 85
unitarianism, strength of, 172–74
unitarianists, 163, 165–66
unitarian nationalists, 173
unitary state system, 163, 166, 167
United Jihad Council (UJC), 189
United Liberation Front of Assam (ULFA), 204, 209, 210
United National Front (UNF) government, 150, 151, 155, 156
United National Party (UNP), 142, 149, 159n2, 165
United Nations Mission on East Timor (UNAMET), 80, 82, 84
United People's Democratic Solidarity (UPDS), 208
United People's Freedom Alliance (UPFA), 152
United Wa State Army (UWSA), 120, 131n9
UNP. See United National Party (UNP)
UN Resolution, 86
UN Secretary General, 85
  auspices of, 78, 79
  report of, 82
UN Security Council, 86
UNTAET, 84
UPDS. See United People's Democratic Solidarity (UPDS)
UWSA. See United Wa State Army (UWSA)

V
Vajpayee, Atal Behari, 188
violence
  in East Timor, 86–88
  election, 270
  endemic, 210
  ethnic, 164, 170
  in Indonesia, 10
  Jammu & Kashmir (J&K), 180, 189
  in J&K, 180
  LTTE and, 144, 146
  in Manipur, 210
  by militias, 87
  against Muslims, 147
  and negotiation in East Timor, 94–101
  in Philippines, 270–71, 271
  in police and civilian population, 189
  political, 218
  protracted cycle of, 242
  resurgence of, 235
  in Satun, 243
  scale of, 63
  in Southern provinces, 252
  in Southern Thailand, 218, 235, 252
  in Sri Lanka, 162, 163, 174
  statist, 4, 39, 299
  terrorist, 189
  in Timor-Leste, 86–88
  in Tripura, 205
Viqueque, 97
vis-à-vis autonomy proposals, 89
Visayas, 279, 289

W
Wahid, Abdurrahman, 41, 44, 47, 64
Wasi, Prawase, Dr., 227–28

WCS. *See* World Conservation
    Society (WCS)
Western Sahara, 77
    case study of, 80–83
    establishment of MINURSO in,
        86
    international law, role of, 86
    parallels and paradox of, 83–84
    self-determination of, 81
West Papua, 27, 89
    autonomy, 19
    peace agreements in, 28
Westphalian states, 16

sovereignty, 22
Wickremasinghe, Ranil, 172
Wilsonian-Leninist reorganization,
    23
World Conservation Society
    (WCS), 12, 13, 132n17
Wospakrik, Frans, 65–67, 71

Y
Yogyakarta, 64, 66
Yom Kippur war, 262
Yubamrung, Chalerm, 228–29, 230
Yudhoyono, Susilo Bambang, 47, 69

www.ingramcontent.com/pod-product-compliance
Lightning Source LLC
Chambersburg PA
CBHW072121290426
44111CB00012B/1730